BIRTH OF WELSH DEMOCRACY

The First Term of the National Assembly for Wales

EDITED BY JOHN OSMOND AND J BARRY JONES

D1407094

INSTITUTE OF WELSH AFFAIRS

The Institute of Welsh Affairs exists to promote quality research and informed debate affecting the cultural, social, political and economic well-being of Wales. IWA is an independent organisation owing no allegiance to any political or economic interest group. Our only interest is in seeing Wales flourish as a country in which to work and live. We are funded by a range of organisations and individuals. For more information about the Institute, its publications, and how to join, either as an individual or corporate supporter, contact:

IWA - Institute of Welsh Affairs
Ty Oldfield, Llantrisant Road, Llandaf, Cardiff CF5 2YQ

Tel: 029 2057 5511

Fax: 029 2057 5701

Email: wales@iwa.org.uk

Web: www.iwa.org.uk

THE WELSH GOVERNANCE CENTRE

The Welsh Governance Centre was established in February 1999 to undertake scholarly research into the operation of the new Welsh political institutions and their role in the evolving policy making process. Academics from a wide range of disciplines – politics, economics and the social sciences, history, law and Welsh – participate in the Centre's activities, which include short conferences, seminars, consultancies and public lectures. The central aim of the Welsh Governance Centre is to study the evolution of the policy process, the inter-action between organised interests and the National Assembly, in the context of the continuing role of the Westminster Parliament and the growing influence of the European Union. The Centre is committed to reaching beyond the academic world and to forging links with its local community and the broader national community of Wales.

WGC - Welsh Governance Centre
Cardiff University, PO Box 908
Cardiff CF10 3YQ

Tel/Fax: 029 2087 4885

Email: welshgovernance@cardiff.ac.uk

Web: www.cf.ac.uk/euros/welsh-governance

The publication of this book and the
project on which it is based have been
undertaken with the support of the
Joseph Rowntree Charitable Trust.

ISBN 1 871726 94 8
© Institute of Welsh Affairs and Welsh Governance Centre, March 2003
Designed by Payne Taylor Design (PTD 2304) 029 2025 5525
Printed in Wales by Coloursmart Print Solutions Ltd. Tel: 01639 896543

CONTENTS

PART 1
THE EMERGING CONSTITUTION

PART 2
POLICY PROCESS

PART 3
POLITICAL PARTIES

PART 4
A CHANGING POLITICAL CULTURE

PREFACE

This is the third volume tracking the development of policy and administration in the National Assembly during the historic early years of its first term. The first volume, *Inclusive Government and Party Management: The National Assembly for Wales and the Work of its Committees*, was published in March 2001; and the second, *Building a Civic Culture: Institutional Change, Policy Development and Political Dynamics in the National Assembly for Wales*, in March 2002.

The project is a joint undertaking between the Institute of Welsh Affairs and the Welsh Governance Centre at Cardiff University. It has been made possible as a result of generous support from the Joseph Rowntree Charitable Trust. This has funded a research student at the Welsh Governance Centre, the organisation of a series of seminars, and this publication. The project builds on the IWA's earlier publication *The National Assembly Agenda: A Handbook for the First Four Years* (November 1998), also supported by the Joseph Rowntree Charitable Trust, which examined the future Assembly's operational processes, policy agendas and its relationship with other tiers of government.

In this third volume examining the Assembly's record, we have taken an overview of the Assembly's first term as a whole. Inevitably, as before, we have found ourselves also considering the impact that devolution is having on wider civil society in Wales. So much so that we believe this is leading to a time when we will be able to speak of a *Welsh civil society*. This testifies to the impact the National Assembly is having.

The book should be read alongside quarterly reports produced by the IWA that also track the progress of the National Assembly. These are published in printed form and also posted on the IWA's website: www.iwa.org.uk . The project is being pursued in association with the Constitution Unit, University College, London, as part of a monitoring exercise of all the UK devolved institutions, together with tracking developments in Whitehall and in the English regions. Our partner organisations in Scotland and Northern Ireland are the Department of Politics, University of Strathclyde, and Democratic Dialogue. The Constitution Unit monitors constitutional changes and responses in Whitehall, while the Centre for Urban and Regional Development Studies at Newcastle University is following developments in the English regions. Further information on this project, including the regular reports from Scotland, Northern Ireland, Whitehall and the English regions can be found on the Constitution Unit's website: www.ucl.ac.uk/constitution-unit/

A project such as this incurs many debts of gratitude. We are grateful to politicians and officials within the National Assembly for their ready co-operation, but especially Paul Silk, Clerk to the National Assembly and Marie Knox, Head of the Committee Secretariat, Office of the Presiding Officer. We are also grateful to Rhys David and Jessica Mugaseth, of the IWA, who handled the proofs.

John Osmond
Director
Institute of Welsh Affairs

J. Barry Jones
Director
Welsh Governance Centre

NOTES ON THE CONTRIBUTORS

David Adamson is a Professor in the School of Humanities and Social Sciences at the University of Glamorgan. He was an External Adviser to the Assembly Government during the development of its Communities First policy.

Denis Balsom is Editor of *The Wales Yearbook* and a political consultant with HTV Wales.

Gillian Bristow is a lecturer in Economic Geography at the Department of City and Regional Planning, Cardiff University. Her research interests are focused on devolution and finance in the UK, the restructuring of regional economies, and the EU Structural Funds. She is currently engaged in a study of partnerships in Wales for the Welsh Assembly Government.

Geraint Talfan Davies is Chairman of the Institute of Welsh Affairs. Since leaving the BBC where he was Controller of BBC Wales throughout the 1990s, he has been heavily involved in the arts in Wales as Chairman of both Welsh National Opera and CBAT, the Arts and Regeneration Agency.

Rhiannon Tudor Edwards is Senior Research Fellow in Health Economics, and Director of the Centre for the Economics of Health, Institute of Medical and Social Care Research, University of Wales Bangor.

David Egan is professor of Education in the Cardiff School of Education at the University of Wales Institute, Cardiff. He is a member of the Education Broadcasting Council for Wales and the Court and Council of the National Museums and Galleries of Wales. With Roy James, he is currently involved with research projects for ACCAC relating to the National Curriculum and Assessment, the General Teaching Council for Wales on teacher professional development and the WAG on headteacher management and leadership training.

Robert Hazell is Director of the Constitution Unit and Professor of Government and the Constitution in the School of Public Policy, University College London (UCL). Originally a barrister, he spent most of his working life at the Home Office. He left Whitehall to become director of the Nuffield Foundation and founded the Conmstitution Unit in 1995.

Roy James is External Professor at the University of Glamorgan. He was previously her Majesty's Chief Inspector of Schools in Wales, 1990-97. With David Egan he is currently involved with the research projects set out above.

Eilidh Johnston is an IWA Senior Research Fellow in association with the University of Glamorgan, specialising in social and environmental issues.

J. Barry Jones is Director of the Welsh Governance Centre, Cardiff University. He edited, with Denis Balsom *The Road to the National Assembly for Wales*, University of Wales Press, 2000.

Mark S. Lang is a research student with the Welsh Governance Centre, Cardiff University, working on the relationship between the Labour Party and the trade unions. Formerly a political researcher at the National Assembly, he was a member of the Wales Labour Party Executive Committee from 1995 until 1998.

Laura McAllister is Senior Lecturer in Public Administration and Politics at the University of Liverpool. Author of Plaid Cymru:The Emergence of a Political Party (Seren, Bridgend, 2001) she is currently Plaid Cymru's representative on the Richard Commission on the Assembly's powers and electoral arrangements.

David Miers is Professor of Law and Deputy Head of Cardiff Law School. He manages Cardiff Law School's website, *Wales Legislation on-line*. He has written extensively on the making and interpretation of legislation and given evidence to the Welsh Affairs Select Committee and the Commons Procedure Committee on aspects of devolution.

John Osmond has been Director of the Institute of Welsh Affairs since 1996. A former journalist and television producer he is the author of many articles and books on Welsh politics and culture, including *Welsh Europeans* (Seren, 1996) and, as Editor, *The National Assembly Agenda*, published by the Institute.

Keith Patchett is an Emeritus Professor of Law at the University of Wales and an international consultant on public law, legislation and legislative drafting, principally for Commonwealth and Central and Eastern European countries. He is a member of the Constitution Unit's Advisory Committee and the IWA's Constitution Working Group.

Nia Richardson is Research Officer with the Universities and Colleges Employers Association. She was a Research Officer with the Institute of Welsh Affairs from June 2000 to December 2002, tracking policy development within the National Assembly

Elin Royles is a research student at the Institute of Welsh Politics, University of Wales, Aberystwyth.

Andrew Scott is Professor of European Union Studies in the School of Law, University of Edinburgh.

Roger Scully is Lecturer in European Politics in the Department of International Politics at University of Wales, Aberystwyth.

Alan Storer is a research student with the Welsh Governance Centre, Cardiff

University, working on the relationship between business and politics in post-devolution Wales.

Gerald Taylor is a Research Fellow at the University of Glamorgan working on the Glamorgan Governance Programme. He has published a monograph Labour's Renewal? The Policy Review and Beyond and edited a research-based volume The Impact of New Labour as well as articles on Labour's policy-making system and Canadian politics. He has been active in the Labour party and was its Parliamentary Candidate for Torbay in the 1987 General Election.

Alys Thomas lectures in Government and Politics in the School of Humanities & Social Sciences at the University of Glamorgan. She has a long standing research interest in Welsh politics and government and, with colleagues, has recently completed a project funded by the Joseph Rowntree Foundation onThe Impact of Devolution on Local Government in Wales. She is currently part of a research team examining the transition period of devolution in Wales.

Jane Williams is a law lecturer at the University of Wales, Swansea. She was formerly in private practice at the Bar, then a member of the Government Legal Service working in the Home Office Legal Advisers Branch, Civil Service College, Welsh Office Legal Group and Office of the Counsel General, National Assembly for Wales. She is founder and general editor of the Wales Law Journal(www.waleslawjournal.org) .

Richard Wyn Jones is Senior Lecturer in the Department of International Politics at University of Wales, Aberystwyth, and Director of the Institute of Welsh Politics.

LAYING THE FOUNDATIONS

John Osmond

Viewed from the vantage point of the last months of the National Assembly's first term it was clear we were witnessing the birth of Welsh democratic governance. Though little noticed outside, the Assembly was transforming itself from an institution subordinate to Westminster into a parliamentary body with the potential, and the intention, of acquiring primary legislative powers. This was not a legal transformation since the Assembly still operated within the terms of the 1998 Government of Wales Act. Nonetheless, it was the reality in practice, and agreed across the parties. A separate legislature now operated, guided by an independent Presiding Office with its own budget of some £22 million a year. On the other side was a powerful executive in the form of the self-styled Welsh Assembly Government, equipping itself with an array of policy interventions increasingly different from those being pursued in Whitehall. This book surveys these developments over the first four-year term and discusses their significance, not just from the point of view of constitutional change, but in terms of their impact on the policy making process and the emergence of an autonomous civic culture.

Part I examines the Assembly's constitutional architecture, taking into account the relationship between Cardiff and Westminster in promoting primary legislation, procedures for dealing with secondary legislation, and the role of the civil service. It describes the main part of the agenda currently being addressed by the Richard Commission on the Assembly's powers, due to report towards the end of 2003. In particular, Professor Robert Hazell's chapter on *Multi-Level Governance* makes a powerful and cogent case for the Assembly to acquire primary legislative powers.

We then explore in Part II the policy processes that have developed, assessing the impact of the Subject Committees and their inter-relationship with the Assembly Government in key areas such as education and health. Attention is given to the promotion of programmes that have in many ways defined the policy output of the first term. Two programmes stand out: the application of European Union Objective 1 structural funds to west Wales and the Valleys, and the ambitious Communities First initiative aimed at tackling social exclusion across Wales.

In Part III we place the political parties under the spotlight, asking how well they have adjusted to the new demands placed on them by the Assembly. An appreciation of the impact devolution has had on the parties adds an essential human dimension to the story of the first term. In one way or another all the parties were put through the mill by the experience. Labour had to cope with the Ron Davies affair, and the consequences of that, in particular the perceived imposition of Alun Michael as leader and his resignation following the vote of no confidence in February 2000. The Conservatives lost their first leader, Rod Richards, within months of the establishment of the Assembly, following his involvement in a court case. Plaid Cymru lost their leader Dafydd Wigley in early 2001 as a result of illness and have since struggled to re-establish their profile under Ieuan Wyn Jones. And the Liberal Democrats saw their leader temporarily forced out of the Coalition Cabinet for a year from July 2001 because of a police investigation into his former role at the Welsh Joint Education Committee.

Finally, in Part IV we analyse how Welsh political culture has been affected by devolution. How far have the aspirations for changing the way politics is conducted in Wales, articulated as part of the case for the Assembly, been realised in the first term? How has the electorate responded? To what extent is the European dimension of Welsh politics gaining ground? And more generally, how far is Wales developing a civic culture, typified by the impact of an increasingly distinctive legal personality?

A DEVELOPING CONSTITUTION

Unlike Scotland, Wales did not have the benefit of a Constitutional Convention to hammer out cross-party agreement before the onset of democratic devolution. Instead, the National Assembly was the best compromise that Ron Davies, as Shadow Secretary of State, could push through the Welsh Labour Party ahead of the 1997 general election. Left to his own devices he would have produced a Scottish-style Parliament. As it was, he was forced to appease devolution-sceptics within his own party and settle for a minimalist Assembly based on a local government model.

This inheritance inevitably cast a shadow across the National Assembly's first four-year term. In so far as it could within the framework of the 1998 Government of Wales Act, the new institution immediately set about digging up its constitutional foundations. By the end of the first term it had re-laid them in such a way that they now had the potential of carrying the full weight of a parliament with legislative powers. The essence of the matter is that the Assembly was established as a corporate body. That is to say, its legislative and executive functions were combined along local government lines rather than separated, as is normal in parliamentary institutions.

The powers of the Assembly are limited to those previously exercised by the Secretary of State for Wales and are derived from specific ministerial functions named in pieces of primary and secondary legislation. Those 5,000 functions are set out in the first Transfer of Functions Order, referred to in the Wales Act, and detail the exact functions the Assembly may carry out. Within the Act these functions had to be transferred to some authority. In the absence of legislative powers, and hence a clearly defined, separate Administration, the drafters of the Government of Wales Bill came up with the notion of the Assembly as a whole, as a corporate body, to which the powers would be transferred.

The constitutional history of the Assembly's opening period was dominated by an emphatic rejection of this mode of operation. Instead, the Assembly moved as far as it possibly could in the direction of separating its administrative and legislative roles. By the time of the establishment of the coalition between Labour and Liberal Democrats in October 2000 these two elements had developed highly distinctive personalities. Representing the legislative side was the Presiding Office, with its own budget. Representing the executive was what became known as the Welsh Assembly Government, supported by the bulk of the civil service. Each acquired separate identities symbolised by distinctive logos.

The main force driving the split in the first period of the Assembly's life was the Presiding Officer, Lord Elis-Thomas[1]. Thereafter, however, it was the Assembly Government, led by the First Minister, that was most anxious to define and emphasise the difference. Part of the motivation was a widespread anxiety that its decisions were being interpreted by the media as coming from the Assembly as a whole. Both Government and Opposition in the Assembly shared an interest in avoiding such confusion.

This development was highly significant, not just because the practical functioning of the Assembly made it inevitable, but because it also confirmed the Assembly was moving in a parliamentary direction. As the Assembly's chief legal officer, the Counsel General Winston Roddick QC, put it in his written evidence to the Richard Commission on the Assembly's powers in December 2002:

"The legislature and the executive have been living apart for more than three years. They remain married but only legally. So far apart have they grown, they have taken different names and different identities. If they were human beings the law would permit them to divorce and thereby formalise the separation."[2]

---

[1] For an account see John Osmond, 'In Search of Stability: Coalition Politics in the Second Year of the National Assembly' in Alan Trench (Ed.) *The State of the Nations 2001: The Second Year of Devolution in the United Kingdom*, Constitution Unit/Imprint Academic, 2001, pages 26-31.

[2] Winston Roddick QC, Evidence to the Richard Commission, December 2002, para. 85.

However, to make the separation legal, so to speak, would mean further legislation, with the Government of Wales Act 1998 either being amended or replaced. The Richard Commission, established as part of the Partnership Agreement between Labour and the Liberal Democrats, began its work against this background. The logic of the Assembly's constitutional progression pointed towards a new Westminster Act that would reconstitute the Assembly as a Parliament. In this sense the Richard Commission was but another stage in an ongoing debate that characterised the first term of the National Assembly as a constitutional convention by other means. The key moments of this debate during the first term were as follows :

- The enforced resignation of Alun Michael as First Secretary in February 2000.

- Creation of the majority Coalition government in October 2000.

- Report of the Assembly's cross-party Procedural Review in February 2002[3].

- Establishment of the Richard Commission in July 2002.

These episodes were disruptive to varying degrees. It is noteworthy, therefore, that the Assembly came into being so smoothly and experienced relatively little conflict in its first term, not least with Westminster and Whitehall. That this was the case was due, in large part, to two considerable advantages:

1. Throughout the whole of its first term the Assembly benefited from an ever rising budget. This central fact contributed more than anything else to the stability of the new institution and its relative harmony with Westminster and Whitehall. It more than counter-balanced the generally acknowledged constitutional inadequacies in the Government of Wales Act, exemplified by frustrations that surfaced from time to time over the lack of clarity of the Assembly's powers.

2. A further important stabilising influence was the maintenance of Labour-dominated administrations in London and Cardiff, notwithstanding underlying tensions that occasionally occurred in relation to specific policy issues such as free personal care for the elderly and student fees.

Imagine the difficulties that would have arisen if these circumstances were different, if say the Assembly had been established in the early 1980s. At that time there was a stridently right wing Conservative administration in Westminster, public expenditure was being cut, and major Welsh industries were being dismantled. In examining the lessons of the Assembly's first term,

---

[3] For an account see John Osmond, 'Constitution Building on the Hoof: the Assembly's Procedural Review' in the previous volume in this series, *Building a Civic Culture*. It is argued there that for much of the time, "... the Review took on the character of an informal Constitutional Convention ..." (page 69).

the Richard Commission should adjust its perspective to take account of the extremely benign circumstances that persisted. It needs to ask how the Assembly and its present constitutional arrangements would fare if the going became a good deal rougher. How would it manage a combination of falling UK public expenditure and party political competition between London and Cardiff? The question was also raised by the House of Lords Committee on the Constitution, commenting on the legislative relationship between Cardiff and Westminster. Its report, following a lengthy inquiry during 2002, put forward a number of constructive suggestions how these might be improved within the present arrangements, but concluded:

> "The problems arising over Westminster legislation cause us to doubt whether the form executive devolution has taken in Wales is sustainable in the long term ... [Underlying the difficulties] is the reliance of the Welsh arrangements on mutually sympathetic administrations in London and Cardiff. We find it hard to see how such arrangements could work satisfactorily if there were major policy differences between the two governments."[4]

THE POLICY PROCESS

If the Assembly inherited a flawed institution constitutionally, it confronted a largely blank sheet of paper so far as policy was concerned. To put it at its kindest the manifesto commitments of the parties lacked specifics. The minority Labour Administration inherited a few broad commitments from the previous Welsh Office – on putting together a framework for Objective 1, for example, and the recommendations of the Education and Training Action Group on recasting the delivery of post-16 programmes – but precious little else.

It has been well rehearsed that the Welsh Office was not a policy making machine, but rather an outpost of Whitehall. A major impact of the first year of devolution was to radically change that impression, at least in terms of presentation. A flurry of policy declarations came from the minority Labour administration, identifying the economy, social inclusion, health and rural Wales as strategic areas where it intended to make a difference.[5] A further major intervention was the coalition Partnership Agreement in October 2000, with its wide-ranging, on the whole, admirable aspirations, driven a good deal it should be said by the Liberal Democrats. However, three qualifications need

---

[4] House of Lords Select Committee on the Constitution, Devolution: Inter-Institutional Relations in the United Kingdom, HL Paper 28, December 2002.

[5] See, for example, the Administration's mission statement, A Better Wales, published in July 1999.

to be made to this endorsement.

The first is that the policy aspirations were generally little more than just that: broad brush commitments aimed at, for example, improving the environment, reducing morbidity or raising education standards. The most notorious, of course, was the commitment to raise Welsh GDP from the current 80 per cent to 90 per cent of the UK average by 2010. This was made with no focused plan how it might be achieved, other than as the overall result of the sum total of the Assembly Government's policies.

The second qualification involves drawing attention to specific policy areas where the Partnership Agreement was reneged upon. The outstanding example is the determination, against all the opposition and all learned experience, to fundamentally re-structure the health service, discussed in Chapter 8.

The third qualification addresses a perhaps inevitable consequence of the Assembly being a young institution and therefore relatively inexperienced. This is the sense that, in key policy areas the Assembly Government is developing long-term, wide ranging, very ambitious, and relatively expensive initiatives that fail to come across as completely wired up. It is as though one wire in the connections is missing. This is the one that connects the policies to earth. It is not that the policies or strategies, or even the priorities, are inherently wrong or misguided. It is rather that there is a lack of coherence to them, little sense of how they are going to be delivered, how they will have a real chance of effectively engaging with, or making a difference to, the problems they are designed to tackle.

This last point can be illustrated by exploring three large–scale policies that were developed by the Assembly Government during the first term: the Basic Skills Strategy; a number of related initiatives in Early Years education ; and the Communities First Programme.

The Basic Skills strategy is attempting to address the fundamental problem that one in ten of young people leave Welsh schools and colleges without any qualifications. By GCSE stage only around 50 per cent achieve A-C grades in English and just 40 per cent in maths. The source of the problem is simple reading and writing, the fact that large numbers of Welsh people – at all ages – perform poorly in these, literally, basic skills. As Professor Kevin Morgan has memorably put it:

> *"One wonders if we have the skills to enter the knowledge economy when one in four of the population is functionally illiterate and one in three functionally innumerate."*[6]

---

[6] Kevin Morgan, 'Over-worked, Under-Resourced and Unloved', IWA, *Agenda* Autumn 2001, as assessment of the first two years of the National Assembly.

The Basic Skills Strategy is designed to tackle these problems. Launched in April 2001, it will have cost £27 million by April 2004. However, by the end of this strategy it is far from clear: (i) How its impact will be assessed; and (ii) how future improvements will be made in pursuing what must be a long-term policy commitment. In early 2003 the Assembly Government were embarking upon an evaluation programme, but the results were bound to be delivered too late to have any impact on the delivery of the Strategy's first three-year period.

There is a growing body of research which testifies that children who receive pre-school education benefit in later educational and developmental progress. There is a growing realisation, too, that investment in early years education, is the most effective way of tackling the basic skills deficit. And, to its credit, the Assembly Government has allocated approximately £34m to develop and expand early years provision . These include

- Every three-year-old in Wales should have the opportunity to receive free half-time education by 2004. The Assembly Government provided £12m in 2002-3 towards this objective and commissioned an audit to identify current provision and estimates of future demand in Wales across all sectors.

- Each Local Authority is to develop at least one pilot integrated early years centre by September 2004. These centres will provide early years education, supplemented by wrap-around day-care together with a range of support services from pre-natal parenting through to adult learning that benefits children and families. Integrated centres will seek to tackle wider social problems in Wales such as child poverty and a high rate of teenage mothers and will be jointly funded by local authorities' social services and education budgets.

- A New Foundation Stage for three to seven year-olds is being developed. The aim is to eliminate the cut-off point between pre-school and school education and will introduce an element of continuity in a child's early years education. A new foundation curriculum will also ensure that nurseries from the voluntary and maintained sectors have a common approach to educating the children in their care.

These are all admirable initiatives. However, no system has been put in place to track their progress or evaluate their effectiveness. What is required is a programme to:

- Assess the impact of the various initiatives envisaged, such as the integrated centres.

- Compare Welsh and English medium provision.

- Investigate curriculum content and methods of delivery.

Communities First is a major programme aimed at tackling Wales' relatively low GDP by addressing high economic inactivity in deprived areas, found largely within the Objective 1 region of west Wales and the south Wales Valleys. Involving expenditure of £83 million over the first three years (2002-05), the programme is targeting 142 of Wales' most disadvantaged communities.

The programme has a lifespan of at least ten years and so aims to have a long-term impact through tackling the factors that contribute to poverty. It is intended that communities themselves, in partnerships with statutory bodies, voluntary groups and the private sector, will identify their requirements and how to address them. Capacity building in the affected communities – that is, building leadership from within – forms a central part of this strategy. Again these are all laudable objectives, but it is far from clear how they are going to be achieved. There are three further, inter-related problems:

1. The programme is being motivated from Finance Minister Edwina Hart's Communities division within the Assembly Government. The Economic Development division has not been centrally involved, yet the programme's underlying objective is to tackle economic inactivity. Overall, this is the Assembly Government's single most important economic objective since it is central to raising GDP levels.

2. The main agents for the delivery of Communities First appear to be local authorities. These are the organisations to which money is flowing and which are doing the recruiting. Yet a central aim of the project is to build leadership capacity from within the affected communities. While local authorities are theoretically representative of the communities because of their democratically elected position, they are often distrusted because of their previously poor service provision to deprived communities. There is a danger that the programme's capacity building objective might end up in communities becoming alienated from the process.

3. It is not clear what the programme's precise targets are, or how they will be evaluated. How can 'capacity building' be assessed? It is true that in early 2003 the Assembly Government put a large-scale Evaluation Project out to tender. But that will not report for some years.

To summarise, a package of policy initiatives and strategies emerged towards the end of the first term across the range of the Assembly Government's responsibilities. However, what was often missing was thought-through consideration of how these initiatives would engage practically with the problems they were meant to address. Only rarely were time-lined targets set. Often missing, too, was how the various initiatives could be evaluated to ensure optimum effectiveness. And often missing, again, was a clear sense of how they would engage with the Assembly Government's central policy objective of raising GDP. All too often we were left with policies that, though admirable in themselves, were largely aspirational. This presents a clear challenge for the Assembly's second term.

CIVIC CAPACITY

The final two sections of the book deal broadly, and from different perspectives, with the development of Welsh civic society. The notion of Wales having a civic culture is novel to a society with such little experience of its own institutions. Before the onset of the National Assembly it could be fairly said that there was a *civil society in Wales* rather than a *Welsh civil society*. This was simply because there was an under-developed civic infrastructure to which Welsh society could respond. During the National Assembly's first term we have seen a civic culture beginning to develop and its clearest manifestation is the Assembly Government.

The most immediate impact, however, has been on the character and strategies of the political parties. Each has had to cope with different challenges. Democratic devolution has radically changed the character of Plaid Cymru. For the first time it has a relatively large and cohesive group of full-time, professional politicians within its ranks, the 17 elected Members in the Assembly together with their support staff. These have altered the balance of forces within the party's traditional structure. At the same time the party's focus of attention has shifted decisively from Westminster to Cardiff Bay. For the first time in its history, too, the party has a sense that it could be a party of government. These changes have created new problems of communication and increased the potential for divisions between the leadership and the wider membership, not least over the party's objectives and how they are articulated.[7]

The onset of devolution has also had a profound impact on the Welsh Labour Party. In the first place it has changed its name to Welsh Labour, from Labour Party Wales (previously the Labour Party in Wales). This registered an

---

[7] See *Plaid Cymru, Towards Full National Status: Stages on the Journey*, December 2000. Beyond Wales achieving parity with Scotland this envisages two broad constitutional scenarios: a democratic, federal Europe of the Regions with a greatly empowered European Parliament and a written constitution within which Wales could find a role; or, failing that, full national status for Wales as a member-state within the European Union. However, these options were sketched out only in broad conceptual terms with little detailed or tactical sense of what the party's preference would be, and how it might influence the course of events in that direction.

important emblematic and tonal change. There is a recognition by all the parties, but especially Labour, that identifying with the national dimension can bring political rewards in post-devolution Wales. There is now a recognisable nationalist, with a small n, wing within the Labour Group in the Assembly that is currently in the ascendant under Rhodri Morgan's leadership. To a large extent this Group is defining itself against the image and policy profile being developed by the New Labour Party at Westminster.[8]

The outcome of the devolution process for Welsh Liberal Democrats hangs almost entirely on the progress of the Coalition. Its constitutional objective of achieving a federation within the UK creates an inherently weak position. Although Britain may be moving in a quasi-federal direction, given the nature of the British state devolution is always likely to be asymmetrical. However, the Welsh Liberal Democrats will be judged on the extent to which they are seen to influence policy development in their direction, and more immediately on the electoral consequences. On this latter score the party will have drawn a good deal of comfort from an HTV poll in November 2002 which saw them edging ahead of the Conservatives in terms of seats in the Assembly in May 2003.

Paradoxically, in electoral terms the Conservatives have benefited most from devolution, achieving significant representation in the Assembly through the operation of the regional list proportional system. There is also a determination on the part of the leadership to identify more with Welsh concerns, develop distinctive Welsh policies, and a more autonomous organisation for the party in Wales.[9] The party's identity as an Opposition party in the Assembly has also been strengthened by the formation of the majority Coalition government. What all this may imply for the party's constitutional thinking has been speculated upon by a number of their new politicians. For example, David Melding, AM for South Wales Central, declared:

> "The party least sympathetic to devolution needs to become its most conspicuous supporter. I believe we have reached a stage where the British state can only survive with devolution. Commentators should not rule out, therefore, the possibility that the next and most vital advance for devolution in Wales will be instigated by the Conservative Party."[10]

Another obvious expression of the emerging civic society has been the way a growing number of organisations are recasting their structures to reflect the

---

[8] See, for example, Rhodri Morgan's 'Clear Red Water' address to the National Centre for Public Policy, University of Wales, Swansea, in December 2002, where he set out the philosophical divide between Welsh Labour in Cardiff and New Labour in London

[9] See Jonathan Evans, *The Future of Welsh Conservatism*, IWA, Gregynog Papers, 2002.

[10] David Melding, 'Conservatives Should Finish the Job', IWA, *Agenda* Autumn 2001.

new Welsh polity, and often appointing National Assembly Liaison Officers in the process. Cardiff is now rarely seen as a branch office for London-based organisations. Instead, organisations are progressively establishing more autonomous Welsh structures to more effectively interact with and influence National Assembly politicians. Examples range from the British Medical Association and the Country Landowners Association to the National Union of Teachers, Confederation of British Industry, Federation of Small Businesses, and the RSPB. By now more than 30 such organisations have appointed Assembly Liaison Officers. In addition the advent of the Assembly has seen the spawning of a growing number of Welsh-based political consultancies.

Perhaps the most important expression of the new civic society is the growing development of distinctively Welsh legal institutions since the onset of democratic devolution. In the first instance the establishment of the Office of the Counsel General within the National Assembly has had a significant effect upon the legal profession in Wales. In Chapter 19 Jane Williams traces the development of 'Legal Wales', identifying five ways on which it is finding expression:

1. The repatriation of law making functions.

2. The development of a system for the administration of justice in all its forms which is tailored to the social and economic needs of Wales.

3. The development of institutions and professional bodies which will provide a proper career structure in Wales for those who want to follow a career in those fields.

4. Making the law accessible to, and readily understood, by the people of Wales.

5. The development of a system which can accommodate the use of either the English or Welsh languages so that they are treated on the basis of equality.

These developments, which will have far reaching consequences for the administration of justice and the legal profession in Wales, are particularly important since they underline the civic character of the devolution process. As the Counsel General Winston Roddick QC has put it:

"It would not be correct historically to say that we are seeing the creation of Legal Wales but it is undoubtedly the case that since the National Assembly for Wales was established we are seeing the reawakening of it after centuries of slumber ... The administration of justice in Wales is closer to the people now than at any time during the 19th and 20th Centuries."[11]

---

[11] Winston Roddick QC, 'Creating Legal Wales', IWA, *Agenda* Spring 2002.

A very large caveat needs to be set against this catelogue of the growth of civic society and identity in Wales during the first term of the National Assembly. This is, quite simply, that by and large it has been confined to an élite strata in Welsh society, the political class. As catalogued by Richard Wyn Jones and Roger Scully in Chapter 16, so far the Welsh devolution experience has been characterised by its weak engagement with the wider electorate. In general, the verdict from the polls is that the Assembly has made very little impact on the lives of ordinary people and there has been disappointment at its record, whether it be in health, education or economic development. However, the response has not been a rejection of devolution. Instead, the polls have shown a remarkable shift in favour of greater powers for the Assembly. A majority of around 40 per cent now favour a Parliament for Wales with powers equivalent to those enjoyed by the Scots. The sentiment appears to be, if we are to have an Assembly, let's make it work effectively. This is an important message for the second term.

PART 1

THE EMERGING
CONSTITUTION

CHAPTER 1

THE NEW CONSTITUTIONAL ARCHITECTURE

Keith Patchett

If the Government of Wales Act 1998 instituted constitutional arrangements for devolution that were without precedent[1], the transformation of those arrangements during the Assembly's first term was even more remarkable. The realities of political practice in the United Kingdom, in which governmental functions are separated from the parliamentary process, coupled with the emergence of coalition politics, led to a pragmatic restructuring of the constitutional architecture of the Assembly. This was undertaken without a single amendment to the original statutory framework. Indeed, the commentator relying essentially on the terms of the Act would see a picture that was seriously misleading.

The objectives of Welsh devolution, as stated in the White Paper[2], were to authorise an elected body to set policies for Wales in a range of subject fields and to hold those taking executive action to account, particularly for the standards and performance in service delivery. The Assembly, as originally conceived, was to be a single corporate body in which all the devolved functions, including that of making secondary legislation, were to be legally vested. It was structured to operate through a series of decision-taking committees, reflecting the party distribution in the Assembly. The aim was to encourage consensual politics and inclusiveness of Assembly Members in executive matters, as well as transparency and improved accountability.

In its passage through Parliament, the Government of Wales Bill was materially altered to allow the Assembly to operate through an Executive Committee. This was to be made up of a number of Secretaries, drawn from the majority party, who would discharge the devolved executive functions. Under this model, the function of the Subject Committees as decision-makers was inevitably displaced, though they retained a role in the development of policy and the formulation of secondary legislation, as well as in holding Secretaries to account. It was not practicable at this stage to rethink the basic scheme of a corporate body. Instead, the Act authorised the conferring of the executive functions on the subject Secretaries through the mechanism of

---

[1] See Keith Patchett, 'The New Welsh Constitution: The Government of Wales Act 1998', in J. Barry Jones and Denis Balsom, *The Road to the National Assembly for Wales*, University of Wales Press, 2000, 229-264.

[2] *A Voice for Wales*, Cm 3718, 1997.

delegation by the Assembly to the First Secretary who was made responsible for onward delegations.

SEPARATION OF POWERS

A trend became evident with the renaming of the Secretaries as Ministers and the Executive Committee as the Cabinet, and the appointment of Deputy Ministers (a group that has no legal status under the Government of Wales Act). The practical separation of the governmental structure was realised in November 2001, when the description of 'Welsh Assembly Government' was ascribed to the Ministers and the Deputy Ministers and the officials in the departments under the subject Ministers, the bulk of the civil service. From the start it appointed a Counsel General, as its legal adviser, and established an important office, the Office of the Counsel General, to provide the legal services of the Assembly. In practice this now principally provides for the legal needs of the Assembly Government. Neither position is referred to in the Act.

From early in its life, under the initiative of the Presiding Officer, the parliamentary functions of the Assembly were treated distinctively and increasingly given support from its own cadre of officials from the civil service. This culminated in the establishment of another non-statutory office - the Presiding Office – with its own budget and personnel function, to provide parliamentary services to all Assembly Members not in government, in the appointment of a Clerk and Deputy Clerk to the Assembly, and in access to independent legal advice. In addition, a House Committee, initially created to provide advice with respect to the operation of the parliamentary services, is being replaced by a Committee that will exercise powers delegated to it directly by the Assembly.

In February 2002, the plenary Assembly unanimously supported the clearest possible separation between the Assembly Government and the Assembly that can be achieved under the legislation as it presently stands. This has been symbolically recognised by the adoption by each body of distinctive logos. Accordingly, within the framework of a single corporate body, Wales now has a distinct governmental structure and another, comprising of the rest of the Assembly, which has features that are generally attributed to parliaments, for example, law-making (though only secondary legislation in the case of the Assembly), scrutiny and holding ministers to account. As the First Minister has stated on many occasions, the elastic of the original statutory model has had to be extensively stretched to allow these developments to take place. In the process, the institution has grown differently and rather beyond what was envisaged in the White Paper.

These developments are reflected in the number of personnel and in costs. Although the White Paper, somewhat unrealistically, envisaged that a further 100 posts would be required in addition to the 2,300 civil servants in the former Welsh Office, in fact some 3,800 now serve the Assembly (of whom 230 work in the Presiding Office), an increase of 63 per cent.[3] The costs of administration for the Assembly have risen from the original estimate of £92m in 1997 to something of the order of £146m.

This restructuring of the Assembly has contributed to a significant strengthening of its capacity for policy making. Within the Assembly Government, a stronger focus on policy formation has been facilitated by the work of a Strategic Policy Unit, the establishment of a Research and Development Group and the recruitment of specialist policy advisers. Moreover, it has provided an appropriate foundation for improved processes for managing and delivering governmental functions, as, for example, the Executive Board set up in October 2001. One result of this centralisation of capacity is that the Assembly Government is beginning to implement distinctive policies in important areas of service delivery. Other chapters explore initiatives that have been undertaken in education and training, educational curricula, student learning grants, health service restructuring, economic development, Welsh language and bilingualism, and the introduction of more personal benefits, such as free eye tests and bus passes for the aged. Indeed, in a number of areas, notably education and aspects of health policy, the Assembly Government has shown an intention not to follow initiatives of the Westminster Government. There is no question that the Assembly Government is developing a capacity for policy formation that is enabling the Assembly to respond to Welsh needs and interests more effectively than was possible under the derivative practices of the previous Welsh Office.

That acknowledged, the Assembly is faced with a number of problems that have constitutional implications. Arguably, these have not seriously impaired its work, in part because it has benefited from rising financial settlements from London throughout the first term. In fact, in the 2001-02 financial year its budget was under-spent. A further factor has been the political congruence between the Assembly Government and the Westminster Government. However, in the longer term neither can be guaranteed . Changes to either are likely to affect the stability of the institution and its capacity for further development. These are matters being addressed by the Richard Commission on the Assembly's powers, established in July 2002 and due to report by the end of 2003. Substantive change, for instance an extension of the Assembly's legislative powers, will call for amendments to the Government of Wales Act.

---

[3] See Written Evidence of the Permanent Secretary to the Assembly to the Richard Commission, December 2002.

RESTRICTIONS ARISING FROM THE CORPORATE STRUCTURE

The original conception of a single corporate entity exercising functions on behalf of the Crown[4] is difficult to justify once the executive functions are treated as the responsibility of a designated part of that body. The case for a formal differentiation of the executive, as distinct from the non-executive functions, has been greatly strengthened by the establishment of the Assembly Government and the Presiding Office. Indeed, separate identification of the Administration from the Opposition and backbench groups makes better sense in order that those actually responsible for governmental decision-making can be made answerable for their actions to the electorate.

The device, necessitated by the Assembly's corporate nature, of fixing the responsibilities of Ministers by a chain of delegation from the Assembly, rather than by direct statutory authority, has therefore little to commend it. Since it is the Ministers who perform governmental functions, the legislation should reflect reality by specifically requiring them to carry out their functions on behalf of the Crown.[5]

Moreover, were primary legislative powers to be vested in the Assembly, it is difficult to see how a single, essentially executive, body could be maintained. Indeed, it would be constitutionally dubious to speak of the Assembly as acting on behalf of the Crown when exercising such powers. Further, it would be highly anomalous if, at least under the present terms of the statute[6], the Assembly, when enacting primary law that delegates power to make general subordinate legislation, would have to delegate to itself. At the same time, the question will still need to be resolved as to whether the Assembly is to continue as the authority with secondary law-making powers, including those that have already been vested in it under current legislation. Except in relation to routine instruments, the removal of these powers from the plenary Assembly, for example in favour of the Assembly Government, would be to dispense with valuable procedures that allow elected members to engage with secondary legislation rather more effectively than is the case at Westminster.[7] An alternative would be to enable the Assembly to operate in two legislative modes.

The corporate concept was originally justified on the further ground that it

---

[4] Government of Wales Act 1998, section 1(3) ('GWA').

[5] The Assembly Secretaries, unlike the other AMs, are treated as Crown servants for the purposes of the Official Secrets Act, *ibid.*, section 53(4).

[6] GWA, section 66, especially s.66(7).

[7] GWA, ss. 58 & 65-66.

enabled all Assembly staff to be civil servants within the Home Civil Service. The emergence of the Presiding Office servicing non-executive functions raises the question whether its staff should continue to be part of the same civil service or whether, as in the case of Scotland, they should be separately employed. As evidence to the Richard Commission has pointed out, current arrangements have moved a good way in this direction, for example formal agreements between the Clerk to the Assembly and the Permanent Secretary grant a considerable degree of autonomy in relation to Presiding Office staff.[8] However, legislation will be needed if the staff are to be legally independent of those who service the Assembly Government, and that is likely to be tied up with the wider question of whether an appropriate career structure can be offered, perhaps as a part of a more extensive reform with respect to employment in the public sector in Wales.[9]

There is now widespread recognition that the single corporate body model should be replaced. There is no reason why the parliamentary parts of the Assembly should not continue as a distinct corporate body under its existing name, but the Government would need to be constituted separately, perhaps under a different name that disassociates it from the Assembly.

COMPLEXITY OF FUNCTIONS

The most trenchant criticisms made about the settlement relate to the complex ways in which functions, both executive and secondary law making, have been conferred on the Assembly. The scheme exhibits a lack of coherence in the extent to which functions under different legislation have been transferred, which still reflects the somewhat arbitrary ways in which functions were vested in the Secretary of State over the years preceding devolution.

The principal source of functions, the first Transfer of Functions Order[10], sets out in particularised and chronological terms the legislative sources of the functions the Assembly was initially authorised to exercise with respect to its subject fields as defined by the Government of Wales Act 1998. Subsequently important modifications have been made by a variety of means.[11] These include:

---

[8] See Written Evidence of the Presiding Officer to the Richard Commission, December 2002.

[9] See Written Evidence of the Permanent Secretary to the Richard Commission, December 2002.

[10] SI 1999/672.

[11] Keith Patchett, *Enhancing Welsh Input into Westminster Legislation*, IWA Discussion Paper No. 14, 2001.

- A small number of subsequent transfer orders.[12]

- Amendments to the legislation listed in the Transfer of Functions Order.

- Vesting of new functions by Acts and secondary legislation directly on the Assembly.

- European designation orders authorising the Assembly to make regulations to implement specified obligations governed by EU law.[13]

This difficulty is compounded by the differing degree to which functions are devolved from statute to statute and by the variety of drafting devices used to express the functions.[14] Keeping track of the instruments used for conferring functions and ascertaining whether or in what form a function exists, as well as any statutory constraints as to its exercise, present real problems for the user.[15] Some aids to finding the legislation which affects Wales do exist, for example the Assembly's own website and the electronic digest managed by the Cardiff Law School.[16] Yet even a glance at the entries in the latter shows how complex the information has to be in order that the contents of particular legislation can be adequately explained.

Recent trends suggest that some of these practices will be improved upon in future legislation as experience of devolution grows. Even so, presentational changes will make only minor improvements to the confusing devolution inheritance. In any case, Parliamentary Counsel find it necessary to handle the Welsh dimension in differing ways, since different legislative schemes require different drafting approaches.[17]

Rationalisation of these features is not easy. In principle, a case can be made for devolution of executive responsibility by reference to subject heads alone. This could be achieved only by a major revision of the Government of Wales Act and would involve renewed negotiation with Whitehall on the limits of the devolution. Such an approach still leaves open the question as to the precise statutory functions that are covered by those heads. The executive

---

[12] SIs 1999/2787, 2000/253,1829 & 1830; 2001/3679.

[13] For example. SIs 1999/2788, 2000/2812, 2001/2555, 2683, 3495 & 3919, 2002/248 & 1080.

[14] For fuller accounts, see David Lambert, 'A Voice for Wales: the National Assembly for Wales', in *Legal Wales: its past, its future*, Welsh Historical Society, 2001, 167-18; Richard Rawlings, 'A Quasi-Legislative Devolution: Powers and Principles', (2001) 52 NILQ 54-81.

[15] See in particular the evidence of the Law Society of England and Wales to the Assembly Review of Procedure, ARP-06-01(P5), 21 March 2001.

[16] David Miers and David Lambert, 'Law making in Wales: Wales Legislation on-line', [2002] *Public Law* 663-669. The web-site is www.wales-legislation.org.uk.

[17] See Evidence of the First Parliamentary Counsel to the Welsh Affairs Committee Enquiry into the Legislative Process as it affects Wales, 16 December 2002, 2001-2002 HC1242–ii.

must be able to know what it is entitled or expected to perform. The Scotland Act 1978, which used this mechanism, refined the listed groups of subject heads at some length by reference to individually identified statutes. Indeed, it was the complexity of that solution, and the need for constant updating that led to its rejection in 1998. Instead, the Scotland Act 1998 conferred on the Scottish Parliament a general legislative competence in all matters except those reserved to the Westminster Parliament.[18] Executive devolution was made to follow legislative competence, and was therefore subject to the same range of exceptions.[19] If this device were to be applied to executive devolution for Wales to replace the present form, the list of subject heads and that of the excepted matters would be more detailed than for Scotland, not least because the coverage of Welsh devolution is necessarily more limited.

Rationalisation might also be achieved without such a radical change to the Government of Wales Act if the Assembly were to be given generalised secondary law-making powers with respect to groups of related matters within the devolved fields. Provided these included Henry VIII powers to amend and replace existing law, this would enable the Assembly to provide greater coherence in relation to those matters. Safeguards might be built, for example by authorising Parliament to scrutinise such instruments and to disapprove any considered to constitute a misuse of the Assembly's authority.

In any case, more could be done under the existing scheme both to standardise the statutory formulae by which functions are transferred and in explaining in individual bills the extent to which Wales is affected. For example, as appears likely to be the case from Session 2002-2003, the Explanatory Notes to Acts will summarise in one place the provisions that are applicable to Wales.[20]

RELATIONSHIP WITH WHITEHALL AND WESTMINSTER

Devolution implies that the devolved authority is entitled to go its own way within pre-determined limits. The extent of that right and the defining of those limits are matters for negotiation between the centre and the devolved body and should be reflected in an overall settlement and the legislation that is subsequently made. In fact, the Welsh devolution settlement is being constantly rewritten as new legislation that affects the Assembly's competence

---

[18] Scotland Act 1998, ss.29-30; Sched.5.

[19] *Ibid.*, ss.52-55.

[20] Evidence of First Parliamentary Counsel (*op. cit*).

is enacted by Parliament. In consequence, the relationship between the Assembly and central Government is the key to the future of the settlement.

Patently, some Whitehall departments, notably those whose responsibilities are principally with non-devolved subject fields, are less comfortable than others with Assembly expectations on working relations. For instance the Finance Minister Edwina Hart has singled out the Home Office as seeming to regard the Assembly as simply a large local authority that was a "nuisance" to deal with.[21]

The pivot of the Assembly's relationship with Whitehall is the Secretary of State, through whom much of what it may want has to be channelled. If the Assembly's requirements for distinctive treatment in primary legislation made by Parliament are to be met, it is difficult to see how under the present settlement that could be done except with the active involvement of a senior member of Government, and a separate office, concerned solely with Welsh matters. But that raises potential concerns for a future where the Secretary of State either through personality or political allegiances is less than sympathetic to those requirements.

The Wales Office is no mere conduit or channel of communication. The Secretary of State is entitled to act on the basis of his own assessment as a Cabinet Minister in central Government, subject of course to collective Cabinet responsibility. The First Minister has indicated an intention that the Assembly will not follow a number of the policy initiatives from central Government in the fields of education and health, a position that may colour future negotiations in those areas.[22] Not to exercise powers that have been devolved is obviously a prerogative of a devolved authority. Difficulties are more likely to arise where a more confident Assembly wishes to acquire additional powers to develop alternative policies that follow materially different directions from those to be taken by Whitehall. We have already seen on the issue of free care for the elderly the discounting by the Wales Office of a policy that was unanimously endorsed by the Assembly.[23]

In fact, during the first term relatively smooth co-operative arrangements have been worked out between the Assembly Government and Whitehall with respect to legislative projects affecting devolved matters, although the processes are largely conducted under the direction of the latter. The Assembly has recommended a series of Guidelines, originally devised by Professor Rick Rawlings, that should be observed in formulating bills that

---

[21] Evidence of the Assembly Finance Minister to the Richard Commission, 6 December 2002.

[22] Speech at University of Wales, Swansea, 11 December 2002. See also IWA, *Dragon Takes a Different Route; Monitoring the National Assembly September to December 2002*, December 2002.

[23] IWA, *Engaging with Europe: Monitoring the National Assembly March to June 2002*, IWA, 2002, 2-3.

touch upon the Assembly's area of competence.[24] These are designed to ensure that future legislation affecting matters within the Assembly's responsibility confers any new functions in sufficiently broad terms to enable the Assembly Government to develop its own policies flexibly. It remains to be seen whether these will be adopted and regularly followed in Whitehall and in any case how compliance will be monitored.

However, the relationship of the Assembly at large with new legislative projects is less satisfactory. The rules of Government confidentiality mean that the rest of the Assembly remains outside the processes for working up a legislative project. Unless Government is prepared to put out a bill for consultation or pre-legislative scrutiny, the Assembly at large only sees the legislation when the bill is made public.

It has now become the practice for the Assembly in the debate on the Queen's Speech to identify those Bills that are of particular relevance to its responsibilities. It then remits these to the relevant Subject Committee for consideration of the Welsh-related provisions and how the Assembly might use the powers conferred.[25] While this process does afford the Assembly an opportunity to react to new legislation, it provides no guarantee that the views of members will carry weight with the Assembly Government or the lead departments. There is no formal machinery for these views to be fed directly to the departments. Instead they must be forwarded through the Secretary of State who may have different views.[26] In any case, they will be subject to evaluation by the lead department and Parliamentary Counsel. The effectiveness of these arrangements depends in part on the committees having adequate time after publication of the bill to receive a briefing on the often complex drafts from officials and to analyse and report on their provisions. This can turn upon the time at which the bill becomes available and the competing commitments of the committees. Assembly Ministers are expected to report to the Assembly as to the extent to which the bills may have accommodated their representations.[27] There is very little that the Assembly can do if those representations have not been successful.

Assembly influence may be more effective if a bill is published in draft for pre-legislative scrutiny, since, unlike bills published after their first parliamentary reading, the legislative scheme has not been finalised. This procedure is being

---

[24] Report of Assembly Procedural Review, 2002, Annex V. For Rawlings' scheme, see 'A Quasi-Legislative Devolution: Powers and Principles', *op. cit*. See also Evidence of the Secretary of State and First Minister to the Welsh Affairs Committee, 16 December 2002, 2002-2003 HC 79–i.

[25] The Assembly Procedural Review recommended that the procedure should be prescribed by Standing Orders: Report, para.4.12.

[26] The Assembly Procedural Review would like to see the Secretary of State or his deputy attending subject committees working on bills: Report, para.4.10.

[27] SO 31.10.

used for a small number of Government bills. A strong case has been made for extension of the practice, particularly to all Wales-only bills, as happened in the case of the NHS (Wales) Bill. Similarly, there is value in the Subject Committees taking part in the public consultation when that procedure is used with respect to a bill that affects Wales, as happened with the Mental Health Bill.[28] Although deadlines will be set, such scrutiny or consultation enables a more considered examination of provisions at a stage when improvements can be more readily accommodated. There is little doubt that Subject Committees would feel that their work in relation to bills in this form would be more productive.

More can be done, also without legislation, to strengthen the relationship between the Assembly at large and Parliament in relation to legislative matters affecting Wales. These were being examined by the Welsh Affairs Committee in its inquiry into the legislative process as it affects Wales.[29] It has heard that there are concerns that the Welsh dimensions of bills now receive less attention than in the past. In particular, there are no formal procedures by which Assembly views or proposals for amendments can be fed into the parliamentary process. The Committee has received a series of proposals to encourage more of a partnership approach between the Assembly collectively and the Welsh MPs and in particular the Welsh Grand Committee and the Welsh Affairs Committee itself. These include procedural changes in the Parliamentary process that would accord a more formal status to the concerns and proposals of the Assembly.

WEAKENING OF THE ACCOUNTABILITY MECHANISMS

The concentration of executive authority and civil service support in the Assembly Government has weakened the capacity of the elected members to hold the executive to account. Especially since the formation of the coalition government in October 2000, the Assembly Government seems to have been able to avoid open debate on some controversial policy issues, such as the health reforms that were pushed through during 2001-2002.

Moreover, the strengthening of the governmental machinery and the concentration of resources for that purpose has induced a serious imbalance in the specialist support upon which institutions must depend. Although it

---

[28] See further Keith Patchett, *Developing a Partnership Approach to Primary Legislation between Westminster and the National Assembly*, IWA, 2002, the IWA submission to the Welsh Affairs Committee inquiry into the Legislative Process as it affects Wales.

[29] Ibid.

must be expected that this will be principally focused in the government machine, Assembly Members outside government are just as reliant upon such services if they are to scrutinise governmental action effectively. Although the need is from time to time acknowledged, for example by the Assembly Review of Procedure, which pressed for significantly greater specialist support for the Subject Committees[30], only one specialist adviser (a lawyer) has been appointed. Generally, the numbers of civil servants in the Presiding Office seem disproportionately small, given the range of parliamentary activities that the Office is expected to support. Any increase in the size of the Assembly or in its powers, not least in the form of primary legislative powers, would impact adversely on the Members' capacity to carry out their functions.

At the heart of the problem is the role of the Subject Committees, since the function of policy formation has passed substantially into the hands of the Assembly Government. With varying degrees of success the Subject Committees have conducted consultations and reviews of specific policy areas that have fed into Government thinking, and they have debated major Assembly White Papers. To that end the membership of the relevant Minister of the committee may allow members to exert some influence on the direction of policy that would not otherwise be possible. At the same time, however, that membership may create inhibitions among members when exercising their scrutiny role. Indeed, without their own sources of expertise, committees are handicapped in their ability to examine their Minister rigorously with respect to the future direction of policy as well as the work undertaken in their subject field.

Moreover, the Committees have generally yet to come to terms with making substantive scrutiny of the increasing body of secondary legislation flowing from the Assembly Government, for instance, they have done nothing in terms of initiating their own drafts, as they are so entitled.

LACK OF ASSEMBLY MEMBERS

All indications are that the number of AMs is insufficient to enable the Assembly to carry out its changing and broadening responsibilities. The relative smallness of the jurisdiction is of little relevance in determining the size of an institution, compared with the range of functions it is expected to perform. Both Scotland, with 129 members, and Northern Ireland, with 108, have a considerably larger membership. From the current 60 members of the Assembly in Wales must be drawn nine Ministers, five Deputy Ministers, a

---

[30] Report of Assembly Review of Procedure, para.6.20.

Presiding and a Deputy Presiding Officer, as well as the membership of numerous committees, many requiring representation according to the party distribution in the Assembly. These include seven Subject Committees, and the Audit, Business, Legislation, Equal Opportunities, European, Planning and Standards of Conduct Committees as well as four Regional Committees. It is hardly surprising if AMs are unable sometimes to develop expertise or even focused interest in the substantive work of all the committees on which they must sit. It means, too, that there are likely to be difficulties in finding, from this restricted choice, AMs of the appropriate quality to occupy ministerial office or positions as committee chairs. There can be no question that 60 would prove to be a seriously inadequate number were primary legislative powers to be conferred.

Yet, proposals to increase numbers, for example to 80[31], will bring problems. The first is acceptance, particularly of the increased costs, by a still cynical electorate. Then there is the issue of their selection: how many will be elected by first-past-the post in constituencies and how many by proportional representation from party lists? A third question is that increasing the size of the Assembly would inevitably open the issue of the appropriate number of Westminster MPs, given that, under the present alignment of constituencies, the number of constituency AMs is dictated by the number of Welsh parliamentary constituencies.[32] There is also the precedent in Scotland that the number of Westminster MPs are being reduced, following legislative devolution.

CASE FOR PRIMARY LEGISLATIVE POWERS

The Assembly has moved on in its policy-making role perhaps further than might have been envisaged when the White Paper was published. Most Assembly Ministers have reported in their evidence to the Richard Commission that few problems have been experienced to date in formulating policy proposals for want of the necessary authority from an Act of Parliament.

However, in principle the Assembly's capacity for initiative is constricted by its dependence on Government and Parliament for providing the legislative framework within which it can advance a distinctive Welsh dimension. It seems probable that there will only ever be room for one Welsh-only bill each Parliamentary session. While this is considerably more than in the past, cases

---

[31] Eighty is the number suggested by the Presiding Officer (See Evidence to the Richard Commission), and is also said to be the number of seats in the proposed Assembly Chamber.

[32] GWA, Schedule 1.

will arise when the Assembly is unable to secure desirable statutory changes as promptly as circumstances demand. For example, in pursuit of a more integrated approach to post-16 education, the Assembly has brought two Assembly sponsored bodies, the National Council for Education and Training in Wales and the Higher Education Funding Council for Wales, under a single administrative umbrella – Education and Learning in Wales (ELWa). The two Councils were established and operate under different Acts of Parliament.[33] Accordingly any steps to restructure them into a single body must be done by Act of Parliament. This largely structural change will come about only if the proposal receives sufficient priority to be included in legislation that finds a place in a future Westminster legislative programme.

A case can be made for an annual Miscellaneous Provisions (Wales) Bill, where a range of lesser Welsh-related changes, such as that just described, could be accommodated. However, other needs, and particularly radical or controversial measures, may have to be met by piggy-backing on to Whitehall-driven projects, and therefore on the central UK Government's priorities.

The alternative is to confer some primary legislative power on the Assembly itself. Constitutionally, it seems odd that the body charged with scrutinising the way services are framed and delivered and holding those who implement those services to account has no formal role in the making of the primary legislation on those issues. At the same time, Whitehall and Parliament, which have no formal role in delivery and holding to account with respect to those services, are finally the institutions responsible for creating the primary statutory framework.

The possession of primary powers would also enable the Assembly to rationalise the present allocation of functions, as well as to pursue coherent policy development without having to fit this within London's priorities. At the same time, if Scotland's experience is any guide[34], there would be many occasions on which the Assembly would be content to allow Parliament to legislate on particular devolved matters for Wales as well as for England. But that would encourage a more level playing field for negotiation as to the legislative content.

Conferment of such primary powers need not take place across the whole range of devolved subject fields at one and the same time. A rolling programme could start with subject fields, or parts of them, in which policy divergence has already taken place, such as education, health, language and culture. It would make sense to ease the change in by stages, given the

---

[33] The Learning and Skills Act 2000 and the Further and Higher Education Act 1992.

[34] A. Page and A. Batey, Scotland's Other Parliament: Westminster Legislation about Devolved Matters in Scotland Since Devolution", [2002] *Public Law* 501-523.

Assembly's lack of experience and the need to develop a cadre of legislative drafters of its own.

In the end, the constraints upon an Assembly with primary legislative power are likely to be financial, rather than legal. It is improbable that the Assembly will pursue policies that it cannot fund. The real negotiation between Cardiff and London should be over the mechanisms and levels of financing Welsh services.[35] If devolution has meaning it is that the devolved body has the right to decide how to spend its income. It follows that it should have the necessary legal powers to do precisely that.

SOME BROADER CONSIDERATIONS

If changes are to be made to the present settlement, they should be fully thought through. The Richard Commission offers an opportunity for a considered review of the possible options and for public participation in working out a more appropriate constitutional model.[36] The inadequacies of the pre-devolution debate must not be repeated, nor should the solutions be dictated by sectional political interests to the extent that occurred then. At the same time, there must be some realism about the likelihood of the UK Government making time for substantial legislative changes. It would be unfortunate if piecemeal amendments were made at irregular intervals rather than a unified new start. As with any other governmental structures, Wales requires a single coherent constitutional document, not a series of amending instruments to the original Government of Wales Act.

We should not lose sight of the possible implications of the emergence of distinctive areas of Wales-only law. As the Assembly has competence to make subordinate legislation "in relation to Wales"[37], it appears that within the unitary legal system of England and Wales two law districts have come into being with respect to the matters covered by the devolved fields. This would be even more marked if primary legislative powers were to be conferred on the Assembly, when, perhaps uniquely, there would be two legislatures with such competence with respect to the single legal system.[38] In principle, it is

---

[35] A power to tax, which is a matter on the Richard Commission agenda, would be unlikely to enable the Assembly to raise sums that make a significant addition to its resources. In any case, the First Minister has made clear that such powers would not be used (see *Western Mail*, 2 December 2002).

[36] See the Commission's consultation paper, issued November 2002, and Keith Patchett, *Issues and Methodology*, IWA website (www.iwa.org.uk), 2002, IWA Observations to the Richard Commission.

[37] GWA, s.22(1)(a).

[38] In the quasi-federal cases of Scotland and Northern Ireland, their legislatures exercise primary legislative authority, in a range of subject fields, over the *entire* legal system.

possible to contemplate conflicts of law where the law enacted by the Assembly in relation to the law district of Wales diverges from that enacted by Parliament for the law district of England.

In similar situations where conflicts arise between two different legal systems as to the law applicable to activities of persons with links to both, a well-established body of conflict of laws rules prescribes the legal connections that determine which law applies. Presumably, the same standard connecting factors would be used to determine the law for parties with links to the two law districts within England and Wales. At least theoretically, cases may arise where it might be necessary to show that a person had, for example habitual residence either in Wales or in England, as distinct from somewhere in England and Wales.

In practice, such conflicts might not arise frequently since much of the law likely to be enacted by the Assembly concerns delivery of services within the geographical area of Wales. On the other hand, were the Assembly within its subject fields to enact regulatory provisions or to confer rights or powers on individuals or firms that are linked in some way with Wales, questions could arise as to whether and when this legislation applied to them rather than any made by the Westminster Parliament. This perhaps raises the related issue of the actual limits of the secondary law-making power. When does (or does not) an instrument make provision "in relation to Wales"? Particularly if primary powers are to be granted, it may be necessary to spell out, more precisely than "in relation to Wales", the connecting factors that bring persons or transactions within the ambit of Assembly-made law. It could be a matter of concern to, for example a company that has its operational base in England, to know in what Wales-related circumstances it might have to comply with different legal requirements enacted by the Assembly. If clear connecting factors are not spelt out, the courts of England and Wales could be faced with resolving conflicts of laws and other problems in circumstances that would be unique in the United Kingdom.

CHAPTER 2

MULTI-LEVEL GOVERNANCE

Robert Hazell

This chapter reviews the machinery of intergovernmental relations which has been developed to mediate the communication between the Assembly Government, Whitehall and Westminster. It focuses in particular on the preparation of primary legislation affecting Wales, providing an example of some of the difficulties faced by the Assembly Government in its dealings with Whitehall and Westminster.

The adequacy of the legislative process as it affects Wales has been investigated by two parliamentary Select Committees: the Welsh Affairs Committee of the House of Commons, and the Constitution Committee of the House of Lords. The adequacy of the Assembly's law making powers is also the central issue to be addressed by the Richard Commission into the Powers and Electoral Arrangements of the National Assembly.

THE FORMAL MACHINERY

The formal machinery of intergovernmental relations post devolution need only be briefly summarised here.[1] The Joint Ministerial Committee (JMC) is the central piece of machinery created to discuss devolution issues and to resolve devolution disputes. It was created under the *Memorandum of Understanding and Supplementary Agreements* agreed between the UK Government, Scottish Ministers and the Cabinet of the National Assembly for Wales, first published in October 1999. The JMC has not yet been tested in dispute resolution mode, and has met relatively rarely in the early years of devolution:

- Once a year as a plenary meeting of Prime Minister and First Ministers.

- Fairly regularly as the JMC (Europe) to discuss the UK position before big meetings of the EU.

---

[1] See the Cabinet Office evidence to the Lords Committee on the Constitution, *Devolution: Inter-Institutional Relations in the UK*, Evidence 10 July 2002, HL 147 p14; R Hazell, 'Intergovernmental Relations: Whitehall rules OK?' in R Hazell, (Ed.), *The State and the Nations*, Imprint Academic, 2000; A Trench, 'Intergovernmental Relations a Year on: Whitehall still rules UK' in A Trench, *The State of the Nations 2001*, Imprint Academic, 2001.

- Occasionally to discuss initiatives of the Prime Minister or the Chancellor - on such matters as health and poverty.

Bilateral and informal contacts are far more important in the day to day business of making devolution work, and these contacts happen on a daily basis between Ministers, senior officials, and those at working level. Here, too, there are texts to provide guidance, in the Concordats appended to the Memorandum of Understanding, the bilateral Concordats agreed between the UK government and the National Assembly, and the Devolution Guidance Notes issued by the Cabinet Office.[2]

Despite the best intentions of both governments and this plethora of guidance, it is hard to pretend that the arrangements for making primary legislation for Wales are working smoothly or delivering satisfactory legislation for Wales. There are three fundamental difficulties which cannot be ignored:

- The Westminster legislative programme is chronically congested, so that it is always hard to find space for Wales.

- The UK government will always have competing priorities.

- Legislation is too often drafted or amended at the last minute, leaving little time for Wales to be properly consulted.

Each of these difficulties will be explored in turn, following an examination of how the legislative programme is put together each year at Westminster.

THE WESTMINSTER LEGISLATIVE PROGRAMME

The legislative programme for Westminster is prepared in an annual cycle culminating in the Queen's Speech each November, when the government announces the programme for the coming parliamentary session. The programme is planned and managed by the Legislative Programme Cabinet Committee, chaired by the Leader of the House and President of the Council, currently Robin Cook. At the beginning of each calendar year the Cabinet Office issues invitations to all departments to bid for space in the legislative programme, and from Easter onwards it begins to prioritise Bills into marshalled lists with four or five different degrees of priority. These range from bills to fulfil international obligations, and Bills to preserve statutory

---

[2] The main texts covering the making of primary legislation for Wales are: DGN 4, on the Role of the Secretary of State for Wales; DGN 9, on Primary Legislation affecting Wales; and the Concordat between the Cabinet of the National Assembly and the Wales Office.

powers about to expire, to programme Bills promised in the manifesto. Bills with high enough priority receive authorisation to be drafted by Parliamentary Counsel over the summer. The rest languish or die. Competition to get into the legislative programme is extremely fierce, with typically only as few as one in four or one in five of departmental bids managing to gain legislative slots. Slots are not awarded simply on merit: it is a rare session when one of the bigger beasts in the Whitehall jungle, such as David Blunkett or John Prescott, does not get at least one Bill into the programme.

The whole process is meant to be kept a tight secret until the Queen's Speech is given and the contents of the new session's legislative programme are unveiled. In November 2002 the Blair government previewed most of the contents in a carefully orchestrated series of announcements in the days before the Queen's Speech that broke with all convention. Who said that for their second term New Labour were abandoning spin?

Into this confidential process have to be inserted the bids for primary legislation that come up from the National Assembly for Wales. Primary legislation is of fundamental importance to the Assembly, since it is entirely dependent on Acts of the Westminster Parliament for the legal framework within which it develops its own secondary legislation and administrative policies. Westminster defines the powers and functions of the Assembly in matters great and small. In the process it can reduce the Assembly's powers - inadvertently or by design - as well as increase them. The Assembly has to be constantly alert to the possibilities of new legislation from Westminster, in terms of the opportunities it may present as well as the risks.

The Government of Wales Act provides a formal piece of machinery whereby once a year the Secretary of State for Wales consults the National Assembly about the UK legislative programme, and attends a debate in the Assembly on the Queen's Speech, after it has been announced at Westminster. In practice, by then it is usually far too late for the Assembly to gain any slots in the legislative programme for the new session just beginning, so the debate is a bit of an empty ritual. However, the Assembly Government is invited to submit bids well before that, in the spring of each year, at the same time as other Whitehall departments; and it is known what bids the Assembly Government has put forward.

So far the success rate of the Welsh Assembly Government has not been high. Rhodri Morgan claims a 500 per cent improvement by comparison with the years pre-devolution, but the figures do not seem that encouraging.[3] For the 2001-02 session the Assembly Government put forward four bids and got half

---

[3] Oral evidence to Lords Committee on the Constitution, 27 May 2002, in Evidence volume published on 10 July 2002, HC 147, p. 236.

a promise on one.[4] For the 2002-03 session they put forward eight bids but didn't improve their strike rate.[5] This may be no higher than the success rate of any other Whitehall department. But is it right, and in the spirit of devolution, to rank the Assembly alongside any other Whitehall department? The contrast with Scotland is particularly stark: the Scots have been passing a dozen bills a session in the Scottish Parliament (details given below).

Whitehall guidance also makes it quite clear where Whitehall's priorities lie: in supporting the interests of the UK Government, not those of the National Assembly. Devolution Guidance Note (DGN) 9, the Cabinet Office guidance on Post-Devolution Primary Legislation affecting Wales, states bluntly that:

> "The purpose of this guidance is to facilitate the efficient conduct by the UK Government of its legislative business. Disagreements are an impediment to that … ."

The guidance goes on to enjoin departments to consult the Assembly Government at an early stage in the development of legislative proposals, in particular those which confer new functions on the Assembly or alter its existing functions. Consultation will be in confidence and may constrain wider consultation by the Assembly Cabinet:

> "… in no circumstances will the Assembly Cabinet circulate or allude to Bill material without the consent of the lead Department."

By the time proposals reach the Legislation Programme Committee, all devolution-related issues are to have been addressed and so far as possible resolved. Memoranda for the Committee must contain a statement to that effect and should:

- "explain any provision proposed in respect of Wales which differs from the proposal for England or the rest of the UK;

- identify any exception to the general rule that a new function created by the Bill will pass to the Assembly in cases where it already exercises similar functions... ;

- identify any change to the existing functions of the Assembly, including any new function being vested in the Assembly which might raise issues of general principle;

---

[4] The bids were for a Health and Well-Being (Wales) Bill; an Education (Wales) Bill; a St David's Day Bill (to make St David's Day a public holiday); and a Census (Amendment) (Wales) Bill, enabling the indication of Welsh national identity in the 2001 Census: Assembly *Record*, 13 March 2001. Approval was given for the first (the Health and Well Being bill) in the November 2001 Queen's Speech, but as a draft bill, with the promise of legislative time in 2002-03.

[5] The 2002 bids were for a Common Land (Wales) Bill; a Sunday Licensing (Wales) Bill; a St David's Day bill; a Land Use Planning bill; an Education Bill; an Audit (Wales) Bill; a Housing Ombudsman bill; and a Passenger Transport bill: Assembly *Record*, 19 March 2002.

- *confirm that the Assembly has been consulted on the draft clauses as necessary."*

Despite this detailed guidance, our Whitehall interviews suggest that in the early days of devolution consultation was sometimes perfunctory. Memoranda for the Legislation Programme Committee adopted a rather tick box approach. The position has improved since, but there is no disguising the weakness of the Assembly's position. Assembly officials are entirely dependent on Whitehall departments to make the first move in informing the Assembly Government about legislative proposals, and they are entirely dependent on departments keeping them in the loop thereafter. Nor is it always possible for the Assembly to negotiate a different policy solution for Wales: in at least one case that was not permitted by the Whitehall department because the difference between the two approaches would have been too glaring on the face of the Bill.

The other fundamental weakness lies in the long and indirect chain of communication between the Assembly Government in Cardiff and those drafting the bill in London. Assembly Government lawyers in Wales are not allowed to instruct Parliamentary Counsel. If a bill relating entirely to Wales is being drafted, the Assembly can second a skeleton bill team to the Wales Office to help with the preparation of the Bill; and they have seconded individual officials to join bill teams in other departments where the Bill has a significant Welsh component. In the main, however, they are kept a long way away from the legislative action, geographically and figuratively, and are heavily reliant on Whitehall goodwill to keep them in the picture.

FRAGMENTED WELSH LEGISLATION

These fundamental weaknesses - the chronic legislative logjam, Whitehall's overriding priorities, and the rush in which Westminster legislation is prepared - lead in turn to a number of undesirable consequences. Legislation for Wales is often fragmented and incomplete, because the Assembly needs to grab every legislative opportunity it can. As a consequence primary legislation for Wales is hard to find and to understand, because some of it is in patchwork instalments in different statutes. Different statutes also treat the Assembly differently, depending on the approach of the individual draftsman. Finally, because the timetables of Westminster and the Assembly do not always coincide, legislation for Wales can fall between the two legislatures and be poorly scrutinised.

The best known example of fragmentation lies in the only Wales-only Bill so far passed by Westminster since devolution, the Children's Commissioner for Wales Act 2001. Despite its title, the Act did not establish the Children's Commissioner for Wales. That was done the previous year, in Part V of the Care Standards Act 2000. In his evidence to the Lords Constitution Committee when they came to Cardiff Rhodri Morgan was quite candid about the reason why:

> "But even that was messy because they said, 'If you would like to have that a year earlier, we can include it in an England and Wales Bill.' That has become quite common. We bid for a bill, they say 'Yes, okay, we will go with that but would you like to tag on the principle and get it established a year earlier than you could otherwise do?' Obviously we grabbed that opportunity."[6]

So fragmented and so hard to find is the law relating to Wales that Cardiff Law School has launched a new public information service, Wales Legislation on-line, with funding from the Arts and Humanities Research Board:

> "The website is updated weekly and is the only known source of information which sets out in one comprehensive source the Assembly's current powers and the general subordinate legislation which it is making."[7]

It says something about the accessibility of primary legislation relating to Wales that this new service is essentially a private initiative, even though its prime mover is David Lambert, former Chief Legal Adviser to the Welsh Office, and now the Legal Adviser to the Presiding Office of the National Assembly.

The next undesirable consequence of dependency on Westminster for primary legislation is the extraordinary variation in how legislation for Wales is drafted, and in particular how new powers and functions are conferred on the Assembly. This was strongly brought out in the evidence to the Welsh Affairs Committee and Lords Constitution Committee inquiries, from independent and official sources. Lord Elis-Thomas said in his evidence to the Lords Committee:

> "At present, there is no consistency of practice and no clear convention on the drafting of Bills which affect Wales - indeed, as the Constitution Unit has argued, each new Bill can be seen as re-inventing devolution."[8]

---

[6] *Ibid* p236.

[7] David Miers and David Lambert, 'Law Making in Wales: Wales Legislation on-line', *Public Law* winter 2002, 663.

[8] Evidence to Lords Committee on the constitution, 10 July 2002, HL 147, p253 para 9.

The point was developed by Professor Keith Patchett in his evidence:

"... the decentralised nature of law preparation in the UK means that devolution arrangements for Wales are being re-written in different ways in each Westminster Bill ... The piecemeal manner in which powers, both executive and subsidiary law making, have been conferred on the Assembly has been widely criticised ... the powers are expressed in a wide variety of forms ... Clarity in distinguishing the Assembly's powers has in a number of cases given way to the overall structural demands of the legislative scheme. Such factors led the Law Society to comment on the absence of any overarching logic in the devolution of statutory powers."[9]

Government guidance in DGN 9, on the making of primary legislation affecting Wales, is silent about any principles to be observed in determining the approach to devolving new powers. To fill the gap Professor Richard Rawlings proposed a set of principles, to ensure greater consistency of treatment and parity with powers conferred on English Ministers. These were adopted with minor variations by the National Assembly Review of Procedure (chaired by Lord Elis-Thomas) which reported in February 2002.[10] The Review urged the First Minister to communicate the 'Rawlings principles' to the UK Government, and to impress on Whitehall departments the importance of adopting the principles. There then ensued a long silence, for which there are several possible explanations. Practice in Whitehall was starting to get better, so Welsh Ministers may have decided not to rock the boat. Some of the Assembly's senior lawyers thought the principles were unworkable. The First Minister may have decided not to force the issue, recognising that UK Ministers were unlikely to agree to be bound in advance by an approach to England and Wales issues which would unduly fetter their discretion. But early in 2003 the issue was forced for him, when the Welsh Affairs Committee was expected also to endorse the Rawlings principles. This in turn will force the UK government in their response to indicate whether they are willing to abide by the principles, or whether they would prefer to continue to allocate powers to the Assembly on a case-by-case basis.

Professor Patchett's comprehensive submission to the Lords Committee contains a powerful critique of the whole law making process in relation to Wales. The final criticism is the inadequate scrutiny of primary legislation for Wales, which is compounded by the difficulties of integrating the operations of two sets of institutions that have different working practices, priorities, resources and timetables. Most legislation for Wales is contained in combined England and Wales Bills, but in practice parliamentary scrutiny at

---

[9] *Ibid* pp 288-9, paras 19, 26, 27.

[10] R Rawlings, 'Quasi-Legislative Devolution: Powers and Principles', 52 NILQ, 54-81, 2001. The modified Rawlings principles are reproduced in Annex 5 of the Assembly Review of Procedure.

Westminster focuses overwhelmingly on the English arrangements. This is perhaps understandable given that England represents 85 per cent of the UK population, and Wales just 5 per cent.

However, even in the rare case of a Wales-only Bill Westminster scrutiny can be seriously inadequate. An outstanding example is the NHS (Wales) Bill, announced in June 2001 with proposals to radically restructure the health service in Wales, replacing the five existing health authorities with 22 new local health boards. Health Minister Jane Hutt said in a press release:

> *"The intention is for the draft bill to be published in the Autumn and the Assembly will have a strong voice in discussing and debating the proposals before they reach the House of Commons. This responds directly to our bid for such a Bill earlier this year and shows how the National Assembly and Westminster can work together for Wales."*[11]

What happened next illustrates very strongly how the Assembly is at the mercy of Whitehall when it comes to negotiating for legislative time. Within weeks the proposals for a separate NHS (Wales) Bill were dropped. Instead they were to be incorporated in an England and Wales Bill, which would provide a more convenient legislative vehicle for the UK government. This meant the proposals went to Westminster before they had been debated in plenary in Cardiff. The results of the Assembly Government's consultation on the proposals arrived in the House of Commons Library on the morning of the Second Reading debate. Former Welsh Office Health Minister Jon Owen Jones was moved to say some strong words about how Welsh MPs were being bounced into approving this particular piece of legislation:

> *"The debate is an opportunity to test whether the present constitutional settlement for Wales provides a means for adequate scrutiny of new Bills. The Welsh Assembly does not have primary legislation powers, but if Parliament simply acts as a rubber stamp for Welsh matters brought to the House, we should dispense with the charade and move towards giving the Welsh Assembly primary legislation powers."*[12]

The solution offered by the UK government to the problems of rushed timing and inadequate consultation is the publication of more Bills in draft - as the NHS (Wales) Bill was to have been. Draft Bills which are subject to pre-legislative scrutiny and evidence from outside bodies allow for much more probing scrutiny, time for second thoughts by government, and make for better legislation. Robin Cook, the new Leader of the House, is strongly persuaded by their virtues, and has promised that in future more bills will be published in draft. But it is not a promise which he alone can deliver. Because

---

[11] Assembly Government Press Release, 20 June 2001.

[12] House of Commons debate 20 Nov 2001 col 252.

of the decentralised way in which legislative proposals are prepared in Whitehall, it is up to his Cabinet colleagues how far in advance Bills might be drafted, and whether that allows time for a draft Bill stage. All too often it does not. The political imperative of getting the Bill through will almost always override the niceties of better legislative scrutiny, as it will override the separate needs of Wales.

THE SCOTTISH EXAMPLE

Wales gets short shrift under present arrangements. The Assembly is dependent for all its primary legislation on finding legislative time at Westminster. Yet it has little or no control on when that time will be found, in what legislative vehicle, and with what degree of scrutiny.

To see how it might be otherwise it is instructive to look at the different practice in Scotland, where the Scottish Executive and Parliament now have over three years experience of making primary legislation for Scotland. In its first three years the Scottish Parliament passed just over a dozen Bills each session. It might be expected that most of these were on matters of Scots law, but in fact such Bills were a minority. Most of the legislation passed by the Scottish Parliament has been in social policy, in subject areas which are devolved to Wales in terms of executive power, but not yet in terms of legislative power. Of the 44 Acts passed by the Scottish Parliament in its first three years (to September 2002), 31 were on subjects which could be devolved to Wales. Seven were on matters of Scots private law, and six were on Scottish criminal law. The full list is set out in table 1.

The categorisation is inevitably arbitrary. Several Acts could have appeared in one or more categories. But the list serves to illustrate the range of matters on which the Scottish Parliament has legislated, and how many of them might be of interest to the National Assembly, because they fall within its executive competence. Three other matters are worth noticing. First is how many are little Bills which are precisely the kind which are so difficult to squeeze into the legislative programme at Westminster. A small change to the census (which the Welsh were denied, despite a specific request); postgraduate medical degrees at St Andrews; closing the loophole over Erskine Bridge Tolls.

Second, is the number of measures to improve governance and accountability in Scotland, in the Public Finance and Accountability Act, Ethical Standards in Public Life, Freedom of Information Act, and creation of the Parliamentary Standards Commissioner and Public Services Ombudsman. The Scots have used their legislative freedom to raise standards in the way Scotland is governed as well as in what the Scottish government does.

TABLE 1: ACTS OF THE SCOTTISH PARLIAMENT 1999-2002

Category	Year	Title of Act
Health	1999	Mental Health (Public Safety and Appeals)
Education	2000	Education and Training
	2000	Standards in Scotland's Schools etc
	2001	Education (Graduate Endowment and Student Support)
	2002	School Education (Amendment)
	2002	Education (Disability Strategies and Pupils' Educational Records)
	2002	University of St Andrews (Postgraduate Medical Degrees)
Environment	2000	Sea Fisheries (Shellfish)
	2001	Salmon Conservation
	2002	Protection of Wild Mammals
	2002	Water Industry
	2002	Fur Farming (Prohibition)
Finance	2000	Public Finance and Accountability
	2000	Budget
	2001	Budget
	2001	Police and Fire Services (Finance)
	2002	Budget
Care/Social Services	2001	Regulation of Care
	2001	Protection from Abuse
	2002	Community Care and Health
Criminal/Judicial	2000	Bail, Judicial Appointments etc
	2000	Regulation of Investigatory Powers
	2000	Adults with Incapacity
	2001	Convention Rights
	2002	Criminal Procedure (Amendment)
	2002	Sexual Offences (Procedure and Evidence)
Transport	2001	Transport
	2001	Erskine Bridge (Tolls)
Parliamentary/	2000	Ethical Standards in Public Life Governmental
	2000	Census
	2001	Scottish Local Authorities (Tendering)
	2002	Scottish Local Government Act (Elections)
	2002	Scottish Parliamentary Standards Commissioner
	2002	Freedom of Information
	2002	Scottish Public Services Ombudsman
Housing	2001	Leasehold Casualties
	2001	Housing
	2001	Mortgage Rights
Land Use	2000	Abolition of Feudal Tenure
	2000	National Parks
International Agreements	2001	International Criminal Court
Civil Law	2001	Abolition of Poindings and Warrant Sales
	2002	Marriage

The third matter worth noticing is not in the table, but is perhaps the most important. Westminster has also legislated for Scotland, including on devolved matters. Under a procedure known as 'Sewel resolutions' (named after Scottish Office junior Minister Lord Sewel, who first announced the convention in debate on the Scotland Bill) the Scottish Parliament can grant consent to Westminster legislating on matters which are devolved to Scotland.[13] Initially it was supposed that this procedure would be used only rarely, but in the first three years of devolution it has become almost routine. In fact, there have been almost as many Sewel motions - 34 to September 2002 - as there have been Acts of the Scottish Parliament. In making primary legislation for Scotland, Westminster is still as important as the new legislature on the Mound in Edinburgh.

Why do the Scots allow Westminster so frequently to legislate for them, when the Scottish Parliament could be doing the job themselves? In evidence to the Lords Constitution Committee Professor Alan Page identified four main reasons:[14]

- First is the need for uniformity across the UK (or Great Britain). Where the Scots accept that a policy needs to be uniform, and Westminster is legislating anyway, there is little point in the Scottish Parliament spending time in passing separate legislation to achieve the same result.

- Second, it avoids disruption to the Scottish Executive's own legislative programme. The Scottish Parliament has a more rigorous and expert process of legislative scrutiny than the House of Commons, which limits the number of Bills which its committees can consider. So the Executive finds it quite convenient to have an alternative legislative channel, especially where its own legislation might be little different from that proposed by the UK government.

- The third reason is when legislation is necessary to give effect to international or EU obligations. In these circumstances the legislation has to be passed, and the international obligation may leave little room for manoeuvre. Westminster is legislating anyway, and the Scots are content to be included in the Westminster legislation.

---

[13] The convention is formally expressed in the *Memorandum of Understanding* between the UK government and the devolved governments as follows: "The UK Parliament retains authority to legislate on any issue, whether devolved or not. It is ultimately for Parliament to decide what use to make of that power. However, the UK Government will proceed in accordance with the convention that the UK Parliament would not normally legislate with regard to devolved matters except with the agreement of the devolved legislature." Cm 4444, Oct 1999, para 13.

[14] Evidence to Lords Committee on the Constitution, 17 May 2002, in the volume published on 10 July 2002, HC 147, p183. There is also a useful list of Sewel motions setting out all the matters on which the Scottish Parliament has consented to Westminster legislating, at page 196.

- Finally there is legislation to close regulatory loopholes, what Professor Page calls the risk of 'regulatory arbitrage' across the different jurisdictions of the UK. If boltholes are being closed, and they need to be closed in a way which prevents people exploiting any potential differences, it might as well be left to Westminster to enact the uniform regulatory regime.

It was not originally expected to happen this way, and some in Scotland like the nationalists (and occasionally the Conservatives) have been critical of how much the Scottish Parliament has been willing to leave responsibility for legislating on devolved matters to Westminster. But to the more distant observer it seems the Scots may have got the best of both worlds. They legislate for themselves on the whole range of social and domestic policy matters which would be of interest to Wales - health, education, social services, environment, transport, housing. They legislate on matters great and small. Although most of the Bills are small scale, a few - such as those on free long term care, and student tuition fees - have made big policy changes. And when it suits them they let Westminster legislate. But even then the Scots are not losing control. If the Westminster Bill is amended they are invited to re-affirm their approval of the policy (which is why one Westminster Bill can be the subject of more than one Sewel motion). And if subsequently they do not like the way the legislation operates they are still free to legislate themselves on the same subject matter. In this case the subsequent legislation by the Scottish Parliament would override the earlier Westminster legislation in which the Scottish Parliament had originally acquiesced.

WORST OF BOTH WORLDS FOR WALES

In February 2003 the Richard Commission visited Edinburgh to see for themselves how the Scottish Parliament uses its powers of primary legislation. It will be hard for them not to have been struck by some pretty stark comparisons. If Scotland seems to be getting the best of both worlds, is Wales perhaps getting the worst?

While the Scottish Parliament passed 44 Acts in the first three years of devolution, in the same period Wales managed to squeeze just one Wales-only statute out of Westminster. All other primary legislation for Wales was incorporated in England and Wales Bills. Even in the most benign of political circumstances, with a sympathetic administration in London, the record in terms of primary legislation for Wales is not exactly impressive.

The National Assembly's policy wishes are generally followed in these combined England and Wales Bills, but the Assembly has no control over how they are expressed by the draftsman. Welsh interests always run the risk of being subordinate to the policy interest of the lead Whitehall department. If the government in London were unsympathetic or hostile, Welsh interests could simply be ignored or overruled. Whitehall decides when and how much to consult with the relevant interests of the National Assembly. Consultation has got much better, and more timely, but there will always be a risk of the Welsh input being too little, too late, especially where the Assembly committees are concerned.

Whitehall sources admit that the complicated nature of the devolution settlement in Wales causes them more problems than the cleaner break of the settlement with Scotland, and requires endless negotiation and consultation. Consultation about legislative proposals is confidential between Whitehall and the Welsh Assembly Government until the bill is published. Unless a Bill is published in draft, publication does not take place until the Bill is introduced into the Westminster Parliament. This allows little time for Assembly committees to look at Bills before Westminster itself engages with them.

It is extraordinarily difficult to integrate scrutiny by two legislatures with separate priorities and timetables. These difficulties have proved hard to overcome between sympathetic administrations; without goodwill they would be quite impossible. Looking at all the contingencies and complications in the existing arrangements, it is hard not to conclude that Welsh interests will always risk being marginal in Whitehall's and Westminster's priorities, and that under the present settlement Wales risks getting the worst of both worlds.

CHAPTER 3

LAW MAKING

David Miers [1]

This chapter has a particular concern: how has the Assembly used its powers to legislate for Wales? More specifically, to what extent has the Assembly achieved a distinctive legislative profile through its enactment of secondary legislation? The principal measure of distinctiveness is the Assembly's main legislative product: statutory instruments.[2]

Whether that measure demonstrates that the Assembly is making law in a quantitatively and qualitatively distinctive manner depends on an understanding of a number of conceptual, legal and empirical issues. It also raises wider issues that are discussed in other contributions to this book.[3] These include the linked questions: what scope is there for the transfer to the Assembly of a more expansively defined legislative capacity, and what would be required to support any such expansion? This chapter does not rehearse these issues, which are well covered elsewhere in this volume. However, the Assembly's law making activity should be understood within the context of two essential elements that warrant reinforcement:

- The *de facto* creation of a parliamentary government within the corporate structure of the National Assembly,

- Constraints in the relationship between the Assembly, Whitehall and Westminster, in particular concerning the promotion of Wales-only Bills and the routine application to Wales of the UK government's legislative programme.

Attention should also be drawn to the complexities of the devolution settlement for Wales. The following section summarises, first, the key statutory parameters governing the transfer of legislative functions to the Assembly; and, secondly, the difficulties that accompany the determination of the legal effect of a transfer in any case.

---

[1] I am grateful to my colleagues David Lambert and Marie Navarro for many helpful comments on earlier versions of this chapter. Remaining errors are mine.

[2] The Assembly also makes other forms of subordinate legislation such as directions, circulars and codes. These are not considered here.

[3] Chapters 1 (Keith Patchett), 2 (Robert Hazell) and 19 (Jane Williams). See also Lords Committee on the Constitution, *Devolution: Institutional Relations in the United Kingdom* (2002-03; HL 28), paras. 119-125.

THE TRANSFER OF LEGISLATIVE FUNCTIONS

The ways which the Government of Wales Act 1998 transfers legislative powers to the Assembly can be summarised as follows:[4]

- Powers in sections 27, 28 and 32 relating to the Assembly's ability to re-organise health and certain other statutory bodies in Wales, and to do anything which may assist matters relating to culture, sport, historic buildings and the Welsh language.

- Power in section 22 to make subordinate legislation in relation to Wales in respect of functions transferred to the Assembly by central government under Transfer of Functions Orders. The first Order transferred pre-devolution ministerial powers contained in primary and secondary legislation within 18 fields set out in Schedule 2 to the Act.

- Section 21 allows the transfer of functions by primary legislation enacted post-devolution. These need not be confined to the Schedule 2 subject fields. For example, a designation order made under sections 111-112 of the Anti-Terrorism, Crime and Security Act 2001 identified the Assembly as "an authorised Minister" for the purpose of implementing any obligation on the United Kingdom under the Third Pillar of the EU.[5]

- A small number of post-devolution Acts confer limited powers on the Assembly to amend primary legislation by order (Henry VIII clauses).[6]

- Power under section 29 for European designation orders to be made under section 2(2) of the European Communities Act 1972 authorising the Assembly to make regulations giving effect to Community obligations.[7]

Both before and since 1 July 1999, when the Assembly formally began its

---

[4] This section draws on the author's co-written evidence (with David Lambert and Marie Navarro) to the Welsh Affairs Select Committee, Enquiry into the Legislative Process as it Affects Wales (2001-02).

[5] See also sections 8-10 of the Electronic Communications Act 2000.

[6] For example, section 147 of the Transport Act 2000 and section 7 of the Local Government Act 2000. These do not permit the Assembly to widen its order making powers. Under section 4(6) of the Regulatory Reform Act 2001 a Minister making a Regulatory Reform Order may designate the Assembly for the purpose of making a 'subordinate provision' order.

[7] In his evidence to the Richard Commission, the Counsel General, Winston Roddick QC observed: "In the case of agricultural, economic development, environmental and food safety matters most, if not all, Assembly legislation and administrative activity in any year is derived from Community legislation. For example, the Assembly is designated to make regulations in relation to the Common Agricultural Policy and the deliberate release of genetically modified organisms." *Commission on the Powers and Electoral Arrangements of the National Assembly for Wales, December 2002*, para. 53. http://www.wales.gov.uk/subirichard/index-e.htm

work, attention has focused on the Assembly's powers within the 18 subject fields listed in Schedule 2. These comprise the areas within which the Secretary of State for Wales exercised ministerial functions prior to devolution. They were included in the Government of Wales Act for the purpose of enabling the making of the first Transfer of Functions Order (the 1999 TFO).[8] They also mirror the areas in which the devolved institutions in Scotland and Northern Ireland have executive and legislative competence.

However, the devolution settlement in Wales differs from these jurisdictions in two fundamental respects. First, both the Scottish Parliament and the Northern Ireland Assembly enjoy primary as well as secondary legislative powers. Secondly, their powers are general rather than specific in nature. They can exercise any powers unless expressly prevented by the provisions of their respective Acts.[9] By contrast, the Government of Wales Act authorises the exercise only of secondary legislative powers, and authorises them only by way of specific provision. As the Counsel General, Winston Roddick QC, put it in his evidence to the Richard Commission in December 2002:

> *"What the Assembly has, therefore, is a collection of powers given to it piecemeal in a number of Acts and transfer of functions orders."*[10]

No entire area of responsibility within the Schedule 2 fields has been transferred, for example for agriculture, education, health or transport. This is so notwithstanding that they constitute the focus of attention for Assembly Subject Committees and for Cabinet Ministers in the Welsh Assembly Government. As the Cardiff solicitor Michael Jones, a member of the Commission that prepared the Assembly's Standing Orders, observed in his 2002 Annual Law lecture at the St Davids National Eisteddfod:

> *"There is a Minister for Education, but she is not responsible for administering every law that deals with education."*[11]

This partial allocation of responsibility is also an obstacle for those seeking to evaluate the Assembly's contribution to the Welsh economy and public life. Two further points need to be emphasised. First, the transfers under primary or secondary legislation that have been made may impose constraints on the Assembly's power to exercise its functions unilaterally. Many of its powers can only be exercised bilaterally, with the consent of, concurrently or jointly with,

---

[8] The National Assembly for Wales (Transfer of Functions) Order 1999 SI 1999/672.

[9] By sections 29-30 of the Scotland Act 1998, the Scottish institutions have competence in all areas that are not 'protected' (Schedule 4) or 'reserved' (Schedule 5). Section 4 of the Northern Ireland Act 1998 provides that a 'transferred matter' means any matter which is not 'excepted' (Schedule 2) or 'reserved' (Schedule 3).

[10] The Counsel General, Evidence to the Richard Commission, December 2002, para. 71.

[11] M. Jones, *Changing a Camel into a Horse*, The Law Society, National Eisteddfod of Wales, Annual Law Lecture, 2002, p.11.

central government or other devolved bodies.

Secondly, by whatever device they are transferred, so far as the subject matter to which the functions relate are concerned, authority to make law for Wales may reside either in the Assembly (with or without any bilateral obligations) or solely in Whitehall.[12] Within agriculture, for example, a Schedule 2 field in which the Welsh Office formerly exercised wide ranging powers,[13] rules having statutory force for Welsh farmers may be made either in Cardiff Bay or by the Department of the Environment, Food and Rural Affairs.[14] To use the analogy of a jigsaw puzzle, in Scotland and Northern Ireland there is a picture of the full agricultural puzzle, from which some pieces have been protected, reserved or excepted. In Wales, by contrast, there is no picture. Some pieces have been transferred; the rest remain in Whitehall. The result, as Professor Keith Patchett told the House of Lords Select Committee on the Constitution, is:

> "… a jigsaw of constantly changing pieces, none of which has straight edges."[15]

As transfers to do with the same subject matter accumulate, they can be categorised as belonging to one of the Schedule 2 fields.[16] Undoubtedly, this assists an informal understanding of the Assembly's powers. However, it is a purely informational technique that cannot in law be equated with the general competence that is exercised by the Scottish or Northern Irish institutions in their subject areas.

A 'HAPHAZARD' SET OF POWERS

When the Assembly took office on 1 July 1999 it assumed its first tranche of transferred functions, effected by the first Transfer of Function Order. This

---

[12] It may not be generally recognised that by virtue of article 3 of the 1999 TFO, all of the existing subordinate legislation made under the Acts which it lists was also devolved to the extent that the primary legislative powers were devolved. It is impossible to say exactly how many statutory instruments or powers this transfer comprises, nor which of them has been amended or revoked subsequently.

[13] In the past functions in agriculture were transferred to the Secretary of State for Wales under the Ministers of the Crown Acts. For this reason the 1999 TFO transfers powers in the pre 1980 Agriculture Acts by a general reference only to the powers which the Secretary of State for Wales had under those earlier Transfer of Function Orders.

[14] For example, in the response to the outbreak of Foot and Mouth disease in 2001, where, even though the Assembly was in practice dealing with its effects in Wales, key decisions were taken by UK Ministers. See Lords Committee on the Constitution, *op.cit.*, pp. 13-14 (Box 1).

[15] Professor Keith Patchett, Evidence to the Lords Committee on the Constitution, *op.cit.*, para. 121.

[16] See Cardiff Law School's website, http://www.wales-legislation.org.uk. See also D. Miers and D. Lambert, 'Law making in Wales: Wales legislation online', *Public Law*, 2002, pp 663-69.

substantial instrument identified some 350 parent Acts in date order; but not, as had been widely assumed would be the case, by reference to the subject matter of the Schedule 2 fields.[17]

With hindsight, the manner of transfer adopted by the 1999 TFO accurately reflected how central government was to approach the implementation of devolution in Wales. Thus, the discrete transfer of functions evident there for the most part continues in the later Transfer of Functions Orders made under the Government of Wales Act and in the primary legislation enacted since July 1999.[18] The manner of transfer occasions two primary issues. In terms of their comprehensiveness, the authorising legislation may:

- transfer all or some of the functions in an Act or section(s) of an Act or in subordinate legislation made under those Acts; or

- transfer those functions with exceptions expressed either numerically by reference to sections, subsections or paragraphs of Schedules or verbally (or in a further sub-category, transfer exceptions to exceptions, which in turn may be effected in a number of ways).

As others have argued, there appears to be no coherent logic to the substantive scope of the functions or group of functions which were initially transferred, or as to those functions in the same authorising legislation which were retained by central government, or which have been transferred or retained since.[19] As the Presiding Officer Lord Elis-Thomas put it, in his evidence to the Richard Commission:

"The powers to make secondary legislation which the Assembly inherited from the Secretary of State for Wales were an almost haphazard accretion of a half-century with little or no coherence of principle underlying them. Little or nothing has been done to introduce coherence in legislation enacted since the Transfer of Functions Order ... "[20]

However illogical the allocation of functions so far transferred may appear to their audience, neither are they necessarily final. As transfers accumulate over time, an increasingly important matter is the effect of amendments in the post devolution primary legislation on the Acts listed in the 1999 Transfer of Functions Order. Four main possibilities arise:

1. Any amendment to the section (or subsection) transferred in the

---

[17] Section 22 is by no means precludes the transfer of functions by reference to subject areas. Two-thirds of the transfers involved the transfer of only a part of the listed Act.

[18] Leaving aside transfers made under post devolution primary legislation, there have been three later Orders; The National Assembly for Wales (Transfer of Functions) Orders 2000 SI 2000/253, 2000 SI 2000/1829; 2000 SI 2000/1830; 2001 SI 2001/3679.

[19] Lords Committee on the Constitution, *op.cit.*, paras. 120-21.

[20] The Presiding Officer, Evidence to the Richard Commission; December 2002, para. 21.

Transfer of Functions Order is likewise an amendment to the Assembly's functions under that section (or subsection).

2. Where the Act listed in the Transfer of Functions Order transferred functions to the Assembly subject to exceptions, a new or an amended function is transferred to the Assembly unless it falls within those exceptions (this may be more complex where the transfer involves exceptions to exceptions).

3. Where the post 1999 Act amends the Act listed in the Transfer of Functions Order by the addition of a new section, the function in the section may be transferred even though it is added after a section or sections which were not transferred in the Transfer of Functions Order if the Act so provides.

4. However, where a subsection is added to a section that was not transferred, the powers in the subsection are likewise not transferred.

It will be plain that the exact identification of the functions that are exercisable by the Assembly is a time-consuming, complex and continuing task. Often they have to be dug out of legislation which on its face, as in the case of the Education Act 2002, generally draws no distinctions by means of separate Parts or a separate section identifying the application of the Act to Wales.[21]

The second issue that is raised by the government's approach is the technical manner of the transfer of functions within primary legislation.[22] This can be more or less helpfully managed. Of the transfers made in the Transport Act 2000, the Lords' Delegated Powers and Deregulation Committee:

> "... noted that in this bill (and others) the powers which were delegated to the Welsh Assembly were scattered throughout the bill, and it was therefore difficult to keep track of them."[23]

On the other hand, the clear sign-posting of the transfer of functions by means of separate Parts in the Learning and Skills Act 2000 and in the Fur Farming (Prohibition) Act 2000 are exemplars of primary legislation in which provisions identify the application of the Act to Wales. Whether there are lessons of general application here, or whether the arrangement of its Parts is to be driven entirely by the exigencies of the particular Bill, is presently a

---

[21] The Presiding Officer, Evidence to the Richard Commission, para. 18. A connected issue is that the National Assembly is itself often obliquely referred to as the 'appropriate Minister' or the 'designated' or 'relevant authority'.

[22] For a detailed account of these difficulties, see David Lambert, 'Legal Wales: Its Past, Its Future' *Welsh Legal Historical Society*, 2001, pages 167-181; and the author's co-written evidence to the Welsh Affairs Select Committee, *op.cit.*

[23] Thirty-seventh Report, 1999-2000; HL 130, para. 70.

matter for the lead department and the draftsman.[24]

Ultimately, the manner in which the transfers are set out is a consideration for central government, mediated by the terms of the 'soft law' agreements between Whitehall and Cardiff.[25] On the question of the working relationship between Cardiff and Whitehall, the House of Lords Select Committee on the Constitution was particularly concerned that liaison over legislation was "… unstructured, almost random [and] highly opaque." It recommended that:

> "… further thought be given to how members of the National Assembly can be afforded the opportunity to consider Westminster legislation that will affect the Assembly and its functions."[26]

THE ASSEMBLY'S LEGISLATIVE OUTPUT

Three kinds of legislation bear upon the subject fields that comprise the Assembly's work: primary and secondary legislation made by central government, and secondary legislation made by the Assembly. The third of these will be dealt with here.

In seeking to answer the question posed at the beginning of this chapter, it is necessary to ask, first, why it might be thought important that the Assembly develops a distinctive legislative profile? For many, not least those who have been elected to, or work for the Assembly, it is important as a signifier of its political independence and its productivity. For others, put bluntly, it is to counter the criticism that it is a glorified local authority. Suppose that the Assembly's legislative products are no different in number and content from the days when instruments were drafted in Whitehall, posted to Cathays Park, and, following a process of 'Walesification', signed by Welsh Office Ministers?[27] What difference, the critic might ask, have the additional 1,500 civil servants and the corresponding increase in public expenditure made to remedy the deficits identified in the White Paper?[28] Far from merely being of parochial and technical interest, therefore, the Assembly's production of statutory instruments is a matter of some political importance. In the same way as Acts

[24] G. Bowman, First Parliamentary Counsel, oral evidence to the Welsh Affairs Select Committee, *op.cit.*, HC 1242-ii (16 December 2002).

[25] See Devolution Guidance Note 9 on Post-devolution Primary Legislation affecting Wales. www.devolution.odpm.gov.uk/dgn/index.htm

[26] Lords Committee on the Constitution *Op.cit.*, paras. 123, 124 (d).

[27] E. Page, *Governing by Numbers*, 2001, p. 123.

[28] *A Voice for Wales* (1997; Cm 1997). On the expansion in the Assembly of personnel and costs see the written evidence of Sir Jon Shortridge, the Assembly's Permanent Secretary, to the Richard Commission.

of the Scottish Parliament comprise a measure of its effectiveness and a possible counter to its critics,[29] so the Assembly's only permissible legislative act constitutes one of its principal measures of success.[30]

Secondly, if that part of the Assembly's subordinate legislative output is to be used for this purpose, it is necessary to elucidate what its distinctiveness might comprise. A starting point is to distinguish quantitative from qualitative distinctiveness. We can count how many instruments the Assembly has made and compare that with the number made each year by the Welsh Office solely for Wales (rather than as an adjunct with England) pre-devolution. A two-fold increase, say, might suggest that the Assembly has been successful in making law to the benefit of Welsh interests. Such an exercise is certainly a proxy for how busy the Assembly has been, but it suffers from the obvious difficulty that it is impossible to know how many Wales–only general instruments the Welsh Office would have been made if the Assembly had not been established. It, too, might have increased its output in response to demand and the growing expertise of its officials.

Imponderables of this kind also affect the utility of qualitative distinctiveness; that is, comparing the content of Assembly Orders with those made under equivalent provisions for England. Nevertheless, this is precisely the comparison that the Counsel General to the Assembly has made, most recently in his evidence to the Richard Commission. Responding to comments about the Assembly's effectiveness, he observed that while only a very few of the first 200 statutory instruments differed in substance from their English equivalents, the content of those enacted in 2001 were notably different. Of 230 general instruments, 31 per cent were:

> "... either unique to Wales or involved significant differences in its content to its equivalents for England."[31]

We examine this claim in more detail shortly.

One final introductory point should be made. The Assembly's legislation may in at least two separate respects be questionably distinctive. First, views may differ on what amounts to distinctiveness in particular cases. There will be different understandings of the proportion of distinctive instruments within the total of the Assembly's output. Beside this definitional issue there is, secondly, a matter of judgment. Distinctiveness is not necessarily a matter for approbation. A legislator may be distinctive for the wrong reasons.

---

[29] See A. Page and A. Batey, 'Scotland's Other Parliament: Westminster Legislation on Devolved Matters since Devolution', *Public Law*, 2002 pp. 501-523.

[30] See, for example, the Counsel General's statement in his evidence to the Richard Commission, "The Assembly's two most important products are its policies and its legislation", December 2002, para.10.

[31] *ibid* para. 11.

Instruments may be inappropriately timed or poorly drafted. There may be excessive regulation. Here too, views may differ.

QUANTITATIVE DISTINCTIVENESS IN SECONDARY LEGISLATION[32]

During the years immediately preceding devolution, the Secretary of State for Wales made around 500 statutory instruments each year. Of these, at least 150 or so would be local instruments relating to road traffic and local health matters. Of the remainder, which would be general instruments, the majority were made by the Secretary of State in relation to Wales in the same instrument as that made by a Minister in England. These instruments were usually drafted in Whitehall. A smaller proportion were made by the Secretary of State for Wales alone. In 1998 the Secretary of State made 66 Wales-only general instruments. There were also 24 local instruments, making a total of 90 for the year.

By contrast, the bulk of the Assembly's general instruments are Wales-only.[33] In 2001 (at the time of writing, the latest complete year), the National Assembly made a total of 331 instruments, of which 241 were general and 90 local. This was an increase of 367 per cent over the number of general instruments made in 1998, virtually all of which were published in the two languages.[34] Between its establishment on 1 July 1999 and 3 December 2002, the National Assembly for Wales made 562 General Statutory Instruments and 330 Local Statutory Instruments. Table 1 analyses these by year.

Manifestly these totals represent a substantial quantitative increase over the Welsh Office's annual figures for Wales-only general instruments. Allowing for speculation that had devolution not occurred, the Secretary of State might have been called upon to increase his productivity, in this respect the Assembly has made a difference. This is true also of its implementation of the statutory principle that the English and Welsh languages are to be treated equally.[35] The Assembly's output in the Welsh language must be regarded as

---

[32] The figures and table presented in this section are drawn from the written evidence of the Counsel General to the Richard Commission.; paras. 35-44.

[33] The Government of Wales Act permits the Assembly to exercise subordinate legislative powers in relation to "an English border area" (sections 22, 29 and 44). The Water Industry Act 1991 transfers functions to the Assembly "in relation to the Dwr Cymru water and sewerage undertaker and its area of appointment", which includes parts of Herefordshire.

[34] The instruments in the two languages share the same SI number, and are distinguished (apart from the obvious linguistic difference) by the parenthetical suffices (W.000) and (Cy.000) for the English and Welsh texts respectively.

TABLE 1: STATUTORY INSTRUMENTS MADE BY THE NATIONAL ASSEMBLY FOR WALES 1999-2002

Year	General Instruments	Local Instruments	Total
1999	29	28	57
2000	119	109	228
2001	241*	90	331
2002 (to 3 Dec)	173	103	276
Totals	562	330	892

*The figure for 2001 includes 45 General Statutory Instruments made by the Assembly in response to the outbreak of Foot and Mouth Disease.

TABLE 2: STATUTORY INSTRUMENTS IN HEALTH MADE BY CENTRAL GOVERNMENT APPLYING TO WALES AND BY THE NATIONAL ASSEMBLY FOR WALES 1999-2001

Year	National Assembly	UK Government
1999	5	22
2000	11	72
2001	18	31
Totals	34	125

TABLE 3: STATUTORY INSTRUMENTS IN EDUCATION MADE BY CENTRAL GOVERNMENT APPLYING TO WALES AND BY THE NATIONAL ASSEMBLY FOR WALES 1999-2001

Year	National Assembly	UK Government
1999	11	12
2000	14	41
2001	14	36
Totals	39	89

quantitatively distinctive.

It would be more were the devolution settlement amended so that it enjoyed full rather than fragmented competence in the Schedule 2 fields. For example, in the case of education and health, both areas in which the Welsh Office had developed distinctive policies and in respect of which a number of functions have been transferred to the Assembly, Whitehall continues to make the bulk of the secondary legislation applying to Wales. The number of instruments made by the Assembly and by central government for the years 1999-2001 for these two subject areas are set out in Tables 2 and 3.[36]

Assuming that it had full competence and wished, as a matter of policy, to introduce the substance of those made by central government, the Assembly would have needed to make a further 125 instruments in health and 89 in education. No doubt this is a somewhat simplistic approach to determining the resource implications of extensions in the Assembly's legislative competence. Nevertheless, the comparative ratio between the number of instruments made over three years in these two areas (34:125; and 39:89) gives a broad indication of the additional resource that would be required to produce the total number of instruments: 367 per cent for health and 228 per cent for education.

QUALITATIVE DISTINCTIVENESS IN SECONDARY LEGISLATION

Are the Assembly's general statutory instruments qualitatively as well as quantitatively distinctive? This question can be tested by an examination of the Assembly's response to transferred functions requiring or permitting it to make subordinate legislation on a matter on which there is an equivalent function exercisable by the UK government. There are two aspects to this response: its substance and its timing. On the assumption that the content of every Assembly Order is the result of deliberate choice, two possibilities arise: the Order is substantively different or it is substantively identical to the English equivalent. These possibilities prompt two further questions: what constitutes a difference in substance, and, where the instruments are identical, why might the Welsh Assembly Government choose that option? The second aspect is that the Assembly may also have discretion as to *when* to legislate.

---

[35] Government of Wales Act, section 47, "in the conduct of its business the Assembly shall, so far as it is both appropriate in the circumstances and reasonably practicable, give effect to the principle that both languages are to be treated equally"; and section 122, "English and Welsh texts of any subordinate legislation shall be treated for all purposes as being of equal standing".

[36] See the author's co-written evidence to the Welsh Affairs Select Committee, *op.cit.*

These matters are considered in turn.

QUALITATIVE DISTINCTIVENESS: SUBSTANCE

SIGNIFICANT DIFFERENCES REFLECTING WELSH CIRCUMSTANCES

The political sensitivity of this heading stems, as noted, from the Welsh Office's practice of adopting *verbatim* the substance of English instruments for Welsh purposes when making instruments together with England. But as implied by the two possibilities outlined above, there may be very good policy reasons for the two instruments to be substantively identical, even where the Assembly is free to pursue its own policies. Nor is there any obvious proportion of the total of instruments in any year which could claim the label, 'made in Wales' that could be used as a measure of distinctiveness in their making.

A former Secretary of State, Lord Morris of Aberavon, while evaluating the Assembly's performance in its first year of law making, suggested that we might annually expect 10 per cent of Assembly Orders to differ in substance from their English equivalents.[37] On the figures given earlier, we saw that about a third of the Assembly's general instruments were

> *"... either unique to Wales or, where they paralleled similar legislation passed in England, involved significant differences in drafting reflecting Welsh circumstances."[38]*

Lord Morris' expectation is, assuming it to be well founded, comfortably exceeded. The details are set out in Table 4.

Discounting the single Order dealing with the Welsh language as not providing a test of potential substantive equivalence with any English instrument, it is arguable that the proportion of instruments that were significantly different was higher. This is because a large number dealt in the same terms with attempts to control the foot and mouth crisis. Discounting them, the Counsel General's conclusion was that the proportion of instruments made in 2001 that were significantly different was 39 per cent.

To assess this claim, it is necessary, first, to identify all the instruments that are included in the 75 'distinctly Welsh' column; and, second, to compare them with the English instrument made under the equivalent provision. At the time of writing, it has not been possible to complete this substantial exercise, particularly as some Assembly instruments combine concepts included in

---

[37] *House of Lords Debates*, vol. 631, col. 1148 (13 February 2002).

[38] Counsel General, Winston Roddick, QC, Evidence to the Richard Commission, December 2002, para. 41.

Subject Area	Orders with distinctly Welsh content (A)	Orders mirroring those for England (B)	Total (A+B)	(A) as a % of total
Transport Planning and Environment	10	12	22	45%
Education and Lifelong Learning	15	15	30	50%
Health and Food Safety	4	34	38	11%
Social Care	6	16	22	27%
Agriculture, Fisheries & Forestry	12	71	83	14%
Local Govt. and Housing, Economic and Industrial Development	27	18	45	60%
Welsh Language	1	-	1	100%
Total	75	166	241	31%

more than one legislative instrument. This exercise also requires a comparison of an instrument's legal effect in terms of the powers used in the primary legislation to make it. That, too, is a major undertaking. It is then necessary to develop criteria by which any differences between them might be judged significant. Based on a small number of randomly selected instruments, the following possibilities arise:

- Technical differences consequent on the legislative authority for the instrument.

- Differences dependent on the existence of differently constituted audiences, but to whom the same message is being sent. Are instruments concerning, for example, health, addressed in Wales and in England to their differently constituted health authorities significantly different where their substance is identical?[39]

- Commencement orders made in England and in Wales may bring provisions into force on different days and sometimes for different purposes. At what point does the difference in days and purposes become significant? We return to this point when considering the timing of instruments.

- Differences are not therefore necessarily matters of categorisation, but as with the number of days elapsing between commencement orders, matters of degree. Judgments should also take into account the impact of differences, however apparently small, on those to whom they are addressed. A difference of 0.5 per cent in a rating discount between local authorities in England and Wales may look very small, but be significant for a local authority budget.[40]

- Identical provision being made in one instrument in Wales to those of two or more in England.[41]

- Bringing the same regulations into force in Wales that were made in England pre-devolution, but with a variation as to their application.[42]

The examples from which these points are drawn unquestionably reflect Welsh circumstances. No doubt they do not exhaust the range of matters on which instruments made in Cardiff and in Whitehall might differ. Certainly it is not suggested that they are representative of those matters, though other examples could be found. Nor has any attempt been made here to compare the extent of any 'Walesification' that was made to Whitehall draft

---

[39] The National Health Service Reform and Health Care Professions Act 2002 creates a different NHS structure in Wales (Local Health Boards replacing health authorities).

[40] Local Authorities (Capital Finance) (Rate of Discount for 2001/02) (Wales) Regulations 2001, SI 2001/1287 (W.75); Local Authorities (Capital Finance) (Rate of Discount for 2001/02) (England) Regulations 2001, SI 2001/384.

[41] On parent governors and Church representatives on school governing bodies; Wales: Parent Governor Representatives and Church Representatives (Wales) Regulations 2001, SI 2001/3711 (W.307); England: Parent Governor Representatives (England) Regulations 2001, SI 2001/478 and the Local Authorities (Alternative Arrangements) (England) Regulations 2001, SI 2001/1299.

[42] England: the Housing (Preservation of Right to Buy) (Amendment) Regulations 1999, SI 1999/1213; Wales: the Housing (Preservation of Right to Buy) (Amendment) Regulations 2001, SI 2001/1301 (W. 78).

instruments pre-devolution. Whether the 75 identified in the Counsel General's evidence "go far beyond merely amending a precedent set in London" is a matter of judgment, but not one which, on this very limited sample, this chapter can make.

CHOOSING THE IDENTICAL OPTION

Whatever the proportion of significantly different Assembly Orders, there will inevitably be a large number identical in substance to their English equivalents; in Table 4, the 166 orders "mirroring those for England". There are good reasons why this should be so. As the Counsel General's evidence shows, the need to control the spread of foot and mouth disease in 2001 required large numbers of emergency orders to be made:

> *"For practical reasons these had to be identical with those in force in England and were often made jointly with the UK Agriculture Minister."*[43]

Secondly, instruments may be identical because they relate to a matter on which the Assembly was required to act bilaterally with central government. Thirdly, even where the Assembly is free to act, the Order may be identical to the Whitehall equivalent because its substance entirely represents considered Assembly policy. If the English equivalent already exists in draft, it is administratively convenient to copy it. Alternatively, they may be identical because the need for uniformity across England and Wales outweighs the Assembly Government's preferred choice, for example in the implementation of Community Directives.

These kinds of reason are themselves very similar to those which lie behind the Scottish Parliament's acceptance of Westminster primary legislation on devolved matters.[44] Not being privy to the decision within the Welsh Assembly Government as to whether any particular instrument is to be drafted in Cardiff, or comprise a cut and paste from Whitehall, it is not possible for this chapter to take this analysis further. What that requires is a full content analysis of all Assembly instruments compared with their English equivalents, together with an analysis of the political choices made.

QUALITATIVE DISTINCTIVENESS: TIMING

Besides decisions concerning how many instruments to make, and with what content, the Assembly may also have discretion as to *when* to legislate. In

---

[43] The Counsel General, Evidence to the Richard Commission, para. 41.

[44] See Page and Batey, *op.cit.*, and see Chapter 2 of this volume.

terms of their legal effect, provisions in primary legislation affecting the Assembly's competencies may, upon their commencement:

- bring into force some new or amended law which neither permits nor requires any further action by the Assembly for it to apply to its subject-matter; or

- require or permit the Assembly to undertake some further action in respect of the subject matter to which they apply.

In each case the Assembly's decision as to when to act depends on a cluster of political and administrative factors. These may include the fact that the legislation makes equivalent provision for England. As with their substance, there may be good reason either for divergence from/or for convergence with Whitehall in the timing of Assembly Orders. Its decision will be distinctive where it:

- brings a provision applicable in Wales into force on a different day than its English equivalent (Commencement Orders); or

- provides for the exercise of a substantive function on a different day in Wales than its English equivalent.

Where they do diverge, this distinctiveness will be questionable if the result is to disadvantage Welsh interests in comparison with those equally placed in England.

COMMENCEMENT ORDERS

A commencement order brings a statutory provision into force. There are a variety of possibilities concerning the making of commencement orders in respect of provisions affecting Wales under post 1999 Acts of Parliament. In short, they may be made by the Assembly or by the UK government, and in some cases by both in respect of different sections of the same Act.[45]

Where the Assembly is the designated authority for Wales, it is possible that it may choose a different day than that chosen by central government for the commencement of the same or equivalent provision applicable in England. Moreover, the Assembly might choose different days for different purposes,[46]

---

[45] The Learning and Skills Act 2000 and the Local Government Act 2000 both contain a significant number of provisions applicable only in Wales, and thus offer the Assembly opportunities for distinctive policy making. In the case of the Care Standards Act 2000, both the Assembly and central government had powers to commence provisions in Wales. The permutations can be complex; see the author's co-written evidence to the Welsh Affairs Select Committee, *op.cit.*

[46] The Education Act 2002 confers wide-ranging powers on both the Secretary of State and the Assembly in respect, for example, of the government of maintained schools. In the exercise of these equivalent powers, the Assembly may choose to introduce quite different provisions for Wales than will apply in England.

or might choose not to make the order at all, or to postpone its making for some time. A further possibility arises where the primary legislation designates central government for the purpose of bringing its provisions into force in both England and Wales. Whitehall might choose different times for the two. In an evaluation of the distinctiveness of Assembly's legislative profile, this possibility is not considered further.

Commencement orders have two operative times: the date on which they are made, and the date that they specify for the commencement of the relevant section. The period of time between making and commencement may be short or long. Some of these possibilities may be depicted as follows, where M1-M3 are alternative dates for making the Order, and C1-C3 are alternative dates for the section to come into force:

Jurisdiction	Making	Into force
England	--------------M--------------------	C ------
Wales	------------- M1 M2 M3 -----------	C1 C2 C3 --

In the case of the Housing Grants (Additional Purposes) Orders made under the Housing Grants, Construction and Regeneration Act 1996, for example, the Assembly acted virtually a year later than the UK government. The affected provisions came into force on 4 July 2000 in England and on 1 July 2001 in Wales.[47] By contrast, the Assembly acted a month earlier than Whitehall in the making of a commencement order under the Countryside and Rights of Way Act 2000.[48] It is also possible that, though orders are made on different dates, they provide for commencement on the same date. Research at Cardiff Law School suggests that approximately 50 per cent of Orders made by the UK government and the Assembly concerning equivalent provisions do this, though, sometimes, for different purposes.

DEVOLVED FUNCTIONS EXERCISABLE BY THE ASSEMBLY

When a section requiring or permitting the Assembly to make subordinate legislation is in force, the question arises, what is the timing of that subsequent action? In particular, if there is an equivalent function exercisable by the UK government for England, are they, or should they be exercised simultaneously?

---

[47] Wales: Housing Grants (Additional Purposes) Order 2001, SI 2001/2070 (W. 142); England: Housing Grants (Additional Purposes) Order 2000, SI 2000/1492.

[48] Wales: Countryside and Rights of Way Act 2000 (Commencement No 1) (Wales) Order 2001, 2001/203 (W.9); England: Countryside and Rights of Way Act 2000 (Commencement No 1) (England) Order 2001, 2001/114.

We considered earlier some reasons for convergence. As with commencement orders, two operative dates may be distinguished: the date on which the Assembly acquires the function, and the date on which it exercises it. These dates may be the same as, or differ from, English only equivalents. In the case of functions transferred under the 1999 TFO, the Assembly's date of acquisition is by definition later than for Ministers in England. However, in the case of transfers under post-devolution primary legislation, it may well be the same, depending usually on the date of the relevant commencement order.

The second variable is the date on which the function, whenever acquired, is exercised. The possibilities that arise from two variables may be depicted as follows, where A1-A3 are alternative dates on which the appropriate authority acquired the function, and E1-E3 are alternative dates on which it was exercised.

Jurisdiction	Acquisition	Excercise
England ----------------A	-------------------E	------
Wales-------------- A1 A2 A3	----------E1 E2 E3	-

An example is the Assembly's exercise some four months after central government of its equivalent power to exempt from rating an additional class of plant and machinery under the Finance Act 1988. Despite the delay, the Welsh and English versions of the Validation for Rating (Plant and Machinery) Regulations 2001 came into force on the same day.[49]

DISTINCTIVENESS IN SUBSTANCE AND TIMING: IMPLICATIONS

Where a provision is brought into force for England but not for Wales, or regulations are made for England but not for Wales, the result is that different laws often contained in different Acts and subordinate legislation apply as between the two. This is so, irrespective of whether central government or the Assembly is the designated authority. Such was the case with the 12 month delay in the Assembly's making of the Housing Grants (Additional Purposes) Order. Another example is the commencement of the Commonhold and Leasehold Reform Act 2002. This was a matter for central government for England, where an order was made and came into force in July 2002, and for the Assembly in Wales, where the order was made in December 2002, coming

---

[49] Wales: Validation for Rating (Plant and Machinery) (Wales) Regulations 2001, 2001/2357 (W.195); England: Validation for Rating (Plant and Machinery) (England) Regulations 2001, 2001/846.

into force on 1 January 2003.[50] There may have been good reasons for the time discrepancy, but for those few months the new rights contained in the Act concerning land purchase were not available to people buying houses in Wales, wherever the purchaser then lived.

CONCLUSION

In summary, where the Assembly has functions to exercise that have equivalents for England, the following permutations in the law applicable in the two jurisdictions are possible:

- The timing and substance for both are the same.

- The timing is the same but the substance is different.

- The timing is different but the substance is the same.

- Both timing and substance are different.

In those three permutations where the law applicable in Wales is for the time being different from that in England in respect of the same or equivalent functions, the question is whether that distinctiveness is a matter for approbation. This judgment cannot be made simply from the fact of the instrument's making, or from a few selected examples. For those reasons alone, this chapter makes no such judgment. It does, however, underline the importance of the following points:

- Agreement about the criteria that make the Assembly's exercise of its legislative functions distinctive.

- The need to determine the reasons for convergence or divergence from England in any case.

- The need for detailed analysis of the content and the timing of statutory instruments made in Whitehall and Cardiff.

The reasons for convergence with/or divergence in any case, and the consequent impact on Welsh interests, are matters that go well beyond the confines of this chapter. But they need to be understood if judgments about the distinctiveness of the Assembly's legislative output are to be made.

---

[50] The Commonhold and Leasehold Reform Act 2002 (Commencement No. 1, Savings and Transitional Provisions) (England) Order 2002, SI 2002/1912 (C.58); the Commonhold and Leasehold Reform Act 2002 (Commencement No. 1, Savings and Transitional Provisions) (Wales) Order 2002, SI 2002/3012 (W.284).

CHAPTER 4

THE CIVIL SERVICE

John Osmond

It was widely acknowledged at the outset of democratic devolution that the National Assembly would create a demand for a new breed of civil servants. This was how former Welsh Office Permanent Secretary Rachel Lomax put it, speaking shortly after the 1997 referendum:

> *"Believe me, a department that answers to sixty politicians who in turn answer to people from all over Wales, is going to respond very differently from one that answers to one Cabinet Minister, whoever he or she is ... We are going to have to get used to explaining ourselves in public."*[1]

An underlying reason was the political change involved in the removal of British Cabinet collective responsibility from the Welsh political leadership. As another senior Welsh Office civil servant argued at the time:

> *"Currently we are working for one Minister whose preoccupations are London rather than Wales centred. But once the Assembly is in being collective Cabinet responsibility will go out of the window. We are very close to being released from the straitjacket of thinking that Britain is a homogeneous community where policy diversity is a dangerous activity."*[2]

It is perhaps too soon to judge whether the onset of democratic devolution has resulted in a different kind of civil servant working in Cathays Park and Cardiff Bay. Certainly there are more of them: over the first term their number increase by about 1,500, or 63 per cent, to around 3,800 full-time equivalents.[3] But whether they are a new 'breed' is another matter. They have inevitably been engaged in more autonomous policy-making than in previous Welsh office days and they have more contact with politicians. Undoubtedly they are becoming more Welsh, in the sense that a cadre of officials is building up whose roots are firmly in Wales. This has the obvious advantage of promoting commitment and loyalty, but at the same time holds out dangers that the service might become inward-looking. In his evidence to the Richard Commission Sir Jon Shortridge, Permanent Secretary at the National Assembly for the whole of the first term, addressed this issue in the following terms:

> *"It is important ... to understand that the market from which the*

---

[1] Rachel Lomax, *Preparing for the Assembly*, IWA: Agenda, Winter 1997-8.

[2] Quoted in J. Osmond (Ed.) *The National Assembly Agenda*, IWA, 1998, page 6.

[3] Sir John Shortridge, Evidence to the Richard Commission, December 2002, para. 5.

*Assembly recruits is largely a Welsh one. It is a feature of the Assembly –
and the Welsh Office before it – that although we are successful in
attracting good quality people back to Wales, comparatively few people
who work for us have much of a desire to move out of Wales, or who see
their future careers as taking them to Whitehall. Partly for this reason
comparitively few people have an appetite for taking on secondments or
short term appointments in Whitehall. Amongst other things, this means
that our stock of people with recent first hand experience of working for
the UK Government is eroding rapidly."*[4]

THE WELSH CIVIL SERVICE IN 1999 AND 2003

At the outset there was a widespread assumption that there would be a large
measure of continuity. For instance, it was decided, that the Welsh Office's
existing 'departmental' organisation would continue relatively undisturbed
after the Assembly was in place. That is to say, although it was acknowledged
that a new dynamic would be given to policy direction from within the
Assembly, driven by the Cabinet portfolios and Subject Committees, there
was no necessary reason for the civil service's departmental arrangements to
follow a similar configuration. Three reasons were offered. First was the virtue
of continuity. Secondly, a concern was voiced that a reorganisation of the
administration would be necessary every time a change was made to the
Cabinet structure. Finally, it was argued that having a functional
administration different from the shape and number of the subject
committees would favour a cross-cutting approach to policy. As Rachel
Lomax put it at the time:

> *"We want to guard against creating a series of self-contained silos within
> the National Assembly where you have got a group of staff, the Subject
> Committee and Assembly Secretary who all talk to one another but
> never talk across the organisation."*[5]

And as her successor, Sir Jon Shortridge, argued four years later, in his
evidence to the Richard Commission:

> *"... given the extent of the uncertainty about how the Assembly itself
> might evolve in terms of the way it exercised its functions, I did not
> consider it sensible to make the official structure of the Assembly
> symmetrical from the outset with the Cabinet portfolios ... My guiding*

---

[4] Sir Jon Shortridge, *ibid.*, para 21.

[5] Welsh Affairs Committee, *The Welsh Office's Organisational Preparedness for the National Assembly*,
Minutes of Evidence, para. 10, 19 January 1999.

principle, therefore, was to maintain as much consistency and continuity as I could at the very top of the organisation. The difference in weight in the various Cabinet portfolios in any case argued against creating separate Departments. The Health and Social Services portfolio, for example, is supported by three Departments - the NHS Wales Department, the Office of the Chief Medical Officer, and the Social Policy Department. The Finance and Communities Minister is supported by the Finance Group and the Local Government, Housing and Culture department - part of which, therefore, serves the Culture Minister. In practice this asymmetry has - from my perspective - worked pretty well.[6]

Even so there were considerable changes in the structure during the first term. Figure 1 on the following page shows the organisation of the Welsh Office as it was in March 1999. This gives the clear impression of a department driven by a culture of administration rather than one that is directly engaged in policy-making. To use Rachel Lomax's terminology, there is an impression of the various departments and units operating within "self-contained silos". Elements driven by the forthcoming National Assembly were creeping in, in particular the appearance of the Counsel General and the Director of Assembly Business. Otherwise, however, the department's organisation was much as it had been for two decades, and plainly the civil servants expected it to continue that way. Nearly four years on the organisation looked substantially different. Figure 2, the organisation of the Assembly civil service in November 2002, shows a structure that is far more policy-oriented and cross-cutting in its appearance and feel. This comes across in at least three ways:

1. The elements which relate to the Cabinet portfolios and the Subject Committees.

2. The work of the Assembly itself flows through the structure, from the centrality given the Counsel General and the seniority of his assistants, to the distinctive nature of the Presiding Office and its significantly renamed Clerk to the Assembly (rather than the previous Director of Assembly Business).

3. The appearance of the Cabinet Executive and the Research and Development Group indicate a new focus on policy-making.

AN EMBRYONIC WELSH PUBLIC SERVICE

One of the more striking commitments in the Partnership Agreement that underpinned the coalition between Labour and the Liberal Democrats was an

---

[6] Sir Jon Shortridge, *op.cit.*, paras. 10 and 11.

undertaking to move the Welsh civil service in a more autonomous direction. Given the sensitivity of the matter, the terms in which this aspiration was couched were remarkable:

> "We will review the existing structures and workings of Assembly officials to ensure they are in tune with the reality of political devolution. We seek to move towards an increasingly independent and Welsh-based civil service – investigating ways of introducing an Assembly 'fast-track' programme to attract and retain high quality staff. We will also investigate extending the Assembly's current policies on mature recruitment and secondment."[7]

The need to ensure that Assembly officials should be "in tune with the reality of political devolution" could only reflect a dissatisfaction with experience hitherto. There was a feeling, certainly on the part of the Liberal Democrats who drafted this clause, that civil servants were continuing the old Welsh Office practice of constantly deferring to Whitehall and being reluctant to countenance Welsh policy initiatives. The unhappiness was not only confined to the Liberal Democrats. First Minister Rhodri Morgan explored the matter at some length in a speech he gave to the Institute of Welsh Politics in November 2000. Recalling his own time as a civil servant at the Welsh Office in the late 1960s he drew a comparison with the relative autonomy of the Scottish Office:

> "In the Scottish Office which had been around for 100 years they had developed a tradition of independent policy. The Welsh Office had no capability of policy-making at all in the late 1960s. Likewise you promoted staff in the Scottish Office on the basis that they had put one over Whitehall. You promoted staff in the Welsh Office on the basis of whether they had kept their nose clean with Whitehall. I hope that's not entirely true today but you are still struggling against a very long tradition where there is not an experience of autonomous policy-making. It was made much worse by the policy top-slicing which occurred under the Redwood cutbacks in the civil service in Wales with the loss of 600 jobs in Cardiff. This led to the loss of the people aged 50-plus, people with experience and capability. Policy-making was top sliced just at the time when it needed to be coming up maximum strength for the incoming Assembly ... What we need now that we have the devolution settlement is to create a positive problem-solving political culture. We need to generate a policy-making ability in a Welsh context and get rid of the old habits which still inhibit that process."[8]

---

[7] Putting Wales First: A Partnership for the People of Wales, Section on Better Government, para. 6, 6 October 2001.

[8] Rhodri Morgan, *Check Against Delivery*, Institute of Welsh Politics Annual Lecture, Aberystwyth, November 2000.

FIGURE 1

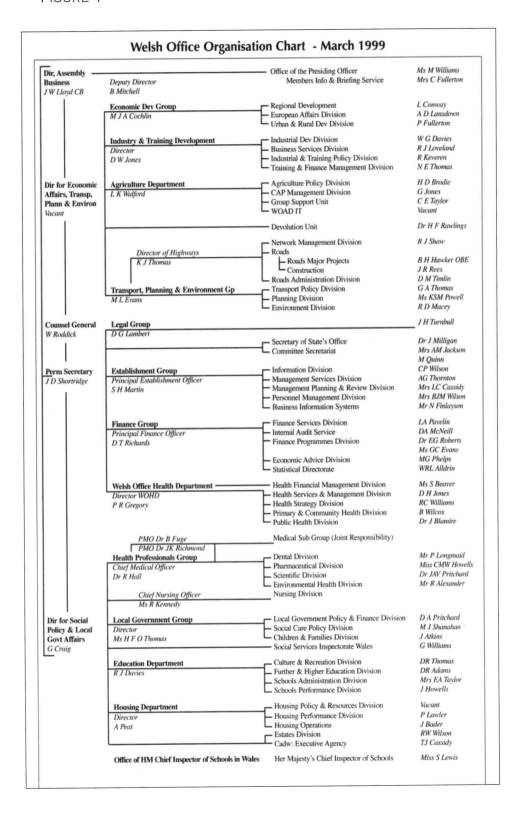

Welsh Office Organisation Chart - March 1999

Dir, Assembly Business J W Lloyd CB		Office of the Presiding Officer — Ms M Williams
	Deputy Director *B Mitchell*	Members Info & Briefing Service — Mrs C Fullerton
	Economic Dev Group *M J A Cochlin*	Regional Development — L Conway European Affairs Division — A D Lansdown Urban & Rural Dev Division — P Fullerton
	Industry & Training Development *Director* *D W Jones*	Industrial Dev Division — W G Davies Business Services Division — R J Loveland Industrial & Training Policy Division — R Keveren Training & Finance Management Division — N E Thomas
Dir for Economic Affairs, Transp, Plann & Environ Vacant	**Agriculture Department** *L K Walford*	Agriculture Policy Division — H D Brodie CAP Management Division — G Jones Group Support Unit — C E Taylor WOAD IT — Vacant
		Devolution Unit — Dr H F Rawlings

	Director of Highways *K J Thomas*	Network Management Division — R J Shaw
		Roads
		  Roads Major Projects — B H Hawker OBE
		  Construction — J R Rees
		Roads Administration Division — D M Timlin

	Transport, Planning & Environment Gp *M L Evans*	Transport Policy Division — G A Thomas Planning Division — Ms KSM Powell Environment Division — R D Macey
Counsel General W Roddick	**Legal Group** *D G Lambert*	J H Turnbull
		Secretary of State's Office — Dr J Milligan Committee Secretariat — Mrs AM Jackson M Quinn
Perm Secretary J D Shortridge	**Establishment Group** *Principal Establishment Officer* *S H Martin*	Information Division — CP Wilson Management Services Division — AG Thornton Management Planning & Review Division — Mrs LC Cassidy Personnel Management Division — Mrs BJM Wilson Business Information Systems — Mr N Finlayson
	Finance Group *Principal Finance Officer* *D T Richards*	Finance Services Division — LA Pavelin Internal Audit Service — DA McNeill Finance Programmes Division — Dr EG Roberts Ms GC Evans Economic Advice Division — MG Phelps Statistical Directorate — WRL Alldrin
	Welsh Office Health Department *Director WOHD* *P R Gregory*	Health Financial Management Division — Ms S Beaver Health Services & Management Division — D H Jones Health Strategy Division — RC Williams Primary & Community Health Division — B Wilcox Public Health Division — Dr J Blamire
	PMO Dr B Fuge *PMO Dr JK Richmond*	Medical Sub Group (Joint Responsibility)
	Health Professionals Group *Chief Medical Officer* *Dr R Hall*	Dental Division — Mr P Longmaid Pharmaceutical Division — Miss CMW Howells Scientific Division — Dr JAV Pritchard Environmental Health Division — Mr R Alexander
	Chief Nursing Officer *Ms R Kennedy*	Nursing Division
Dir for Social Policy & Local Govt Affairs G Craig	**Local Government Group** *Director* *Ms H F O Thomas*	Local Government Policy & Finance Division — D A Pritchard Social Care Policy Division — M J Shanahan Children & Families Division — J Atkins Social Services Inspectorate Wales — G Williams
	Education Department *R J Davies*	Culture & Recreation Division — DR Thomas Further & Higher Education Division — DR Adams Schools Administration Division — Mrs EA Taylor Schools Performance Division — J Howells
	Housing Department *Director* *A Peat*	Housing Policy & Resources Division — Vacant Housing Performance Division — P Lawler Housing Operations — J Bader Estates Division — RW Wilson Cadw: Executive Agency — TJ Cassidy
	Office of HM Chief Inspector of Schools in Wales	Her Majesty's Chief Inspector of Schools — Miss S Lewis

FIGURE 2

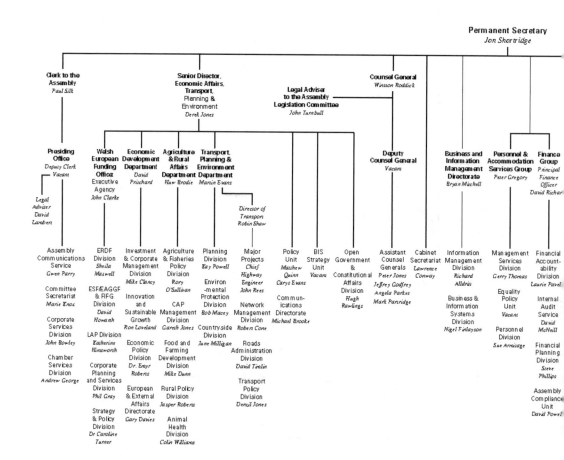

CYNULLIAD CENEDLAETHOL SIART TREFNIADAETH
NATIONAL ASSEMBLY FOR WALES ORGANISATION CHART

Cynulliad Cenedlaethol Cymru
National Assembly for Wales

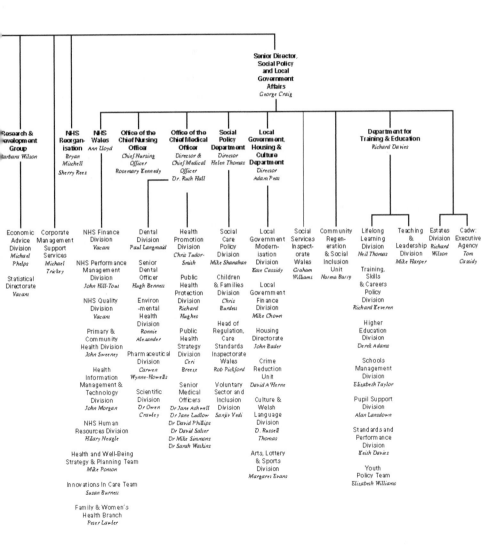

Senior Director, Social Policy and Local Government Affairs
George Craig

Research & Development Group
Barbara Wilson

NHS Reorganisation
Bryan Mitchell
Sherry Rees

NHS Wales *Ann Lloyd*

Office of the Chief Nursing Officer
Chief Nursing Officer
Rosemary Kennedy

Office of the Chief Medical Officer
Director & Chief Medical Officer
Dr. Ruth Hall

Social Policy Department
Director
Helen Thomas

Local Government, Housing & Culture Department
Director
Adam Peat

Department for Training & Education
Richard Davies

Economic Advice Division
Michael Phelps

Statistical Directorate
Vacant

Corporate Management Support Services
Michael Trickey

NHS Finance Division
Vacant

NHS Performance Management Division
John Hill-Tout

NHS Quality Division
Vacant

Primary & Community Health Division
John Sweeney

Health Information Management & Technology Division
John Morgan

NHS Human Resources Division
Hilary Neagle

Health and Well-Being Strategy & Planning Team
Mike Ponton

Innovations In Care Team
Susan Burnett

Family & Women's Health Branch
Peter Lawler

Dental Division
Paul Langmaid

Senior Dental Officer
Hugh Bennett

Environ-mental Health Division
Ronnie Alexander

Pharmaceutical Division
Carwen Wynne-Howells

Scientific Division
Dr Owen Crawley

Health Promotion Division
Chris Tudor-Smith

Public Health Protection Division
Richard Hughes

Public Health Strategy Division
Ceri Breeze

Senior Medical Officers
Dr Jane Ashwell
Dr Jane Ludlow
Dr David Phillips
Dr David Salter
Dr Mike Simmons
Dr Sarah Watkins

Social Care Policy Division
Mike Shanahan

Children & Families Division
Chris Burdett

Head of Regulation, Care Standards Inspectorate Wales
Rob Pickford

Voluntary Sector and Inclusion Division
Sanjiv Vedi

Local Government Modern-isation Division
Kate Cassidy

Local Government Finance Division
Mike Chown

Housing Directorate
John Bader

Crime Reduction Unit
David A'Herne

Culture & Welsh Language Division
D. Russell Thomas

Arts, Lottery & Sports Division
Margaret Evans

Social Services Inspectorate Wales
Graham Williams

Community Regen-eration & Social Inclusion Unit
Norma Barry

Lifelong Learning Division
Neil Thomas

Training, Skills & Careers Policy Division
Richard Keveren

Higher Education Division
Derek Adams

Schools Management Division
Elizabeth Taylor

Pupil Support Division
Alan Lansdown

Standards and Performance Division
Keith Davies

Youth Policy Team
Elizabeth Williams

Teaching & Leadership Division
Mike Harper

Estates Division
Richard Wilson

Cadw: Executive Agency
Tom Cassidy

19.11.02

TABLE 1: CHANGE IN WELSH CIVIL SERVICE STAFF NUMBERS (FULL-TIME EQUIVALENTS) OCTOBER 1998 TO OCTOBER 2002*

	Net Staff	New Tasks	Presiding Office	Additional Bodies	Total
October 1998	2,295	0	0	0	2,295
October 2002	2,617	324	229	582	3,752
Increase	322 (14%)	-	-	-	1,457 (63%)

* Source: Sir Jon Shortridge, Evidence to the Richard Commission, December 2002.

As has been noted, the first response during the first term was to increase considerably the size of the administrative machine, by the 63 per cent shown in Table 1.

The increases came as a result of the creation of the Presiding Office (discussed below), the generation of new areas of work, and the absorption of bodies that merged with the civil service during the period. The 'new tasks' were Private Office support for Ministers and the creation of a Central Policy Unit, management of European funding, overseas trade functions, expanded legal support, and new policy areas including community regeneration, culture and young people. These changes involved a number of significant staff expansions. For example, Wales Trade International employed 73 staff at the end of 2002, compared with 33 spread between the Welsh Office and the WDA in 1999; while the Wales European Funding Office, the Assembly Government's new in-house agency responsible for managing the structural funds, employed some 200. The bodies that merged with the central civil service during the establishment of the Assembly and in its first term were:

- Tai Cymru/Housing for Wales - 65 staff
- Welsh Health Common Services Agency - 67 staff
- Health Promotion Wales - 68 staff
- Farming and Rural Conservation Agency - 100 staff
- Care Standards Inspectorate for Wales - 204 staff

This process is continuing, driven in part by Ministers' wishes to reduce the number of Assembly Sponsored Public Bodies, (ASpBs), as the Quangos have become known. By April 2004 the following will be incorporated: functions currently exercised by the Health Authorities which are being abolished (40 staff); the Rent Officer Service (57 staff); and the Council of Museums (10 staff).

The rapid growth in the civil service, combined with the absorption of so many outside organisations prompted the Permanent Secretary to describe the result as a:

> "… melting pot … in a constant state of development, and in which boundaries are continually shifting".[9]

He analysed the breakdown of the Assembly's civil servants as: former Welsh Office 60 per cent; new recruits 25 per cent; and former employees of merged organisations 15 per cent:

> "Many of the staff in these latter two groups, it is worth noting, probably regard themselves primarily as Assembly officials and not civil servants at all."[10]

A further characteristic, as noted above, was that recruitment to the civil service was overwhelmingly within Wales. A consequence was that the Assembly was in danger of offering too narrow a career path for aspiring civil servants. To address this an effort is underway to widen the recruitment pool within Wales through an Assembly Government 'public service management initiative'. This entails the creation of common leadership and management training for staff working in all parts of the public sector in Wales - the Assembly civil service, the National Health Service, Local Authorities, and the sponsored bodies. As Sir Jon put it, in effect describing an embryonic Welsh public service:

> "This should mean that over time Wales will develop its own cadre of public servants with experience in and understanding of different parts of the public sector in Wales. They should also have an established network of contacts in different parts of the Welsh public sector. This, coupled with the policy on open recruitment, should mean that there will increasingly be a common set of values and experiences amongst staff in the Welsh public sector."[11]

And looking ahead to the Assembly's second term First Minister Rhodri Morgan declared:

> "We need to invent a new form of public service in Wales, in which individuals are able to move far more easily than now between one form of organisation and another. Local government employees, Assembly civil servants, health service administrators, ASpB staff should all be able to map out career paths which move between these bodies, developing

---

[9] Sir Jon Shortridge, *op.cit.*, para 24.

[10] *Ibid.*

[11] *Ibid.*

expertise and cross-fertilising from one place to another ... We need a Welsh public service, rather than a Welsh civil service. "[12]

CREATING A POLICY-MAKING CULTURE

Despite all these changes the Permanent Secretary has pursued a deliberate policy of maintaining continuity and accruing policy experience at the top of the office. As he said in his evidence to the Richard Commission:

> *"Fine tuning aside, I have replaced only two policy Department heads since the Assembly was established. This means that most of the Department heads have at least three years experience in their present jobs and some have much more ... I have similarly maintained continuity of employment at the crucial [48] Heads of Division level as well ... One consequence of this stability at the top is that the Assembly now has a much greater policy knowledge and capacity than existed in the Welsh Office. This - coupled with the existence of the Strategic Policy Unit, the presence of Special Advisers actively involved in policy issues, the establishment of a new Research and Development Group, and our growing experience of partnership working - means that, in my judgement, it is no longer true to say that the Assembly does not have the capacity to develop distinctive policies attuned to the needs of Wales.* "[13]

Undoubtedly the biggest change hastening this process was the creation of a new Executive Board in October 2001, in succession to the Management Board inherited from Welsh Office days. This comprises all the Assembly Government's Departmental Heads and has a strengthened communications and policy role, emphasised by the inclusion of two political advisers as members. Its role is to deliver on Assembly Government policies as well as dealing with management issues. The Permanent Secretary described its work in the following terms:

> *"The one thing I have done is establish an Executive Board which meets every Tuesday morning. I have as observers one special adviser from the Labour Party and one from the Liberal Democrats who sit on that Board and on a Tuesday morning what we are doing is looking at the issues of the day which are flowing through the Assembly. It meets on a Tuesday morning because the Cabinet has met on the Monday afternoon.* "[14]

---

[12] Rhodri Morgan, Third Anniversay Lecture, National Centre for Public Policy, University of Swansea, 11 December 2002.

[13] Sir Jon Shortridge, *op.cit.*

[14] *Ibid.* p. 279.

The creation of the Executive Board was a step change, marking the emergence of an administrative machine geared to policy and driving policy through. As Nick Bennett, the Liberal Democrat's Special Adviser who sat on the Board during its first year, explained, the objective was "to ensure a longer term and more corporate response to policy development."[15] In this task a major tool is the Strategic Policy Unit whose role is to take the long view on policy issues. It comprises ten officials plus five Special Advisers – four Labour and one Liberal Democrat. The following four examples of its work provide an indication of the Assembly Government's policy preoccupations as the first term drew to a close.

- *Strategic Priorities*: a paper setting out policy priorities ahead of the 2002 three-year Comprehensive Spending Review, with contributions from finance officials and Special Advisers.

- *Economic Regeneration*: a mapping exercise analysing economic inactivity in Welsh communities.

- *Community Investment Authority*: development of a new institution to assist new firms and community enterprises by channelling community investment tax credits and creating local investment funds.

- *Bilingual Future*: development of a comprehensive language policy across government.

This sense of a Welsh policy-making machine, combined with the mechanisms and determination to drive through change according to a worked through set of priorities, is something completely new in Welsh life. Specifically, it reflects the emergence of the Welsh Assembly Government in the middle period of the National Assembly's first term.

THE CORPORATE BODY

The National Assembly's inaugural four-year term falls neatly into three phases. The first 18 months saw a new and unstable institution finding its feet and personality, a process that culminated in the vote of no-confidence in Alun Michael as First Secretary in February 2000. In turn, this led to the formation of the majority Labour/Liberal Democrat Coalition in October 2000. The new administration headed by Alun Michael's successor, Rhodri Morgan, as First Minister, and the Liberal Democrat leader, Mike German, as Deputy First Minister, provided a more coherent government and programme.

---

[15] Nick Bennett, 'Developing Welsh Policy Capacity', in IWA: Agenda, Winter 2002/03.

The final year of the first term was inevitably dominated by the politics of the forthcoming Assembly election in May 2003. In addition it was characterised by preparations for the second term with the drafting of far more elaborate manifestos than had been tabled at the first 1999 election. At the same time the Commission on the Assembly's powers under Lord Richard began its work, establishing the framework of constitutional debates that would be major preoccupations across the parties.

In between these initial and final periods were some 18 months during which the Assembly self-consciously paused for reflection about its internal procedures. The mechanism was the Review of Procedures, which brought all four parties together under the chairmanship of the Presiding Officer.

The Review soon focused on the many anomalies in the Assembly's constitution as established by the 1998 Government of Wales Act. The core difficulty was the Assembly's creation as a corporate body – 'a single legal personality' as the Counsel General, Winston Roddick, has put it[16] – in which its legislative and executive functions were combined rather than separated, as is normal in parliamentary institutions and is the case in Scotland and Northern Ireland. The second phase of the Assembly's first four-year term was dominated by an emphatic rejection of this unitary mode of operation. Instead, the Assembly moved as far as it possibly could in a parliamentary direction through separating its executive and legislative roles. From October 2000 onwards these two elements had developed highly distinctive personalities in the form of the majority Coalition Administration on the one hand, and the independent Office of the Presiding Officer on the other.

The main force driving the split in this period of the Assembly's life was the Presiding Officer, Lord Dafydd Elis-Thomas.[17] This was dramatised by a dispute between him and the Permanent Secretary during Autumn 2000. It was sparked by a minor amendment to an Assembly resolution on Sustainable Development, passed by a combination of Plaid Cymru, Liberal Democrat and Conservative votes in September 2000 (before the Coalition was in place). The amendment required that the civil service Sustainable Development Unit, housed within the Agriculture Department of the Assembly, be relocated to the Central Policy Unit. The objective was to give sustainable development policy greater prominence and enable it to operate within a cross-cutting milieu, to reflect its impact across the range of the Assembly's responsibilities.

---

[16] Winston Roddick QC, *Crossing the Road*, Law Society lecture, National Eisteddfod, Ynys Mon, August 1999.

[17] For an account see John Osmond, 'In Search of Stability: Coalition Politics in the Second Year of the National Assembly' in Alan Trench (Ed) *The State of the Nations 2001: The Second Year of Devolution in the United Kingdom* (Thorverton: Imprint Academic, 2001) pp. 26-31.

However, the Permanent Secretary objected to the move, partly on grounds of cost but, more fundamentally, because he felt it should be for himself rather than politicians to make operational decisions on how the Assembly's civil servants should carry out their duties.[18] Certainly this was the reason why the Labour side opposed the change in the debate. The Permanent Secretary also questioned the legality of the decision but was advised by Office of the Counsel General that the Assembly had operated within its powers in passing the amendment. There may, in fact, be an inherent conflict within the 1998 Government of Wales Act between the general competence of the Assembly to exercise its functions and Section 63 (2) which confers on the Permanent Secretary the right, in relation to staff, "… to make arrangements as to which member or members is or are to exercise [a delegated] function."

The issue came to a head in November 2000 during a meeting of the party leaders in the Assembly at which both Lord Elis-Thomas and Sir Jon Shortridge were present. There were exchanges between the two men which, the following day, caused the Presiding Officer to send the Permanent Secretary a letter defending his right to uphold Assembly decisions and criticising the civil servant for seeking to circumvent them.[19]

THE WELSH ASSEMBLY GOVERNMENT

There seems little doubt that this argument was merely the culmination of a succession of disputes between the Administration and the Presiding Officer that reached back the best part of a year. Underpinning them were different perceptions of the Assembly's role and the way it should develop. From the point of view of the Presiding Officer the higher echelons of the civil service were endeavouring to operate as though the old Welsh Office was still in existence, with the Assembly itself as merely an add-on, essentially an advisory body. It would follow the advice of the Assembly as and when it pleased. On the other hand, from the point of view of some in the Administration, the Presiding Officer was seeking to push the remit of the Assembly beyond what was laid down or envisaged in the Government of Wales Act.

However, there is no doubt that following the establishment of the Coalition, in October 2000, disagreement about the nature of the different roles of the civil service serving the Presiding Office, and those serving the Assembly Government diminished rapidly. There was now a common acceptance of the

[18] Clive Betts, *One Battle the Civil Service Cannot Win*, Western Mail, 11 November 2000

[19] The text is contained in J. Osmond (Ed.) *Coalition Politics Come to Wales: Monitoring the National Assembly September to December 2000*, IWA.

de facto separation between the two sides, an acceptance that was reflected in the report of the Assembly's Review of Procedures in February 2002.[20] Certainly, by the Assembly's middle period it was the Administration, led by the First Minister, that was most anxious to define and emphasise the separation. Part of the motivation was a widespread anxiety that the Administration's decisions and actions were being interpreted by the media as coming from the Assembly as a whole. Both Government and Opposition in the Assembly shared an interest in avoiding such confusion. The result was the emergence of an administrative entity called the 'Welsh Assembly Government' with 'Ministers' and 'Deputy Ministers' in an Assembly Cabinet, determined to be the decisive hand in shaping the future of the country.

One indication was a transformation in the relations between the Assembly Government and its executive agencies. Pre-devolution, organisations such as the Welsh Development Agency, the Health Authorities, the Education Funding Councils, the Arts Council and the Wales Tourist Board led relatively autonomous lives. Apart from delivering annual reports and agreeing broad outline targets they were largely unmolested by the old Welsh Office, and only rarely interrogated by MPs at Westminster.

All this has changed. Instead of one Secretary of State for Wales there are now nine Ministers and five Deputy Ministers who keep a constant watch on the activities of the ASpBs. They meet formally with the Administration at least quarterly, and their activities are also reviewed by the Subject Committees. There is a sense that they are being corralled and disciplined, becoming more like state departments along Whitehall lines than free-standing, arms-length organisations. No longer do they project their own corporate image, separate from that of the Assembly Government, and their plans and strategies are ever more closely aligned with those of the Assembly Government. The new relationship was spelt out by Sir Jon Shortridge, responding to the House of Lords Committee on the Constitution during an oral evidence session at the National Assembly in May 2002:

> *"I think one of the features of the Assembly [Government] is that there is a greater intensity and proximity, politically driven throughout the relevant structures associated with the Assembly, and because of that there is a sharper edge to my relationship with the sponsored bodies."*[21]

---

[20] For a full account of the Review see J. Osmond, 'Constitution Building on the Hoof' in the previous volume in this series, *Building a Civic Culture*, IWA, March 2002.

[21] House of Lords Constitution Select Committee on the Constitution Session 2001-02 *Devolution: Inter-institutional relations in the United Kingdom* Evidence complete to 10 July 2002 HL Paper 147, p.280.

THE PRESIDING OFFICE

A far-reaching constitutional dimension of the Coalition Partnership Agreement was its concern with the role of the Presiding Office as the interface between the Assembly and the Administration. As we have seen, its determination to "... secure the independence of the Office of the Presiding Officer and the civil servants that work there" was a decisive move away from the Assembly's legal status as a corporate body. It put in place a defining characteristic of a parliamentary body since the Presiding Officer's independence is necessary if a clear separation of powers between the executive and legislature is to apply. Within weeks of the Agreement being signed the Assembly overwhelmingly approved a new Standing Order establishing the new structure for the Presiding Office. The changes were substantial.

- A separate budget for the Office (£24.3m for 2001-02) out of which is paid Members' and officials' pay and allowances, Assembly accommodation and associated IT and general administration.

- The Clerk to the Assembly, the Office's chief official, became a deputy Accounting Officer (responsible for the budget) working under the general aegis of the Permanent Secretary (under the terms of the Government of Wales Act he remains the Accounting Officer for the Assembly as a whole). The areas for which the Clerk is directly responsible were also increased, providing scope for a distinctive approach to staff recruitment and deployment within the Office.

- A House Committee as an advisory body to oversee the Office was established, chaired by the Presiding Officer with representatives from all parties in the chamber.

These developments marked a highly significant moment in the evolving constitutional architecture of the National Assembly. In so far as the Assembly could act to change its own constitution without achieving an amendment to the 1998 Government of Wales Act, it has done so. *De facto*, though not *de jure*, it put in place a structure to ensure the independence of the Presiding Office. In turn this cleared a path towards achieving a separation of functions between the executive and the legislature and the creation of a body more parliamentary than corporate in character. This process was underlined in December 2001 when the Presiding Officer, Lord Elis-Thomas, announced the appointment of Paul Silk, a clerk in the House of Commons, as the new Clerk to the Assembly in succession to John Lloyd, a former Welsh Office official.

Finally, in December 2002, the Assembly's Business Committee agreed a change in Standing Orders to reconstitute the House Committee as a

Committee with powers delegated to it by the Assembly under the terms of the Government of Wales Act.[22] That is to say, its position would be entirely autonomous and separated from the Administration. Henceforth, the powers of the Assembly would flow in two streams:

1) the governmental, to the First Minister supported by the Cathays Park officials; and

2) the parliamentary to the Assembly in Cardiff Bay with the House Committee responsible for providing the services and accomodation necessary to support the work of the AMs.

ACCOUNTABILITY

A special issue of their newsletter *Links Dolenni* floated across the desks of the 4,000 or so civil servants in Cathays Park and Cardiff Bay on St David's Day, 1 March 2002. It announced that the vast majority of them no longer served the National Assembly for Wales as a whole. Instead their new master was to be the Welsh Assembly Government, complete with a new logo. As the Permanent Secretary Sir Jon Shortridge put it:

"This new identity is aimed at making a clear distinction between the actions and decisions of the Cabinet and the work of Assembly members as a whole."[23]

On first reading the constitutional implications were unclear. The change could be laying the foundations for the future development of the Assembly in extending its functions and acquiring primary law-making powers. On the other hand, the stage could be set for the bulk of the Welsh civil service reverting to type, in effect reconstituting the old-style Welsh Office in Cathays Park. In this scenario the Assembly would be left as the smaller arm in the Bay, inconvenient at times but generally a forum in which Ministers make pronouncements rather than being held to account.

"Who do I work for now?" was a question posed by one headline in the newsletter. So far as the strict legal position was concerned, the response was that civil servants

"... are still bound by the Civil Service Code which requires us to be accountable to 'Assembly Secretaries and the National Assembly as a body'."

---

[22] John Marek, Deputy Presiding Officer, *Report of the Business Committee: Proposal to Change Standing Orders*, December 2002. The changes were agreed by the Assembly on 18 December 2002.

[23] Welsh Assembly Government newsletter, *Links Dolenni*, 1 March 2002.

In practice, however, this was not to be the case. As the Newsletter continued:

"… most civil servants except for those in the Presiding Office, work most of the time either for the Assembly Government or provide corporate services across the whole of the Assembly."[24]

The newsletter is significant because it marked the point where the idea of the National Assembly as a corporate body was formally abandoned - *de facto* if not *de jure*, since the latter would require amendment to the 1998 Government of Wales Act. The stage is set for further development of a conventional parliamentary institution along Westminster lines, with the executive on one side, based in Cathays Park, clearly separated from the Assembly in Cardiff Bay on the other.

There is no doubt that the vast majority of politicians across the parties have welcomed this development. Greater clarity of function and clearer lines of accountability have ensued. The establishment of the independent Presiding Office with its own £23 million budget, together with the creation of the majority coalition between Labour and the Liberal Democrats, made it inevitable in any event.

However, a danger arises because of the disproportionate size of the two arms of the government of Wales. On the one side there is the Welsh Assembly Government, the Cabinet of nine Ministers and five Deputy Ministers serviced by some 3,500 civil servants. On the other there are the backbench Assembly Members serviced by the Presiding Office. Although this has some 200 civil servants working for it, in practice only around a quarter provide direct administrative services for the Assembly, including research and policy support for backbench members and the Committees. Even comparing the respective libraries, the one in Cathays Park, which is now part of the Assembly Government, has more staff than the one serving the Assembly in Cardiff Bay.

In these circumstances the question arises whether the Assembly is equipped to hold the Welsh Assembly Government effectively to account. In the Wales Act, and the relevant Standing Order Number 9, it was envisaged that Assembly Committees would have access to the full range of civil service support and back up. This was to enable them to contribute to policy making and to question Ministerial proposals. However, under the new dispensation this is now simply not the case. The *Links Dolenni* newsletter suggests that in future officials in Cardiff Bay will be dealing with those in Cathays Park as though they are negotiating with a separate government department.

The Review of Procedures report recommended a modest increase in the

---

[24] *Ibid.*

Presiding Office's staff. However, there is a need for this to go further if it is to service members effectively, a need that would be much greater if the Assembly's competencies were to be extend to primary legislation. The outstanding contrast is with the Scottish Parliament which, during the first term, dealt with some ten pieces of primary legislation a year. To deal with this, together with making the Parliament as effective as possible in holding the Scottish Executive to account, the Scottish Presiding Office has a staff of 463 with more than 100 directly supporting and advising its Committees and backbenchers.

To this it should be added that officials within the Presiding Office remain civil servants, answerable finally to the Permanent Secretary. This is in contrast with the position in Westminster and in the Scottish Parliament where parliamentary officials are entirely separate from the civil service with their own career structures.

DIRECTIONS OF CHANGE

Future administrative and legislative development of the National Assembly will depend on the recommendations   that emerge from the Richard Commission in late 2003. In his evidence to the Commission the Permanent Secretary made it clear that the civil service, as it had developed during the first term, could cope with primary legislative powers:

> "... compared with the changes that have already taken place, the acquisition of further powers, including those of primary legislation, would represent a manageable progression, not a major step change, in terms of the demands made upon us ... Policy officials and the Office of the Counsel General already undertake all the work needed to instruct Counsel on Assembly legislation. So the additional work should be confined to the drafting of primary legislation itself and the additional capacity required to achieve an agreed throughput of primary legislation ... were the Assembly to settle down to producing, say, no more than four or five important pieces of primary legislation a year, then it is my judgement that the Assembly Civil Service would, without much further enhancement, have the capacity to cope - not least because we would no longer have to devote the time to negotiating with Government Departments on the need for, and then the composition of, particular Bills."[25]

The Permanent Secretary added that the major impact of the acquisition of primary powers would be upon the Presiding Office, acknowledging that this

---

[25] Sir Jon Shortridge, Evidence to the Richard Commission, December 2002.

would raise the question of whether its officials should continue to be civil servants. The case for change was argued by the Presiding Officer himself in his evidence to the Commission. He argued that the Assembly should create a separate parliamentary service, as is the case in London, Edinburgh and Belfast, as well as in most Commonwealth and European systems:

> *"We have moved a considerable distance in this direction under current arrangements by developing a set of formal agreements between the Assembly's Clerk and its Permanent Secretary which protect the independence and semi-autonomy of staff in the Presiding Office ... But there remains a concern among some Members and outside commentators that staff may not be whole-hearted in their commitment to serve all elected Members impartially if they believe that their careers could be jeopardised if they, for example, help a Committee to subject senior officials of the Assembly Government - who might be their line managers in their next job - to uncomfortably searching scrutiny."[26]*

The terms of this evidence to the Richard Commission, with both the executive and legislative sides of the Assembly inviting consideration as to the future status of officials in the Presiding Office if primary legislative functions were devolved, was testimony to how far the Administration had travelled in the first four-year term. It had inherited a junior Department of the British State, fully integrated into a Whitehall milieu, with little experience of policy making and without the means of driving forward a distinctive agenda. In just four years a transformation had taken place as far as was possible within the constraints of the Government of Wales Act. In place was a growing parliamentary system, a separation of powers, and an increasingly confident policy-making machine ready to take on board the acquisition of more powers. Not only that, but in the words of the Permanent Secretary, the major changes to make this possible had already happened. For the Assembly's civil service the acquisition of legislative powers would entail a "manageable progression" rather than a "step change" in its operation.

---

[26] Lord Elis-Thomas, Evidence to the Richard Commission, December 2002.

PART 2

POLICY

PROCESS

Chapter 5

FINANCE

Gillian Bristow

Finance is an important determinant of the Assembly's policy processes and underpins all major policy decisions. It is no surprise, therefore, that the allocation of financial resources both to and within Wales has dominated debates in the National Assembly from the start. While the way in which UK central government expenditure is allocated to Wales has changed little under devolution, with continued reliance being placed upon the Barnett formula, scrutiny of its mechanics and its implications for spending totals and autonomy in Wales has massively increased. In addition, the expenditure demands wrought by the EU's Objective One programme, coupled with generally rising levels of UK public expenditure have had a significant impact on the budget available within Wales. At the same time, devolution has radically changed the process by which the budget is allocated across the different spending priorities and programmes within Wales. The whole process is now subject to much greater transparency and consultation.

This chapter provides a summary review of the major finance issues, debates and developments which occurred within the Assembly during the first term, and concludes with a critical reflection on their implications.[1]

THE SPENDING REVIEWS: BYPASSING BARNETT

While the allocation of public expenditure within Wales is for the National Assembly to decide, the total budget it has available is determined within the framework of UK public expenditure planning and control. As a consequence, the Treasury's bi-annual Spending Review settlements, which set a rolling programme of three-year limits for the spending totals of all UK departments and devolved administrations, have provided a critical focus for the Assembly's budgetary negotiations with Westminster.

The mechanism by which Wales' allocation of UK public expenditure is determined has changed little since devolution, although its operation has become more transparent and, perhaps, better understood. In short, the bulk of the Assembly's budget is provided via a block grant from central

[1] Much of the chapter is based on the IWA's quarterly monitoring reports, Monitoring the Assembly during the first term, and in particular Adrian Kay's tracking of finance policy, available on www.iwa.org.uk.

government, the annual changes in which are determined by the Barnett formula. The formula operates by allocating a proportion of every increase in public spending in England, to Scotland, Wales and Northern Ireland. The amount allocated is based on the proportion of each country's population to the population of England.[2]

One of the main advantages of this system, as far as the UK government is concerned, is that it is perceived to reduce the need for annual bargaining between Treasury ministers, the Secretary of State for Wales and Assembly Ministers. However, in practice the Assembly's first term was characterised by a significant degree of behind-the-scenes negotiation and political bargaining over spending totals. The impact of the 2000-06 Objective One programme for west Wales and the Valleys provides the main explanation. This generated a unique public expenditure problem for the Assembly in its first year, and an unprecedented requirement for a step change in the budget made available to Wales in the July 2000 Spending Review.

The detailed twists and turns of the ensuing debate and negotiations around this issue have been explored at length elsewhere.[3] In summary, a breaking or "busting" of the Barnett formula had to occur in the 2000 Spending Review if significant extra funds were to be found to both draw down the European element of the Objective One monies available to Wales, and to match them with domestic public sector funding. As First Minister Rhodri Morgan and the then Secretary of State for Wales Paul Murphy put it, in an article in the *Western Mail*:

> "*In England the Objective One area only constitutes eight per cent of the population ... In Wales 65 per cent of the population, 1.9 million out of 2.9 million, are in Objective One areas. That is why Wales' case for different treatment was so strong.*"[4]

The UK government ultimately agreed to the Assembly's demands to bypass the Barnett formula and also transferred control of European Social Fund resources in Wales to the Assembly, thus providing a further increase in funding. As a result of the review, the Assembly budget was increased by 5.4 per cent in real terms over the 2001-02 to 2003-04 period. Table 1 gives the National Assembly's block grant for this period, together with the extra

---

[2] For further explanation see HM Treasury, *Funding The Scottish Parliament, National Assembly For Wales and the Northern Ireland Assembly: A Statement of Funding Policy*, 2002 (available at: www.hm-treasury.gov.uk/media//5A6F9/funding_devolved.pdf)

[3] See, for example, Bristow G. and Blewitt N., 'The Structural Funds and additionality in Wales: devolution and multi-level governance', *Environment and Planning* A 33 (6), 2001, pages1083-1100; and Bristow, G. and Kay, A., 'Spending Autonomy in Wales: Setting the Budget within the Framework of the Barnett Formula', in Osmond J. and Jones B. (Eds.) *Building a Civic Culture: Institutional Change , Policy Development and Political Dynamics in the National Assembly for Wales*, IWA, 2002; pages 83-96.

[4] Rhodri Morgan and Paul Murphy, 'Once-in-a-generation chance in our hands', *Western Mail*, 19 July 2000.

TABLE 1: JULY 2000 COMPREHENSIVE SPENDING REVIEW SETTLEMENT FOR WALES			
	2001 – 2002	**2002-03**	**2003-04**
Assembly Block	£8.4bn	£9.1bn	£9.8bn
Spending Review Extra allocation	£480m	£1.173m	£1.821m
Of which: Structural Funds	£113m	£148m	£160m

amounts resulting from the Review and the allocation within these for the Structural Fund Programmes.

This episode set a significant precedent, and the events and debates that surrounded it drew attention to a number of wider questions about the Assembly's powers and resources. First and foremost, the relationship between the Assembly and UK central government was thrown sharply under the spotlight. The Assembly leadership and Secretary of State for Wales were quick to claim that the settlement represented a victory for the Assembly, although whether such a fortuitous outcome would have been achieved in a more cash-strapped public spending environment is open to question. Nevertheless, as a directly elected body, the Assembly was able to demonstrate resources of political legitimacy. The Economic Development Committee of the Assembly played an important role in raising the profile of the debate and securing answers to key questions. The status of the Assembly as an elected body also ensured a level of coverage of events that helped elevate the significance of the issue. In other words, it became more difficult for Treasury ministers to ignore the voice of the Assembly. The political consequences for Labour of this power struggle were demonstrated when the Opposition parties combined to force the resignation of the Assembly's first Labour leader, Alun Michael.

However, while the Assembly was able to secure additional resources from the Treasury, it proved very difficult to achieve open and transparent information on precisely how the increase in resources was calculated. The additional financial support the Treasury provided in this period could feasibly be removed in a different political environment, for example, if there was a Conservative Westminster government dealing with a Labour-led Assembly. In acknowledgement of this, the House of Lords Constitution Committee has recently recommended that:

"... information about changes to public spending for England should be made available in a manner that relates directly to the categories attracting consequential payments under the Barnett formula; and ... the statistics collected and made available by HM Treasury to the devolved administrations be reviewed so as to ensure that all the information needed by the devolved administrations is available to them."[5]

Furthermore, the July 2000 Spending Review did not put an end to the debate within the Assembly itself as to the availability of resources to meet Structural Fund commitments in Wales. The Barnett-plus settlement provided additional funding to cover the European grants earmarked for projects in Wales. However, the total increase provided was based on cautious assumptions about the spending profile under the Objective One programme. This means at the very least that there will be a build up of funding pressure towards the end of the programming period and at the very worst, that a proportion of the European funds available risk being returned to the Commission.[6] Moreover, no additional contribution was made to support the substantial increase in public sector match funding, most of which has to be found from within the Assembly's block budget. According to the Opposition parties in the Assembly, this is likely to create very severe pressures on other areas of spending in Wales.

Nor were these concerns addressed by the subsequent Spending Review, the results of which were announced in July 2002. The Chancellor announced an increase in the Assembly's budget of £1.7 billion over the three years covered by the review, that is 2003-04 to 2005-06. This included an extra £164 million per year to 'cover' European grant receipts, inclusive of European Social Fund receipts. As in 2000, the Treasury provided no additional money for public sector match funding.

The response of the Assembly Government to this criticism was identical to that in 2000. The large overall increases in public expenditure generally, and for economic development in particular, should provide sufficient extra resources for matched funding purposes. An alternative line is to note that underspend across the Assembly's budget over the past few years is of sufficient magnitude to comfortably provide matched funding. This reduces the force of the Opposition's argument that the demands of matched funding are actively drawing resources away from other areas of the Assembly's budget.

---

[5] House of Lords Committee on the Constitution, *Devolution: Inter-Institutional Relations In The United Kingdom*, Second Report, January 2003, para. 93.

[6] See Chapter 9 for an account of the administration of the programme during the first two years.

SUSTAINABILITY OF THE BARNETT FORMULA

The July 2000 and 2002 Spending Reviews also served to intensify the already growing debate as to whether the Barnett formula provides a sustainable mechanism for allocating public expenditure in a devolved polity. As well as demonstrating the relative inflexibility of the population-based formula in respect of large increases in European Structural Fund allocations to UK regions, the Spending Reviews highlighted that the application of the formula is highly politicised, complex and opaque. Despite the Barnett formula, the Welsh block is a negotiated settlement between Whitehall and Cardiff. The sense of scientific objectivity or rigorous accuracy implied by the word formula is spurious. The Barnett formula sets the framework for discussions at official and ministerial levels. But these remain intensely political. As a result, it is highly likely that other regions will be encouraged to present the Chancellor with equally persuasive demands for additional resources from the public purse.

This scenario is especially likely once the process of devolution in the UK spreads to those English regions already disaffected by Barnett. Devolution has already provoked much wider scrutiny of the real and perceived inequities in the funds available for regional spending across the UK. There are, indeed, substantial differences in levels of per capita spending across different parts of the UK at present, with the most notable of these occurring between Scotland and the neighbouring North East region of England. For example, Scotland spends 11 per cent more per head than the North East, even though its GDP per head is some 25 per cent higher.[7] Such anomalies are destined to accelerate demands for the introduction of a new, more transparent and fairer fiscal settlement based on a thorough review of expenditure needs. In addition, there are calls for the introduction of a broader legal or institutional framework for resolving any conflicts or perceived inequalities that might arise. In short, it will make it imperative that the UK introduces a fiscal constitution. Indeed, the House of Lords Committee on the Constitution has recently made this recommendation:

"We recommend that where discrete disputes arise, they should be referred to an independent body, such as a Devolution Finance Commission, with that body then making a recommendation to the Cabinet. To the extent that macro-economic management requires control by the Treasury of the aggregate amounts of funding involved, such amounts could be set as the total value of a settlement to be

---

[7] HM Treasury, *Prudent for a Purpose: Building Opportunity and Security for All*, Spending Review 2000: New Public Spending Plans 2001-2004, CM 4087, The Stationery Office, July 2000.

allocated by the same body without the Treasury being able to determine the way in which it is allocated."[8]

Within this context, political debate within Wales has begun to focus on whether Wales would benefit from the removal of the Barnett formula and the introduction of a new needs-based system for allocating UK public expenditure. Opinion is sharply divided on this issue. The Assembly Government is unwilling to open discussions with the UK Government on a needs-based replacement for the Barnett formula on the grounds that it cannot be absolutely certain that the outcome would be favourable for Wales. This stance can be explained by virtue of the fact that the current system for allocating funds to Wales has provided a relatively generous settlement, certainly in comparison to Scotland and Northern Ireland where the so-called 'Barnett squeeze' is being felt. This describes the process whereby strict application of the formula ensures that those areas that enjoy higher levels of per capita expenditure, receive slightly lower proportionate increases in spending than those with lower levels of spending per head (such as Wales). Indeed, in the words of Lord Roberts of Conwy, Wales is currently experiencing not so much of a 'Barnett squeeze' as a "Barnett hug". It is also highly likely, of course, that political motives are at work. The question of whether to replace the Barnett formula with a model based on needs is a highly politicised and sensitive one at Whitehall, where the Labour government itself is divided over the need for and desirability of change. With the Treasury still ultimately holding the purse strings, it is not surprising that the Labour-led Assembly Government is unwilling to be seen as responsible for opening up this particular Pandora's Box.

This view is strongly challenged by others within the Assembly, particularly Plaid Cymru members, who believe that given the demands on public services associated with the high proportion of elderly people in Wales, there is a strong needs-based case for higher levels of public expenditure.[9] Similarly, former Secretary of State Ron Davies has drawn attention to the way in which the formula directly squeezes health expenditure in Wales. In essence, the formula translates any increase in health expenditure in England into the same cash increase per capita for Wales, irrespective of health needs in Wales and the historical imbalance of health expenditure in favour of England. As Ron Davies put it:

> *"For every £100 per capita spend in England, our poor health status requires us to spend £114 in Wales. However, under Barnett as year-on-year health expenditure increases we only receive £100 from the Treasury*

---

[8] House of Lords Constitution Committee, *op.cit.* , para. 102.

[9] Professor Phil Williams AM, *The Case for Replacing the Barnett Formula: A Submission to the Treasury Select Committee Inquiry into Regional Public Expenditure by the Plaid Cymru / Party of Wales Group at the National Assembly for Wales*, 2002.

*for every £114 we spend. Welsh policy makers face an unenviable choice,
either increase health expenditure at a lower level of increase than
England (so worsening the health divide) or maintain expenditure at
existing comparative levels to try to maintain health conditions. Not
unnaturally the policy, hitherto, has been to do the latter. But you can't
spend the same pound twice. That extra £14 has to come from other
budgets within the Welsh block, that is environment, education, local
government or economic development."[10]*

Thus, if the Assembly wants to match the current percentage rate of increase
of health spending in England, the inevitable corollary is reduced spending in
other areas. The end result is to reduce autonomy over policy choices.

At present, however, there is only partial and incomplete evidence on which
to review public expenditure needs in Wales. A comprehensive needs
assessment has not been conducted for over 20 years and much more research
is required into how needs could and should be assessed in the UK and how
this will impact upon Wales.

THE BUDGET SETTING PROCESS

As indicated earlier, once the overall budget for Wales has been determined by
central government, the Assembly has the freedom to make its own spending
decisions on devolved programmes within the overall total. This has
dramatically changed the process of allocating public expenditure within
Wales. Commenting on the Assembly's first budget in the plenary debate in
December 1999, Finance Secretary Edwina Hart noted that:

*"... this is an entirely new and radical way of producing a budget. It is
designed to promote inclusiveness, accountability and consensus among
us."[11]*

Few could argue with her. Before devolution, the budget round was
conducted behind closed doors and involved only the Secretary of State for
Wales, two junior Welsh Office Ministers and Welsh Office Group Directors.
The process is now open to debate by Assembly Ministers and Committees,
and is subject to wide public consultation. As well as becoming more
transparent, spending decisions and priorities are also subject to a much
greater degree of political scrutiny. Indeed, whereas previously the Secretary
of State for Wales simply presented the budget as a *fait accompli*, the final
budget now has to be ratified by the Assembly although no amendments can

[10] Ron Davies, 'Where Needs Must', IWA, *Agenda*, Winter 20002/03

[11] Assembly *Record*, 1 December 1999.

be made at that stage. These changes have significantly lengthened the budget process in Wales. Figure 1 sets out the process the Assembly followed in allocating its budget for the 2001-02 financial year.

FIGURE 1: BUDGET PLANNING ROUND FOR 2001 - 02

- Paper issued by the Finance Minister Edwina Hart on 18 May 2000 outlining the strategic context for the budget process (as defined by the Better Wales document), the financial background to the process and initial issues for consideration. Public responses were invited by 14 July 2000.

- Ministers invited to submit issue papers to appropriate Committees in order to focus discussion by 14 July 2000.

- Committees formally responded to their respective Assembly Ministers in July and August 2000 setting out priorities for the Budget and Strategic Planning Round.

- The Preliminary Draft Budget was published on 26 October 2000 and debated in plenary session on that date.

- Subject Committees discussed their particular budget allocations and were asked to present their views to the Finance Minister in November 2000.

- Finance Minister prepared Final Budget by 29 November 2000.

- Final budget ratified by Assembly in plenary session of 7 December 2000.

Plainly, the Subject Committees have an important role to play in the budget setting process. In the debate on the first Assembly budget round in November 2000, Finance Minister Edwina Hart noted that of the 33 budget recommendations that had been formally made by the Committees, the Preliminary Draft Budget had met 29 of them, whilst two had been partly met.[12] Although there was some disagreement over the extent to which the budget allocations reflected the Committees' degree of priority on certain issues, the Committees' views do appear to have been influential in affecting the distribution of resources. Furthermore, the discussions which took place during November resulted in further allocations to a number of the Subject Committees' priority areas.

---

[12] Assembly *Record*, 10 November 2000.

During successive budget rounds, a more effective opposition in the Assembly also appears to have emerged. The 2001-02 budget round was the first budget of the Coalition government in the Assembly. There were a few areas where spending was explicitly linked to the Partnership Agreement that underpinned the Coalition, but the main effect seems to have been to sharpen the public scrutiny of the budget. Relieved of the requirement to manufacture a cross-party consensus to pass the budget, the parties slipped easily into the roles of Government and Opposition.

It could be argued that the scrutiny of the Welsh budget would be further increased if the Assembly were to establish a Finance Committee. This is perhaps an issue for the Assembly to consider in the future.

CHANGING BUDGET PRIORITIES

The end of the Assembly's first term provides an appropriate opportunity to consider how spending priorities have changed under this new, more open and democratic régime. Table 2 summarises the outcome of the Assembly's first budget round, and provides a useful indication of the early priorities identified.

This first budget was significant because it demonstrated that despite working within a fixed level of funding, there were opportunities for the Assembly to make significant changes at the margins. Thus, it demonstrated that health and social services were a priority area for the Assembly administration with the budget here being increased by £12.1 million in 2000-01 and £10.1 million in 2001-02, compared with the inherited Welsh Office plans. Similarly, compared to the inherited Welsh Office baselines, around £14.5 million extra was transferred to the Local Authority Revenue Settlement for 2000-01 and over £27 million in 2001-02, for the costs of teachers' pay and appraisal arrangements arising from the Green Paper The BEST for *Teaching and Learning*.

Not surprisingly, the main focal point of this budget was the issue of finding appropriate funding to support Wales' Structural Fund commitments in the first year of the programme, that is before the outcome of the July 2000 Spending Review. To cover this expenditure, the inherited Welsh Office baseline of £19 million was supplemented by £56 million of unspent 'cover' of Structural Funds provision carried forward from previous years. Leaving aside the increased European Regional Development Fund provision, the Economic Development baseline within the Draft Budget was actually reduced by £6.2 million to £315.5 million, when compared with the original Welsh Office baseline for 2000-01. The Economic Development Committee's

TABLE 2: DRAFT BUDGET BY MAIN EXPENDITURE GROUPS. APPROVED BY THE ASSEMBLY IN PLENARY SESSION ON 1 DECEMBER 1999 (£000s)

	2000-01		2001-02	
	Approved Changes[1]	Approved Plans	Approved Changes[1]	Approved Plans
Health and Social Services	12,100	2,880,162	10,100	3,065,622
Local Government	16,740	2,693,305	36,908	2,820,457
Housing, Transport and Environment	2,600	714,561	6,050	733,130
Agriculture and Rural Development	5,880	282,746	5,500	307,007
Economic Development (ED including ERDF carried forward)	-6,203 (49,400)	315,468 (371,071)	-11,352 –	329,999 –
Education and Training (E & T budget pre transfer to Local Government)	-12,766 (2,324)	882,675 (897,765)	-28,474 (6,784)	932,921 (968,179)
Chief Inspector of Schools	0	9,509	800	10,566
Auditor General for Wales	1,551	1,961	1,651	2,061
Assembly Costs	0	26,822	0	22,173
Central Administration	0	101,904	0	108,688
Capital Modernisation Fund / Invest to Save Budget	-17,936	115	-20,391	345
TOTAL ASSEMBLY EXPENDITURE	1,966	7,909,228	792	8,332,969
Office of the Secretary of State for Wales	200	2,862	200	3,096
TOTAL WELSH BUDGET	2,166	7,912,090	992	8,336,065

[1]Approved Changes are the changes, relative to the inherited Welsh Office plans.

response was highly critical. The Committee's Chair, the late Val Feld, said that:

"... the Committee believes that cutting the Economic Development budget sends the wrong messages about how seriously the Assembly takes the task of raising the GDP of Wales. This is a time when greater flexibility, rather than tighter funding constraints, is appropriate. The Committee wishes to see the cut in the budget restored."[13]

The backdrop to the second Welsh budget (debated in the Autumn of 2000) was a large increase in public expenditure in England over three years, which accordingly provided a large increase in the block grant available to the Assembly to allocate. An indication of the degree of largesse available to the Finance Minister, Edwina Hart, was her claim that she had met 54 of the 55 priorities given to her by the Subject Committees during the budget consultation process. This was a budget settlement in which all the major policy areas received significant increases in funding, as shown in Table 3.

In this budget round, the Assembly Government set out its spending plans for the three year period covered by the July 2000 Spending Review, that is 2001-02 to 2003-04. Table 3 demonstrates the impact of the July 2000 Spending Review settlement and the additional funding for the Structural Fund programmes in Wales, with a 55.6 per cent increase in the economic development budget for the year 2001-02. However, this budget also allocated the block in line with the priorities of the UK government. For example, large increases in health and education expenditure in England have also generated large increases in health and education expenditure in Wales. It is difficult to see from the figures that the pattern of funding allocation is any different than it would have been under the Welsh Office in the sense of reflecting the central government's priorities. This is hardly surprising since the big increases in expenditure by the UK government that produced the big increases in expenditure in Wales represent Labour Party priorities. Labour holds a majority of Welsh seats both at Westminster and in the Assembly.

The budget for 2002-03 was revised slightly in the Autumn of 2001. Substantial increases in public expenditure had already been planned for this year. Nevertheless, the revised budget contained some increases on top of those already in the system: There was £53.8 million more for health and social services on top of a £327.5 million increase already announced, and £19 million for education on top of the existing planned £44 million increase.

However, the extra expenditure for 2002-03 was not new money. It was funded from underspending in previous financial years. Indeed, in presenting the budget, Edwina Hart stated that the major public spending issue facing

---

[13] Val Feld AM, Economic Development Secretary, Letter to Rhodri Morgan, 25 November 1999.

TABLE 3: NATIONAL ASSEMBLY BUDGET 2000: MAJOR
EXPENDITURE GROUPS (£M)[1]

	2000-01	2001-02	annual % change	2002-03	annual % change	2003-04	annual % change
Health and Social Services	2986.5	3248.8	8.8	3559.6	9.6	3840.8	7.9
Education and Lifelong learning	877.4	932.4	6.3	975.5	4.6	1032.0	5.8
Economic Development	263.2	409.6	55.6	449.2	9.7	485.8	8.1
Agriculture and Rural Development	231.1	258.4	11.8	247.2	-4.3	247.6	0.2
Environment, Planning and Transport	275.8	294.3	6.7	350.6	19.1	379.5	8.2
Housing	530.4	563.0	6.1	585.7	4.0	594.2	1.5
Culture, Sport and the Welsh Language	55.5	56.5	1.8	59.9	6.0	62.9	5.0
Local Government	2712.0	2852.4	5.2	3022.7	6.0	3194.9	5.7

Source: National Assembly Budget 2000: Final Budget for 2001-02 to 2003-04.1.

Figures for 2002-03 and 2003-04 are indicative.

the Assembly was its capacity to fully spend the available budget and to ensure that all resources reached the frontline services for which they were intended. Underspend in 2001-02 amounted to three per cent of the Assembly's budget with a cumulative underspend of £387 million being carried over to be re-allocated in 2002-03 as 'end-year flexibility'. Edwina Hart set a medium-term target for the Assembly of reducing underspend to one per cent of the budget.

Issues surrounding underspending provided much of the focus for the debates on the draft and final budget. The Opposition parties raised concerns about the procedures for identifying and dealing with areas of underspend as well as the potential for underspend to jeopardise the Assembly's case for additional resources in negotiations with the Treasury. Concerns were also expressed about the lack of transparency in the way underspend is re-allocated which may create the perception that the Assembly Government is continuously re-announcing existing pots of funding. The Assembly Government's progress in spending under the Objective One programme and its Communities First initiative are likely to bring these issues sharply into focus.

In October 2002 Edwina Hart promulgated the Assembly Government's draft budget for 2003-04 and indicative budgets for the two subsequent years.[14] In many ways, the announcement was similar to the previous two years: another generous Spending Review settlement leading to substantial increases in the headline budgets of the major areas of Assembly expenditure. The figures for the main Major Expenditure Groups are set out in Table 4.

The consistent theme of Edwina Hart's budget speech was the need to

TABLE 4: ASSEMBLY GOVERNMENT'S DRAFT BUDGET 2003-04 (£ MILLION)						
Major Expenditure Group (MEG)	2002-03	2003-04 Draft budget	% change	2004-05	2005-06	% change 02/03 to 05/06
Health and Social Services	3,749	4,158	+11	4,345	4,427	+18
Local Govt	2,995	3,203	+7	3,277	3,467	+16
Housing*	507	506	0	491	471	-8
Communities	79	98	+24	122	131	+66
Environment, Planning and Transport	917	968	+6	1,002	1,042	+14
Agriculture and Rural Affairs	227	250	+10	248	258	+14
Economic Development	536	568	+6	572	579	+8
Education	1,072	1,171	+9	1,245	1,386	+29
Culture, Sport, Language	75	93	+24	101	108	+44
OVERALL TOTAL**	10,518	11,333	+8	11,931	12,745	+21

* The apparent fall in spending in housing seems to be due to moving budget lines between MEGs, in particular to the new 'Communities' heading.
**The MEGs referring to administration, inspection and forestry have been omitted. Consequently the columns do not sum to the overall total.
Source: Assembly Government Draft Budget 2002.

[14]Assembly *Record*, 15 October 2002.

connect extra finance with improved performance, a departure from her previous two budget speeches. To this end, she committed the Assembly Government to the position that:

> "... allocation of resources beyond the end of the next financial year will be determined by the direction that the review can lead us in ensuring that investment is matched by reform and delivery."[15]

The health budget illustrates this commitment. The Finance Minister labelled the increase in 18 per cent health spending over the three-year period 2002-03 to 2005-06, shown in Table 4, as "relatively modest".[16] Instead, she has put aside substantial reserves to be spent according to the recommendations of a Review Team looking at health spending.[17] It will be important to chart whether this principle - that reform should accompany extra resources - will bring Welsh health policy more closely into line with England or will represent the development of a genuinely distinctive health system in Wales.

CONCLUSION

To conclude, the advent of the National Assembly has elevated the importance of finance questions in Wales. In theory not much has changed in the way the Welsh budget is determined. The Barnett formula has been retained and the Assembly largely remains subject to the decision-making processes of UK central government. In practice, however, the financial relationships between central government and the devolved administration have been tested and challenged significantly. The Assembly Government managed to secure an increase in resources to support its European funding commitments, which at the very least has thrown the whole question of the future of the Barnett formula into sharp focus.

In terms of budget priorities within Wales, the whole process has become much more democratic, open and transparent, with the Subject Committees playing an important role in determining priorities. Even here, however, the influence of UK central government cannot be ignored. Westminster priorities for rising health and education expenditure have largely been followed, although the Assembly has benefited from the generally rising tide of UK public expenditure. With world events generating political and economic uncertainties, who is to say that the Assembly's second term will be so fortuitous.

---

[15] Assembly Government Press Notice, 'Major investment in frontline services to be matched by improved delivery, says Edwina Hart', 15 October 2002.

[16] Assembly *Record*, 15 October 2002.

[17] The Adviser to the Review is Derek Wanless, author of the Treasury's influential report on the future of the NHS, published in April 2002.

CHAPTER 6

THE SUBJECT COMMITTEES

Mark S. Lang and Alan Storer

The ambiguity and complexity of the Welsh devolution settlement resulted in some uncertainty about how the subject committees in the Assembly would operate. They are intended to combine policy development with scrutiny of the executive and also some engagement with the legislative process. However, the extent to which they can engage in policy development when faced with an increasingly strong executive, certainly since the formation of the Welsh Assembly Government, is one question. Another is the how effectively they can hold the executive to account so long as they include Cabinet Ministers among their membership.[1]

Members of the Assembly underwent a steep learning process on the nature of the subject committees during the first term. Inevitably there were some mistakes, but there were also successes. This chapter analyses the development of the subject committees as institutions within the wider Assembly policy process. This task is complicated by the degree of flexibility in their operation permitted by standing orders, which has led to a variety of interpretations by different committees.

The analysis presented here is divided into five sections. The first addresses policy development and the second scrutiny, bearing in mind that there is a close relationship between the two. The third section examines the impact of the coalition from October 2000. The fourth relates to the committees scrutiny of secondary legislation, while the fifth deals with resource constraints.

POLICY DEVELOPMENT

Two main approaches to policy development within the subject committees can be identified. The *policy review* approach is characterised by a subject committee undertaking an extended review of one particular topic over a period of weeks or months. The second is characterised by *short discussions*

---

[1] For a full discussion of these issues see the earlier volume in this series, *Inclusive Government and Party Management: The National Assembly for Wales and the Work of its Committees*, IWA, 2001, especially the concluding chapter.

within the committee on policy documents presented by the Minister as part of a strategy being developed by the civil service. Each of these approaches has had its advantages and disadvantages.

POLICY REVIEWS

The policy review approach requires members to prioritise certain policy areas above others. Due to the constraints that such an in-depth review places upon the time of a committee, there is little opportunity to cover a broad range of topics. Committees that have adopted this approach have sacrificed quantity at the expense of quality. In addition, time is also taken away from scrutiny of the Minister. On the other hand, the policy review approach does produce a weighty report that has been carefully prepared, over which the committee has ownership. Unlike the short discussions approach that rarely amount to more than a 20-minute discussion and involve mainly the first reactions of committee members to a policy issue, a policy review carries much more weight. It is much more difficult for the Minister to ignore.

Of course, a policy review could ultimately be in vain since the committees do not have legislative initiative. The successful implementation of a policy ultimately depends on influencing the Minister to implement a policy in full, in part, or more commonly to redistribute resources in favour of a particular policy area the following year. This last influence was the case following the Culture Committee's review of the Welsh language.

At the same time, policy reviews have other benefits that are not necessarily dependent on the implementation of policy. They educate committee members and generally improve the knowledge of the wider policy community around the committee.

There are more fundamental weaknesses concerning the use of policy reviews. In order to be most successful a given policy review should be carefully chosen. Many policy areas are not within the power of the Assembly to influence. The early example of the Agriculture and Rural Development Committee's beef on the bone inquiry, conducted in the opening months of the first term, could never have influenced the executive nor succeeded in lifting the ban on beef on the bone because it was not within the power of the Assembly to do so. Likewise the Local Government and Housing Committee's review of housing stock transfer as a means to deal with the backlog of repair and maintenance of council housing, recommended that the rules should be changed to allow local authorities to borrow the money they needed to fund maintenance of their housing stock. However, such a policy was not within the power of the Assembly.

Some policy areas are only partially devolved and consequently involve a dialogue with Westminster through the civil service, as was the case with the

Economic Development Committee's energy policy review. This is a complicating factor and limits the choices available to the committees. There are also fundamental weaknesses to reports published as a result of policy reviews. A committee of amateurs and a clerk is simply not in a position to get to grips with some complex policy issues, as was the case with the Post-16 Education and Training Committee's review of Higher Education. In many cases, therefore, the published reports are in effect contributions to debates rather than authoritative documents.

These weaknesses not withstanding, many policy reviews have ultimately overcome the difficulties involved and been successful. Amongst the first successes was the Post-16 Education and Training Committee's review of the Education and Training Action Plan. This policy document emanated from the Welsh Office and considered the reorganisation of post-16 training in Wales. The Administration was anxious to close down debate and push the plan through quickly. It put the proposals to the Committee in June 1999 hoping for an immediate ratification. However, under the experienced chairmanship of Cynog Dafis, the committee insisted that the Plan should be thoroughly examined. During the following six months it took evidence from a wide range of bodies. The Committee's report on its investigation proved highly influential in reworking the Education and Training Action Plan. Whilst retaining the broad thrust of the original proposals, the final version contained a number of significant amendments that were incorporated into primary legislation.[2] These included:

- Funding of sixth forms through local education authorities.

- Provision for the Council for Education and Training Wales to have regional offices and advisory panels instead of regional groups with their own budgets.

- The needs of Welsh education and training to be considered.

- A Welsh baccalaureate to be considered within the post-16 qualifications framework.

SHORT DISCUSSIONS

An alternative approach to policy development undertaken by the committees is characterised in the form of short discussions. Typically these entail discussing policy documents tabled by the civil service. This activity is less time consuming than undertaking full-scale inquiries and enables the committees to cover a much wider area of policy. On the other hand, the process entails much less active engagement with policy development and

[2] Egan, D. and James, R., 'Driving a Policy Agenda: The Post-16 Education and Training Committee', in: J. Barry Jones and J. Osmond (Eds.) *Inclusive Government and Party Management: The National Assembly for Wales and the work of its Committees.* IWA, 2001, pages 63-78.

consequently gives the committees far less 'ownership'. The committees that adopted this approach were accused of doing very little in the way of policy development. However, in their defence the Panel of Subject Committee Chairs argued that:

"… by looking briefly at a number of initiatives as they emerge, subject committees are acting as a kind of democratic litmus test … fulfilling this sounding board function is a valid role for committees."[3]

The approach also enables committee members to respond to current issues and provides more opportunities to scrutinise Ministers and their departments. Some AMs argue that although policy discussions are less visible than policy reviews, this does not mean they are less effective. Also, given the restrictions on subject committees' time and resources, they are a useful way of instigating executive reviews of policy, as for example the Townsend Review of resource allocation within NHS Wales, which leads to a needs-based system being adopted from 2003-04. On the other hand, some AMs have argued that subject committees cannot simply endorse policy papers from the executive that they have had no part in developing.

Nevertheless, this avenue for policy development has allowed subject committees to influence policy, usually in small incremental ways. For example, as Chairman of the Economic Development Committee Ron Davies was able to use this mechanism to elicit information from the civil servants that revealed where funding cover for Objective One programmes would come from, and that EU money earmarked for Wales was not added to the baseline defined by the Barnett Formula.[4]

POLICY SCRUTINY

In contrast with their approach to policy development, the subject committees adopted just one main approach to policy scrutiny. This is essentially a week-by-week approach, centred on questioning Ministers on their monthly committee reports. It has the advantage of allowing committee members to scrutinise Ministers on contemporary issues. However, as with the short discussions approach to policy development, it runs the risk of subject committees becoming involved in operational matters. In turn, this can lead to a blurring of the distinction between implementation of policy and scrutiny of policy implementation. The

---

[3] Minutes of the Panel of Subject Committee Chairs, *The Role of the Subject Committees*, 10 February 2001.

[4] See Chapter 9 for a discussion of this episode.

approach also lacks a strategic focus, with the committees channelled into reactive responses to Ministerial statements.

Some AMs have claimed that Ministers' membership of subject committees has led to a flaw, which makes the process of scrutinising them seriously ineffective. Unlike House of Commons select committees which have a 'hunt in a pack' mentality when scrutinising Ministers, Assembly committees tend not to have this attitude. Instead, it is common for other members of a Minister's party, or their coalition partners, to defend them during questions, or even to ask 'friendly questions'. This is a direct result of Ministers' membership of the committees and is a serious flaw given that the Minister's report is a committee's main focus for scrutiny.

Ministerial committee membership also means that the clerks cannot prepare a brief in advance of the report, as in the House of Commons, because the Minister would get hold of it. In some instances Deputy Ministers, who do not have a formal role in the subject committees other than their ordinary membership, have acted to defend the Minister. However, removing Ministers as members of subject committees would not be an option unless the size of the Assembly were increased, as there would not be enough backbench AMs to fill the committees. One option might be to allow the Ministers to remain as members of the subject committees, but be much stricter about their specific involvement. Rules could be drawn up to prevent a Minister from obtaining committee briefings in advance of their monthly reports, though how effective these would be is open to question.

An alternative approach to policy scrutiny, as identified by the Panel of Committee Chairs, would be to adopt a more strategic, proactive and in-depth approach to scrutiny, similar to the policy review approach to policy development. This would involve the committees deciding their priorities for a year ahead and, ideally, linking them to their policy development work. At an early stage in the development of a policy the committees would need to identify the outputs they would expect to see. At the end of a three to four year period the committees would measure the impact of the policy against those targets. There are obvious limitations to such a strategic approach. One is the long lead-time involved before a committee could get to grips with policy outcomes. Another is the greater demands on a committee's time that would be involved.[5] However, this is an approach the committees could usefully experiment with in the second term.

---

[5] Minutes of the Panel of Subject Committee Chairs, *The Role of the Subject Committees*, 10 February 2001.

IMPACT OF THE COALITION

Coalition government has had a significant impact on the operation of the National Assembly subject committees. In important respects the Assembly has come to resemble the Westminster model. It now has a number of features associated with a parliamentary system:

- A governing coalition: Labour-Liberal Democrat since October 2000.

- A recognisable opposition, led by Plaid Cymru.

- An executive branch in the form of the Welsh Assembly Government.

- A legislature in the form of the Assembly Members and the Presiding Office.

However, the Assembly does not have the checks and balances of Westminster. Power of legislative initiative lies exclusively with Ministers and the executive. With the advent of the coalition many Assembly Members began to argue that the scrutiny function of the subject committees should be improved, though this has not been a uniform view. Members of the Economic Development Committee have tended to favour a greater scrutiny role since the coalition, while members of the Health and Social Services Committee have continued to emphasise a consensual approach. Other committees have continued to attempt to balance the policy development and scrutiny functions. The Agriculture and Rural Development Committee, for example, has decided to split its meetings into two halves, with the Minister being subject to scrutiny in the first half, whilst acting like an ordinary member of the Committee in the second half.

These changes have not had the effect of reducing Ministers' attendance at the subject committees, mainly because, as discussed above, there would otherwise not be enough backbenchers to fill the committees. It also remains the case that Ministers' attendance gives the committees greater access to the civil service, and certainly more than in the House of Commons.

Apart from the changing role of Ministers, there are also indications that committee members themselves have been less consensual since the coalition. As the Assembly Government now has a majority on every subject committee and in plenary, there is no need to build a consensus in the committees. This has led to a breakdown in the cross-party consensual approach previously adopted, though some committees have continued this tradition to a greater extent than others.

The trend towards confrontation is as apparent in committee scrutiny as it is in committee policy reviews. The first two policy reviews of the Post-16 Committee prior to the coalition, on the Education and Training Action Plan and Culture in Common, were characterised by the cross-party consensus that emerged. On the other hand, the two inquiries that followed the coalition, into Higher Education and the Welsh Language, produced cross-party divisions.

More generally, prior to the coalition, committee decisions were commonly seen as Assembly decisions, partly due to the consensus support that was needed for the Assembly to operate without a majority. Since the coalition this is no longer the case. Instead, there is an increasing distinction between executive decisions, made by the self-styled Welsh Assembly Government, and committee decisions.

SCRUTINY OF SUBORDINATE LEGISLATION

The Assembly Review of Procedure concluded that the subject committees should scrutinise Assembly and Westminster legislation more systematically and on the basis of better advice. It added that any involvement in legislation would need to be at an early stage to be effective. The bulk of subordinate legislation will not be priorities for subject committees, due to their technical or non-controversial nature. However, the Panel of Committee Chairs considered it important that committees should have the opportunity, and sufficient time, to consider whether they would like to examine forthcoming items of subordinate legislation in detail and if necessary to recommend amendments to them. Early notification would allow the committee time to adjust its forward work programme to include secondary legislation and enable Ministers to build consultation into the timetable for managing the legislation.

For this arrangement to work the committees would need access to the Assembly legal advisers or have their own legal advisors, perhaps in the way they currently employ special advisers for one-off policy reviews. The Panel of Committee Chairs also envisaged a more involved role for the subject committees in the development of primary legislation, commenting:

> "The crucial stage for the subject committees to influence primary
> legislation is when Ministers are in negotiation with the UK
> Government or at least at the Green or White Paper stages: the reality is
> that once a Bill has been published there is only limited scope for
> amendments to be made to it during its progress through Westminster. It
> does not mean that committees should not take an interest in Bills
> passing through Westminster, simply that they are more likely to have an
> influence on proposals at an earlier stage in the process."[6]

---

[6] Submission from the panel of Chairs to the Assembly Review of Procedures, February 2001.

Secondary legislation is more of an issue for some committees than others, partly because the Assembly's powers over secondary legislation vary from policy area to policy area. For example, in the field of economic development hardly any secondary legislation exists, whereas health and education have large quantities. During the third and fourth years of the first Assembly term, the Heath and Social Services Committee led the field in examining secondary legislation. However, until recently most has been short notice and highly technical. 'Framework legislation' that allows the Assembly to look at wide areas of policy has been lacking. If the deployment of draft legislation increases then there will be a chance for weightier policy issues to come before the committees. Only if secondary legislation becomes more important will it become a priority for the subject committees.

RESOURCE CONSTRAINTS

Assembly Members have a limited amount of time to give to Subject Committee work. Many are on several committees at once and have to balance competing demands. Whilst it may be argued that membership of several committees can lead to a more cross-cutting approach to policy development, it remains the case that many AMs are simply overloaded. This is not helped by the frequency with which AMs change their membership of different committees. As soon as they get to grips with a particular policy area they may be moved to another committee.

AMs sit on Assembly committees other than the subject committees, have party obligations and constituency days. These obligations have the additional restriction of having to be fulfilled within the discipline of 'family friendly hours'. In addition, AMs have a relatively small budget to employ support staff. As a result of these constraints it is only practical for subject committees to meet once every two weeks for three to four hours. Family friendly hours in particular have limited the ability of subject committees to set-up sub-committees or joint working groups with other committees. Additionally, although they have undergone an expansion, the committee secretariat and library research service for members remain relatively small.

While committee agendas are consistently overloaded, it is not exclusively the fault of the committee chairs. It remains the case that a large proportion of the work undertaken by the committees is obligatory. For example, the Economic Development Committee has scrutiny oversight for a significant number of Assembly Sponsored Public Bodies, many of which have significant budgets, and it has an obligation to scrutinise the annual reports of each one. As a result, much of what is on the committee agenda simply has to be on it. Since the scope for additional committee meetings is severely limited, this prevents a division of the workload over a larger number of committee meetings, as well as limiting the scope for joint committee meetings. Time constraints are a large part of the explanation for overloaded agendas.

The size of a committee budget to employ special advisers and to undertake policy reviews would not appear to be much of an issue. Each year a central pot of money is held by the committee secretariat, from which committees can fund policy reviews and other work. Although it is notionally allocated to individual committees for the purposes of forecasting, in practice it is pooled and used by committees when needed. No committee has ever been told that they cannot undertake a project due to lack of funds, and there has always been enough.

However, it is interesting to note that committee chairs tend not to know what their notional budget is. It is believed to be in the region of £40,000 per committee. Part of the reason why the budget has never been an issue is because committees do not have the time to engage in additional projects or policy reviews and therefore to spend additional money. The ultimate restraint is the size of the Assembly: 60 AMs are simply not enough to have an effective, and comprehensive committee system.

CONCLUSION

The Assembly's subject committees operate within a constitutional framework unique in the UK context. The decision to create a corporate body and place the subject committees at the centre of both decision making and scrutiny was taken against a background of rhetoric that assumed all-party inclusiveness and a 'new politics'. However, the advent of the coalition government altered this scenario significantly.

The first impact was to add policy substance to the Welsh agenda and the development of a Westminster parliamentary model. Alun Michael's short-lived minority administration struggled to produce a policy programme that was tailored to the needs of Wales. Initiatives were constantly watered down by day-to-day wrangling with the other Assembly parties. Furthermore, the civil service struggled to come to terms with the policy making role that was assigned to it. One Assembly Member summed up both these problems aptly. When asked whether the scrutiny and policy development roles of the subject committees had changed after the formation of the coalition government he replied:

"During Alun Michael's time there was no policy and therefore very little to scrutinise. The committees had to come up with the big ideas to fill the vacuum. Policy making was very much to the fore. Now we need to scrutinise the executive far more consistently as well as come up with policy reviews that offer the Welsh public and the Welsh Assembly Government options that feed into the policy debate."[7]

Herein lies the paradox of the shift to a majority coalition government. The subject committees are now even more important due to the increased desire for effective scrutiny and the need for informed debate on the alternative options available to policy makers in Wales. Yet it is debatable whether the subject committees and, indeed, the Assembly as a whole have sufficient resources, both in terms of Members and civil servants, to reap the benefits.

[7] Authors' interview, November 2001.

CHAPTER 7

EDUCATION

David Egan and Roy James

Our groundbreaking education initiatives do indeed prove the effectiveness of devolution.

Jane Davidson, Minister for Education and Lifelong Learning
***Western Mail*, 10 January 2003**

This claim by the Welsh Education Minister could be dismissed as mere self-congratulation. Yet, it follows earlier and more independent praise directed towards the Assembly Government for its work in the field of education. Indeed, for many commentators Wales appears as nothing less than a left wing Utopia for teachers. *The Guardian* and the *Times Educational Supplement* have lauded the Minister and her officials for 'daring to be ever more different'. Jane Davidson's panegyric, also chimes with the contemporaneous claim of First Minister, Rhodri Morgan, that 'clear red water' existed in policies between England and Wales, with the field of education providing one of the best examples.[1]

'Distinctive' and 'innovative' are certainly new descriptions for educational policies in Wales. Just as the new devolution settlement was being launched in Wales, there appeared, from the University of Wales Press, the most authoritative interpretation of education policy making ever produced in Wales.[2] It recorded how educational policies followed in 20th century Wales largely mirrored those of the Westminster Parliament and the Whitehall-centred state. In a few instances, linked to language and culture, it identified policies that were exclusive to Wales. In general, however, whether *differentiated* (as in the existence of separate agencies) or *mediated* (for example, through the less regulatory approach which had been adopted for school inspection and improvement), the lack of policy difference had created a system which was firmly 'England and Wales'. Whilst this interpretation would not be totally acceptable to those who have operated at a high level within the pre-devolution policy process, it nevertheless provides a stark contrast to the almost triumphalist tone of Jane Davidson and the education

---

[1] See his 'Clear Red Water' speech to the National Institute for Public Policy Research, University of Wales, Swansea, December 2002.

[2] R. Daugherty, R. Phillips and G. Rees, *Education Policy Making in Wales*, University of Wales Press, 2000.

media today.

Against this background, this chapter assesses the claims made for educational progress during the Assembly's first term. It reaches two broad conclusions:

- The first is that much has, indeed, changed in the education policy making process, leading to considerable achievements.

- Secondly, however, and deriving from the inevitable lack of evidence of successful implementation of these policies, given their recent origins, caution needs to be exercised in claiming that significant improvements have yet been produced.

Moreover, we suggest that whilst there has been a significant and impressive commitment to shaping educational policies suited to the needs of Wales, these are often 'borrowed' from elsewhere, with their innovation lying simply in their application to Wales. Finally, we argue that, whilst many facets of educational provision in Wales are in a process of change and flux, this does not yet constitute the emergence of a distinct or separate educational system. In the quotation at the head of this chapter, Jane Davidson supports her claim by pointing to policy initiatives in the following areas:

- A new Foundation curriculum for early years
- Special Educational Needs
- Disaffection, absenteeism and poor behaviour
- The Curriculum
- The Welsh Baccalaureate
- Information and Communications Technology
- Modern Foreign Languages
- Key Stage 3
- Capital investment
- Reducing the bureaucratic burden
- Partnership working

There has undoubtedly been considerable policy activity in each of these areas. In some instances, however, it might be contended that activity remains ahead of achievement. For example, there is the oft-repeated barb that the papers sent out by the Assembly on the reduction of bureaucratic burdens, constitutes one of the biggest files in a headteacher's office. A more rigorous evaluation of what has been achieved can be gauged from an exploration of four of the examples, each illustrating slightly different policy processes at work: Early Years, Information and Communications Technology, the

Curriculum, and Partnership Working.

EARLY YEARS

The development of an Early Years policy was one of the first tasks taken on by the Pre-16 Education Subject Committee. This priority was supported by research showing that involving children in schooling as early as possible produces the greatest gains in lifelong learning and educational achievement. The social inclusion aspects of this policy resonated strongly with one of the Assembly's cross cutting themes and the work of other Subject Committees.

The extensive written and oral evidence submitted to the Committee revealed a surface topography of education provision and opinion that had previously been largely submerged. The scale of the response prompted the Committee to appoint the Assembly's first expert adviser, Margaret Hanney, a Lecturer in Education at the University of Wales Institute, Cardiff. Her role was to assist the Committee in analysing the evidence, placing it in the context of global best practice, and preparing its report. A major lesson was drawn from this experience. Committees subsequently embarking on such large policy inquiries generally appointed expert advisers from the outset.

The Committee's report was presented in December 2000 when the Administration accepted its major recommendations in full. The 2001 strategic policy document *The Learning Country*, and the Assembly Government's budgetary commitments took the recommendations forward. There was a commitment to provide early years education for all three year old pupils. This was to be achieved through partnership working between educational and childcare providers at local authority level. In addition an Early Years Advisory Panel was set up to advise the Minister on the strategic development and implementation of the policy.

The Learning Country committed the Assembly Government to ending the National Curriculum's Key Stage 1 for five to seven year olds in Wales. In its place a new Foundation Stage for 3-7 year olds would be introduced to 'join-up' Early Years provision with the existing system of schooling. The nature of the Foundation Stage and the curriculum it will follow is currently in the process of development. It is likely that it will be built on the structured experiential approach to learning set out in the guidance produced by the Curriculum and Assessment Authority in Wales, known as 'Desirable Outcomes'. This will take the place of the current subject-based National Curriculum. Whilst a full analysis must await the finalisation of this process, it appears that a radically different educational philosophy is emerging in Wales for three to seven year olds from that which is current elsewhere in the

United Kingdom. Instead, Wales appears to be moving closer to countries such as Scandinavia and Italy where formal education is delayed, although schooling starts as early as possible.

This initiative represents a notable turning away from the previous 'England and Wales' model for Early Years provision. It is also underpinned by a new educational philosophy. In this area devolution has enabled Wales to look at and borrow from best practice on a wider European basis. Two other things are also apparent. Firstly, the initiative has been strongly influenced by the experience and beliefs of practitioners and experts in the field. As a result the policy development, has been undeniably inclusive and participative in its genesis. Secondly, though its ultimate value and success must await future evaluation, it is likely, over time, to have a profound affect on the rest of the education system in Wales.

INFORMATION AND COMMUNICATIONS TECHNOLOGY

The development of Information and Communications Technology policy had also been led by the Pre-16 Subject Committee, moving on from its Early Years work. In this case an initial study of local education authority co-operation in the procurement of Information and Communications Technology, led to a much wider study of its impact on schools education more generally.

Again the committee collected a wide range of evidence and found it necessary to appoint an expert adviser. In the process it brought together the experience of local education authorities and national agencies to an unprecedented degree. It was noteworthy that two AMs from opposite sides of the political spectrum, Labour's Huw Lewis and the Conservative Jonathan Morgan, took a leading role in the work. Their activity included visits to Scotland and a conference to test out preliminary findings.

The final report, presented to the Assembly in March 2001, proposed a three-year development programme to advance Information and Communications Technology education and a National Grid for Learning designed to provide bilingual curriculum support. Though enthusiastically received, progress with these initiatives was frustratingly slow, partly due to procurement regulations and the need to create appropriate infrastructures. However, the policy is now fully developed and budgetary support has been approved. In particular, at school level the provision of interactive whiteboards has been warmly welcomed.

Though the impact of the policy can only be evaluated in the longer-term, there is no doubt that schools have been transformed in their capacity to utilise Information and Communications Technology over the past five years. Pupils are becoming much more confident in and familiar with the way technology is capable of assisting their learning. Nationally-funded training opportunities for teachers have also been successful.[3]

Again, what marked out this exercise was the way in which partnership and co-operation, channelled by the Subject Committee, created the possibility of a joined-up policy suited to the interests of Wales. In the past such co-operation was non-existent. There was nothing startlingly new or innovative about the policy that resulted. What was achieved was an eminently sensible assembling and adapting good practice seen to be effective elsewhere. In the view of one commentator with experience of the British Educational and Communication Agency, the results represented 'a discourse, policies and practices ahead of those prevalent in England'. For this to be achieved so quickly, was indeed an achievement of which the Assembly could be proud.

CURRICULUM

The third area highlighted by Jane Davidson and considered here, is the curriculum. In addition to the two policy fields considered above, work has been undertaken in a number of other major areas affecting the school curriculum. These include:

- A survey of the national curriculum and assessment arrangements, currently being undertaken by the Curriculum and Assessment Authority in Wales.

- Work designed to identify excellent practice in the Key Stage 3 curriculum, led by the Schools Inspectorate, Estyn, and the Curriculum and Assessment Authority in Wales.

- A study on how gaps in pupil attainment between schools might be narrowed, led by the Assembly's Education and Training Department and the Welsh Local Government Association.

- Work on developing a new range of learning pathways for 14 to 19 year-olds, a development led by a secondary headteacher whose secondment was funded by the Assembly Government.

These initiatives are generally at a development or consultation stage, which

---

[3] One indication was that a history teacher from a south Wales comprehensive school, where Information and Communications Technology was strongly exploited in the curriculum, won the Lloyds/TSB Teaching Awards category for the best secondary teacher in the UK in 2002.

makes a definitive analysis of their impact premature. Nonetheless, they are likely to prove influential. For example, the proposals set out in the 14-19 Learning Pathways consultation document suggested that traditional 'academic' examination routes for pupils through Key Stage 4 (GCSE) and Key Stage 5 (A and AS levels), be joined by vocational and hybrid pathways. There would be much stronger work-related experience for all pupils, a community based approach to offering out of school learning and the availability of educational counselling and mentoring support. If these proposals are accepted it would mark a fundamental change to the existing curriculum for 14-19 year olds in Wales. In combination with the introduction of the Foundation Stage and the possible changes that might now take place in Key Stages 2 and 3, this promises to see in Wales the demise of the National Curriculum framework created by the Education Act of 1988. The possibility of distinctiveness in the curriculum in Wales is provided by the 2002 Education Act.

How innovatory these proposals are should be considered in context. In many ways, they reflect curriculum and assessment policies that have long been established in many European countries and in other parts of the world. In January 2003 it was announced that a task group with a similar policy brief was to be created in England, suggesting that similar curriculum reforms are likely there. In fact, there may well have been a prior cross-territorial agreement to pursue this area of policy development between the Westminster, Cardiff and possibly the other devolved governments. Policy development may be piloted in Wales and then picked up in England, reversing the trend of pre-Assembly times.

PARTNERSHIP WORKING

In the three examples considered above, consultations took place with a wide range of opinion, experience and expertise in the fields being investigated. This contrasts very strongly with the situation that applied before devolution. Whilst the Welsh Office consulted on its policy initiatives as a matter of course, it was never evident what the outcomes were. Whatever might have happened behind the scenes, it was not the practice to overtly involve stakeholders, interest groups and national agencies in the development of policy. This was regarded as the prerogative of the civil service.

In contrast, policy work is now carried out in partnership, sometimes led by officials themselves, but more usually by the Subject Committee, involving a group created by the Assembly Government and one of the national education agencies. Two examples illustrate the process at work and how impressive it can be. In the case of the Early Years policy review, more than 60 organisations and individuals provided evidence and at all stages there was a full consultative process with all interest groups. The Learning Pathways proposals were developed by a project team made up of representatives of schools, local education authorities, higher education, voluntary organisations such as the Royal National Institute for the Blind, business, careers organisations, ELWa, further education, and the teacher associations. There was also a Reference Group that allowed the views of the General Teaching Council for Wales, Princes Trust Cymru, Directors of Education, Estyn and the Welsh Local Government Association to be added to the organisations and interest groups represented on the project team. Additional inputs came from training organisations, the Wales Youth Agency, the Curriculum and Assessment Authority in Wales, the Council for Wales of Voluntary Youth Services, Atlantic College, and pupils from ten comprehensive schools. The proposals were widely circulated to all secondary schools and other stakeholder organisations and a number of consultation events were held. It is difficult to conceive how such partnership and participation could be improved upon.

CREATION OF ELWa

What is perhaps just as interesting in Jane Davidson's article, quoted at the outset, is the things she does not include. The work of the Post-16 Education and Training Committee, in carrying out its first policy review of the Education and Training Action Group report inherited from the Welsh Office, is a case in point. Although it faced initial resistance from the Administration, the Committee insisted on re-opening the policy investigation, led by its impressive and effective chair, Cynog Dafis AM. In the process it achieved far greater transparency and refined the recommendations to a significant extent.

The result was the creation of the National Council for Education and Training in Wales. Combined with the Higher Education Funding Council, this also saw the creation of an umbrella body, ELWa, responsible for both further and higher education. With a budget of £811 million (2002-03) this has become by far the largest Assembly Sponsored Public Body (or Quango). At the local level, Community Consortia for Education and Training (CCETs) were to be created as the main planners of post-16 education outside the Higher Education sector. At the same time funding for school-based 16-19 provision would continue to be channelled through the local education authorities. For the first time a national careers and guidance service, Careers Wales, was set up. In addition, the need for a credit-based qualifications framework, Welsh-medium provision and the possibility of a Welsh Baccalaureate, were also accepted. Whilst there have been difficulties faced in the operation procedures of ELWa[4] , there is no doubt that lifelong learning and the status of post-16 education outside the universities has been significantly heightened as a result.

Again this appears to have been a piece of policy development where Wales led the way for England, possibly by agreed intent at British Cabinet level prior to devolution. In any event, the Learning and Skills Council in England soon followed the National Council in Wales. Arguably, the Post-16 Committee's changes to the Education and Training Action Group's proposals resulted in the most fully developed structural and philosophical change achieved in education during the first term of the Assembly.

REVIEW OF HIGHER EDUCATION

The review of Higher Education in Wales begun by the Post-16 Committee and taken forward by the single Education and Lifelong Learning Committee from October 2000, is also an area not mentioned by the Minister. Yet the scale of the review, the amount of Committee and Assembly time it took up, together with the political infighting it provoked, were unprecedented. Sessions were held *in camera* and draft reports were leaked prompting censure motions in the Committee. All testified to the sensitivities involved in interfering with Higher Education.

The 13 Welsh Higher Education institutions had already been made to feel insecure by a pre-Assembly paper by the Higher Education Funding Council for Wales suggesting that their number might be reduced to five or six. Using all his adroit skills Cynog Dafis, in his final act before stepping down as chair of the Subject Committee, steered through recommendations that looked to collaboration between the institutions as the key to creating a sector strong enough to face the challenges of wider participation and the need to create a world-class research base.

Dafis knew the politics of Wales well enough not to be surprised by the sophisticated in-fighting that ensued. In the process, the Higher Education institutions could be accused of being the least signed up to the 'new Wales' of partnership, inclusion and sustainability. Although the Assembly Government has set in train a process of reorganisation, this has hardly been an example of successful policy development. The wisdom of intervening in

---

[4] See Hugh Rawlings (a senior Asssembly Government civil servant), ELWa: a Review of Senior Structure, September 2002, reported in John Osmond(Ed.), *Dragon Takes a Different Route: Monitoring the National Assembly September to December 2002.* IWA, December 2002.

such a contentious and charged area by means of a Subject Committee policy review is to be wondered at. As the Assembly's first term drew to a close the Higher Education sector appeared citadel-like, resisting the forces of change that have impinged on all the other education sectors in Wales.

STUDENT FINANCE

The work of the Independent Investigation Group on Student Hardship and Funding provides another example of a 'task and finish' approach to the policy development process. It is one that has captured a great deal of attention across the British Isles, in a feverish debate that has been taking place on Higher Education funding and student finance. Chaired by Professor Teresa Rees of Cardiff University, the Group was set up by the Minister in December 2000. In part it was a consequence of the Partnership Agreement between the Liberal Democrat and Labour parties which underpinned Coalition Administration in October 2000. Its formation can also be seen as the result of strong and growing public opinion, such that student funding might become a significant factor in future Assembly elections. The most important recommendations of the report, presented to the Minister in June 2001, included:

- Expansion of the budget available for student hardships.
- Replacement of a variety of grants with two new ones.
- Introduction of means-tested Learning Grants for students normally resident in Wales.
- Creation of a Financial Contingency Fund for cases of hardship.

An interesting feature of the report was the way in which it delineated those areas of policy which were within the power of the Assembly, those which only the UK Government could act upon and, finally, areas where the Assembly might persuade others to act, either singly or in partnership with the Assembly. Here, again, was an example of bold policy making. It was responsive to public opinion, innovative (alongside comparable development in Scotland), and strongly participative and inclusive in nature.

As this chapter was being written 'top-up' higher education tuition fees were being proposed by the UK Education Secretary in his January 2003 White Paper. These were strongly resisted by the Higher Education sector in Wales, and by the Assembly Minister who called for additional powers to allow the Assembly to abolish tuition fees.

WELSH MEDIUM EDUCATION

The Assembly Government's policy 'Iaith Pawb ('Everybody's language'), which seeks to create "a truly bilingual Wales", was presented to the Assembly at the end of November 2002. Described by Culture Minister Jenny Randerson as the "most radical comprehensive and far-reaching policy ever produced for the Welsh language" the aim is to increase the number of Welsh speakers by 5 per cent by 2011 – from around 20 per cent to 25 per cent.[5]

The action plan builds on the blueprint *Bilingual Future* published by the Assembly Government in the summer of 2002 in response to the Education and Culture Committees' review into the Welsh language.[6] It is based around three main strands, the national level, the community and the individual, and is supported by an extra £26.8 million funding. The third strand, empowering individuals to speak Welsh, is supported by £9.5 million funding. The greater part of it will go towards increasing the availability of early years provision through the medium of Welsh and increasing the number of staff available to teach in Welsh.

In the main, this work was characterised by consensus. With the assistance of its Special Advisor, the Education and Culture Committees again demonstrated enthusiasm for looking at best practice across the world, taking evidence from experts from Catalonia and Canada. As the difficulties apparent in English-medium secondary schools in Wales in persuading pupils, parents and teachers of the worth of studying Welsh at non-examination level in Key Stage 4, make clear, far from everything in the garden is rosy in this area of education. However, the work of the Committees on behalf of the Assembly created a clear, positive and inclusive agenda for the future development of the Welsh language.

THE LEARNING COUNTRY

The Learning Country, a ten-year strategy published by Jane Davidson in September 2001, is regarded by many commentators as one of the most significant and exciting policy statements ever produced on education in Wales. Its immediate origins were conversations between civil servants in Cardiff and Whitehall in the summer of 2001, to identify those areas where

---

[5] These percentages were estimates, pending publication of the 2001 census in the early part of 2003.

[6] For an account see the quarterly report, *A Bilingual Future: Monitoring the National Assembly: May to August 2002*, IWA, August 2002.

Wales might 'opt out' of a Green Paper being prepared for England. It was also a repository of much thinking that had taken place in the pre-devolution Welsh Office. To some extent, however, it also appears to draw greater inspiration from Scottish, Irish, and wider European models and cultures than the established 'England and Wales' continuum. In the process it established six major principles which appear likely to guide Welsh education policy for the foreseeable future:

- Commitment to state education, publicly funded and provided through local education authorities, in stark contrast to policy promoted by 'New Labour' for England;
- Distancing from the 'third way' approach to public service provision.
- Affirmation of the comprehensive principle in education.
- An end to the publication of examination and assessment results.
- An end to statutory national tests for 7-year olds.
- Rejection of specialist schools.

AN ASSESSMENT

The analysis presented here has been generally supportive of claims made for a progressive educational policy during the first term of the National Assembly. At the same time, it will need longer term and robust, longitudinal evaluation and research before the efficacy of the changes can be fully assessed. This is particularly so in respect of the impact they have upon learners and on the teaching professions.

It is a common criticism of policy interventions in the educational, as in other public policy fields, that they are not piloted, or given sufficient implementation time, to allow them to be properly judged. This was captured in the USA by President Clinton's plea for politics to 'stop at the schoolroom door' and for policy and policy-making to be less fickle and transitory. Whilst the present Assembly Government may have an impressive record in policy continuity and participation, it remains to be seen how far successors, whatever their political hue, feel obliged to accept a policy continuum.

This is as true of the policy making process, as it is in relation to the policies themselves. Academic observers have always pointed to the complexity of these processes and the way in which they challenge the 'assumptive worlds' of politicians, and civil servants. Professor Gareth Rees, in his consideration of the effects of devolution on post-16 education and training, maintained that:

> *"... policy outcomes continue to reflect highly complex processes of negotiation and brokering between, for example, political parties, professional bodies, interest groups, civil servants and so forth. Whilst the new constitutional arrangements have opened up new mechanisms ... they have not removed the indeterminacy of the outcomes which emerge."*[7]

It is clear that in some areas success in developing policy is more intractable and hard-won, than in others. The extent to which the Assembly is capable of effecting major changes to the teaching profession, is one of these. The desirability of change is widely accepted in Wales, as it is in England. Undertaking it in a way that reflects the different history and present relationships that exist between the profession, its representative bodies and government in Wales, is also a strongly held ambition. The existence of the General Teaching Council for Wales as a separate entity, has made possible, for example, a different approach to teacher professional development from England.

On a number of occasions, however, there has been dissonance. A 'cause célèbre' during the first term was the issue whether the Assembly had powers in relation to the pay and conditions of schoolteachers, in particular over 'performance related pay'. Following a protracted wrangle it became clear that the Assembly did not, in fact, enjoy the power to implement the newly introduced 'threshold' policy in a different way.

More recently the Assembly has taken a different approach in relation to the position of enhancing the role of teaching assistants and in reducing teachers' workloads. It is clear that the Assembly does not intend to follow the policy agreed with the teacher associations, other than the NUT, in England. What is not so apparent is what they intend to do positively to create a distinct policy in Wales. Establishing a separate teaching profession would be a high risk policy, largely because, as Cynog Dafis has pointed out, in this respect Offa's Dyke represents "a long and highly permeable border."

The same applies to school funding. This has been a source of irritation between the Assembly and the representatives of headteacher associations that continued throughout the first term. The Minister has forthrightly defended her view that schools in Wales receive at least the same levels of funding as their counterparts in England. On the other hand, the schools

---

[7] Gareth Rees, 'Devolution and the Restructuring of Post-16 Education and Training in the UK', in John Adams and Peter Robinson (Eds.), *Devolution in Practice: Public Policy Differences Within the UK*, Economic and Social Research Council and Institute of Public Policy Research, 2002.

remain steadfast in their view that they are denied both regular and initiative funding opportunities of the kind that benefit schools in England. Of course, this links to the support given by the Assembly Government to its partnership with local authorities with whom it wishes to participate closely in the governance of Welsh education. This is in contrast with the weakened position of local education authorities in England. Set against this, of course, is the antipathy which many Welsh secondary headteachers feel towards local government, and especially the channelling of their funding through its treasuries. In itself this must qualify any positive analysis of partnership working in the field.

One final example of the more difficult terrain on which policy has to operate should suffice. This is the area of school performance. It is well recognised that, under both Labour and Conservative administrations, the former Welsh Office mediated a distinctive line in policy areas such as school inspection, the publication of performance tables, grant maintained status for schools, and parental choice. In England these policies were part of a market-driven approach, designed to apply pressure to schools to improve standards. In Wales the same policies were either eschewed or ameliorated to make them more amenable to the prevailing culture of Welsh education.

Under the Assembly this dichotomy has continued apace, although it might be argued that the practical effect is as much cosmetic as real. The examples of performance tables and school inspection can be taken to illustrate these trends. In the 1990s the Welsh Office compiled and published growing amounts of information on school performance. Yet, these were not presented as league tables where schools and local education authorities could be compared one with another. They could, however, easily be presented in this way and this is what the press and media, as well as those within the educational system itself, were able to do. The Assembly has recently decided to cease publishing the information, making it extremely difficult, therefore, for the press to publish league tables.

At the same time this does not mean that the information does not exist and cannot be used to measure school performance and apply pressure to the system. In the case of the inspection systems of the two countries, it is possible that significant differences in philosophy and approach have now been mainly eradicated. Following the departure of Chris Woodhead as Chief Inspector in England, the public profile of OFSTED has, with almost certain intent, been lowered. There is now a discernible attempt to work closely with schools and other educational partners to move the system forward by much greater use of self-evaluation as the basis for external inspection. The same impulses are clear within Estyn in Wales, but they are no more strikingly apparent than those in England. It is almost inevitable, perhaps, that the present devolution settlement will constrain the Assembly in how far it can make different policies in these areas. This is partly to do with the determination of Westminster and Whitehall to retain some territorial parity in these sensitive areas. There is also, of course, the political reality that no party can be seen to be 'weak' on matters such as parental choice and the attainment of pupils.

A final qualification should be made to the Assembly Government's claims made for the distinctiveness and radicalism of its policies. This is the political realities of the continuing UK system of government which make it difficult for radically different philosophical approaches to co-exist. In turn this makes separate policy making difficult and, in some circumstances may even preclude it. It should come as no surprise, therefore, that many key Welsh policy initiatives have approximated to the New Labour agenda pursued in England. An outstanding example is the shared belief that we need to improve our economic performance through creating a knowledge-based economy. To achieve that we must improve training and the esteem of vocational education. This was the driver of the Education and Training Action Plan and, more recently, the *Learning Pathways* consultation document, as much as equivalent initiatives in England.

CONCLUSIONS

None of this should detract from the extent to which the Assembly Government has produced radical policy positions in areas such as Early Years and Information and Communications Technology. However, the challenge is now for the Assembly Government to become proactive. As Professor David Reynolds has pointed out, the need is for it to move from a position where it decides *what not to do* in relation to New Labour paradigms, to one where it moves to *what to do*, based upon distinctive policies.[8] He points to four areas where new thinking is pressing:

- The first is the matter of who, or what, will drive future educational change. If that is not to be market pressure or performance data and instead to be the teaching profession, how can such a change be motivated and resourced?

- Second, how will we inform change and ensure standards are raised? What is the role of educational research in this process?

- Thirdly it will become necessary to replace the OFSTED/ESTYN type

---

[8] David Reynolds, 'Education in England, Wales, Scotland and Northern Ireland'. in John Adams and Peter Robinson (Eds.), *Devolution in Practice: Public Policy Differences Within the UK*, Economic and Social Research Council and Institute of Public Policy Research, 2002.

inspection system, with some form of 'school based review'. But how might this be achieved?

- Fourth, the relationship between the central state and other stakeholders within the education system needs to be redrawn. In the context of Wales this implies that the relationship between the Assembly and 22 local education authorities needs to be reviewed.

In the book that they produced on the eve of the Assembly's birth, Daugherty, Phillips and Rees indulged in some crystal-ball gazing on the changes that might result from devolution.[9] They wondered about the political culture that would emerge, influenced perhaps by the presence of so many women AMs and the determination to be transparent and inclusive. They also speculated that education policy would to a large extent, continue to be subservient to the needs of economic and social policy, as it had been under successive political régimes at the Welsh Office. They asked whether the existence of a different set of cultural and value positions would continue to be influential. Finally, they pondered the extent to which the profession would itself be made central to the policy debate, both as focus of it and as participants. The analysis offered in this chapter is likely to do much to assuage them. The National Assembly for Wales, the Welsh Assembly Government, its Ministers, the various Education Subject Committees and the civil servants have much of which they should feel proud.

Tensions that exist in the current constitutional settlement will, however, need to be resolved for truly radical and distinctive policies to be forged. Put simply, the Assembly will need to have the necessary political will and power. As the Education Minister Jane Davidson put it, in the introduction to *The Learning Country*:

> *"We share strategic goals with our colleagues in England. But we often need to take a different route to achieve them."*

---

[9] R. Daugherty, R. Phillips and G. Rees, *op.cit.*

CHAPTER 8

HEALTH POLICY

Rhiannon Tudor Edwards

Taking over responsibility for health policy was arguably the greatest challenge facing the National Assembly. In 1999-2000 health care accounted for £2.7 billion, or 34 per cent of the Assembly's budget, greater than any other policy area.[1] As an employer of some 65,000 staff across Wales, the NHS represents an important contributor to the state of the Welsh economy.

THE HEALTH CARE INHERITANCE

The National Assembly inherited an NHS which, in real terms, had experienced a fall in spending as a proportion of GDP. In Wales, total NHS expenditure fell from 8.3 per cent to 8.0 per cent in these terms in the three years 1996-7 to 1998-9. This compared with a fall in England from 5.7 per cent to 5.5 per cent in the same period. Likewise, spending on capital investment in the NHS in Wales fell from £111m in 1996-7 to £104m in 1999-2000 and £73m in 2000-1.[2]

The Welsh NHS was long used to the tension between the need for localised comprehensive services and pressure for centres of excellence, for example, in cancer care. The National Assembly inherited a service faced with difficulties in recruiting consultants in specialised clinical areas and in enticing GPs to work in remote, socioeconomically deprived areas such as the south Wales Valleys.

It also inherited a spending deficit by Welsh Health Authorities and Trusts of £72 million in 1998-1999.[3] The previous Conservative government's introduction of the NHS internal market into Wales had further left a legacy of competition and lack of transparency between hospitals across Wales. It can be argued that this was part of the democratic deficit which devolution was aimed to address. In his review of the NHS in Wales, Sir Graham Hart,

---

[1] John Osmond, *Monitoring Devolution and Health: Baseline Report*, IWA, 1999.

[2] *NHS Resource Allocation Review Targeting Poor Health:* Professor Townsend's Report of the Welsh Assembly's National Steering Group, 2001.

[3] Cabinet Strategic Policy Unit, *Stocktake of NHS Wales*, Assembly Government, 1999.

former Permanent Secretary at the Department of Health in Whitehall, described the distant nature of administration from Westminster under the prior Conservative government and John Redwood. He also observed the lack of Welsh Office personnel working in health policy who had prior experience of the NHS.[4] Notable was the abolition in 1995 of the Welsh Health Planning Forum which had been established in 1988, and the slimming down of the health policy function of the Welsh Office at this time. Sir Graham noted the lack of interaction between government departments on health issues, arguing the need for what has since become termed 'joined-up working' not only at a local government level, but also within the Welsh Office, later to become the National Assembly.

In 1999, spending per head in Wales was 13 per cent above that in England (see Table 1). Hospital admissions, including accident and emergency and prescribing costs, are relatively higher in Wales than in England. The reasons for this are not straightforward. Undoubtedly, however, they derive from a combination of factors, including:

- The relatively poor health of the people of Wales, rooted in inequalities in socio-economic deprivation.

- The need for large urban hospitals as well as smaller hospitals to serve sparse rural populations.

- The relatively higher proportion of elderly people living in Wales.

- Possible inefficiencies in service provision.

TABLE 1: TOTAL MANAGED EXPENDITURE ON HEALTH AND PERSONAL SOCIAL SERVICES, 1998-9

Country	£ (million)	£ (per head)	% of total UK Health and Personal Social Services expenditure
United Kingdom	58,935	995	100
England	47,677	963	81
Wales	3,274	1,116	6
Scotland	6,130	1,197	10
Northern Ireland	1,854	1,098	3

Source: Public Expenditure Statistical Analyses 2000-1,
HM Treasure 2000, cited in: Office for National Statistics, 2001.

---

[4] Sir Graham Hart, *The Health Responsibilities of the National Assembly for Wales*. Unpublished, but circulated from 1998. For a partial account see John Osmond, *Adrift But Afloat: The Civil Service and the National Assembly*, IWA, 1999

Table 1 shows total managed expenditure on Health and Personal Social Services for countries of the UK. In 1998/9, the latest date for which comparative figures are available, spending per capita was highest in Scotland, followed by Wales and Northern Ireland. Of all the regions, spending per capita was lowest for England.

AN AMBITIOUS HEALTH PROGRAMME

The Assembly Government has pursued an ambitious and wide-ranging programme of policies spanning the structure and administration of the NHS, clinical standards and health targets. It has also reached outside the NHS to begin to recognise and tackle the underlying root socio-economic causes of inequalities in health. However, much of this programme was already in train, based on preceding Welsh Office NHS policies since the mid-1990s. It may be argued that the long-term direction of health policy in Wales was set out under John Wyn Owen's leadership of the NHS in Wales in the Strategic Intent and Direction Programme. Unlike the Conservative administration's unwillingness to address inequalities in health, New Labour's commitment was clearly set out in *Better Health - Better Wales,*[5] and later taken up by the Assembly as the fulcrum of its *NHS Plan for Wales.*[6]

The NHS Plan for Wales 2001 promised a 7.7 per cent increase in health funding for 2001-2, with further increases of 7.6 per cent and 7.9 per cent for subsequent years, this took NHS spending from £2.6 billion to £3.6 billion in 2003-4, an increase of 37.4% over the four years. The Plan indicated that Wales would follow Tony Blair's commitment to increase health spending as a percentage of GDP to European levels. In April 2001, a further boost of £20 million was announced by Jane Hutt for the NHS in Wales.

While welcoming additional promises of resources for the NHS, health service managers and directors of finance have warned that they may not be able to meet the Assembly Government's ambitious policy objectives and may only be able to operate the NHS at its present levels of services. The following excerpt from a Western Mail report from February 2002 illustrates this point.

> *"A damning report into NHS funding warns that the National*
> *Assembly's efforts to improve the service next year are doomed to failure.*
> *Health officials have leaked a report being circulated among NHS Trusts*
> *in Wales that claims the promised 9.7 per cent increase in funding next*
> *year is not even enough to keep the service running at a standstill let*

---

[5] Welsh Office, 1998.

[6] *Improving Health in Wales: A Plan for the NHS with its partners*, Assembly Government, 2001.

*alone bring in a raft of promises made by the National Assembly. It
warns that expected improvements in waiting list times, A+E and cancer
services cannot be delivered without an even bigger cash injection. Under
the title National Targets and Priorities 2002-3, the report paints a
sometimes alarming picture of the NHS in Wales, particularly in terms
of manpower. It also worries about the degree of upheaval taking place
over the next three years as Health Minister Jane Hutt pushes through
her reforms."[7]*

It is interesting to note that Finance Minister Edwina Hart found it necessary
to follow England's example to the letter by committing Wales's share of a
windfall of almost £50 million announced by the UK Government in
February 2002 to an expansion of spending on health services. This money
was not ring-fenced and arguably could have been spent by other
departments, either to boost the economy directly or to improve health
through housing, transport or environmental initiatives.

STRUCTURAL CHANGE

In February 2001, Health Minister Jane Hutt announced the abolition of the five
Health Authorities and their replacement by 22 Local Health Boards,
coterminous with local authorities, to take place by April 2003. This radical
restructuring constituted an abandonment of the October 2000 Coalition
Partnership Agreement which called for a period of stability in the NHS to allow
health care professionals to pursue their priorities for improving patient care.

Jane Hutt sought special dispensation from Kirsty Williams, the Liberal
Democrat Health Spokesperson and Chair of the Health and Social Services
Committee, to pursue the structural change. Consent was given, but arguably
not in anticipation of the radical changes eventually put forward by Jane
Hutt. Her insistence on pushing through structural change strained relations
between Labour and the Liberal Democrats in the Coalition. The episode
revealed how consultation, although widespread since devolution, failed in
probably the most significant policy initiative of the first term, certainly in the
health field. Indeed, given the coalition's near split, it is ironic that Rhodri
Morgan's preface to the plan describing the structural change declared:

> *"...this Plan is a product of the Partnership Government ... and draws
> regularly and directly on the Partnership Agreement."[8]*

Following consultation, the Liberal Democrats sided with Plaid Cymru and

---

[7] *Western Mail*, 8 February 2002.

[8] *Improving Health in Wales: A Plan for the NHS with its partners.* Assembly Government, 2001.

the Conservatives on the Health Committee, forcing the Health Minister to concede a plenary statement and full debate on her proposals. In their formal submission, the Liberal Democrats outlined their concerns about the proposed restructuring of the NHS as follows:

- The changes imposed major disruption to a health service struggling with rising waiting lists at a time when stability was necessary.

- The number of 'Quangos' would increase from 20 to 37 (five Health Authorities and 15 Trusts to 22 Local Health Boards and 15 Trusts).

- The Minister insisted that there would be no additional cost to the health service despite no cost analysis having been performed.

- More power would accrue to the centre, in particular to the National Assembly's NHS Directorate.

- With respect to the openness and transparency of health policy-making, concerns were raised that while in the past the public had been able to attend open Health Authority meetings, in future there may be a loss of public involvement. This reflects the role of the NHS Directorate as a non-publicly accountable body and arbiter in disputes over service level agreements.[9]

Notably, a number of Welsh Labour MPs spoke in Westminster against the changes, focusing in particular on the number of administrative bodies that would be responsible for running the NHS. These would be 52 in total, comprising 22 Local Health Boards, 15 Hospital Trusts, 12 Health Partnerships, and three regional offices of the Assembly's NHS Directorate. This was described by Jon Owen Jones, Labour MP for Cardiff Central, as "the most bureaucratic health service in western Europe".[10]

During the consultation period, serious criticisms were voiced by NHS managers and clinicians. The NHS Confederation in Wales found that:

- 69 per cent of managers believed that the 22 new Local Health Boards would be difficult to sustain.

- 87 per cent thought that accountability would be less clear.

- 81 per cent thought that the NHS would find it difficult to manage or understand the structure put before it.[11]

A number of senior clinicians have voiced concerns that the Health Minister has

---

[9] *Welsh Liberal Democrat Assembly Group's Response to 'Improving Health in Wales – Structural Change in the NHS in Wales: A Consultation Document'.* Available online at: http://www.cix.co.uk

[10] See John Osmond (Ed.) *Coalition Creaks Over Health: Monitoring the National Assembly September to December 2001*, IWA, 2001, for a full account of this episode.

[11] *Ibid.*

a misplaced preoccupation with restructuring the NHS rather than acknowledging and tackling what they view as a manpower crisis. That is to say, a lack of sufficient consultants, GPs, nurses and professions allied to medicine necessary to meet the ambitious waiting list targets set by the Assembly. In her plenary debate, Jane Hutt stood steadfast to her view that the abolition of Health Authorities would remove an "unnecessary tier of administration", bringing resources and decision-making powers closer to local populations through Local Health Boards staffed largely by health care professionals.[12]

Nevertheless, she had to concede to pressure from the Liberal Democrats to establish an all-Wales commissioning body, the Specialist Health Services Commission for Wales, with responsibility for tertiary services and enhanced capacity to advise, guide and facilitate commissioning of secondary care. Simultaneously the Minister was forced to concede that the 22 Local Health Boards would no longer be overseen by three regional health organisations alone. Alongside there would be the creation of between ten and twelve Local Partnerships involving collaboration between two Local Health Boards, two Local Authorities and one NHS Trust.

At both a grass roots party level and an Assembly level, the Liberal Democrats felt strongly that there had been a lack of prior consultation on such a major structural change to the NHS. Many AMs across the parties begged Jane Hutt to go back to the drawing board with respect to her plans for the future structure of the Welsh NHS. However, the restructuring did not meet with universal criticism. Amongst others, the British Medical Association supported the abolition of Health Authorities.

Abolition of the five health authorities across Wales has brought into question the structure and function of public health in Wales in the future. Following wide consultation, it has been agreed that the public health function within the NHS will be delivered through the All Wales Public Health Service. Specialist epidemiology and research will be supported through the establishment of the Wales Centre for Health.

RESOURCE ALLOCATION

The Review of the Resource Allocation Formula in Wales, under the chairmanship of Professor Peter Townsend, illustrates the extent to which consultation has been a central part of the policy-making process.[13] However,

---

[12] Assembly *Record*, 27 November 2001. See also her article in the *Western Mail* the same day: 'The birth of a new NHS beckons'.

[13] *NHS Resource Allocation Review Targeting Poor Health : Professor Townsend's Report of the Welsh Assembly's National Steering Group on the Allocation of NHS Resources*, National Assembly for Wales, 2001. Available online at: www.wales.nhs.uk

the extent to which consultation has influenced final policy decisions is arguable. The Resource Allocation Review, which took place during 2000/2001, involved a National Steering Group headed by Professor Townsend and a Project Review Group, together with task groups responsible for the following areas:

- Review of research
- Social deprivation
- Rural/remoteness
- Teaching and tertiary services
- Prescribing, General Medical Services (GMS), community services, family health services

A research team, under the direction of Dr David Gordon, from Bristol University, was commissioned to advise the committee and respond to the research questions of the task groups.[14] The research team proposed a radical move away from the resource allocation formula used in Wales (and still used in England and Scotland). The move was from a formula which deploys hospital utilisation as an indirect proxy for need, towards one which uses data from the 1998 Welsh Health Survey as a direct measure of health at small area level. Serious concerns were raised by task groups over the proposed formula change and the speed with which it was to be implemented. There were also wide-ranging calls for further research into issues such as reasons for cost differentials between small and large hospitals, and appropriate indicators of both urban and rural socio-economic deprivation. Despite this, Professor Townsend's final report recommended the formula change. It is difficult to see how the consultation process ultimately changed the recommendations of the Bristol Research Team.

THE PRIVATE FINANCE INITIATIVE

In contradistinction to Westminster the Assembly Government has proved notably cautious on pursuing capital projects through utilising the private finance initiative route. In late 2001 it announced that two new community hospitals, in Porthmadog and Rhondda, were to be financed entirely through the public sector. During 2001, too, Finance Minister Edwina Hart re-branded PPPs and PFI schemes in Wales as 'investment partnership'. She described this as a pragmatic 'Welsh way' embracing the four principles laid out in Table 2.[15] The approach would limit the use of PFI to large-scale

---

[14] *Wales NHS Resource Allocation Review Independent Report of the Research Team*, National Assembly for Wales, 2001. Available online at: http://www.wales.nhs.uk/Publications

[15] Edwina Hart, *Statement on Investment through Partnerships in Wales*, Assembly *Record*, 13 December 2001.

schemes that were clearly within the public interest.

Edwina Hart also promised to widen the categories of staff who would remain within the public sector when a PFI was under way. At present employees such as doctors who are involved directly in providing a public service remain within the public sector when a facility is operated under PFI.

TABLE 2: THE ASSEMBLY GOVERNMENT'S FOUR PFI PRINCIPLES

- All PFI schemes should be governed by the public interest in the quality of public services.

- The relationship with the private sector should be based on partnerships that improve services rather than arrangements to access finance only.

- The interests of employees should at least be maintained.

- Partnerships between people who work together to serve the public should be enhanced rather than diminished.

On the other hand, staff who are involved in the upkeep of a facility - such as porters, cooks and cleaners - are transferred to the private sector. As Edwina Hart put it, addressing an Assembly plenary session in December 2001:

"We must continue to be prepared to finance a large part of our capital investment through conventional means ... The Assembly does not intend to privatise public services. Rather, it seeks to deliver those services by the most efficient and effective means available under the direction of the relevant public body ... We aim to maintain the public sector ethos, which we value, in all public services ... we would not expect clinical, professional, or front-line staff, such as doctors, nurses and teachers, to transfer to the private sector as part of any PPP or PFI project in Wales. I want to ensure that the concept of the clinical team in this context is not defined by status. We will aim to redefine that which makes up the clinical team so that staff such as porters, cooks, and cleaners would not transfer to private sector employment but would remain employees of the National Health Service."[16]

It is clear, therefore, that the Assembly Government is pursuing PFI less aggressively than the Labour administration at Westminster. As First Minister, Rhodri Morgan, put it, speaking to the Wales TUC in May 2002:

"Our decision, jointly made by Finance Minister, Edwina Hart, and

---

[16] *Ibid.*

*Health Minister, Jane Hutt, to build the second Rhondda hospital and
the hospital at Porthmadog entirely through the public sector is not some
opportunistic aberration."*[17]

The less enthusiastic approach to PFI in Cardiff Bay compared with Whitehall
is perhaps not surprising, given the importance of the public sector in Wales
and the degree of antipathy to the private sector. At the same time it holds out
the prospect of a more measured approach to the implementation of a policy
that has proved highly controversial, with notable concerns coming from
Wales's health economists.[18]

WAITING LISTS AND WAITING TIMES

Despite the establishment of a Waiting Times Strategy Development Group in
1999, the Assembly Government has failed to get to grips with increasing
NHS waiting lists and waiting times. The Office of National Statistics
recommends caution in making comparisons between countries, due to
differences in the ways waiting times are calculated. Nevertheless, Figure 1
shows Wales's proportion of patients waiting 12 months or more to be
substantially higher than in both England and Scotland. In January 2002 it
was reported that:

> *"... there are now 210,816 people waiting to see a consultant in Wales,
> nearly 30,000 more than this time last year and double the number
> when Labour came to power in 1997."*[19]

If the Minister were prepared to stand by her commitment to reduce waiting
lists to the extent that Tony Blair has committed himself to resolving the issue
by the next general election then she will be held very visibly accountable for
the success or failure of her policies. After all, waiting lists and times are very
visible performance indicators for the health service and they make good
media headlines.

It may be that some of the problems facing the Assembly result from the time
lag required to build up Wales's service capacity. Wales has a high prevalence
of heart disease when compared with the rest of the UK. To meet its waiting
time targets for heart disease, the Assembly has funded patients to travel to
London for heart surgery. This was criticised by some Plaid Cymru AMs as
making a mockery of devolution. For instance, it has been suggested by Dr

---

[17] *Western Mail*, 3 May 2002.

[18] *Western Mail*, 3 September 2001.

[19] *Western Mail*, 31 January 2001.

FIGURE 1: NHS HOSPITAL WAITING LISTS: PATIENTS WAITING
12 MONTHS OR LONGER

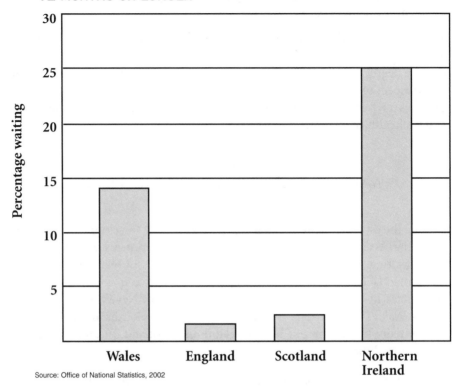

Source: Office of National Statistics, 2002

Dai Lloyd, Plaid Cymru's health spokesman in the Assembly, that

> " ... we are knee deep in task forces yet they are unworkable because we
> haven't got the surgeons, theatre space or expertise." [20]

The reality may be that the time lag needed to create sufficient capacity within
Wales to meet ambitious Assembly pledges makes such interim arrangements
inevitable. If England is sending patients to France, then why not send
patients from Cardiff to London?

FINITE RESOURCES, INFINITE DEMANDS

The establishment of the National Institute for Clinical Excellence (NICE) for
England and Wales, offered an opportunity for the NHS to make and enforce
explicit rationing decisions about the introduction of potentially expensive
new drugs and therapies for which there was little evidence of clinical and

---

[20] *Western Mail*, 11 October 2001.

cost effectiveness. Health Authorities have set in place systems to adhere and monitor NICE guidelines for prescribing.

At Health Authority level, the need for explicit priority setting or rationing has been accepted, with the establishment by a number of Welsh Health Authorities of priority setting committees and protocols. However, there is little sign at Assembly Government level of open acknowledgement that the NHS cannot deliver all potentially beneficial interventions to patients and that rationing, either through waiting lists or limiting prescription formularies is inevitable. Nor is a clear distinction made between needs, wants and demands for health care. The NHS *Plan for Wales* is full of the language of wants.[21] It promises to meet patient wants rather than meet professionally judged patient needs. The present situation of insufficient capacity to meet rising waiting lists for elective care, together with persisting winter pressures means that the NHS will face impossible strain until the Assembly is prepared to engage in an open public debate about what the NHS can afford to provide and what services it cannot provide in future.

Perhaps politicians have to sound positive about their policies and perhaps people working in the health service will always bemoan their lack of resources and increasing workloads. However, to the concerned commentator, there does seem to be a gap between what the Assembly Government is saying about its health policy and how patients and health care professionals are feeling about the state of the NHS in Wales. Jane Hutt declared in January 2002 that Labour had

"… delivered its manifesto on health in every significant area".[22]

However, managers in the NHS fear for the sustainability of Local Health Boards and the extent to which the public will understand the structure of the new NHS. Finance directors in the NHS warn that additional resources promised to the NHS will only just be sufficient to maintain the status quo given recent pay awards. Leading health professionals believe the Minister's focus on structures to be misplaced. Shortages of manpower, beds and theatres are repeatedly given as the reason for the continued increase in NHS waiting lists in Wales.

Perhaps this perceived reality gap is the result of a time lag between Assembly Government intervention and outcomes. There is an inevitable gap between consultation, the establishment of task groups, and training health professionals and the eventual increase of NHS capacity.

The Assembly may not have as many choices as it might have hoped. Would it be politically tenable for the Assembly to opt to spend windfall monies on

---

[21] *Improving Health in Wales: A Plan for the NHS with its partners*, Assembly Government, 2001.

[22] *Western Mail*, 29 January 2002.

other government areas which address the socio-economic causes of inequalities in health, when such equivalent monies are promised to health care in England? Even if Wales, with its historical commitment to socialised medicine, were to resist the temptations of following England down the route towards the incorporation of the PFI into future NHS capital spending decisions, could the National Assembly for Wales sustain such a decision were people in Wales to look over the border at new, shiny hospitals in England and compare them with older publicly financed hospitals in Wales?

MEDIA ENGAGEMENT

The Welsh media, as is the case with the media generally, has judged health issues, particularly special interest stories, as fair game for harsh criticism. The *Western Mail*, in particular, has drawn attention to the Minister's failure to meet waiting list targets. And the UK press has latched on to the medico-legal repercussions of rare but high profile cases, such as that of Mr Graham Reeves whose death occurred as a result of the removal of a healthy kidney at Prince Philip Hospital in Llanelli.[23]

The following are examples of a series of headlines appearing in the Western Mail describing Assembly health policy and its implications for the NHS over the winter of 2001-02.

- Waiting lists grow as the NHS flounders (1 November 2001)
- NHS reforms 'unworkable' (5 November 2001)
- Health shake-up alarms managers (6 November 2001)
- Services 'not affordable' (8 November 2001)
- It's simple: the NHS needs more beds (5 December 2001)
- Health pledges fail to match rhetoric (2 January 2002)
- Waiting list 'a national disgrace' (31 January 2002)

Such stories, with their persistently negative slant, tend to build up an impression of failure which is probably unfair to underlying progress and the everyday accomplishments of a service under constant pressure. It is bad news that tends to capture the headlines. At the same time it is possible to argue that, as a result of the Assembly, those who read the *Western Mail*, and in north Wales the *Daily Post*, are better informed about NHS issues than they were prior to devolution.

The Minister's decision to centralise control of many of the activities carried

---

[23] *The Guardian*, 16 November 2000.

out in the past by Health Authorities while devolving other responsibilities for commissioning to Local Health Boards may remove a buffer, bringing public and media criticism more directly to the Assembly.

THE FUTURE

During the first term the Assembly Government published two key documents with the potential to influence the health of the people of Wales. These were the *NHS Plan for Wales* (February 2001), which set out an agenda for health policy, and *A Winning Wales* (January 2002), which set out a programme for economic regeneration.

The Assembly Government has an opportunity to bring these two goals for economic regeneration and an improved health service together to tackle the root socio-economic causes of inequalities in health. Figure 2 sets out a diagrammatic representation contrasting Wales at 2001/2 with what Wales might potentially become by the year 2020. The diagram proposes policies for

- An increase in workforce participation.
- Reduction on reliance on benefits.
- Diversification of the Welsh economic base.
- Less reliance on heavy industry.
- Greater penetration into service, financial and e-commerce markets.

In parallel, the diagram illustrates the need for a health service that appreciates its role in economic regeneration, workplace and school-based health promotion and in responding flexibly to keep the workforce working. Joined-up working at an Assembly Government level as well as at a more local level is needed in order to improve the health of the present and future generations of the people of Wales.

Much data on morbidity, mortality and health service utilisation is only available up until 1998/99. It will be another three or four years until it is possible to examine the trends in order to establish whether the health of the people of Wales has improved post-devolution. Even if it has, then it would be difficult to identify whether such an improvement has resulted from changes in health care policy. A key question is whether health improvements arise more from health policy as such, that is to a Welsh NHS tailored to the specific needs of the Welsh population, or more from economic regeneration. One suspects that increases in workforce participation, falls in unemployment and increases in disposable income are more effective in alleviating the root socio-economic causes of inequalities in health. If such a conclusion were to arise from properly researched outcomes then the impact for policy making, and in

FIGURE 2: INTEGRATED POLICY

Wales 2001

Compared with the rest of the UK, Wales has:

- economically inactive workforce
- reliance on declining heavy industry
- less penetration into expanding markets, e.g. financial services, e-commerce
- lower GDP per head
- lower literacy skills
- high longstanding limiting illness

- an elderly population

Wales has:

- inequalities in health between areas within Wales
- inequalities in prosperity between regions within Wales
- inequalities in access to health services

Economic Policy

- Encourage economic activity amongst population of working age
- Encourage inward investment from abroad
- Substantial job creation
- Diversify Wales's economic base to encompass green energy, tourism
- improve uptake of technological advance, e.g. e-commerce
- Improve opportunities for workforce re-entry skills
- Ensure benefit structure supports workforce re-entry

Health Care Policy

- Redistribute health care resources to more closely match health care needs based on direct measures of mortality and morbidity
- Increased role for workplace health promotion
- Increased role for schools-based health promotion
- Ensuring health care available to keep workforce economically active, e.g. waiting list policy
- Flexibility of primary/secondary health care services to meet needs of economically active

Wales 2020

Compared with the rest of the UK, Wales has:

- Increased participation in the workforce
- Less reliance on declining heavy industry
- Increased penetration into expanding markets, e.g. financial services, e-commerce
- Increased GDP per head
- Improved literacy skills
- Reduced longstanding limiting illness

- Better able to support an elderly population

Wales has:

- Less inequalities in health between areas within Wales
- Less inequalities in prosperity between regions within Wales
- More equitable access to health services

particular allocation of resources, would be profound.

It is said that a week is a long time in politics, but evidence shows that three years is not a very long time to see the results of devolved policy-making. The National Assembly inherited an NHS which had experienced real reductions in both capital and revenue expenditure, a population with relatively poor life expectancy, relatively high morbidity, and significant inequalities in health and socio-economic determinants of health across Wales.

Devolution has enabled the Assembly Government to put into place a mechanism for making health policy and for fostering a culture of consultation. It has also ignited a Welsh consciousness and a nation's sense of responsibility for its own health. As in other countries, there is a reality gap between the optimism of the Minister and her ambitious commitments for service improvement and the very real capacity and manpower crisis being felt on the ground by health care professionals, especially Trust managers and directors of finance. No doubt, as argued in the *NHS Plan for Wales*, it will take time. But this is an NHS suffering from 'change fatigue', in the throws of yet another major reorganisation, which many doubt will bring the improvements promised by the Welsh Assembly Government. One cannot help but wonder what the NHS in Wales would look like today if the Minister had honoured the Coalition commitment to a period of stability to allow the NHS to try to meet its priorities for patient care.

CHAPTER 9

OBJECTIVE 1

Elin Royles

A major first term priority for the National Assembly was Objective 1 for West Wales and the Valleys. This was the European Commission's largest Structural Funds programme in the UK and one of the largest in the European Union as a whole. With a £1.2 billion potential investment to be made between 2000-06, the programme provided the Assembly with an opportunity to demonstrate that it could make an impact upon Wales's economic future. The challenge was a one-off opportunity since Wales is unlikely to receive such a significant injection of funding from the European Union following enlargement and the inclusion of applicant countries from eastern Europe.

This chapter first examines the preliminary stages of developing Objective 1, taking the process to the approval of the Single Programming Document by the European Commission in July 2000. It then examines the decision-making processes involved in the implementation of Objective 1, addressing the programme's management and administration. The chapter concludes by providing an overview of Objective 1 during the Assembly's first term.

THE OBJECTIVE 1 PLANNING PROCESS

In the Autumn of 1998, following concerted lobbying, the Office of National Statistics confirmed that the GDP per head for west Wales and the Valleys was below the 75 per cent threshold necessary for Objective 1 designation. Immediately, the then Secretary of State for Wales Ron Davies established a European Task Force which included representatives of the public, voluntary and private sectors in Wales.[1] As well as being responsible for developing an ambitious national economic development strategy, the Task Force was the main body charged with preparing the Objective 1 Single Programming Document. Its Secretariat was provided by the Welsh Office European Affairs Division and Hywel Ceri Jones, formerly a high ranking official with the European Commission, was appointed as an adviser. As part of the process

---

[1] Ron Davies declared that, "Wales is ready for the European Challenge": Welsh Office European Affairs Division Press release, 22 October 1998. For an account of securing Objective 1 status, see Morgan, K., 'How Objective 1 Arrived in Wales: The Political Origins of a Coup', *Contemporary Wales 15*, 2003. For membership of the Task Force see Appendix 1.

two regional partnerships were established, one in west Wales and the other in the Valleys.

A draft of the Single Programming Document for the Objective 1 region was issued in July 1999. It proposed packages of national and local programmes to be co-ordinated by appropriate 'lead bodies', at the national level by bodies such as the Welsh Development Agency, and locally by local authorities.[2] It was anticipated that this approach would be more effective than the previous 1994-99 Structural Funds period when individual projects lacked overall co-ordination. However, the different levels soon produced a struggle for ownership of the Objective 1 process. Devolving decisions to local partnerships allowed local authorities to become the main players and gave priority to locally driven regeneration. At the same time the regional partnerships demanded a robust role for national organisations such as the Welsh Development Agency and they resisted pressure coming from below. The tension that resulted created problems that were not addressed in the preliminary stages. As one community sector representative put it:

"... the conversations that people avoided was how the relationship between the partnerships would happen. As a consequence, there was no clear guidance on the remits of the partnerships at the local or regional level."[3]

The struggle for influence over Objective 1 was played out within the Task Force. As with previous Structural Funds programmes in Wales, its composition was largely public-sector based 'usual suspects', but also included some voluntary organisations and trade union representatives (see Appendix 1). The Task Force itself was not equipped to develop Objective 1. It was too big and unwieldy to develop a strategic approach. The two regional partnerships were heavily dominated by local authorities with some voluntary sector representation but minimal private sector involvement.

The two regional partnerships established the teams that drafted the Single Programming Document and the Programme Complement from March to October 1999. Key organisations, such as the Welsh Development Agency, the Countryside Council for Wales, and some voluntary organisations such as Wales Council for Voluntary Action and Chwarae Teg (European Equality Partnership) also contributed to detailed drafting while Assembly civil servants co-ordinated the production of the overall Document.

The Task Force did not fulfil expectations and a decision to wind it up was announced in September 1999.[4] The Programming Document was taken over

---

[2] See minutes of the Assembly's Economic Development Committee, April 1999.

[3] Author's interview, June 2002.

[4] McAllister, L., 'Devolution and the New Context for Public Policy-making: Lessons from the EU Structural Funds in Wales', *Public Policy and Administration*, Volume 15, No. 2., 2000, page 46.

and revised by the civil service between October 1999 and April 2000. They listened to comments from the consultation process held from July to October 1999 and from a detailed critique of the Document by the European Commission received in December 1999. A Shadow Monitoring Committee was convened in March 2000 to continue the work on Objective 1.[5] Following endorsement by a plenary session of the National Assembly, the Single Programming Document was finally submitted to the Commission in April 2000.

In May 2000, a Structural Funds Working Group was established by the Assembly to advise the Shadow Monitoring Committee.[6] This smaller group had a reduced public sector and increased voluntary and private sector representation.[7] It reflected a new 'Team Wales' approach following the creation of the National Assembly. Members of the working group formed a small delegation that participated in negotiations with the European Commission. This was led by the Assembly Government and included the Welsh Local Government Association, the Wales Council of Voluntary Action and representatives from Higher Education. The document was eventually approved by the Commission in July 2000.

THE ASSEMBLY'S INHERITANCE

Despite Ron Davies' declaration in 1998 that Wales was ready for the European challenge, in many respects the country was ill prepared. The early stages of developing the Objective 1 programme revealed a number of 'teething troubles', some of which failed to be resolved as the programme progressed.

Firstly, the Welsh Office European Affairs Division and the Wales European Programme Executive were not adequately equipped to deal with such a large scale programme. Its size also meant that only limited lessons could be learnt from previous programmes. Secondly, the European Affairs Division was simultaneously concluding the 1994-99 programmes and agreeing a number of other programmes for 2000-06. This further reduced the resources available for dealing with Objective 1.

More generally, pre-devolution the Welsh Office had been dependent upon Whitehall for policy direction. As a result, the 1997 policy document *Pathway to Prosperity* was inadequate as a comprehensive economic plan for Wales

---

[5] See Appendix 2.

[6] McAllister *op.cit.*, page 46.

[7] See Appendix 2.

under which the Structural Funds programmes for 2000-06 could be developed. This created the need for a National Economic Development Strategy to be put in place as a context for developing the Objective 1 Single Programming Document. In the event this also failed to provide an effective framework for the post-devolution European Programmes.

Equally significant was the impact on the civil service of having to make the transition from the previous Welsh Office style of running Wales to responding to the requirements of the National Assembly. The demands of having to cope simultaneously with devolution and the early stages of planning Objective 1 created an overload. As one civil servant involved explained:

> "At the time nearly all our focus was on devolution. You're setting up the Assembly which was an enormous project. You can't imagine how much of a project it was really. In the early stages the Objective 1 programme was significantly under-resourced and not properly planned. I don't think there was a coherent learning process."[8]

Consequently, the Objective 1 project lacked the necessary resources for the formulation of policies. For instance, only a small team of civil servants worked on the Single Programming Document. Deficiencies were particularly evident in community and sustainable development. As a result the input of outside experts became essential. Even so, lack of capacity led to civil servants making decisions without adequate information. Working practices further exacerbated the difficulties. The frequent transfer of staff between Welsh Office departments made it difficult to build organisational memory and learning in policy development. Yet there was little attempt to tackle these problems. As one civil servant observed:

> "There was very little attempt to create organisational capacity in the Welsh Office or the Assembly."[9]

The coming of the National Assembly politicised the Objective 1 process. The winding up of the Task Force by the First Secretary Alun Michael in September 1999 signalled that a new political force was in charge. The balance of influence was shifting from the local to the national level. As one observer judged:

> "... many local authority partners in particular regarded the winding-up of the Task Force as a calculated and pragmatic political snub,

---

[8] Author's interview, June 2002.

[9] Author's interview, June 2002

designed to reinforce the ultimate authority of the Assembly over the planning process."[10]

Meanwhile, consultation on Objective 1 had been delayed by Alun Michael until the National Assembly was up and running in July 1999. While this slowed the process down, it was a sensible move as it avoided the programme becoming politicised during the first Assembly Elections. Once the Assembly was in being the Economic Development Committee contributed to the early shaping of the programme. It received evidence from other Objective 1 areas, such as Ireland and Merseyside, and organised joint 'roadshows' with the Assembly's Regional Committees around Wales to hear evidence from the public, private and voluntary sectors. The Committee emphasised the importance of partnership between the public, private and voluntary sectors, and, in another significant contribution, urged that gender balance should be 'mainstreamed'.[11] This commitment to partnership and equality reflected the background of many AMs. It also demonstrated that the Assembly was predisposed to greater openness than was the case under the old Welsh Office system.

MATCH FUNDING

Objective 1 was assured of a high profile during the early months of the Assembly's life due to the contentious dispute over match funding. The central issue was whether the Treasury would find the money to match the £1.3 billion European Commission investment over the next seven years. The Chair of the Economic Development Committee during its first meetings was Ron Davies.[12] He revealed that in his former position as Secretary of State for Wales he had made bids to the Treasury for additional financial cover for EU receipts. He had asked for £3m for the 1999-2000 financial year, rising to £54m for 2000-01, and £263m for 2001-02. All were turned down, with the Treasury saying the Assembly would have to find cover and matched funding for EU receipts from within its existing £7.5 billion block grant.

Under close cross-examination civil servants revealed where funding cover for EU Objective 1 spend in the first year of the programme would come from. Questions prised out the information that a total of £75 million had been allocated, made up of the following:

---

[10] McAllister, L., 'Devolution and the New Context for Public Policy-making: Lessons from the EU Structural Funds in Wales', *Public Policy and Administration*, Volume 15, No. 2, 2000, page 46.

[11] See Minutes of the Assembly's Economic Development Committee, March, April and June 1999.

[12] This was before his forced resignation in July 1999 as a result of fall-out from his Clapham Common incident the previous October

- £19 million was already allocated in the budget.

- £21 million from European Regional Development Fund monies under-spent on programmes in Wales over the previous three years.

- £35 million re-allocated from other parts of the Welsh block compared with the previous year.

It was also revealed that EU money earmarked for Wales was not added to the baseline defined by the Barnett formula, according to which central government expenditure is distributed between Wales, Scotland, and Northern Ireland. In other words, the whole spending on EU projects in Wales would come out of the Barnett block, calculated by comparison with English spending departments and without reference to those EU projects. The official explanation was that spending departments in England used to calculate the Barnett formula had some EU funding themselves. Therefore, spread over the whole of the UK the sums balanced, with some winners and some losers. Yet, along with North East England, Wales was one of the poorest economic regions in Britain, with low GDP, high unemployment and high economic inactivity rates. Consequently Wales would lose all the time under this dispensation.

Plaid Cymru did some quick calculations and claimed that Wales had lost out on EU funding by some £50m a year over the previous five years. With the extra money that could be drawn down for the Objective 1 region between 2000 to 2006 the problem could only get worse. Speaking in a plenary debate Professor Phil Williams, Plaid Cymru's Economic Development spokesman, paid tribute to the work of the Committee and its chairman:

> "In the first two meetings of the Economic Development Committee, the whole matter has been largely cleared up. These two meetings have justified the cost of the Assembly many times over. I pay tribute to the Welsh Office civil servants and the Chair, Ron Davies. It was due to how those meetings were handled, with a judicious mix of informed pugnacity and constructive discussion, that the right questions were asked and the right answers given."[13]

In this plenary debate, Labour attempted to amend a Plaid Cymru motion by watering down its insistence that adequate match funds be found in addition to the Welsh block and that the operation of the Barnett formula should exclude all EU-supported expenditure in the English departments or in Wales. However, the key Labour amendment was lost by 26 votes to 25 with Plaid Cymru, Conservative and Liberal Democrats combining to oppose the Government. This was a harbinger of things to come.

---

[13] Assembly *Record*, 14 July 1999.

Following attacks on the minority Labour administration in November 1999, the three opposition parties tabled a joint four-page paper with annexes, *Explanatory Guide to European Structural Funds*, laying down their shared understanding of how the structural funds applied to Wales. It explored a range of questions including match funding, additionality, and the need to maintain a spending profile across the six-year Objective 1 period. In addition it addressed the complex inter-relation of EU funding and the Barnett Formula with the Welsh block. On match funding it concluded that the UK Government was expecting 'the lion's share' to come from existing Assembly budgets and that this was unacceptable for the following reasons:

- *"Because it breaches the core principle of additionality on which all programmes are based.*

- *Because it is an impossible expectation on budgets already stretched to their limit."*[14]

The moment of truth came the following February, at the end of the process establishing the Assembly's budget for the 2000-01 financial year. The Opposition combined to force the resignation of the First Secretary, Alun Michael, after he could give no assurances on match funding. Subsequently, in July 2000, the Comprehensive Spending Review did produce additional funding to provide a measure of match funding, though the amount and whether what it provided was adequate was disputed. Throughout this period, therefore, the match funding issue ensured that Objective 1 remained securely within the political and media limelight.

THE DECISION-MAKING PROCESS

The Programme Monitoring Committee's membership was constituted on the basis of equal representation for the public, private and voluntary sectors – that is to say, on a 'one-thirds' each principle (for the membership see Appendix 3). The implementation structure was to be 15 local partnerships, one for each local authority within the Objective 1 area, together with ten regional partnerships based upon specific sectors of the economy. The local authorities questioned the practicability of implementing the 'one-thirds' at all levels and argued for some flexibility. Nevertheless, the Shadow Monitoring Committee decreed that:

"… the clear view of the Committee was that the 'one-thirds' principle should be adhered to in all partnership groups."[15]

---

[14] See John Osmond, *Devolution 'A Dynamic, Settled Process?' Monitoring the National Assembly July to December 1999*, IWA, page 38

[15] Minutes of the Shadow Monitoring Committee, March 2000.

It is noteworthy that the 'one-third' principle was not imposed by the European Commission. In general the definition of partnership in European regulations remained unchanged between 1994-99 and 2000-06. The one exception was that the 2000-06 regulations extended the recommended composition of partnerships further than the public, private and voluntary sectors. Now they also referred to:

> "... those responsible for the environment and for the promotion of equality between men and women, and other competent bodies."[16]

It was the National Assembly that was pivotal in ensuring that the 'one-third' principle became enshrined in Objective 1. The Economic Development Committee, especially when the late Val Feld, the former Director of the Equal Opportunities Commission in Wales, was its Chair, was a strong advocate of the 'one-thirds' principle.[17] It may well have been that the principle would not have been implemented at all had it not been for the active endorsement of influential politicians. As one voluntary sector representative explained, the 'one-thirds' principle:

> "... was ultimately a political decision in the early euphoric days in the Assembly. It simply would not have happened had it still been left to the Welsh Office."[18]

The notion of partnership and inclusiveness permeated the work of the Assembly as a whole. This was due partly to the stress placed by the National Assembly Advisory Group in preparing the ground for the Assembly, but also the results of the National Assembly's first elections, which left the Labour Party without an overall majority.

Nevertheless, there was some frustration that the Objective 1 Partnership had a greater role in developing the Single Programming Document than the Assembly itself. There was an attempt to gain greater control of the Objective 1 decision-making structures. The main means was by ensuring a greater role for Assembly Members on the Programme Monitoring Committee, and not least by appointing an AM as its Chair. As one participant explained:

> "It was one of the first issues on the Assembly's desk and a really difficult one for them. They [the politicians] were bound to want to put their mark on it."[19]

In short, the 'one-thirds' principle requiring a partnership approach to the

---

[16] European Commission, *Structural Actions 2000-2006 Commentary and Regulations*, 2000, page 36.

[17] Minutes of the Economic Development Committee, July 1999.

[18] Author's interview, June 2002

[19] Author's interview, local authorities, June 2002

administration of Objective 1 was a direct consequence of the intervention of politicians and is a striking example of the impact the advent of devolution has made. As Bachtler argues:

> "… with the exception of Northern Ireland, no other UK programme experiences this degree of 'politicisation' of the Structural Funds."[20]

Despite this, and the emphasis on partnership, there were wide variations in the local and regional operations. Generally, the secretariat for local partnerships was made up of local authorities, while Assembly Sponsored Public Bodies provide secretariats for the regional partnerships. Consequently, the public sector remained the key player. In large part this reflected its being the main source of match funding, but also its previous Structural Funds experience.

Despite the importance of the private sector in in efforts to increase GDP, its involvement in the Objective 1 partnerships was less significant than expected. Some private sector members had an impression that they could directly access Objective 1 funds which raised false expectations. The reality was that private sector representatives on committees were less experienced and could not match the technical back-up of their public sector colleagues. As a result they tended to be less engaged, and more easily frustrated with the process. In fact, some private sector representatives felt that their representation on the committees was little more than a token gesture, designed to meet European Commission requirements.

On the other hand, civil society organisations tended to be more involved. In part this was because they had access to the support of national organisations, such as the Wales Council for Voluntary Action, which employs staff dedicated to European issues. Such organisations have levels of expertise that compare with the public sector. At the same time, smaller community and grassroots organisations experienced capacity difficulties similar to the private sector. In general, the 'one-third' principle led to many participants feeling over-stretched. As one put it:

> "I think what has happened is that partners who do not have the wherewithal to support the demands that have been put on us over the last three years, are starting to buckle under the weight."[21]

Undoubtedly, the large number of partnerships in Objective 1 created systems overload. It had simply been assumed that all partners could participate effectively and disparities in experience, skills and resources were not recognised. Neither did all agree that the 'one-thirds' principle was beneficial.

---

[20] Bachtler, J., 'Objective 1 in Wales: A Comparative Assessment', *Contemporary Wales* No. 15, 2003, page 36.

[21] Author's interview, July 2002.

To some public sector representatives it was too rigid. The public sector, the main driver of European funding, felt under-represented and the expectations of other partners were too high. The process did broaden perspectives and improve expertise in policy-making. It also promoted joint working and networks. However, not all who participated are convinced that the partnership approach has improved the effectiveness of Objective 1.

IMPLEMENTATION

At an early stage, the Economic Development Committee decided to take a relatively hands-off approach to the work of the Programme Monitoring Committee's work.[22] Nevertheless, as Bachtler observed, west Wales and the Valleys proved different from the other UK Objective 1 regions in having politicians directly engaged in the implementation process.[23] The Chair of the Programme Monitoring Committee continued to be the Cynon Valley Labour AM Christine Chapman. And the Economic Development Committee continued to be proactive in policing the rules of engagement. So, for instance, it held meetings with European Commission representatives and was supportive of decisions taken by the Programme Monitoring Committee on the 'one-thirds' principle. It also voiced concern to the Wales European Funding Office about adherence to maintaining gender balance within the partnerships.[24]

By November 2000 political concerns about the complexity of implementation led to the then Economic Development Minister, Mike German, establishing a Task and Finish Group to undertake a review. In July 2002, the National Audit Office Wales published a report on maximising the benefits from Objective 1. Together they provide key insights into problems around the implementation of the programme.[25] The Task and Finish Group report noted that a lack of expertise and informed guidance has affected Objective 1 programme development and delivery. It recommended that a policy group be established to advise the Programme Monitoring Committee on policy issues and programme management, concluding that:

"… decision-making has been at best based on inclusivity and the working groups from the European Task Force onwards have tended to

---

[22] Minutes of the Economic Development Committee, March, 2000.

[23] Bachtler, *op. cit.*, page 36.

[24] Minutes of the Economic Development Committee, September and December 2000.

[25] Benfield, G, et. al., T*ask and Finish Group Report on the Implementation of Objective 1 Structural Funds*, Wales European Funding Office, 2000; and Auditor General for Wales, *EU Structural Funds: Maximising the Benefits for Wales*, National Audit Office Wales, 2002.

be representative rather than capable of taking strategic decisions. In the absence of clear leadership this has led to a decision making style aimed at achieving consensus rather than clear policy as its overwhelming aim. "[26]

Both reports identified problems with the operation of Wales European Funding Office. Established as an executive body of the Assembly in April 2000, it combined the former Wales European Programme Executive and part of the old Welsh Office European Affairs Division. All its staff became Assembly civil servants. This was a necessary overhaul in the way the Structural Funds had been managed and administered. The Wales European Programme Executive had been managing just £395 million in the six years between 1994-99, while it was anticipated that some £1.4 billion of EU funding would be available to Wales in the seven years 2000-06.[27] However, the timing of the creation of the new Wales European Funding Office caused a good deal of disruption. This happened at a critical point in developing Objective 1. As Bachtler states:

"... the creation and then abolition of WEPE and then creation of WEFO has inhibited continuity of learning and lost a significant part of the institutional experience accumulated in recent years. "[28]

The Wales European Funding Office also faced severe staffing and technical problems. Due to uncertainty and the lure of job opportunities elsewhere, many of the old Programme Executive staff left and the remaining core staff of the new organisation had a very heavy workload. By the time of the Auditor General report, recruitment had improved, but its staffing levels were still below complement.[29] Moreover, it had inherited inadequate information systems which were not designed to cope with the much larger work programme.[30] All this meant that the necessary management structures and plans for deciding on selection criteria were not in place when the Office was established. In turn this slowed down the Objective 1 process, particularly in the first round of fast-track applications.

The Task and Finish Group made recommendations to address the cumbersome nature of the application process. This was characterised by complexity, jargon, delays and uncertainty, making the process far more onerous than accessing funds from other sources, for example Communities

[26] Benfield, G, et. al., *Task and Finish Group Report on the Implementation of Objective 1 Structural Funds*, Wales European Funding Office, 2000, page 26.

[27] Auditor General for Wales, *EU Structural Funds: Maximising the Benefits for Wales*, National Audit Office Wales, 2002: page 1.

[28] Bachtler, *op.cit.*, page 36.

[29] Auditor General for Wales, *op.cit.*, page 28.

[30] *Ibid.* page 29.

First or the National Lottery. Many potential applicant groups were put off by the bureaucracy, together with the length of time it took for committed funds to be actually paid. The Task and Finish Group called for an application process offering:

> "... simplicity of access and speedy, effective decision making which puts the need of the applicant first."[31]

Specific measures were also recommended to address the problems of the private and voluntary sectors. These included improvements to a private sector unit set up within the Wales European Funding Office in September 2000, and the creation of a Voluntary Sector Support Unit at the Wales Council for Voluntary Action. The Auditor General for Wales commended the setting up of these two units and discussed match funding problems that particularly affected the voluntary sector. His report noted that the Assembly Government had established a number of match funding sources and was working with European Funding Office to provide guidance on potential sources of match funding.[32] Both reports raised the use of key funds to simplify the engagement of private and voluntary actors in the programme, though only a few of the local partnerships have taken this up.

Both reports also acknowledged tensions between local and regional partnerships. The Task and Finish Group stated:

> "... one of the most contentious issues surrounding the process has been the lack of clear direction with regard to the interface of these crucial elements of the Programme."[33]

It provided its own definitions of the roles of local and regional partnerships. It was also decided to set up four strategy partnerships to be the final arbiters on project applications. Their membership was determined on the basis of equal representation of local and regional partnerships and the 'thirds' principle. It was claimed that:

> "... their existence [would] make competition between local and regional partnerships redundant."[34]

Since their establishment in 2001, these strategy partnerships have improved implementation and contributed to refining the partnership structures within the programme. According to one voluntary sector participant:

> "... the only way of dealing with the conflicts between local and regional

---

[31] Task and Finish Group report, *op. cit.*, page 5.

[32] Auditor General for Wales, *op.cit.*, page 38.

[33] Task and Finish Group report, *op. cit.*, page 8.

[34] *Ibid.*, page 22.

partnerships was by creating the strategy partnerships. You have a way of resolving everything. But you also have a very complicated system. "[35]

Undoubtedly, the strategy partnerships added another tier to the decision-making process, lengthening it and increasing the bureaucracy. The Task and Finish Group attempted to address this by setting timescales for the different bodies to process applications. According to the Auditor General for Wales there has been an improvement in applications processing. He noted that the 90 days appraisal period was in line with other Objective 1 regions in the UK. However, it was difficult to address the call for a simplified and shortened application system since, as he states:

"There will always be a degree of tension between a user-friendly application process and the need for the Wales European Funding Office to carry out a rigorous appraisal of projects against the selection criteria specified by the Programme Monitoring Committee, according to European Commission regulations and to the standards expected of a public body." [36]

This requirement for sound management of public money means that, as Bachtler put it, bureaucracy is endemic to Structural Fund implementation.[37] Nonetheless, an early indication of the successful implementation of Objective 1 occurred on 31 December 2002 when there was a possibility that funds would be de-committed under the n+2 rule, defined as:

"... all programmes are expected to pay out expenditure for project commitments made in the first year of operation ... Failing that, expenditure not paid out on commitments will be 'de-committed' or lost to the programme." [38]

The principle is new to the current programming period and places greater pressure to ensure spending conforms to the stricter financial control regulations and monitoring obligations. There was initially considerable speculation that there would be de-commitment. However, the Auditor General assessed that there was little risk of claw back in spend on the European Social Fund and the European Regional Development Fund, though he expressed concern at a higher possibility of de-commitment on agriculture and fisheries funds.[39] In December 2002, Andrew Davies, Economic Development Minister announced that Wales had met all its

---

[35] Author's interview, June 2002.

[36] Auditor General for Wales, *op.cit.*, page 37.

[37] Bachtler, *op.cit.*, page 37.

[38] Bachtler, *op.cit.*, page 34 and 35.

[39] The European Agricultural Guidance and Guarantee Fund (EAGGF), and the Financial Instrument for Fisheries Guidance (FIFG): Auditor General for Wales, *op.cit.*, page 3.

spending targets for all EU Structural Funds programmes for 2002 and that none of the funds earmarked for Wales would be lost.[40] In addition to the n+2 rule, the Commission have established a process which rewards the best performing regions. The Auditor General's report concluded that Wales should be well placed to qualify.[41]

CONCLUSION

A major challenge facing the National Assembly in 1999 was the successful development and implementation of Objective 1. In doing so it faced formidable problems. These included inadequate staffing and a lack of policy development capacity and expertise within the civil service in Wales. There was also considerable conflict between various sectors in terms of ownership of the Objective 1 programme. The new Administration found it difficult to address these at a time when it was preoccupied with its own untried processes. As Bachtler states:

> "Wales is unique (not just in the UK, but possibly across the EU as a whole) of having to accommodate so many institutional shifts and challenges at one time, especially in a programming period when the management requirements (financial management and control, monitoring, evaluation etc.) are much more demanding than previously."[42]

It was inevitable that devolution would open up the process of Structural Funds policy-making to greater political influences. This created more openness and scrutiny in the formulation of programmes. As we have seen, the Assembly was also the main driver for more inclusive partnerships in all aspects of Objective 1. As a European Commission official, Manfred Beschel, observed:

> "I do think that devolution creates a different kind of visibility for people. Partnerships in a devolved region, where the link to political representation is much closer, does make a difference, I can quite clearly say that."[43]

Furthermore, as the Auditor General remarked:

> "… the high degree of commitment to partnership working at all levels,

---

[40] Assembly *Record*, 18 December 2002.

[41] Auditor General for Wales, *op.cit.*, page 3.

[42] Bachtler, *op.cit.*, page 36.

[43] Select Committee on Welsh Affairs, *Second Report Objective 1 European Funding For Wales*, 2002.

particularly in the Objective 1 programme, represents an up-front investment in time and effort that will pay off … and will build capacity for the long term."[44]

The end of the National Assembly's first term corresponds with the commencement of the mid term review of the Objective 1 programme in 2003. This will be an acid test of the effectiveness of Objective 1. What is clear, however, is that the programme met its spending targets for the first year and there will be no de-commitment.

---

[44] Auditor General for Wales, *op.cit.*, page 21.

APPENDICES

Appendix 1: European Taskforce Membership

	October 1998	May 1999
Politicians	1 MEP	2 AM/MP, MEP
Government Actors	5	8
Government Agencies	6	13
Regional Agencies	1*	4***
Local Authorities	2	5
Private and Third Sector	5 Federation of Small Businesses (FSB); Confederation of British Industry (CBI); National Farmers Union in Wales (NFU); Farmers Union of Wales (FUW); Wales Trades Union Congress (WTUC)	5 FSB; CBI; NFU in Wales; FUW; WTUC
Higher Education	2	2
Voluntary Sector	1 WCVA	2 WCVA; Disability Wales
Other	1**	1**
Total	24	42

* North Wales Economic Forum on behalf of all Regional For a.

**Hywel Ceri Jones was European adviser to Ron Davies, the Secretary of State for Wales.

***The four Economic Regional Fora.

Source: North Wales Economic Forum - Minutes European Task Force Meeting 16 October 1998 and Minutes European Task Force Meeting 14 May 1999 ETF (99)

Appendix 2: Shadow Monitoring Committee

March 2000

Politicians	2
	AMs
Government Actors	4
Government Agencies	7*
Local Authorities	2
Social Partners	6
	British Telecom; Federation of Small Businesses; North Wales Chamber; Transport and General Union; NFU Cymru; Wales Co-operative Centre
Higher Education	1
Voluntary Sector	6
	WCVA x 2; Chwarae Teg; Wales Wildlife Trust; Groundwork Wales; Cymad
Total	28

* One was from the European Programme Executive.
Some of these were included as specialist statutory bodies

Source: WEFO website: Minutes Meeting Shadow Monitoring Committee, 7 March 2000

Structural Funds Working Group

Government Actors	1
	National Assembly
Public Sector	6
	3 Local Authorities; 2 Government Agencies; 1 Higher Education
Social Partners	6
	FSB; CBI; Chamber Wales; Wales TUC; NFU Wales; FUW
Voluntary / Community	6
	WCVA x 2; Chwarae Teg; Wales Wildlife Trust; LEADER; Groundwork
Specialist Statutory Bodies	8
Total	21

Source : WEFO website: Minutes Shadow Monitoring Committee June 2000

APPENDIX 3: PROGRAMME MONITORING COMMITTEE MEMBERSHIP

Government Actors	8	
	2 AMs; 6 WEFO Officials	
Public Sector	5	
	2 Local Authorities; 2 Government Agencies; 1 Higher Education	
Social Partners	4	
	FSB; CBI Wales; Chamber Wales; NFU Cymru	
Voluntary / Community	6	
	WCVA x 2; Chwarae Teg; Wales Wildlife Trust; LEADER; Groundwork	
Specialist Statutory Bodies	7*	
Total	30	

* These include 3 European Commission officials

Source: WEFO website: Minutes of PMC meeting 22 June 2001

CHAPTER 10

COMMUNITIES FIRST

Dave Adamson and Eilidh Johnston

During its first term, the Assembly Government placed a high priority on tackling social disadvantage through its Communities First programme. This will receive £83 million between 2002-2005 and spending will continue through the rest of the decade, making the initiative a long-term commitment. The aim is to regenerate 132 of the most disadvantaged single wards or groups of wards in Wales, and ten further 'communities of interest' spread over wider geographical areas.

The communities themselves will identify their requirements and how to achieve them, by producing a Community Action Plan. In the process they will create partnerships with statutory bodies, voluntary groups and the private sector. Capacity building forms an important part of the strategy. Each of the communities involved must produce a Capacity Building Plan which addresses their staffing, training, and infrastructure requirements.

Though *Communities First* in Wales is broadly comparable with initiatives in other parts of the UK – specifically *Neighbourhood Renewal* in England, *Social Justice* in Scotland, and *Targeting Social Need* in Northern Ireland – it is distinctive enough to warrant examination in its own right. The emphasis placed on involvement of community and voluntary representatives in the Communities First partnerships is stronger than in England or Scotland. There also appears to be less willingness to let the Welsh partnerships be controlled by local authorities. The identification of small pockets of deprivation also appears to be at a more advanced stage in Wales, with communities identified at ward and sub-ward levels, rather than at a local authority level as in England, or at postcode level in Scotland. The funding and long-term commitment offered in Wales also indicates an acceptance that tackling social exclusion will require considerable investment over time.

This chapter first examines how the idea of 'social exclusion' came to influence policy makers during the 1990s. It then examines the Welsh experience of community regeneration before analysing the development of Communities First by the Welsh Assembly Government. Finally, it highlights what was distinctive in the policy development process and assesses the impact of this 'made in Wales' policy on the National Assembly.

SOCIAL EXCLUSION

By the time of the Labour victory in 1997 the issue of poverty and disadvantage was beginning to reassert itself on the political agenda. During the Conservative years a pattern of denial had led to a policy vacuum. In the mid 1990s in Wales there was a 'hidden' poverty crisis which was being ignored not just by the Welsh Office but across the political parties as well.[1]

The landslide Labour victory effectively transformed the political climate and allowed poverty to move to the centre of the political stage. The creation of the Social Exclusion Unit in the Cabinet Office in 1997 heralded the beginning of a major policy development phase in England, with similar processes running in parallel in the devolved administrations. In England, 18 Policy Action Teams identified a range of social problems which characterised poor communities throughout Britain.[2]

The term 'social exclusion' entered the UK political lexicon via Brussels. Its increased usage in European Union policy began to establish a different understanding of poverty. With origins in French Catholic and socialist thinking,[3] the concept of social exclusion was taken up by the new Labour government. In contrast to an 'Anglo-Saxon' view of poverty, which historically has blamed the poor for their poverty, European understanding is based on analysis of structural factors such as the processes of global economic change. Poverty's existence is seen as a failing of the state rather than of the individual.

The term social exclusion also embraces the relationships the poor have with wider society. These are characterised by powerlessness, stigmatisation, lack of political participation and economic marginalisation.[4] The combined result of these experiences is social exclusion, whereby individuals, families and whole communities become unable to participate in the wider social and economic experiences of the society in which they live.

This analysis of poverty led to an emphasis being placed on 'social inclusion' to remove barriers to participation and allow poor populations access to mainstream society. The objective is to change the relationship between the poor and society. This is in contrast to the response that is confined to redressing the economic and financial disadvantages of the poor.

---

[1] Adamson, D., *Living on the Edge: Poverty and Deprivation in Wales*, Llandysul, Gomer Press, 1995.

[2] Social Exclusion Unit, *Policy Action Team report summaries: a compendium*, London, 2000.

[3] Silver, H., 'Social Exclusion and Social Solidarity: Three Paradigms', *International Labour Review* 133 (5-6), 1994, pages 531-578.

[4] Room, G., *Poverty in Europe: competing paradigms of analysis. Policy and Politics*: 23, 1995, pages 103-113; and *Poverty, policy and evaluation: lessons from Europe*. Southampton, Centre for Evaluative and Developmental Research, University of Southampton, 1998.

Conventional policy has focused on redistributing income through the welfare state benefit system. In contrast, social inclusion policies attempt to empower marginalised groups and re-establish their participation in society. They are less concerned with underlying economic disadvantage and more concerned with the social disadvantages that result in disengagement, marginalisation and disaffection.

In Britain social inclusion is envisaged as being primarily achieved by promoting participation in the labour market. An orthodoxy grew in New Labour thinking during its first term of office that it is largely exclusion from the labour market that promotes exclusion from all other aspects of society.[5] The argument was that those outside the labour market have no stake in society . Consequently, policies at the UK level focused on the creation of a 'stakeholder' society in the form of the New Deal which aimed to return the long-term unemployed to the workplace.

At the same time, there was government recognition that communities that have experienced long-term unemployment also have other problems. These include lack of basic skills and soft working skills, absence of qualifications and hard skills, and, above all, collapsed self-esteem and confidence. All are characteristic of marginalised populations and present major barriers to labour-market entry.

Poverty was also seen to be concentrated in key locations, typically large housing estates in urban peripheries.[6] In response the Policy Action Teams produced the Strategy for Neighbourhood Renewal, a programme founded on area-based regeneration projects with high community participation. Its central belief was that those experiencing social exclusion were best placed to identify their problems and propose solutions:

> *"A comprehensive regeneration programme cannot be imposed on local communities. Significant time and effort needs to go into building the capacity of local individuals and organisations so that they can be involved in the design and implementation of a programme to maximise its success. Moreover, involvement and ownership by the community is needed to sustain the improvements after time-limited programmes have ended. Where communities were not involved a number of difficulties arose".[7]*

This community model of regeneration had emerged from the experience of

---

[5] Levitas, R., 'The concept of social exclusion and the new Durkheimian hegemony', *Critical Social Policy* 16, 1996, pages 5-20.

[6] Power, A., *Area-based Poverty, Social Problems and Resident Empowerment,* Welfare State Programme Suntory-Toyota International Centre for Economics and Related Disciplines, London School of Economics, 1994.

[7] Department of Environment, Transport and the Regions, *The Strategy for Neighbourhood Renewal,* 2000.

urban regeneration policies such as the City Challenge programme and the Single Regeneration Budget, neither of which were applied to Wales. Although they were primarily property-led regeneration schemes, greater success was apparent where a community component was present.[8] The primary delivery vehicle for such actions was a multi-agency partnership bringing together public, private and voluntary sector agencies.[9] The model quickly established itself as an effective way of achieving the 'joined-up' approach the government was looking for, notwithstanding difficulties in its implementation.

The government was also seeking to replicate the advantages in regeneration associated with the burgeoning community development sector. Since the early 1990s this had created a diverse range of 'grass roots' projects that were spontaneously tackling serious social problems left untouched by the statutory agencies.[10] Faced with abandonment by public services, many communities were providing a portfolio of their own support mechanisms. By the mid-1990s many of these had multi-million pound budgets, were limited companies, or had acquired charitable status. They were providing training, housing, adult education, leisure facilities, cafes, crèches and much more. Many were trading and producing surpluses that were re-invested for community purposes. Such experiences influenced policy makers in the devolved administrations to develop their own regeneration programmes which placed an emphasis on community involvement.

EARLIER WELSH COMMUNITY REGENERATION

Policy diversion between England and Wales did not begin with the advent of the National Assembly. Regeneration processes in Wales had always differed from policies pursued in England. Thatcherism had been tempered by the realism shown by the majority of the Conservative Ministers who served as Welsh Secretary. On the whole they recognised the need to build some relationship with local government and the voluntary sector in Wales. The

---

[8] Russell, H., *A Place for the Community: Tyne and Weir Development Corporation's approach to regeneration.*, Joseph Rowntree Trust with Policy Press, 1998. Ginsburg, N., 'Putting the Social into Urban Regeneration', *Local Economy* 14(1), 1999, pages 55-71.

[9] Geddes, M., *Partnership against poverty and exclusion? Local regeneration strategies and excluded communities in the UK*, Policy Press, 1997. Carley, M. and Chapman M., et al. *Urban Regeneration through partnership. A study in nine urban regions in England, Scotland and Wales*, Policy Press and Joseph Rowntree Trust, 1997.

[10] See McArthur, A., 'Community Partnership – A Formula for Neighbourhood Regeneration in the 1990s?' *Community Development Journal* 28(4): 1993, pages 305-315; Morgan, K and Price A., *Re-Building our Communities. A New Agenda for The Valleys*, The Friedrich Ebert Foundation, 1992; and Adamson, D.L., *Social and Economic Development in Wales: the Role of Community Development*, Community Enterprise Wales, 1997

distinctive problems of the Valleys had also long been recognised. Nevertheless, by the time the National Assembly began its work successive policies had hardly scratched the surface of social deprivation in many Welsh communities.

The extent and seriousness of Welsh poverty levels in the Valleys has been documented elsewhere.[11] By the time the National Assembly of Wales inherited the problem rural poverty was also beginning to climb higher up the policy agenda. There is a polarisation of wealth and opportunity between the relatively affluent M4 and A55 corridors and their rural and post-industrial hinterlands. Along the coastal belts there is an impression of a buoyant Wales, enjoying economic recovery derived from inward investment together with a thriving service and financial sector. At the same time, however, unemployment in the hinterlands has remained consistently above the UK average. Whole populations have been unable to take advantage of new employment opportunities. During the Conservative years the expected 'trickle down' effect of growth on the coastal belts did not materialise[12] and the poverty of much of Wales remained an intractable problem. Against this backdrop a radical shift of policy away from the Welsh Development Agency's reliance on inward investment became essential.

Early policy statements from the National Assembly identified the problem. In particular, the Better Wales document highlighted three key themes that would inform the work of the Assembly Government through the whole of the first term: sustainable development, tackling disadvantage and equal opportunities.[13] All focused attention on the levels of deprivation in Wales. The argument for Objective 1 status highlighted the unfavourable comparison between Wales and the relative prosperity of much of the rest of the UK. A new Multiple Index of Poverty, commissioned from a team at Oxford University, changed the poverty map in Wales and introduced rural poverty to the political agenda. The crisis of poverty was now fully evident. Effective policies were desperately needed.

Although lacking policy development experience in many areas the Welsh civil service had already developed and implemented an earlier community regeneration scheme. Begun in 1998 the *People in Communities* initiative had

---

[11] See Adamson, D., 'Poverty and Social Exclusion in Wales Today' in Dunkerley D. T. (Ed.), *Wales Today*, University of Wales Press, 1999, pages 41-56; and Adamson D., 'Social Segregation in a Working Class Community. Economic and Social Change in the South Wales Coalfield' in Guyes G.V., Witte H.D. and Pasture P., (Eds.) *Can Class Still Unite: The Differentiated Workforce, Class Solidarity and Trade Unions.* Aldershot, Ashgate, 2001, pages 101-127.

[12] See Imrie, R.T.T., 'The Limits of property-led regeneration' in *Environment and Planning C: Government and Policy* 11, 1993, pages 87-102; Lovering, J., 'Celebrating Globalisation and Misreading the Welsh Economy: The New Regionalisim in Wales' *Contemporary Wales*, 1999, pages12-60; Boland, P.L.G., 'Regional Development Agencies: The Experience of Wales' in Bettey G.G.; and Ashgate J., (Eds.) *Regional Development Agencies and Business Change*, 2000, pages 89-108.

[13] *www.betterwales.com*, National Assembly, July 2000.

funded 16 community regeneration projects in Wales. A Social Exclusion Group of outside organisations had been established to advise the programme, including representatives from the Wales Council of Voluntary Action, the Welsh Local Government Association, Community Enterprise Wales, and a number of experienced individuals. They added to the knowledge base of the civil servants involved in the development of the policy. Originally located in the Families Division of the Welsh Office, once the Assembly was established the initiative was relocated to the Housing Division. There it was merged with expertise on housing deprivation and soon an analysis based on social exclusion and multi-dimensional poverty began to inform future policy development.

The *People In Communities* initiative successfully identified the emerging promise of community regeneration as a means to tackle social inclusion. It recognised the need for changed relationships between local authorities and communities. Phase One of the initiative, which funded eight projects, made the money conditional on partnership between local authorities and the voluntary sector.

In Phase Two, which funded a further eight projects, the lead could be taken by voluntary sector organisations. At the same time the requirement to demonstrate partnership with a local authority maintained the commitment to multi-agency working. The programme appointed co-ordinators in each locality to promote community participation at a grass roots level.

Many community organisations encountered major barriers to their development from the 'silo' character of local authority organisational structures. As a result each funded local authority had to designate a senior officer to act as a Social Exclusion Champion with the role of cutting through red tape and raising the profile of social inclusion across the range of its services. In this the programme pre-empted the 'new governance' debate which eventually moved the majority of Welsh local authorities to a Cabinet governance model.

DEVELOPING COMMUNITIES FIRST

There is no doubt that *People In Communities* was a forerunner for *Communities First*. Although not formally evaluated there was sufficient anecdotal evidence that community-based regeneration was effective in engaging excluded populations. There was also a growing academic and practice-based literature presenting favourable arguments for the promotion of community-led solutions to poverty and disadvantage.

In January 2000 a team in the Assembly Government's Housing Division was established to take the process forward. Two external advisers were appointed to provide academic support and practice-based expertise. One of the current authors (Adamson) was seconded from the University of Glamorgan, building on his participation in the development of the *People In Communities* programme and its evaluation framework. The other appointment was Barbara Castle, a community regeneration practitioner with considerable experience of regeneration issues in south Wales.

In March 2000 the National Assembly published a consultation document which outlined the core objectives of a regeneration strategy and some of the underlying principles which would inform its development.[14] In contrast to past consultations this did not set out specific policies but instead asked for advice in developing an appropriate policy model. This document launched a consultation process that would continue for nearly eighteen months. It sought opinion about how the regeneration objectives of the Assembly could be met and set out to build a consensus around the policy development process. It was recognised that a diverse range of interests existed. An effective approach would rely on bringing together the local authority and voluntary sectors which had not enjoyed a good working relationship in many parts of Wales.

Alongside the consultation a review of international best practice in community regeneration was undertaken. This drew on contemporary academic and practice-based publications to derive 32 principles that appeared to underpin successful community regeneration. Examples were drawn from Europe and the United States as well as elsewhere in the UK and Wales. It drew on similar policy development processes in England and also on the considerable output of evidence-based research emanating from the Joseph Rowntree Foundation's Neighbourhood Programme. The review provided effective guidance internally for the interpretation of submissions to the consultation process and was published in January 2001.[15]

The extent of the consultation in which the Assembly Government engaged in developing the Communities First policy was unprecedented. The initial consultation paper was released in March 2000 and accompanied by national conferences in north and south Wales. Development seminars were held in the 22 local authority areas, while the two external advisers undertook a programme of community level focus groups in all parts of Wales. Over 170 written submissions were received. Meetings were held with key agencies such

---

[14] *Communities First. Regenerating our most disadvantaged communities – a consultation paper*, Welsh Assembly Government, 2000.

[15] The National Action Plan on Poverty and Social Exclusion identified the review as an example of best practice within the UK: "... the way in which Communities First incorporates the principles into a workable programme serves as a good example of best practice for others working in community regeneration."

as the Welsh Council for Voluntary Action and the Welsh Local Government Association to establish a basis of support with key policy actors in Wales.

The immediate feedback demonstrated considerable consensus and support for the objectives outlined in the first consultation document and a surprising degree of agreement in the written submissions. There was broad support and commitment to the community regeneration approach. The main issues raised were over how it could be best achieved rather than any disagreement over its value.

This exercise led to the publication of a second consultation paper in December 2000. This outlined the main policy recommendations and sought opinion on a range of issues that had been identified in the responses to the first consultation paper. The 'hallmarks' of the Communities First approach were set out as follows:

- Community partnerships should develop and manage the process of renewal.

- Long-term "visions" for communities should be provided from within.

- Communities should produce a local delivery plan to implement their vision.

- Long-term support and funding would be provided by the Assembly Government.

- Emphasis was placed on 'capacity building' for sustainable change.

- The need for a high level 'Champion' for each community was identified.

- Each community should participate in a monitoring and evaluation scheme based on benchmarking.[16]

The programme would support the 100 most deprived communities in Wales, determined by the Multiple Index of Deprivation. The consultation paper also raised the possibility of supporting 'communities of interest', following concern over the spatial emphasis of the first consultation paper. A further 160 written submissions were received and the final proposals were tested on a national conference audience held in Builth in January 2001.

The final policy framework derived from the full consultation exercise was published as a guidance document in September 2001. This guidance document was supported by further guidance for local authorities published in July 2002.

---

[16] *Communities First. Regenerating our most disadvantaged communities – a consultation paper,* Welsh Assembly Government, December 2000, para 2.5.

PARTICIPATION

It is too soon to judge the impact of the Communities First programme.[17] A detailed evaluation programme was being commissioned by the Assembly Government in the Spring of 2003. The results of this will not be available for some years and it will probably be longer than that before any impact the programme might make on poverty statistics becomes evident. However, it is not too soon to assess the Communities First policy development process undertaken by the fledgling Welsh Assembly Government. In the first instance, its outstanding feature was the extent to which the policy makers collaborated, through consultation, with outside interests. There were three main dimensions to this:

1. The deployment of external consultants was a self-conscious strategy on the part of the Assembly Government to build a bridge with the outside policy community. In particular, the mistrust and suspicion generated within the voluntary and community sectors during 17 years of Conservative administrations at the Welsh Office had to be overcome. Both consultants had established reputations in the field and were trusted within the community and voluntary sectors. Credibility also had to be built for the innovative community-led regeneration approach to convince powerful opinion in local government that it was realistic and grounded in a reasonable body of evidence. The Review of Best Practice fulfilled this objective and gave authority to the belief that both politicians and civil servants had placed in the approach.

2. The volume of public consultation was unprecedented anywhere in the UK. Involvement of key personnel from organisations such as the Wales Council for Voluntary Action gave a channel for wide-ranging views to be expressed. Opportunities for influence were provided at community, county and regional level and written submissions were received from powerful organisations as well as ordinary individuals. The many opportunities for public engagement in the process ensured it delivered more than the token consultation that often characterises such exercises. Identified themes were presented as a thirty-three page appendix to the second consultation paper.[18]

3. This extensive consultation allowed the emergence of a consensus at each stage of the policy development cycle. Participants were able to

---

[17] See Adamson, D., *Communities First: Contemporary Community Regeneration Policy in Wales.* The Journal of Community and Development Work , 2003 (Forthcoming) for an early assessment.

[18] *Communities First. Regenerating our most disadvantaged communities – a consultation paper,* Welsh Assembly Government, 2000.

assess the influence of their previous engagement with the policy makers and were assured that the policy structure was taking their experience and professional values on board. By the time of the release of the detailed guidance document in September 2001 there was a sense of common ownership throughout the many agencies that would be involved in the delivery of Communities First. As the Assembly's Local Government and Housing Committee's review of community regeneration reported in 2002:

"Despite the diversity of organisations presenting evidence there is a clear consensus on several key issues ... The consensus also extends to agreement over key issues in the regeneration process and there has been a high degree of consistency in the written and oral presentations received."[19]

This 'participative' process has set a clear precedent for the future development of major policies in Wales. It may be a precedent that civil servants live to regret since it creates large expectations in the wider policy community, expectations which future policy makers may not be able to meet.

The highly participative approach to the writing of the Communities First programme reflects a wider trend in social policy evident in the UK as a whole. The increasing importance of a 'stakeholder' perspective in British politics is driving a more negotiated pattern of policy design and delivery. Governments are tending to operate more as a broker of views and pressures from the policy community than the originator of clear policy frameworks and principles. As one observer has described it, this:

"... emphasises the legitimate interest of citizens around the development and delivery of public services and places the focus on how citizens should be involved in debate and decisions about such services."[20]

In this emerging pattern of policy design and delivery the state by-passes traditional agencies. Instead it engages directly with and manages a complex network of relatively autonomous providers and clients. This new governance is seen to be emerging at both central and local government levels and across a range of policy arenas.[21] In the process it contributes to the social capital necessary for successful policy outcomes by creating a 'soft infrastructure' for

---

[19] National Assembly Local Government and Housing Committee, Community Regeneration Policy Review, 2002, paras 2.2 and 2.3.

[20] Sanderson, I., 'Participation and Democratic Renewal', *Policy and Politics*, 1999, 27 (3), page 326.

[21] Chandler, D., 'Active Citizens and the therapeutic state: the role of democratic participation in local government reform' *Policy and Politics*. 2001, 29(1), pages 3-14.

the emergence of collaborative policy.[22] What emerges is a 'negotiated' policy process:

> *"A focus of analytical attention is the interface between various groups and players involved in the policy process. Here the strategies of the various players, state and non-state, and how these strategies are shaped by broader social processes are of interest."*[23]

This suggests that the differing political cultures and constitutional frameworks in the devolved administrations will equally lead to a differentiation in the emergence of an 'interactive state'. The pace and nature of change is likely to diverge across the UK. It is to be expected that community development and regeneration strategies will be at the leading edge of any move to 'interactive' processes since this policy domain is underpinned by beliefs in participation, empowerment and partnership.[24]

Current policy in this area is targeted at challenging patterns of social exclusion, seen as a multi-dimensional consequence of long-term poverty. Compounded problems of high unemployment, poor housing, poor physical and mental health and low educational achievement are believed to manifest themselves in youth disaffection, low self-esteem, criminality and substance misuse.[25] Involvement of communities in the design and delivery of policy and services is seen as a necessary element of social inclusion strategy. This inevitably imposes a more interactive process of policy development:

MADE IN WALES

Communities First was the Assembly Government's first major 'made in Wales' policy. Whilst more has been made recently of the 'clear red water' approach to Welsh politics,[26] from the outset there was a strong political imperative for the Assembly's credibility for it to demonstrate that it could provide leadership and government in Wales. Communities First is a

---

[22] Pennington, M and Ryden, Y., 'Researching social capital in local environmental policy contexts', *Policy and Politics* 2000, 28(2) page 234.

[23] O'Donovan, O., 'Re-theorising the interactive state: reflections on a popular participatory initiative in Ireland', *Community Development Journal*, 2000, 35(3) page 227.

[24] Adamson, D (2001). Social Segregation in a Working Class Community. Economic and Social Change in the South Wales Coalfield. *Can Class Still Unite. The Differentiated Workforce, Class Solidarity and Trade Unions.* GV Guyes, HD Witte and P Pasture. Aldershot, Ashgate: 101-127.

[25] Adamson, D (1999). Poverty and Social Exclusion in Wales Today. *Wales Today.* DT Dunkerley, A. Cardiff, University of Wales Press: 41-56

[26] Rhodri Morgan, speech to the National Centre for Public Policy, University of Wales, Swansea, December 2002.

powerful example of devolved powers being used to create an innovative social policy which is subject to some envy in the community regeneration sector in England.

Whilst the consultation process did not produce the policy quickly, it did clearly establish that the Assembly Government was developing policy independently, in partnership with the Welsh public. Whilst the policy falls within a broad UK approach to area and community-based regeneration (for instance, there are clear similarities with the New Deal for Communities in England) there is sufficient difference to mark it out as a specifically Welsh policy. In particular, Communities First can be distinguished from other approaches by its commitment to long-term funding, the clear community component of the partnerships and the smaller-scale spatial pattern of delivery.

At the same time there were some casualties as a result of the pursuit of a distinctive Welsh agenda. One was the failure to adequately incorporate the Policy Action Team reports into the Communities First portfolio. Some of the valuable lessons derived from the extensive research which fed into these reports has been effectively lost to Welsh policy. There is also a danger that too firm a commitment to Welsh policy development can lead to isolation and a failure to incorporate best practice from other UK initiatives.

Nevertheless, Communities First demonstrated the ability of the Welsh civil service to develop major social policy without the support of their counterparts in Whitehall. Whilst in the early stages of the policy development process there was limited availability of personnel who were familiar with the community regeneration and voluntary sector, the civil service team quickly developed appropriate expertise and knowledge.

A more fundamental challenge came in the second year when an internal re-organisation to create a Communities Directorate resulted in an almost complete change of personnel in a period of several weeks. Whilst the speed with which the new staff gained sufficient expertise was exemplary, the episode raised questions about the continued viability of the civil service belief in the 'generalist' civil servant. Civil servants are expected to move between departments to acquire a range of skills and knowledge. For many external agencies this raises a major difficulty of constantly working with Assembly contacts that are learning their new role. Few stay in a single position long enough to be recognised externally as expert. Whilst this may have been acceptable in the purely administrative days of the former Welsh Office, it has major consequences for the quality of policy development in the context of democratic devolution.

A final reflection is on the response of Communities First to the large place that the concept of community occupies in Welsh politics and culture.

Whether in rural Wales or the urban Valleys, the role of place is extremely powerful in constructing Welsh identity. A policy so centred on the notion of community simultaneously responds to this cultural attribute and recognises the need to address poverty at a community level.

The impact of economic change in Wales has been enormous. Whilst it is experienced at both individual and family level it is the community experiences of unemployment, social decline, rising crime and decaying housing that have formed the most powerful images in Wales in the last decade. Poverty has been seen as a challenge to a way of life and to core cultural values. The growing awareness of crime, disaffection, drug use and anti-social behaviour has been seen as a challenge to a 'traditional' way of life based in mutuality, self-help, and cohesive communities. That traditional way of life may be based on a myth of a 'golden age', but nonetheless it has mobilised a process of policy development and provided a consensus that would be hard to replicate in any other policy area. It is illustrative of the powerful attachment to community that transcends the political divide in Wales. Whether it proves to be a substantive enough basis for a policy to eradicate poverty remains to be seen.

PART 3

POLITICAL
PARTIES

CHAPTER 11

LABOUR

Gerald Taylor

If any organisation can claim to have determined how devolution came to Wales, it is the Labour party. In the 1979 referendum, attacks by Labour MPs rebelling against their party's position ensured that the Assembly proposed at that time would not win support. In 1997 such opposition was not repeated and in its absence, the narrow victory for the Yes campaign was achieved.[1] The main reason for the change was the intervening period, in which a succession of Conservative governments had come to be seen as lacking legitimacy in Wales.[2]

By 1997 Labour Party opinions on devolution had altered but were still not unanimous. While an Assembly might be preferable to a Conservative government, was it better than Labour rule from Westminster? The party never resolved this question, either in the 1997 general election or the subsequent referendum. Nonetheless, Labour emerged as the largest Group in the Assembly, and albeit in partnership with the Liberal Democrats following the Coalition in October 2000, its guiding hand.

As an institution the Assembly has certainly left its mark on the Labour party, and not just the Welsh Labour party. The experience of managing relationships between Westminster and Cardiff Bay, and of running Wales in a radically different political context, all had their effect. At the same time, whether Labour had done enough to establish the Assembly in the hearts and minds of the people of Wales remained an open question as the first term drew to a close.

BAD BEGINNINGS

The election of Welsh Secretary, Ron Davies, as Welsh Labour leader in September 1998 suggested a smooth transition to devolution could take place. Bridges had, indeed, to be built, candidates selected and a manifesto pulled

---

[1] See J. Barry Jones (Ed.) 'The "No" Campaign: Division and Diversity' in J. Barry Jones and Denis Balsom (Ed.) *The Road to the National Assembly for Wales*, University of Wales Press, Cardiff, 2000, pages 84-5.

[2] Ron Davies, *Devolution A Process not an Event*, IWA, 1999, page 5.

together. Yet for the most part mechanisms were in place and the road ahead appeared clear. That was until 27 October when Ron Davies became the:

> "... *first Cabinet Minister ever to resign for not having done anything wrong.*"[3]

The immediate problem facing the party in the aftermath of Ron Davies' 'moment of madness' on Clapham Common, was the selection of his replacement. This prompted the 'New' Labour government in Westminster to sanction some 'Old' Labour practices in the months leading up to the second leadership election. If the first leadership election between Ron Davies and Rhodri Morgan in 1998 had been bruising, it paled into insignificance when compared with the second campaign in early 1999, between Morgan and Alun Michael.[4]

Michael's victory led to a widespread perception that he had been imposed by the Labour party machine and backed by the London government against the wishes of Welsh Labour activists. This was hardly a glorious start to the first Assembly election campaign. However, this was not the only example of what were perceived as old Labour-style deals, stitch-ups and backroom fixing. Apparently well-laid plans dealing with candidate selection and the manifesto were blown significantly off course by events in the months before the Assembly election.

The party's élite saw the new institution as offering a fresh start to introduce selection procedures that would encourage candidates from outside the normal channels and orbits. Rather pretentiously this was justified as an attempt to fill the Assembly with the best talent in Wales. It also reflected a desire to avoid the Assembly becoming packed with Labour local councillors seeking a more secure political career or party workers rewarded for their endeavours. The fear that this might be the case pandered to the perceptions of many in London, and some in Wales, that not only was patronage endemic to the Welsh Labour Party, but that its local councillors were also generally poor in quality.

The selection of women was another issue. It emerged as a result of Labour's success in achieving an historically high proportion of successful women candidates in the 1997 General Election. This naturally fuelled a wish that the success be emulated in the National Assembly elections.

These two objectives were pursued by different means. The first prompted the creation of a closed list of approved candidates. The list was compiled by a rigorous and well thought-through procedure that involved candidates being ranked against a set of criteria. This was based on an application form and an

---

[3] Patrick Hannan *Wales Off Message: From Clapham Common to Cardiff Bay*, Seren, 2000, page 14.

[4] For an inside view see Paul Flynn *Dragons Led by Poodles*, Politico's, 1999.

interview with a selection panel. On the whole, it was widely seen to be a fair process and led to the approval of a list of 151 hopefuls by August 1998. However, this judgement was overturned for many by the actions of the appeals panel. It granted the appeals of twelve members, but provided no apparent reason nor any obvious criteria for allowing candidates back on to the list. It was widely observed that though some of these candidates had failed on the criteria initially set by the panel, they had strong personal connections within the party.

The integrity of the process was further dented by the re-opening of the panel in November 1998 to allow the candidature of Alun Michael. Now that he was seeking the Welsh party leadership, he needed an Assembly seat in order to become First Secretary. His eventual selection at the head of the list for Mid and West Wales, did nothing to lessen suggestions of fixing and stitch-ups.[5]

Women candidates were promoted through a process of 'twinning', which paired two constituencies so that one would select a male candidate and the other a female. The decision on who was to fight in which constituency was left until after the selection process itself.[6] Opponents argued that constituency 'sovereignty' was being eroded, with four constituencies - Blaenau Gwent, Cynon Valley, Islwyn and Llanelli - threatening to fund legal action against the device, and then being threatened themselves with an imposed selection by the Welsh Labour party. Two of the constituencies, Islwyn and Llanelli, were to fall to Plaid Cymru during the Assembly election, as was Cynon Valley's neighbour, Rhondda. The eventual result of the Labour selection was a gender balanced, public sector weighted list of candidates, eventually announced in November 1998. The constituency selections then rumbled on until well into February 1999, leaving only a few months before the election itself.

The party's manifesto became another victim of Labour's leadership woes. Welsh Office Minister Peter Hain had presented a draft manifesto for discussion on the day of Ron Davies' election as Welsh Party leader. However, this was rapidly engulfed in the events which followed. The party's final manifesto, written by Welsh Labour party officials following a truncated consultation process, only appeared on 14 April 1999, three weeks before polling day.[7]

In essence, Labour, the deliverer of devolution and overwhelmingly elected in a General Election two years earlier, appeared before the Welsh electorate in May 1999 as a party in disarray. Its leader bore all the hallmarks of

---

[5] *Ibid.*

[6] For a discussion of the twinning process see Julia Edwards and Christine Chapman, 'Women's Political Representation in Wales: Waving or Drowning?' *Contemporary Politics* Vol. 6, no. 4, 2000.

[7] See Kevin Morgan and Geoff Mungham, *Redesigning Democracy: The making of the Welsh Assembly,* Seren, 2000., pp. 173ff.

having been imposed by London and machine politics. Its candidates were tainted by controversies over their selection process. Many of its constituency parties were divided. Finally, it had a manifesto which had been hastily brought together and published with minimal consultation. Considering all this, the result might be thought of as something of a victory. Certainly commentators, not least within the party itself, came to see Labour's poor showing as being a direct result of the damage done by Alun Michael's leadership campaign and the perception that he had been imposed from London.

TAKING CHARGE

To say that the results of the election were a disappointment to the Welsh Labour party would be a massive understatement. In the constituency seats it polled 37.6 per cent of the vote, matching its performance in the disastrous General Election of 1983. In the regional lists, where voters were supposedly voting for parties rather than candidates, it fared slightly worse. The one seat it did win on the list, Alun Michael's in Mid and West Wales, was only possible because of the party's poor performance in the constituencies, in particular Llanelli where it lost to Plaid Cymru.

The fact that Labour's major rival at the UK level, the Conservatives, also substantially under performed, and that the Liberal Democrats only managed to replicate their disappointing General Election performance, was completely overshadowed by the phenomenal success of Plaid Cymru. With 28.4 per cent of the vote it practically trebled its 1997 General Election performance and won seats which had previously been safe Labour constituencies. While Labour won 27 of the 40 constituency seats, and a single list seat, this left them three short of a majority in the Assembly.[8]

These results provided a considerable culture shock for the party, particularly at the local level. It probably helped bring in a new generation of parliamentary candidates who had not been part of the 'favoured son' system so prevalent in the Valleys. They included Huw Iranca Davies in Ogmore, and Chris Bryant in the Rhondda.

Within the Assembly it meant Labour had to govern as a minority administration, a novel experience. A majority of the Labour Group (16) were women, some of them selected because they were not 'typical' politicians. Many had to create a new political institution and develop their skills and understanding of politics 'on the job'. Some possessed experience at

---

[8] See *The Wales Yearbook 2001*, Aberystwyth, Francis Balsom Associates, 2000, pages 33 and 179.

Westminster or at local government level, including a majority in Alun Michael's first Cabinet. In this context the worst possible leader to have chosen was one who gave the impression that he was a reluctant AM. Temperamentally he was unsuited to the notion of 'inclusive politics' that was current, tending always to dominate decision-making.

This is not to say that Michael did not have many virtues as Wales's first First Secretary. He was hard-working, diligent, and embedded in the Welsh Labour party. His Cabinet attempted to achieve a regional balance, including AMs from north and west Wales. Unfortunately, this meant the Cabinet had a distinctly 'old' Labour feel. It was male led and included individuals well placed in their local party communities. However, they were hardly representative of the mould-breaking type of personality that the party's selection process had aimed at producing. In addition, Michael's insistence on running the show in a very personal way, wanting to see every piece of paper and be party to every decision, meant that few of his Cabinet were able to establish themselves as independent personalities. He gave them only limited opportunities to develop the skills and responsibilities of ministerial government.

This approach excluded much of his own party as well as other parties, in a body that was designed as a 'corporate' entity charged with 'inclusiveness'. At the outset Michael refused to countenance a coalition with the Liberal Democrats whose early offer was rejected out of hand. All of this led to an initial period when the minority Administration was more concerned with obtaining a majority on each particular vote than with developing a programme for government. Strategic politics became virtually impossible. The widespread feeling of stagnation and drift that resulted was only resolved by Michael's forced departure in February 2000, less than a year after the Assembly's creation.

Ironies abound in Labour's role in the National Assembly. A leader promoted in the party by the supporters of New Labour, not least Tony Blair himself, operated politically in a way that greatly resembled Wales's 'old' Labour mechanisms. In short order he was replaced by a leader who, although denounced as inveterate 'old' Labour, managed to build a Cabinet that represented the inclusive and 'meritocratic' virtues supposedly advocated by New Labour. Another irony was the fact that Alun Michael, who as the Prime Minister's choice was seen as the ideal candidate to guarantee Westminster co-operation, was brought down as a result of the Treasury's refusal to grant 'match funding' to support the Objective 1 programme.[9]

These events came to a head with the vote of no confidence in Alun Michael

---

[9] For an extended argument along these lines see Patrick Hannan, *op cit*, pp. 72ff.

on 9 February 2000. It prompted one of the strangest pieces of political theatre of the first term, played out before an eager press in the Assembly and the House of Commons. With little or no consultation, Michael decided to hand a letter of resignation to the Presiding Officer during the debate, thereby aiming to forestall a vote of no confidence. This would perhaps have allowed him to be re-nominated as First Secretary, as he would not have been formally removed by a vote.[10] Meanwhile, Tony Blair was answering parliamentary questions in London, apparently ignorant of Michael's intentions until a Conservative backbencher alerted him. In the event, the Presiding Officer, Plaid Cymru's Lord Elis-Thomas, decided not to read Michael's letter of resignation. Instead he allowed the vote to proceed, so frustrating Michael's manoeuvre.

Alun Michael's short tenure as First Secretary and his departure from Cardiff Bay back to Westminster, raised questions of party loyalty within the Assembly's Labour Group. To a large extent, his predicament stemmed from lukewarm support among his backbenchers. Once the motion of no confidence was passed, the majority of Labour AMs deserted him. They were, in fact, torn between loyalties in at least three different directions: between their own Administration and the wider Assembly, between the Assembly and Westminster, and between the party in Wales and the party in the UK as a whole. These fissures could not be resolved on the basis of one issue or event, even one of the magnitude of Michael's ignominious exit from the Assembly. Nonetheless, Welsh Labour activists have not always taken their lead from the UK party. More than once Labour Governments in Westminster have found themselves in conflict with Labour councils in Wales. In general, however, the importance of these dilemmas is that they are pushing Welsh Labour in the direction of seeking greater autonomy for the Assembly.

POWER SHARING

Though they were low key and did not grab the headlines, early changes initiated by Rhodri Morgan as Labour's new First Secretary were significant. His appointment of Sue Essex to the Cabinet gave it a female majority, reflecting that of the Labour Group itself. He also created three Deputy Minister posts extending front bench experience to a broader range of the Labour Group. Within a few months, too, he had appointed four special advisers to support the Cabinet and oversee policy development. Meanwhile, at its Llandudno Spring conference in March the party re-branded itself as

---

[10] Michael later said the manoeuvre was to ensure that only Labour party members would have a hand in deciding who should be the Labour First Secretary.

'Welsh Labour: the true party of Wales', a move clearly aimed at contesting the perceived threat from Plaid Cymru.

Despite these changes Labour's underlying problem of operating as a minority Administration within the Assembly remained. This was only resolved by the launch of the 'partnership' coalition with the Liberal Democrats in October 2000.[11] Not surprisingly the coalition created problems for the Labour party on a number of fronts. An immediate cause of dissension was the changes to the Cabinet that the coalition required, in particular the offer of two Cabinet posts to the Liberal Democrats. These were two steps too far for many in the Labour party. Resentment was also stoked up by the fact that while the Liberal Democrats called a special party Conference to agree the coalition, Labour's involvement was merely rubber stamped by the Welsh Labour Executive Committee. Irritation was also caused by the Liberal Democrats' claim that the bulk of the Partnership Agreement reflected their policies. This prompted Labour to publish a pamphlet that traced the policy options agreed back to Labour's 1999 manifesto.[12]

Power sharing also meant a complete restructuring of the Cabinet. Tom Middlehurst, Peter Law and Rosemary Butler, were replaced by the Liberal Democrat leader, Mike German, and his colleague, Jenny Randerson, with Jane Davidson being promoted as a new Labour Minister. This left just four survivors from Alun Michael's original Cabinet of May 1999: Rhodri Morgan himself, Andrew Davies, Edwina Hart and Jane Hutt.[13] Throwing three ministers overboard in a Labour Group of 28 created a potential focus for backbench dissent. Yet despite some public criticisms by Law this has not happened, largely because of the benefits the coalition has brought in getting business through the Assembly.

The reshuffle also ended any pretence of regional balance within the Cabinet, a fact recognised in Morgan's adoption of ministerial responsibility for north Wales. In addition, the number of Deputy Ministers was increased from three to five, with one being allocated to a Liberal Democrat, Peter Black, as shadow to Finance and Communities Minister Edwina Hart. This last appointment was resented by the Labour elements in the Welsh Local Government Association, who found the relationship between the Labour Minister and her Liberal Democrat Deputy difficult to understand. But this grievance was overshadowed by the Partnership Agreement's commitment to appoint a

---

[11] The agreement was set out in a 25-page document *Putting Wales First: A Partnership for the People of Wales*, published on 6 October. For an outline of the ground rules of the coalition and the agreed policies see 'The Coalition Government' in John Osmond (Ed.) *Coalition Politics Come to Wales: Monitoring the National Assembly September to December 2000*, IWA, 2000.

[12] *The Partnership Agreement and the Labour Party Manifesto*, Welsh Labour Party, 2000.

[13] Sue Essex had been promoted immediately after Rhodri Morgan became First Minister, while Carwyn Jones replaced Christine Gwyther as Minister for Rural Affairs in July 2000.

Commission to consider the introduction of proportional representation in local government. Predictably, however, the eventual Commission, chaired by Professor Eric Sunderland, former Vice Chancellor, University of Wales, Bangor, was unable to come to a unanimous agreement on the central point of proportional representation for local government elections.[14]

NEW WAYS OF WORKING

In the wake of the Assembly Labour has developed new policy structures to ensure wider party debate on the content of its Welsh manifesto. These are based on the newly created Welsh Policy Forum, Policy Commissions and Welsh Joint Policy Committee, paralleling the UK Policy Forum structures that developed the 2001 General Election manifesto. Welsh Policy Forum papers were debated at Welsh Labour's annual conference at Llandudno in 2002, leading to the pre-manifesto document *Labour's Priorities for Wales* in early 2003.

Following these changes the Assembly has had a significant impact on Labour's Welsh policy-making process. This is now separated from the UK policy system in an entirely different way from the English regions. The former policy-making role of the Welsh Labour Party Executive Committee has been largely supplanted by the Welsh Joint Policy Committee The latter is now the dominant body in Labour's policy-making for the National Assembly.[15]

In addition, reforms to the selection process have ensured that all candidates are 'endorsed' by a vote of party members in their constituency. The main mechanism has been the adoption of an affirmative nomination process. If sitting Labour AMs wished to remain and received the nominations of more than 50 per cent of the party units in their constituency they are deemed to have been selected. At the time of writing none who had been through this process had failed to be reselected.[16]

Following this process the party was left with 16 vacancies: the 13 first-past-the-post seats they failed to win in 1999, and three additional resulting from

---

[14] See Denis Balsom, 'A Report destined for the Long Grass', IWA, *Agenda*, Summer 2002.

[15] For a fuller outline of the new processes see Gerald Taylor, 'Welsh Labour's Expanding Policy Process', *Agenda*, IWA, Summer 2002, pages 23-6.

[16] However, in early 2003 re-selection loomed for Deputy Presiding Officer John Marek, Labour's Wrexham AM, despite his affirmative nomination. This arose from disciplinary hearings that were due to be arranged following complaints by the ruling Labour Group on the local council that he had brought the party into disrepute. Marek was offered an opportunity to forestall the disciplinary process by standing again for affirmative nomination. This he lost, triggering a selection process in Wrexham in which he remained eligible to stand.

retirement. It was calculated that six needed to agree all-women shortlists to ensure a gender balance of candidates. These were agreed through negotiations between the constituency parties and Welsh Labour Party officials. Finally, the list selections were circumvented by the simple means of using already selected constituency candidates to fill the list positions.[17]

A noticeable aspect of the closing months of the first term was the re-ordering of relationships with Westminster, most visibly through the replacement of Paul Murphy as Secretary of State for Wales by Peter Hain. While Murphy is a quiet and careful negotiator, Hain has a much stronger political image and is more at ease in the public eye. Whether this new dynamic will provide a fresh impetus or create greater tensions in the relationship between Cardiff Bay and Westminster remains to be seen. Undoubtedly, one of the major resentments Labour MPs have felt towards the Assembly has been the media attention it has attracted, which many feel has been at their expense. It is worth watching whether Hain's stronger media image will enable Labour's Welsh MPs to regain some of this lost ground.

There have been attempts to improve communication links between the Assembly's Labour Group and the Welsh Parliamentary Labour Party, for instance joint meetings to conduct pre-legislative scrutiny of new policy proposals. However, these efforts have been hampered by the logistical problems of organising meetings.

There have also been other attempts to mobilise collaboration at the constituency level. A good example is the Valleys Forward initiative, aimed at bringing together Valleys MPs and AMs. This organised a fringe meeting at the Welsh Labour Party's Annual Conference in 2002 which was addressed by an AM, MP and an MEP. Nonetheless, there has been little involvement by AMs in the organisation which has been largely promoted by MPs. Valleys Forward did stimulate a response in the form of a North Wales Group, but so far this forum is solely for MPs.

'CLEAR RED WATER'

With the Assembly elections approaching, the party felt it necessary to re-affirm the autonomy of the Welsh Labour Party and the Labour Group in the Assembly. In large part this took the form of Labour leadership at Westminster and Cardiff acknowledging that devolution meant the opportunity to do things differently. So, for example, Tony Blair's statement

---

[17] A complicating factor was the desire to promote ethnic minority candidates by including one such candidate on each regional list. Party endorsement was obtained by tagging a vote for five such candidates on to the ballot papers for the selection of the party's European election candidates.

in his 2002 October party conference speech that schooling was entering a 'post-comprehensive era' immediately drew a disclaimer from First Minister Rhodri Morgan. He was Prime Minister in Wales as far as schools and hospitals were concerned, he said, and he would never use the phrase 'post-comprehensive' to describe the Welsh education system. And he added that there was no demand in Wales for alternative selective secondary schools, such as city technology colleges.

Similarly, following the Queen's Speech in November, the First Minister distanced himself from the notion of foundation hospitals, making it clear that the 'consumerist' agenda being pursued by the government in England had little relevance in Wales. He said that University top-up fees would also be rejected as unsuited to Welsh needs:

> *"We are neither going down the foundation hospital route nor the top-up fees route. We are still for universal provision rather than a variation of provision."[18]*

And he forecast that divergences between Cardiff and London on such issues would widen over the years:

> *"That is what devolution is all about."[19]*

In this he was echoing an acknowledgement made by Prime Minister Blair at the Labour Conference that differences between public services in the two countries were the inevitable result of devolution. Asked whether he was now effectively premier for England on these matters Blair responded:

> *"I agree with him [Rhodri Morgan] that the Welsh health service and schools are matters for the Assembly and the Welsh executive. If people in Wales want to do it in a different way they can – and it will be the people of Wales that will be the judge of that."[20]*

Rhodri Morgan's views on foundation hospitals and top-up fees were underlined by his Ministers the following week. Health Minister Jane Hutt declared:

> *"The foundation hospital programme is a policy being pursued in England, not in Wales. Foundation hospitals are not part of our reforms here in Wales. We want an NHS based on co-operation between hospitals, not competition."[21]*

Education Minister Jane Davidson said:

---

[18] Guardian, 15 November 2002.

[19] *Ibid.*

[20] Western Mail, 4 October 2002.

[21] Assembly *Record*, 19 November 2002

"I do not believe we should have fees in advance of receiving an education at higher education level because that is a disincentive and what we want to do is create incentives. I do not see it as an issue benefiting our sector in Wales when one of our biggest agendas is about widening participation. The issue about up-front student fees does not just put off those who would have to pay them, it puts off those who don't have to pay them in large numbers as well."[22]

In his address to the National Assembly on the Westminster Queen's Speech in November, the newly appointed Secretary of State for Wales Peter Hain acknowledged, and endorsed, these differences:

"The Assembly Cabinet has made it clear that you will not follow the same path as the Government intends pursuing in England by, for example, the creation of foundation hospitals. Why should this be a problem? It is devolution in action. That is why we campaigned so hard to win that referendum: to enable the people of Wales to meet the different needs and values of our nation in different ways from England."[23]

However, the clearest statement of this position was articulated by the First Minister in what became known as his 'Clear Red Water' address at Swansea University in December 2002. This set out his aspirations for the Assembly's second term, emphasising the philosophical distinctiveness of Welsh Labour from New Labour. The most quoted passage reiterated his opposition to Foundation hospitals:

"… our commitment to equality leads directly to a model of the relationship between the government and the individual which regards that individual as a citizen rather than as a consumer. Approaches which prioritise choice over equality of outcome rest, in the end, upon a market approach to public services, in which individual economic actors pursue their own best interests with little regard for wider considerations … My objection to the idea of Foundation Hospitals within the NHS is not simply that they will be accessed by those public service consumers who are already the most articulate and disadvantaged, and who can specify where they want to be treated, but that the experiment will end, not with patients choosing hospitals, but with hospitals choosing patients. The well-resourced producer will be choosing the well-resourced consumer as the kind of patient they want – the grammar school equivalent in hospitals."[24]

---

[22] Western Mail, 20 November 2002.

[23] Assembly *Record*, 26 November 2002

[24] Rhodri Morgan, Speech to the National Centre for Public Policy, University of Wales, Swansea, 11 December 2002.

CONTINUING DIFFICULTIES

The Assembly has had an enormous impact on the Welsh Labour party. Its failure to win an overall majority in the 1999 Assembly elections coupled with the debacle of the Alun Michael leadership election, fundamentally altered Welsh Labour's relationship with the UK party. It is difficult to imagine that Tony Blair and Rhodri Morgan would be going quite so far to publicly distance themselves from each other in terms of policy if the 1999 result had been different. Indeed, if a majority had been secured then Alun Michael would still been in place as First Secretary and it is unlikely he would have recast himself as First Minister. What this would have done for the public image of the Assembly is difficult to assess. However, it is unlikely for example, that the profile of Labour Ministers such as Carwyn Jones, Jane Davidson, and Edwina Hart, would have developed in the way they have. The failure to achieve a majority also led to the coalition and the need for UK Ministers to negotiate with Welsh Liberal Democrats over policy and legislation.

At the same time the ability to lay the blame for electoral failure at the door of internal party conflicts has masked wider problems Labour is facing. It is by no means clear, for instance, that Plaid Cymru's performance in 1999 was solely due to Labour's problems in Wales. Surveys suggest that Plaid's performance reflects a feeling among Welsh voters that they are more relevant at Assembly level than they are at Westminster level.[25] In addition, while Blair has been an electorally successful politician in the UK as a whole, the fall in turnout and lack of enthusiasm for Labour in 1999 and in the 2001 general election in Wales suggests that he is not necessarily a popular one. UK policies have not been wholeheartedly embraced by Labour, or floating, voters in Wales. The fact that Morgan wishes to distance himself from the Blair government suggests that Welsh Labour is conscious that too strong an association may be a vote loser. However, it remains to be seen whether such a separation will appear credible to Welsh voters.

Labour's local party organisation in Wales has also suffered. The leadership contests and candidate selection rows leading up to the 1999 Assembly elections, the shock of losing key seats and councils, such as Rhondda Cynon Taf, to Plaid control, had an effect on local morale and organisation. Most significantly, the 'new politics' forced by devolution have eroded the traditional forms of paternalism and patronage which have been a main feature of Labour party organisation in Wales. In one sense this is no bad thing and was occurring anyway as a result of the decline of the traditional

---

[25] See the Assembly Electoral Study, Institute of Welsh Politics, University of Wales, Aberystwyth, reported in Agenda, IWA, Summer 2000.

industrial base, particularly in south Wales. It was a stated intention of Labour's candidate selection procedures for the first Assembly elections to select a different type of candidate. Labour leaders such as Ron Davies articulated an aspiration to establish a 'new' politics.[26] However, little attention has been given to the effect this has had on the party's grass roots party organisation.

The culture shock of the loss of key seats in the 1999 election has had a sobering effect on local parties, particularly in Valleys seats where it was reinforced by significant local council losses to Plaid Cymru. Nonetheless, the parlous and declining state of the party's organisation in many areas of Wales, in terms of membership, finance and organisational integrity, may have real implications for the campaign the party is able to muster for the May 2003 Assembly elections.

Of course, one reason why Welsh Labour has a history of paternalistic and patronage politics is because of the intimate nature of Welsh politics. If anything the arrival of the Assembly has reinforced this intimacy. For senior Welsh politicians and party organisers, dealing with 40 constituencies and 22 unitary local authorities is a far cry from the prospect facing a Minister or senior party official in England having to deal with hundreds of organisations. Moreover, the Labour Group of 28 AMs resounds to completely different dynamics compared with the 400-plus Parliamentary Labour Party.

One consequence is that a hectoring political style is less likely to obtain results in Wales. It also makes internal political intrigues far more difficult to pursue or to bring to fruition, no doubt to the considerable disappointment of the many journalistic observers of the Assembly. This has tended to create a distance between Labour politicians in the Assembly and in Westminster. The potential for collaborative policy development and political activity have not been fully realised on either side. While some MPs have seen this as an introverted trend in Assembly politics, AMs have not fully grasped the concerns of their parliamentary colleagues.

This dislocation between Labour's MPs and AMs has been exacerbated by the fact that contact between them is restricted to Ministerial negotiations or constituency issues. While the fact that all but one of Labour's AMs were elected as constituency representatives has strengthened the links between themselves and their Westminster counterparts, this has focused the relationship on local issues and constituency postbags rather than on wider political and policy discussions. How this will play out if the Assembly Government really does create 'clear red water' between itself and the Blair government is impossible to guess. It is noteworthy, however, that some MPs

---

[26] See Chapter 15 in this volume.

are already concerned about the differences in policy outcomes between England and Wales in areas such as health care and over policies such as PFI.[27] How will constituency postbags impact on such concerns as diverse policies develop, and to what extent will voters punish, or be perceived to punish, Welsh Labour MPs for the perceived failings of the Assembly, or AMs for those of Westminster?

CONCLUSION

For Labour, devolution has been dominated by the personalities of its leaders and the relationships between them. The relations of first Alun Michael, and then Rhodri Morgan, with the Prime Minister, Tony Blair, were crucial to the events of the opening years of the National Assembly. As we have seen they did much to ensure, first Alun Michael's election as First Secretary and subsequently his downfall. Perhaps helped by his period as Alun Michael's Economic Development Secretary and his willingness to remain loyal to the Michael cause, Morgan was able to establish his credentials as a 'safe' pair of hands in Welsh politics.

The character of Paul Murphy, the Secretary of State for Wales for most of the first term, as a negotiator and well respected behind-the-scenes politician also served well in this regard. The arrival of Peter Hain as Murphy's replacement offers a very different prospect for the future of a more dynamic and public relationship. But it also needs to be remembered that British government is departmentally based. The different personalities and personal politics of individual Ministers, particularly in Westminster but to some extent at Cardiff as well, can have a big impact on outcomes.

The National Assembly has presented Labour with as many questions and dilemmas as it has resolutions. Many of these have been of Labour's own making. Even so, devolution was always going to raise the fundamental question of the relationship between the party in Wales and the party in the UK. The development of this relationship is not entirely in Labour's own hands. It depends crucially on the perception and reactions of voters in Wales to the performance of Labour in government at Westminster and Cardiff Bay.

---

[27] See Jon Owen Jones (Labour MP for Cardiff Central), 'The Price of Saying No', IWA, *Agenda* Winter 2002/03.

CHAPTER 12

LIBERAL DEMOCRATS

Alys Thomas

The Welsh Liberal Democrats have, in a curious way, emerged as both losers and winners in the first term of the National Assembly. On the one hand, they picked up fewer seats than hoped in the first elections in May 1999 and fared badly in the second preference votes.[1] The six-strong Liberal Democrat Group was the smallest in the Assembly. On the other hand, their entry into coalition with Labour in the Autumn of 2000 saw them become partners in Government with two Ministers in the Cabinet.

This chapter will examine how devolution and the entry into coalition in October 2000 has impacted on the Welsh Liberal Democrats in terms of representation, their organisation in the Assembly, the party's organisation and policy-making machinery, and its electoral prospects.

A FEDERAL PARTY

As part of a federal party with a commitment to proportional representation the Liberal Democrats found it easier to adapt to the new devolved politics than other Britain-wide parties. Indeed, in the first elections the party presented itself as the true party of devolution. This was in contrast to what it declared to be a separatist Plaid Cymru, 'oppositionist' Conservatives and a Welsh Labour Party subordinate to London.

The advent of devolution can be said to have "brought the [Liberal Democrat] Constitution to life".[2] The Party has a federal structure, comprising the three 'State' parties for Scotland, Wales and England. The Federal Party is responsible for the preparation of UK-wide policy, Parliamentary elections and fund-raising. The 'State parties' separately are responsible for the operation of local parties, selection procedures for prospective parliamentary candidates and membership issues. They also deal with policy matters relating specifically to their 'State', although English policy-making powers have been

---

[1] A Thomas, 'The Liberal Democrats: Losing to Win', *Contemporary Wales*, Vol.14., 2001. pp.121-126.

[2] Interview with Chris Lines, Chief Executive of Liberal Democrats Wales and Head of Assembly Group Office, Cardiff Bay, 10 September 2002.

passed up to the Federal party.[3] Two representatives from the Welsh party sit on the Federal Policy Committee as of right, and Welsh party members can also stand for election to the Committee. Its determinations must then pass through the Federal Conference before becoming official party policy.

The Welsh Liberal Democrats were founded in 1988, although the genealogy of the party can be traced back further to the creation of a distinct Welsh Liberal Party in the 1960s. The main organs of the party in Wales are the Conference, National Executive and Policy Committee which has the responsibility under the constitution of producing Welsh manifestos. There are other key committees concerned with Campaigns and Elections, Finance and Administration, and Candidates. The basic unit of local organisation is a single constituency, known as the Local Party which is responsible for selecting Parliamentary and local government candidates. Parliamentary candidates must be drawn from a list of approved candidates, drawn up by the Welsh Party. In September 2001 the party's membership stood at 2,800.

The experience of devolution led to a review of some internal processes. In the run up to the Assembly elections in 1999 the Policy Committee had taken on the role of policy development. However, once the Assembly was up and running a 'major operational weakness' was identified in the fact that, of the AMs, only Mike German sat on the Policy Committee, and then in an *ex officio* capacity. It was judged that this was hampering a co-ordinated approach to policy development. As a result a number of Policy Development Groups were established, each involving an Assembly Member, which would present policy proposals to the Policy Committee.[4]

The Welsh party headquarters had been upgraded after 1992, becoming a full-time office with a party manager.[5] The advent of devolution naturally required a further review of the staffing at headquarters and in 1998 Chris Lines was appointed Chief Executive, with responsibility for party organisation, staff and resources. Since May 1999 he has combined these with a role as Head of the Group Office within the Assembly itself, co-ordinating the Liberal Democrat research staff and chairing group meetings.

Before devolution and up until 2001, the Leadership of the Welsh Party was held by Richard Livsey, MP for Brecon and Radnor. However, with the advent of devolution the constitution was amended to create the post of Assembly Leader, with Mike German elected Assembly leader designate in November 1998. Although German is the leader in the Assembly and bears the title Deputy First Minister in addition to his Cabinet portfolios, it is Lembit Opik,

---

[3] Liberal Democrats Policy Unit , *A Party For All Its Members:* Policy Briefing 41, 2000.

[4] Liberal Democrats Wales, Annual Report, 2000.p.9

[5] R. Deacon, 'The Hidden Federal Party: The Policy Process of the Welsh Liberal Democrats', *Regional Studies*, Vol. 32, No. 5. 1998.

MP for Montgomery who is currently the Welsh Leader, having been elected in 2001. In the Liberal Democrat 'Shadow Cabinet' at Westminster he has the Wales and Northern Ireland portfolios. The constitution of the Welsh party was changed in 2001 so that the Leadership may be held by an MP, AM or MEP. The reasoning behind this change was that each has sufficient status to lead the Party as a whole. The constitution requires that there should be leaders in Parliament and the Assembly, but one of these may also be Leader overall.

Analysis of the Assembly election result raised concerns within the party about its Welsh profile. As one policy document put it, in 1999:

> "Many voters switched to the Liberal Democrats in the Assembly elections. However the reasons for switching did not include a recognition that the Liberal Democrats were a party which could take decisions in Wales. This belief is totally at odds with the reality of our federal party, and clearly demonstrates that we must make more effort to demonstrate that we are a Party for Wales."[6]

While the party continues to make much of its distinctively Welsh Liberal heritage, a growing body of survey evidence suggests that it draws its support and activist base from people originating from outside Wales. For example, of the candidates standing in the 1999 Assembly election only 38 per cent were born in Wales. This contrasted with 64 per cent for Labour, 68 per cent for the Conservatives, and 79 per cent for Plaid Cymru.[7] Yet, as far as activists are concerned, the ideological commitment to federalism and decentralisation is complementary to the idea of Welsh autonomy. As a party document put it:

> "Being Welsh is not just about the language and culture. It is also about being seen as capable of deciding on Welsh solutions for Welsh problems."[8]

However, a glance at the voting base throws up another picture. In their analysis of the Welsh referendum result Richard Wyn Jones and Dafydd Trystan correlated party identification, national identity and the referendum vote. Designating the Liberal Democrat voters in the sample as whether they identified themselves as 'primarily Welsh', 'equally Welsh and British' and 'primarily British', the figures revealed that all three groups recorded a strong

[6] Welsh Liberal Democrats, *Building Community Politics: Liberal Democrats Wales' Party Strategy into the Millennium*, 1999.

[7] J Bradbury, L Bennie, D. Denver and J. Mitchell, *Party Attitudes and the Politics of Devolution: An Analysis of Candidates at the 1999 Scottish Parliament and Welsh Assembly Elections*, Paper to Political Studies Association Territorial Politics Workshop, Cardiff, January 2001.

[8] Welsh Liberal Democrats, *Op.Cit.*, 1999.

No vote in the referendum.[9] This reveals an interesting gap between stated desire of the party for a strongly devolved constitutional settlement for Wales and the inclinations of its core electorate.

THE ASSEMBLY GROUP

A major challenge for the newly elected Liberal Democrat Group in the Assembly was the distribution and management of portfolios. The internal machinery of the Assembly had been designed with the intention of building party balance into the structures. This was a process in which Liberal Democrats had previously been directly involved through its participation in the National Assembly Advisory Group and the Standing Orders Commission.[10] However, given the large number of committees, in practical terms this presented a tall order for a group of six. As has often been observed, with just 60 members in total there is no such thing as an Assembly 'backbencher'. This became even more of a challenge for the Liberal Democrats after the party became a partner in the coalition government.

Mike German, the party Leader in the Assembly, became the inaugural Chair of the Legislation Committee and sat on the Economic Development Committee, which was dominated by the crucial question of Objective One funding. Kirsty Williams, Liberal Democrat AM for Brecon and Radnor, took the chair of the Health and Social Services Subject Committee. Of the other members, Mick Bates (Montgomery) sat on the Agriculture and Rural Affairs Committee, and after February 2000, the Environment and Planning Committee. He also sat on the European Committee and succeeded Mike German as Chair of the Legislation Committee. Peter Black, a List member for South Wales West, originally sat on the Local Government, Environment and Housing Committee. Later he became a Deputy Minister with responsibility for Local Government and Housing following the coalition. Before becoming a Minister Jenny Randerson (Cardiff Central) had sat on the Pre-16 Education Committee. The North Wales List member Christine Humphreys sat on the Post–16 Education Committee and after, February 2000, the Education and Life Long Learning Committee and Environment, Planning and Transport Committee. In April 2001 she retired from the Assembly due to ill health and was replaced by Eleanor Burnham who became spokesperson for Transport and the Environment.

---

[9] R. Wyn Jones and D. Trystan, 'The 1997 Welsh Referendum Vote', in B Taylor and K Thomson (Eds.) *Scotland and Wales: Nations Again?*, University of Wales Press, Cardiff, 1999.

[10] M Laffin and A Thomas, ' Designing the Welsh Assembly', *Parliamentary Affairs*, 53.3, 2000. pp.557-576.

As can be seen in the chart below, the group is represented on all Assembly committees and each member speaks across a range of responsibilities. This was further complicated following the advent of the Coalition, since German and Randerson then took their places in Committee by virtue of their role as Ministers. As a result their roles on 'backbench committees' such as German's chairmanship of the Legislation Committee had to be taken over by other Liberal Democrat Members. The following chart describes Liberal Democrat AMs responsibilities in the Assembly in January 2003.

LIBERAL DEMOCRAT AM RESPONSIBILITIES IN THE NATIONAL ASSEMBLY, JANUARY 2003

Mike German, Leader	Deputy First Minister, Minister for Agriculture and Rural Affairs and Wales Abroad.
Jenny Randerson	Minister for Culture, Sport and the Welsh Language
Peter Black	Deputy Minister, Local Government and Housing, Local Government and Housing Committee, Local Government Partnership Council.
Mick Bates	Spokesperson on Education and Economic Development, Education and Life long Learning Committee, Economic Development Committee, Chair of the Legislation Committee, Voluntary Sector Partnership
Eleanor Burnham	Spokesperson on Environment, Planning and Transport, Environment, Planning and Transport Committee, Equal Opportunities Committee, Audit Committee.
Kirsty Williams	Chair of Health and Social Services Committee, Spokesperson on Health and Social Services, Chief Whip, Business Committee, Standards Committee

---

THE COALITION

The prospect of a Labour coalition with the Liberal Democrats had been discussed immediately following the Assembly elections, with the Liberal Democrats offering similar terms to those underpinning the Scottish arrangement. However, this was considered a step too far by the Labour leader Alun Michael who felt that he could not sell it to the group or the party as a whole. A major problem was the prospect of giving two cabinet seats to the Liberal Democrats. Labour judged that it could proceed as a minority administration after it became clear that Plaid Cymru would give it a fair wind, at least initially. When Michael faced his vote of no confidence in February 2000, ostensibly on the issue of European funding, there had been last ditch attempts to get the Liberal Democrats to shore up the administration, including the offer of the two seats which had been unacceptable in May 1999. At that stage, however, given the public nature of the stand off on European funding, it was impossible for the Liberal Democrats to enter a coalition with any credibility.[11] For the Liberal Democrats nothing could be done in terms of pursuing a coalition until the forthcoming Comprehensive Spending Review in July which was expected to address the Objective 1 question.

Alun Michael's pre-emptive resignation in the face of the vote of no confidence saw a shift in the political landscape in Wales, with his successor as First Minister, Rhodri Morgan, operating in a very different style. Relations between Mike German and Alun Michael had not been good. Michael reserved some of his most savage invective for the Liberal Democrat leader, on one occasion claiming that:

"... his natural role is Paperclip Counter General to the Universe."[12]

Nonetheless, there had been a 'growing synergy' between some key players in the Liberal Democrat and Labour camps within the Assembly even before Michael's Assembly demise. Moreover, there was a feeling by some Labour figures that the minority administration was unsustainable. The Welsh administration was attempting to manage from day to day, unable to plan ahead. Instead they were faced with constantly shifting alliances and deals amongst the opposition parties. A coalition was not an option in February. However, at the Welsh Labour Spring conference a motion vetoing pacts with other parties was defeated. This allowed for the possibility of coalition without an explicit endorsement. Then in July the Comprehensive Spending Review included a commitment that Wales would get extra money to allow it to deliver European funds. This was a turning point as the Liberal Democrats were then in a position to indicate that the demands they had made in February had been fulfilled.

Presenting the coalition to the Cabinet and both parties' Assembly Groups and the wider parties was always going to be difficult. In early September formal overtures were made when Rhodri Morgan wrote to Mike German. For some Cabinet members the prospect of Liberal Democrats as Ministers in the Cabinet was a step too far. Tom Middlehurst, Minister for Post-16 Education, resigned in protest. His sentiments were echoed by Peter Law

---

[11] A Thomas and M Laffin, 'The First Welsh Constitutional Crisis: The Alun Michael Resignation', *Public Policy and Administration* 16:1, 2001.

[12] Alun Michael MP, Speech at University of Glamorgan, 18 May 2000.

who was subsequently sacked from the Cabinet in the reshuffle to make room for the Liberal Democrats. He has remained a constant critic, drawing a rebuke from the Presiding Officer when he described them as "toe-rags" in the Chamber.[13]

Indeed, the creation of the coalition and the earlier removal of Alun Michael revealed interesting contrasts between the cultures of the two parties. In the run up to the vote of no confidence in February 2000 Tony Blair called Charles Kennedy on three occasions in an attempt to secure Liberal Democrat support.[14] Kennedy indicated that it was a matter for the Welsh party to decide. With the exception of the critics mentioned above, the Assembly Labour Group acquiesced to the coalition idea. However, there is opposition elsewhere in the party. This is largely concentrated amongst local government activists and MPs less familiar with the problems faced by the Labour minority administration.

The Labour Group approved the coalition proposals after they had been past by the Cabinet. On the other hand, the Liberal Democrats sought the approval of the party through a special one day conference. In the week before, Mike German travelled around Wales selling the deal to the local parties. The biggest concern was opposition in some rural strongholds where suspicion of Labour was deepest. In the event, the coalition was strongly endorsed, not least because of claims that the *Partnership in Power* document that underpinned it was dominated by Liberal Democrat policies. Not surprisingly, this caused some exasperation within Labour circles, especially the commitment to a Commission on Electoral Arrangements in Local Government with the implicit acknowledgement that proportional representation was on the agenda.

One of the terms of the Agreement was that the Liberal Democrats should have two seats on the Cabinet. Mike German became Minister for Economic Development and Deputy First Minister, which gave him the freedom to comment across a range of issues. Jenny Randerson took on the Culture, Sport and Welsh Language portfolio. However, the arrangement came under threat almost immediately as Mike German was investigated by his former employers, the Welsh Joint Education Committe for alleged irregularities when he was in charge of its European Unit. The WJEC handed its report to the police and in the summer of 2001, German stood down on a temporary basis pending the outcome of the police enquiry.

No alternative Liberal Democrat Minister was appointed and Rhodri Morgan again took over the Economic Development portfolio, arguing with Plaid and Conservative critics that the investigation into Mike German would be over

---

[13] Assembly *Record*, 30 October 2002.

[14] A Rawnsley, *Servants of the People: The Inside Story of New Labour*, Penguin, 2001.p.359

by the new year. In the event, this was not the case and in March 2002, Andrew Davies became Economic Development Minister and Carwyn Jones took on his duties as Assembly Business Minister alongside his existing portfolio. Finally, in June 2002 German was cleared and was reinstated to the Cabinet, this time taking over the Agriculture and Rural Affairs portfolio from Carwyn Jones who became Minister for Open Government. German also acquired the additional responsibility for 'Wales Abroad'.

There is no doubt that this episode, particularly the impact of its dragging on through the best part of a year, placed a large strain on the coalition. First Minister Rhodri Morgan had to fend off constant attacks, both from the Opposition and from within his own ranks, by those hostile to the coalition, that combining the Economic Development portfolio with his own was unsustainable. Yet throughout the period he remained implacably loyal to Mike German, insisting that in due time he would be cleared of the allegations against him and would return to the Cabinet. This loyalty was returned in full measure when the coalition came under pressure in the latter half of 2001 from a different direction, due to a sharp policy divergence between Labour and the Liberal Democrats over re-structuring the health service. Only top-level, last minute negotiations kept the Liberal Democrats on side.

Radical proposals to abolish the five Welsh health authorities and replace them with 22 Local Health Boards, coterminous with the 22 local authorities, were presented to Cabinet in early July 2001 without prior consultation with the Liberal Democrats. This attempt to railroad the proposals through the coalition resulted in the Liberal Democrat group in the Assembly taking the extraordinary step of making its own response to the formal consultation process that ensued. In it the group called for substantial modifications to the coalition policy, specifically an all-Wales Health Authority to keep the administration of the Welsh health service at arms length from the Assembly.

The background to the row was a key health component of the Partnership Agreement that established the Coalition between the Liberal Democrats and Labour in October 2000. This stated that the new Administration would:

> "Seek a period of organisational stability within Health Services in
> Wales to allow staff to prioritise the delivery of better health care."

In December 2000 Health Minister Jane Hutt sought the agreement of the Liberal Democrat health spokesperson Kirsty Williams, Chair of the Health Committee, for this clause to be set aside. Her consent was given but not in anticipation of the radical proposals that subsequently emerged, and certainly not in the expectation that there would be no further consultation[15]. The issue came to a head in mid November 2001 when a crisis meeting to thrash out a

---

[15] See Chapter 8 of this volume

compromise was held between First Minister Rhodri Morgan, Health Minister Jane Hutt, the Deputy First Minister, Jenny Randerson, and the Liberal leader, Mike German. The Press Association quoted 'a senior Liberal Democrat source' as claiming the Health Minister had learned a lesson in partnership:

> *"We have been screaming blue murder about this for three weeks telling her she must stop and talk to us before going ahead. But she kept on going, digging herself deeper and deeper into it. There was no ideological split, it just comes down to practical solutions. There will be some bruised people on both sides after this, but we have always said partnership government is not comfortable or easy."*[16]

The advent of coalition government coincided with the process of the strengthening of the executive/legislative spilt in the Assembly, for example through a re-branding exercise which brought forth the 'Welsh Assembly Government'. This raised interesting questions with regard to the principle of collective responsibility and spawned frequent debates about when Liberal Democrat members, especially Ministers, were speaking as party spokespeople or for the 'Government of Wales'. Peter Black, as Deputy Minister with responsibility for Local Government, has trodden a particularly awkward line, taking his seat on the Partnership Council as a Liberal Democrat and facing a substantial amount of hostility from Labour council leaders. The situation is further complicated by the fact that he remains a Swansea City Councillor.

There are also the inherent tensions of, on the one hand, maintaining the partnership with Labour in the Assembly and, on the other, highlighting the gains made by the party in local by-elections for the consumption of activists and with the 2003 Election in view. This was demonstrated when Mike German, the day before the publication of the First Minister's second Annual Report in October 2002, claimed that of the leading eight achievements listed therein, "six came directly from the Welsh Liberal Democrats manifesto."[17] To some Labour critics this underlines what they consider to be the fundamental indiscipline of the Liberal Democrats as a party and as an Assembly group, as summed up by Tom Middlehurst's condemnation of the Assembly Group as *"ragtag"*.[18] More often than not, however, such critics are also opposed to the Additional Member electoral system and the whole idea of coalition.

Partisan observations aside, to what extent do the Assembly group deserve the reputation of being 'undisciplined'? Their relatively small number means

---

[16] Press Association report, 14 November 2001. For a full account of this episode see the monitoring report, *Coalition Creaks Over Health*, Cardiff: IWA, December 2001.

[17] *Western Mail*, 29 October 2002.

[18] Assembly *Record*, 30 October 2002.

their dynamics vary greatly from those within the larger Labour or Plaid groups. The fact that the group has to cover a wide range of portfolios and responsibilities means that patronage and the hope of preferment, traditional weapons in the enforcement of party discipline, are relatively meaningless.

Furthermore, as already mentioned, the group is evenly split between list and constituency members. Many list members of all parties, including Mike German (South-east Wales), take an 'entrepreneurial' approach and campaign aggressively across the region to the frustration of many constituency members (as well as MPs and Councillors). On the other hand, the Liberal Democrat constituency members are concerned to defend and consolidate their positions. Kirsty Williams (Brecon and Radnor) and Mick Bates (Montgomery) both represent rural constituencies and face their own 'entrepreneurial' Conservative list rivals. Williams' appearance on the Epynt Mountain during protests about the burial of animal carcasses during the foot and mouth crisis was an example of pitting local interests against the Welsh Assembly Government.

A third factor is a strain of individualism and independence which has traditionally characterised Liberal and Liberal Democrat representation in the House of Commons, associated with the 'luxury' of a distance from power.[19] For the Liberal Democrat AMs in the National Assembly, the realities of being in power have to be balanced against party traditions of individualism and localism and the smallness of their group, which automatically endows them with more clout. This point should not be over-stressed as some members have extensive experience of group dynamics in local government. Nevertheless, as the Welsh Assembly Government steadily evolves a tradition of responsible government, the impetus for discipline becomes stronger.

ELECTIONS AND CAMPAIGNS

One of the concerns about the coalition was how it might affect the Liberal Democrats' standing in the polls. In the 1997 Westminster election the party had taken 12.4 per cent of the vote. In the 1999 Assembly elections, this improved only marginally to 13.5 per cent and still saw them lagging in fourth place behind the Conservatives. The party acknowledged that political progress had been slower than in England, and to some extent slower than in Scotland, but took heart from a local government presence in different parts of Wales:

---

[19] V. McKee, 'British Liberal Democrats: Structures and Groups on the Inside', *Contemporary Political Studies*, Proceedings of the Political Studies Association Conference, 1994.

"We are the principal political opposition to Labour in Cardiff, Swansea and Bridgend. We share power in Wrexham. We have substantial representation on Powys, Conwy and Ceredigion Councils. We have a newly established Group on Caerphilly Council. All this represents a move forward."[20]

The party's 1999 strategy identified the 2001 Westminster election as a building block for May 2003 Assembly elections. The long term objective was defined as being:

" … in 10 years from now, the Liberal Democrats control at least five councils in Wales, are within striking distance of 20 Assembly Members, and have 6-8 Members of Parliament."[21]

In the event the 2001 General Election saw the Liberal Democrats improve on 1997, with 15 per cent of the vote, holding Brecon and Radnor and Montgomery, running Labour very close in Cardiff Central, and increasing its share of the vote in Ceredigion.

By November 2002 an HTV/NOP poll put the Welsh Liberal Democrat share of the Regional List vote at 19 per cent which would possibly yield an additional two seats.[22] At the same time the first-past-the-post vote was polled at 13 per cent, down on the 2001 general election. This suggests the electorate is becoming more sophisticated in distinguishing between the first-past-the–post and list votes. It will encourage party strategists to campaign on persuading voters casting their first votes for other parties to vote Liberal democrat on the list.

EVALUATING THE FIRST FOUR YEARS

Russell Deacon has identified what he considered to be the strengths and weaknesses of the policy process in the Welsh Party.[23] Strengths identified included *policy coverage and distinctiveness*, in that its policies were wider ranging and more distinctive from its English counterpart in comparison with Welsh Labour and the Conservatives. He also noted that:

"… policy is nearly always derived and shaped directly from the Welsh party's own membership."[24]

---

[20] Welsh Liberal Democrats, *Op.cit.*, 1999.

[21] *Ibid.*

[22] Denis Balsom, 'Public Attitudes', in John Osmond (Ed.), *Dragon Takes a Different Route: Monitoring the National Assembly September to December 2002*, IWA.

[23] Deacon, *Op.Cit.*, 1998.

[24] *Ibid.*

At the same time, the many weaknesses he identified include a paucity of resources which has hampered promotion and dissemination of policy. He also noted that a lack of direction or interest from the top was a problem, with the two MPs at Westminster being over-stretched. In addition he highlighted an urban-rural cleavage which created competing policy demands. More generally was a marginalisation of the Welsh party in the broader context of the UK party. These issues provide a useful framework to evaluate the extent to which the first Assembly term, and especially participation in the coalition government has impacted on the Welsh Liberal Democrats.

As discussed above, the Liberal Democrats' federal constitution allowed the party to adapt to devolution with greater ease than Labour. The 1999 and 2003 Assembly Manifestos were produced autonomously by the Welsh party while the leadership made much of its claim that the Partnership Agreement was dominated by Liberal Democrat policies. In Labour's view many of the policies were already being developed within the Assembly on a consensual basis, while the key concessions – the Commission on Electoral Arrangements in Local Government and the Commission on the Assembly's Powers (the Richard Commission) – could be seen as exercises of kicking the ball into the long grass.

The claim of Welsh autonomy seems relatively sound, although Liberal Democrat MPs at Westminster did vote against the Health Bill incorporating clauses for reform of the NHS in Wales endorsed by the Coalition Government. However, this perhaps is a reflection of the inherent complexity of the current devolution settlement and other parties have experienced similar difficulties. What sets the Liberal Democrat experience apart is the reality that the devolved administrations in Wales and Scotland are enjoying power. That remains a distant prospect for the party at the UK level. This means that the balance of the relationship is different from that in other parties. The federal conference has become a 'sharing experience', with Welsh and Scots Ministers and spokespeople taking a prominent role. Conference agendas are marked so as to distinguish between devolved, UK and English only matters. Nevertheless, there are occasions when the Federal party can fail to distinguish between the UK and England.[25]

Liberal Democrat parliamentary representation increased significantly in the 1997 Westminster election, establishing a momentum that was sustained in 2001 when the party emerged with 52 seats.[26] A critical mass of MPs now represent seats across England with the result that the 'Celtic fringe' no longer wields the disproportionate influence it once did. There is certainly a possibility that divergent agendas might emerge in the future to test the

---

[25] Chris Lines, *Op.Cit.*,2002.

[26] *Ibid.*

federal structure of the party. For example, the Peel Group has been set up by some MPs who are concerned with holding the ground against a Conservative revival and has recruited disillusioned Tories such as the former MP Anthony Meyer to the party. The marginalisation of the Welsh Party identified by Deacon may have been reduced, but fundamental questions remain about the future evolution of the party on a UK basis.

Deacon highlighted the paucity of resources as a constant challenge and this remains a problem for the Welsh Party.[27] A Five Year Budget and Development Plan has been put in place and a Finance Committee sets the budget accordingly. The hope is that this will allow the party to take a longer term view of its work and aims.[28] The challenge of managing two electoral cycles is also making an impact, with plans for a Fund Raising Strategy derailed by the 2001 General Election.

Financial issues also reveal tensions with the Federal headquarters in Cowley Street. Improved communication has been reported but problems persisted with the timing of payments to the Welsh Party. The Electoral Commission has made Policy Development Fund money available to political parties for long term research but there have been questions about how this will be filtered through the UK party headquarters. A Welsh Liberal Democrat representative reported that despite pressures on federal finances she had won "a battle to secure a staff person in Wales to help our manifesto development work".[29]

At the Cardiff headquarters, apart from Chris Lines, the part-time Chief Executive, there are policy and campaigns officers, a party administrator and a party liaison post aimed at bringing MPs and AMs together. Within the Assembly, the Group receives a core amount of funding as a governing party for support staff and employs a group administrator, two researchers and a press officer. AMs also have their own support staff. There are also two political advisers who work for the Liberal Democrat Ministers, although they are technically Assembly Government appointments.

Deacon's critique of leadership refers specifically to the policy development process in the party. However, there are also wider issues about how the leadership of the Welsh party will develop. Devolution and the existence of six AMs have galvanised the policy development process and AMs are enjoying a higher profile within the party. Eleven papers based on the work of the policy working groups were published in 2002 and debated at the two Welsh conferences.

---

[27] Liberal Democrats Wales, Annual Reports 2000,2001.

[28] *Ibid.* 2000.

[29] Liberal Democrats Wales, Annual Report, 2001.

Regarding the broader context of the Welsh party leadership, Lembit Opik MP, enjoys a high profile, partly deriving from his media-friendly and sometimes idiosyncratic approach. Relationships between the two MPs and AMs are reportedly good and they attend group meetings via video link, while German and Opik meet regularly. The fact that Chris Lines combines a party and an Assembly support role provides an additional link. However, there is a question whether having an MP as Welsh leader is sustainable in the long term. Unlike the Welsh Labour Party, Liberal Democrat AMs outnumber MPs and as actual and potential coalition partners and participants in Welsh Government, the logic for combining the Assembly and Welsh leadership may well prevail.[30]

Deacon also highlighted the impact of the rural-urban cleavage within the party and its influence on policy development. As seen in the discussion on the Assembly group, this is still detectable but also coincides with the concerns of constituency-based AMs. Nevertheless, the success of the leadership in securing endorsement of the Partnership Agreement demonstrated an ability to fulfil the aspirations of the party across Wales. Arguably, it is another area where the reality of power has ameliorated a traditional weakness of the Welsh party.

LOOKING AHEAD

In Spring 2003 the Welsh Liberal Democrats will enter an election campaign with a manifesto which has emerged from the work of 11 policy working groups and a consultation process both within the party and with organisations outside. A pre-manifesto document was discussed at the Spring conference in March 2003.

Forward thinking has taken place about how the establishment of a second coalition will be approached with issues such as an increased investment in public services and the strengthening of Welsh communities regarded as central to talks over a new coalition administration. The terms of any such pact are to be in writing, made public, and to run for a specified time only.[31] There is a question of whether the Electoral Reform Commission findings will be implemented in the teeth of opposition from Local Government. At the Autumn conference in 2002 it was intimated that any renewal of the pact in 2003 would not be conditional on proportional representation for local authority elections, but the party would want Labour to move significantly

---

[30] The fact that Opik became leader in October 2001 was arguably as much a response to German's unavailability for office, due to his being subject to a police investigation at the time.

[31] BBC Wales News Web Page, 20 October 2002.

towards this.[32] Regarding the Richard Commission, due to report after the election, even Labour supporters of extending Assembly powers question whether that could occur without another referendum.

However, firstly the party faces the challenge of entering a competitive election against its erstwhile coalition partners. The response of the opposition parties, some Labour members and sections of media to this prospect indicates the extent to which Welsh political culture must catch up with the realities of the new political and electoral system. All parties may aspire to an overall majority but even Labour, with its overwhelming hegemony, failed to obtain that in 1999 – though its 'poor' showing needs to be seen in relative terms. In this respect the Liberal Democrats, more than Labour, find themselves as the 'guinea pigs', acknowledging coalition as a realistic outcome of the forthcoming electoral contest. It is hard to argue with the view of Chris Lines, the Welsh Liberal Democrats' Chief Executive, that devolution and, in particular the coalition, has:

> "… energised the party in terms of policy development, the profile of our elected representatives, organisation and the engagement of our activists."[33]

Moreover, polling evidence suggests modest gains in public support, demonstrating that the coalition with Labour has not been costly in those terms. How Welsh Liberal Democrats fare in the 2003 Assembly Election will contain lessons not only about the development of the party but also about wider public perceptions of the new Welsh politics.

---

[32] *Ibid.*

[33] Chris Lines, *Op.Cit.* 2002.

CHAPTER 13

CONSERVATIVES

John Osmond and J. Barry Jones

The Conservatives entered the first general election to the National Assembly in 1999 with two severe handicaps. The first was the years of Conservative government in the previous two decades. The Welsh electorate had overwhelmingly negative memories of these. They had seen the virtual closure of the coal-mining industry and a draconian rationalisation of steel production. Popular attention had also focused on a growing democratic deficit. There had been increased centralisation at the expense of Welsh local authorities, and an erosion of accountability through the creation of a range of quangos composed largely of Conservative nominees.

The second handicap was the product of these experiences. In the 1997 general election the Conservative Party lost all its Welsh seats. In parliamentary terms, Wales became a Tory-free zone. Welsh Conservatives were traumatised by the scale and depth of their rejection by the Welsh electorate. Consequently the party kept a low profile during the subsequent referendum campaign.[1] Nonetheless, their unambiguous, if muted hostility to devolution, inevitably compromised the party's strategy for the Assembly elections. It is difficult to rubbish a policy and then ask for support to make the policy work. While campaigning for election to the new body, many Conservative activists still shared the party's long-standing opposition and fully subscribed to the view that it would lead inexorably to the 'slippery slope of separation'.

Some Conservative AMs now acknowledge that changing these deep-seated perceptions was bound to be an impossible task in so short a time. Looking back at the National Assembly's first term they still doubt whether even four further years provided enough time for the party to adjust. Yet, to a great extent the leadership of the party did, and set about re-shaping the organisation and policies to better deal with the new realities. However, while the leadership was conscious of the need for change and began to work out a strategy for achieving it, the wider party membership remained largely disengaged. The party remained in retreat and suffered low morale throughout the whole period. The 2001 general election repeated the rout of

---

[1] See David Melding, 'The Conservative Party's Shy and Muted Campaign' in J. Barry Jones and Denis Balsom (Eds.) *The Road to the National Assembly for Wales*, University of Wales Press, 2000.

1997, leaving the Conservatives without any Welsh constituency MPs in Westminster. These were not good times to be forging a new identity.

'AN ENGLISH PARTY'

The Conservative Party is fundamentally 'Unionist', dedicated to preserving the United Kingdom as a political entity. Over more than a century its social and economic policies have swung across the spectrum, from liberal to the autocratic, according to political and electoral circumstances. As regards the Union, however, it has remained steadfastly consistent. For much of the time this stance paid handsome electoral dividends in Scotland and Northern Ireland where Conservatives managed to play the Unionist card and also develop distinctive local identities.

In Wales, however, this never happened in quite the same way. Since the beginning of the franchise in 1865, Conservatives in Wales have been widely regarded, and disregarded, as 'the English Party'. The explanation is partly historical. In the 19th Century Conservatism was inextricably associated with landlords and the Anglican Church. Tales of tenant farmers being evicted by Conservative landlords for daring to vote Liberal may have been exaggerated, but they cast a long shadow. Equally, the fact that though Winston Churchill, as Home Secretary in 1910, sent in troops to quell riots in the Rhondda, they did *not* shoot at unarmed miners is not what matters. The point is that for decades voters believed that they did.[2]

Throughout much of the 20th Century the Englishness of the Conservative Party was underscored by two further factors. In rural Wales they were marked out because most of their representatives did not speak Welsh, while in industrial Wales they were marginalised because of the overwhelming dominance of Labour. Such conditions tended to obscure the reality that throughout this period Conservatives were the main opposition party in Wales, consistently securing around a quarter of the vote. Indeed, during the 1980s the party's support exceeded 30 per cent, and in 1983 it won 14 parliamentary seats.

---

[2] In The *Future of Welsh Conservatism* (IWA Gregynog Paper, 2002) the Welsh Conservative MEP Jonathan Evans reports that, "During the 1999 local government and Assembly elections, which Wayne David was defeated in the Rhondda, one Plaid Cymru candidate complained to me that Labour canvassers were desperately urging elderly voters to stick with Labour and '*vote against the Tories for what Churchill did at Tonypandy*'." During November 1910, on the command of Churchill, infantry and detachments of cavalry, the 18th Hussars, were stationed at Pontypridd and for several weeks patrolled the Rhondda. On one occasion infantry with fixed baynets were used at Penygraig, after police had been stoned by the local population: Kenneth O. Morgan, *Rebirth of a Nation, Wales 1880 to 1980*, Oxford University Press, 1982, page147. It is worth noting that Churchill was Home Secretary in a Liberal Government.

Nevertheless, the perception of the party as English and because of that an alien force, persisted. In this it did not help itself. During the 18 years of Conservative rule between 1979 and 1997 only one out of five Secretaries of State at the Welsh Office sat for a Welsh constituency. The most stridently English was, of course, John Redwood who, during his relatively short sojourn between 1993 to 1995 appeared to use Wales as a laboratory for his particular form of free market economics. He will be remembered for returning under-spent funds to the Treasury and for his expressions of puzzlement at a Conservative conference during a rendering of the Welsh national anthem.

Of course, the Conservatives consistently and viscerally opposed devolution as a threat to the Union. But this, too, underlined their appearance as an English force. In the 1997 referendum campaign they were the only one of the four main parties to be aligned with voting No. However unjustly, this marked them out as 'anti-Welsh'. All of which proved a handicap when it came to fighting the first Assembly elections in 1999. In the wake of the 2001 Westminster general election Conservative AM David Melding told a party meeting:

> "Time and again on the campaign trail I was told that the Conservatives are an 'English' party."[3]

In a groundbreaking lecture in November 2002, Lord Griffiths of Fforestfach, formerly head of Mrs Thatcher's Policy Unit at Number 10 in the 1980s, observed:

> "Too often in the past, the Conservative Party in Wales has been seen as a regional branch of an English institution. For many in Wales, the word Tory has a distinctly foreign, if not hostile ring, to it. It is a brand with a history to which people do not relate." [4]

And Greg Walker, Conservative candidate in Cardiff Central in the 2001 general election, a constituency where the party has slipped into third place behind Labour and the Liberal Democrats, but held in the 1980s, reflected:

> "… there is still a widespread misconception among the electorate that the Conservatives are somehow 'un-Welsh'. We know this not just from overwhelming anecdotal evidence but also from objective statistical analysis derived from the comprehensive British Election Survey up to and including the 2001 election. We also know that this misconception deters a very large number of Welsh voters from voting Conservative, even after taking into account social and economic factors. The average

---

[3] David Melding AM, Speech to South Wales Central Conservatives, 21 June 2001.

[4] Lord Griffiths of Fforestfach, *A Conservative Agenda for Wales*, Institute of Welsh Politics Annual Lecture, University of Wales, Aberystwyth, November 2002.

middle income, middle class voter in Wales is significantly less likely to vote Conservative than an English voter in the same socio-economic position. This electoral dead weight cannot be allowed to persist."[5]

THE 1999 ELECTION

It has been widely remarked that the coming of the National Assembly rescued the Welsh Conservatives from oblivion. That is to say, despite the party securing an historically low 16.5 per cent of the vote, the Additional Member proportional system gave it eight AMs on the regional Lists. Added to their single constituency seat in Monmouth this produced the third largest Group in the Assembly and an opportunity for the party to rebuild its fortunes.

This relative success was achieved in spite of the election campaign itself. Former Welsh Office Minister Rod Richards had been voted as 'leader of the campaign' by the party membership in place of the establishment favourite, Nick Bourne. There was no campaign committee as such but, instead, a series of ad hoc discussions with regional groups of candidates. Rod Richards personally controlled preparation of the manifesto *Fair Play for All: Your Voice in the National Assembly*, giving it an uncompromising right wing edge with little concession to the Welsh dimension. He also 'fronted' all the important radio and television appearances, attracting considerable coverage with his trenchant attacks on the Labour Party. However, his authority was significantly qualified. He was not the leader but simply in charge of the campaign. Even with this limited role he was afforded only a grudging acceptance. Candidates on the 'centre-left' wing of the party generally ignored the Richards' manifesto, issuing their own personalised election addresses.

While Rod Richards's belligerent and confrontational style gave life to the campaign there was little evidence that it motivated core Conservative voters. Indeed, it might well have alienated more moderate elements. More importantly, the party fell into the trap of treating the Assembly election as a 'mini UK' general election and thus failed to develop fully the Welsh dimension. The party focused instead on a bilateral debate with Labour, the traditional basis of British party politics, to the almost total exclusion of other parties. Consequently, most Conservative candidates failed to anticipate the rise of Plaid Cymru, a massive and near-mortal miscalculation.

Lastly, the Conservatives failed to involve sufficient English incomers who, while willing to vote Conservative in a British general election, apparently

---

[5] Greg Walker, 'Status Quo Will Undermine the Union', IWA, *Agenda*, Winter 2002/03.

regarded the Assembly elections as the concern of the Welsh with little relevance to them. And indeed, in his analysis of the poor result, Rod Richards himself ascribed it to Conservative supporters' hostility towards devolution:

> *"A lot of Conservative voters who didn't want devolution in the first place made the positive decision not to vote. This was their second opportunity to demonstrate their dissatisfaction with the Assembly."*[6]

A CONSTRUCTIVE OPPOSITION

This was hardly a promising starting point for the new Conservative Group to set about building a constructive opposition. How genuine was the party in its stated aim of wishing to 'make the Assembly work'? How capable was it of learning the lessons of past defeats and creating a more authentically Welsh party with a distinctively Welsh policy platform? To a great extent these questions were resolved within a few months when Rod Richards resigned as a result of a police charge of serious grievous bodily harm against him following of an incident in London.[7] Elected in his place was Nick Bourne, previously a Professor of Law at Swansea Institute of Higher Education, and now a List Member for Mid and West Wales.

This was a significant change since the Conservatives now had an opportunity to present a more moderate approach to policies, for example on the Welsh language. It was important, too, because there was now the possibility that the Conservatives would collaborate with the other opposition parties in a more formal way. And, indeed, this proved the case within a matter of months on the Objective 1 issue when the Conservatives co-operated closely with Plaid Cymru and the Liberal Democrats in engineering the vote of no confidence against Labour's First Secretary Alun Michael. If Rod Richards had remained the leader it is doubtful whether the Opposition Parties would have united on their core concern of challenging Michael's style of minority administration. As it was, the relatively high media profile that Nick Bourne achieved during the affair helped to re-position the Conservatives as a more distinctively Welsh party.

At the same time, from the point of view of the Conservative Group the eventual outcome of the episode, the formation of the majority coalition between Labour and the Liberal Democrats, was wholly positive. It chimed with their approach of wishing to separate the executive from the legislature,

---

[6] *Western Mail*, 8 May 1999

[7] Though Richards eventually won the court case he never returned to front rank politics. In February 2000 he was voted out of the Conservative Group for failing to follow the whip, and in 2002 resigned his North Wales List seat due to illness.

Westminster style, rather than become embroiled in any hint of coalition politics themselves. As Glyn Davies, the Conservative member for Mid and West Wales put it, in a plenary debate on the implications of the coalition:

> " We have always viewed it as our job to test the Government, their proposals, and to see what individual ministers are made of. We will carry on doing that. We will fit into these new arrangements as if they were made to measure for us. "[8]

Under Nick Bourne's leadership a high proportion of the Conservative Group have achieved significant prominence within the Assembly Chamber. As Chair of the Agriculture Committee Glyn Davies has had a leading role in some of the more contentious debates of the first term, not least on GM crops and the outbreak of foot and mouth disease which lasted during most of 2001. David Melding, AM for South Wales Central, is widely acknowledged as being the leading Opposition spokesman on health issues. Alun Cairns, AM for South Wales West, emerged as a key member of the Economic Development Committee, while Jonathan Morgan, AM for South Wales Central, the youngest member of the Assembly, established a profile as the party's Education Spokesman. Between them these members managed to project a mainstream centre-right position on a range of social and economic issues. Within the Assembly at least, the party went unchallenged in occupying firm and distinctive territory on the centre-right. It also grew more confident in asserting its Welshness. So, for example, Glyn Davies used the party's second large-scale defeat of the 2001 general election as a platform to make the case for a stronger Welsh identity for Welsh Conservatism:

> "Our attitude towards the National Assembly is the key to convincing the Welsh people that we are totally committed to 'sticking up for Wales'. Whether we like it or not, the National Assembly is here to stay and the Conservative Party's commitment to it is the measure by which our commitment to Wales will be judged ... Our strategy for Wales may include a Welsh political leader and may involve more autonomy for the Welsh Conservative Party, but at the heart of any strategy must lie a 100 per cent commitment to an effective Assembly."[9]

THE PROCEDURAL REVIEW

An opportunity to demonstrate this commitment came with the year-long Procedural Review of the Assembly's operation that began work under the

---

[8] Assembly *Record*, 19 October.

[9] Glyn Davies, 'Time to play as a team for party's sake', *Western Mail*, 11 June.

chairmanship of the Presiding Officer in January 2001.[10] During May 2001 the Review took on the character of an informal Constitutional Convention with substantial submissions made by each of the parties, not least the Conservatives. Given their previous hostility to the devolution project, their submission was surprisingly hard-edged, containing a series of on the whole radical ideas for improvement and demonstrating in practice their commitment to 'making the Assembly work'.

Taken together, the submissions of the four parties to the Operational Review revealed a frank acknowledgement on all sides that there were serious flaws in the basic design of the Assembly machine. Three substantial areas – relations with Westminster and Whitehall, the work of the Subject Committees, and the Assembly's dealings with European affairs - illustrated this and on all of them the Conservatives had trenchant observations to make. On the first, relations with Westminster and Whitehall, the party's submission commented:

> "The liaison between the Assembly and Whitehall Departments has left much to be desired. On a range of issues – from the planting of GM crops to incarceration of asylum seekers in Cardiff prison – information and consultation with the Assembly has appeared to be an afterthought. This has not only caused embarrassment to Assembly Ministers but also calls into question the commitment of some Ministers in Westminster to the success of devolution."

And it recommended:

- That an all-party ad hoc Concordats Committee be set up and allocated one year to review each departmental protocol that has been established with a view to strengthening their provisions and ironing out any weaknesses.

- Consideration ought to be given to appointing a senior figure – perhaps a former civil servant or judge - to be an independent arbitrator in the event of disputes between the Assembly and Whitehall departments.

The work of the Subject Committees also drew a good deal of input from the parties, with most debate concentrating on the problems of their combining scrutiny of the Administration with joint policy making work. The Conservative Group made the following constructive suggestions for dealing with the difficulty:

> "The dual role of the committees, as scrutinisers and policy makers has

---

[10] For an account of the Review see John Osmond 'Constitution Building on the Hoof' in the previous volume in this series, *Building a Civic Culture: Institutional Change, Policy Development and Political Dynamics in the National Assembly for Wales, IWA, 2002. Pages 67-80.*

sometimes been a difficult one to reconcile. This dual role reflects the ambiguous nature of the Government of Wales Act, which tried to tread a 'third way' between a local government committee model, and the classic parliamentary executive-legislative split. The Group is of the view that this compromise can be made to work - though we recognise that a great onus is on committee chairmen to give clear direction to their committees. However, it is instructive that in the Government's proposed model for local government 'Overview and Scrutiny Panels' executive members are barred from membership of such committees ... The Group believes that committees achieve their best results when focussing on specific policy areas. Committees that have decided to deal with six or seven issues simultaneously have often not had the impact that they might have wished."

Dissatisfaction with the working of the European Affairs Committee was voiced by all the parties, with the Conservative Group's submission commenting:

"Against expectations the European Affairs Committee has not turned out to be a high profile committee. Though much attention has focused on the way in which Wales could enhance its relationship with the European Union post-devolution, the European Committee has been relatively low key. This reflects more the infrequency of its meetings and the selection of agenda items than on the quality of its membership. Its treatment of pressing European issues, such as preparations for the Nice Treaty, has been a serious disappointment. The Group believes that measures could be taken to correct this underachievement."

Generally, there was a consensus on these issues. However, this broke down at the end of October 2001 when the Opposition parties together with the Liberal Democrats refused to endorse a draft final report put together by civil servants. Instead, Deputy Presiding Officer John Marek set about a series of negotiations with the party leaders and business managers to achieve a harder hitting report with more focused recommendations. As Nick Bourne explained:

"We did not think the report was nearly radical enough. Our main concerns were the lack of clear division between the Executive for the Government of Wales, and the National Assembly in its legislative mode; little or no movement on family/friendly hours; the unfocussed way that the Regional Committees operate; and the need for a clearer role, in policy development terms, for Subject Committees. Other concerns that have been raised are the need to give all members the opportunity to put forward secondary legislation during a four year term, improve liaison in terms of influencing primary legislation at Westminster, and sharper plenary sessions."[11]

---

[11] Nicholas Bourne AM, electronic communication with the authors, 15 November 2001.

It is worth recounting the Conservative Group's participation in the Procedural Review in some detail since it shows the party getting to grips with the Assembly's operation. It also provides substantial evidence that the party was, by now at any rate, committed to making the new institution work more effectively.

PARTY ORGANISATION

Another sign that Welsh Conservatives were rapidly adjusting to the post devolution era was their establishment of a Commission on the future organisation of the party under the chairmanship of the veteran party loyalist Lord Roberts. During his long period as Minister of State at the Welsh Office, serving for 16 years under successive Secretaries of State, Wyn Roberts had shown himself to be highly sensitive to Welsh aspirations, not least the Welsh language. In the wake of the 1997 general election he was among the first of the Party's strategists to appreciate that it would have to adjust fundamentally to the new realities.

Immediately after the Scottish referendum and before the Welsh referendum the recently elevated Lord Roberts promised to use his position in the upper chamber in an effort to 'upgrade' the Welsh Assembly. He was unhappy with Labour's proposed committee system (based on local government practice) and instead wanted the Assembly to have 'Cabinet government' like that proposed for the Scottish Parliament. In his judgement, such a change would:

> "… make all the difference between [the Welsh Assembly] being a proper government and a grand regional council."[12]

He stopped short of advising Conservatives to vote 'Yes', but his intervention undoubtedly boosted the 'Yes' campaign. He intervened again after the Welsh referendum on the eve of the Conservative conference. Describing the possible future of Conservatism in Wales, he pulled no punches. His argument was based on two propositions: the referendum result was final and could not be overturned, and the Conservative Party in Wales must begin 'to think the unthinkable'. He noted that in terms of votes the Conservatives were still the second largest party in Wales, but warned that if they refused to have anything to do with the Assembly, or attempted to rely on the blind adherence of members, then Conservative support could continue to seep away and its traditional base in parliamentary constituencies would crumble. The solution, he argued, was a party with a strong Welsh dimension. In short, Lord Roberts was suggesting that the Conservative Party should accept devolution

---

[12] *Western Mail*, 13 September 1997.

and establish a more autonomous Welsh party. Consequently, when he was later appointed to chair the Commission on the party's organisation there could be no doubt as to the outcome.

In 1998, in the wake of the referendum and ahead of the first elections the Conservative Party in Wales renamed itself the Welsh Conservative Party. However, this was not reflected in a new organisational structure with significantly devolved powers. The new UK Conservative Party constitution of 1998 granted the Board of the Welsh Conservative Party scarcely more powers than an English Area Council. The ability to shortlist candidates in Wales, determine how the budget of the Welsh party is spent, and other executive functions were not devolved explicitly to the Welsh party in the constitution. According to Greg Walker, the party's candidate for Cardiff Central in the 2001 general election, Lord Roberts's Commission had a choice of four options for the future structure of the Welsh party :[13]

1. **Status quo** – the Welsh party would remain encompassed within the wider UK party constitution, with its powers dependent on delegation from the UK party board. Parliamentary candidate selection would remain in the hands of Conservative Central Office in Smith Square.

2. **A devolved party** – the Welsh party would be given broad powers vested in it as of right by the UK party constitution – not dependent on ad hoc delegation. Parliamentary candidate selection and the power to refer members to the Ethics and Integrity Committee would be transferred to the Welsh party.

3. **An autonomous party** – the Welsh party would become 'sovereign' with its own distinct constitution. It would choose to remain intimately affiliated with the wider British Conservative movement, similar to the way that the Scottish Conservative Party is organised.

4. **An independent party** – often called the 'Bavarian option' after the CSU. The party would be separated from the wider party issuing its own manifesto and sitting as separate group in Parliament, albeit in coalition with other Conservatives.

The third option would seem to afford the greatest flexibility and freedom of action consistent with remaining an integral part of the British Conservative movement. However, when the Commission's recommendations emerged they did not chart the way forward in such overt terms. Instead, they recommended a dozen detailed changes which together would undoubtedly move the party in a more autonomous direction. They included:

- A leadership election within the National Assembly should only occur if a majority of the Conservative Group called for one. At present a

---

[13] Greg Walker *op.cit.*

contest can be triggered if just two of the Conservative AMs wish one to take place.

- Distinctive policies for the party to be developed by a "high quality, high powered think tank which will not be distracted by day-to-day matters."[14]

- A panel to vet all candidates seeking to stand for Parliament in Wales - a process that would have the effect of barring candidates with few local roots.

- An independent disciplinary committee to be set up with a legally qualified chairman to deal with complaints against members in Wales – a recommendation prompted by the experience of dealing with the former party leader, Rod Richards.

Undoubtedly, underlying the reluctance to press for more substantial change is a worry that the Welsh Party could be cut off from the UK party financially. At present most of the costs of the Welsh organisation, the salaries of permanent staff and so on, are paid directly from the Conservative's UK headquarters, Smith Square in London. There is not an agreed budget set out in advance of the financial year. This has created an atmosphere of dependency. However, it ignores the fact much of the money Conservatives raise in Wales bypasses the Welsh party and makes its way directly to Smith Square accounts. However this question is addressed it can only lead in the direction of greater autonomy. As a senior figure in the party, Jonathan Evans MEP, has argued:

> "… further organisational changes will be required if we are to meet the challenge of making the Conservatives the leading force in Welsh politics. Central to this project must be the organisation of the way the Party is run from within Wales. Ron Davies has rightly pointed out the contradiction of Labour facilitating the transfer of powers from Westminster to Cardiff and then not exercising parallel decision-making in respect of its own party organisation. Conservative Central Office in London appears to have adopted a somewhat ambivalent approach towards autonomy in the party structure in Wales and the English regions. For many years the party organisation was run on a regional basis with strong regional offices. As the Party finances have contracted and the Party machine in London has grown, we have gradually seen the erosion of the Conservative Party's regional structures. I believe that we are now at the time when Central Office staff in Wales must come fully under the control and remit of the Welsh Conservative Party."[15]

---

[14] Quoted in the *Western Mail*, 2 May 2002.

[15] Jonathan Evans, *The Future of Welsh Conservatism, op.cit..2002.*

However, autonomy for the Welsh Conservatives is part of the agenda for the second term, kicked firmly into touch to avoid dissension in the run up to the second Assembly election. Meanwhile, the party has been repatriating its policy-making process. From the Autumn of 2001 the Assembly Conservative Group began a year-long comprehensive and unprecedented consultation on its 2003 election Manifesto. This took place internally, within the party, and with outside interests. Consultation documents were issued addressing the policy areas broadly covered by the Subject Committees in the Assembly. They were circulated to the 40 constituency associations and to some 500 outside organisations covering the private, public and voluntary sectors. They contained a summary of the present state of policy formation and delivery in their respective areas and asked for responses to a range of questions. Internal party meetings and seminars were held across Wales, while policy spokespeople in the Assembly engaged outside interest groups on a one-to-one basis. Policy Director South Wales Central AM David Melding said that, though drawn out, it was a worthwhile exercise:

> "For us as a party it was an opportunity to simultaneously improve our image with outside organisations and strengthen our policy development process. It was also important because our manifesto is something we can control as a party. It also enables us to project ourselves as a party capable of participating in government, with a credible agenda of our own which can be tested. We attracted a high response rate from our constituency associations with more than 30 responding to the consultation. The questionnaire sent to outside organisations received a response rate of about 30 per cent. Most interest was in health and education, though great attention was also paid to issues concerning the Welsh language and law and order, even though the latter are outside the remit of the Assembly."[16]

The final draft Manifesto, running to some 30 pages, was approved by the Assembly Group in early February 2003. It then went through a Strategy Policy Group of senior party figures, including the Assembly leader, Nick Bourne, David Melding, Nigel Evans, the Shadow Secretary of State for Wales, Carol Hyde, Chair of the Welsh Party, Lord Roberts, and Jonathan Evans MEP.

Meanwhile, a draft Manifesto had been published for consultation in October 2002. It was entitled *Fighting for the Vulnerable*, and presumably designed to emphasise a softening of the Conservative's stance on social questions. In this there is no doubt that it reflected the wide-ranging consultation that had taken place. The draft Manifesto contained more than 50 commitments

---

[16] Interview, February 2003

across the range of the National Assembly's responsibilities, including the following:

- Establish an independent all-Wales health Authority free of political interference, with the Assembly restricting itself to setting strategic objectives for the NHS.

- Fully fund a children's hospital for Wales

- Abolish tuition fees for Welsh students.

- Target resources for Welsh medium teaching at pre-school and primary levels.

- Limit increases in business rates to give a competitive advantage to those operating Wales.

- Improve the A470 road between north and south Wales.

- Establish a National Art Gallery for Wales.

A problem area for the party was the constitutional question and the Assembly's future. What will the party say to the Richard Commission, currently examining the Assembly's powers and due to report by the end of 2003? The draft manifesto is blunt, stating that the party will:

"Oppose primary legislative and tax raising powers for the Assembly."

This left Policy Director David Melding with the task of defining how executive devolution could be made to work effectively within the framework of the 1998 Government of Wales Act, widely considered to be seriously flawed in the way it shares power between Westminster and Cardiff Bay.[17] However, the Conservative Group had endorsed the final report of the Assembly's own Procedural Review. This contained a radical set of proposals setting down how primary legislation should be drafted at Westminster to ensure maximum discretion and autonomy for the Assembly. Some commentators argued that if implemented wholeheartedly these proposals would allow primary legislation for Wales to be devolved by the back door.[18] In any event they allowed sufficient flexibility for the door Welsh Conservatives had begun to open on constitutional policy to be kept ajar.

Although the question of coalition was not openly addressed in the manifesto, the wide ranging discussions leading up to its publication concentrated the minds of the leadership. Proportional representation makes it highly unlikely for any one of the parties in the Assembly to achieve an outright majority. To

---

[17] See Chapter 2 in this volume.

[18] Known as the Rawlings Principles after their author Rick Rawlings, Professor of Public Law at the London School of Economics: see Chapter 1 in this volume for a discussion, and also John Osmond, 'Constitution Building on the Hoof', an account of the Procedural Review in the previous volume in this series, *Building a Civic Culture, ibid,* 2002.

participate in government, therefore, all the parties have to consider with whom amongst their opponents they might be able to collaborate. David Melding acknowledged they would be examining the other party manifestos closely, commenting:

> "We take the view that it is question of thirds in our own Manifesto: a third that we must have in any deal, a third that would be highly desirable, and a third that could be jettisoned. The same, I guess, applies to the other parties. For my part I regard the Conservatives as a natural party of government not opposition. Our aim should be to reach a position of being strong enough numerically as a group to have these discussions on potential coalitions within eight years."[19]

DISESTABLISHMENT

Conservatives can never cease being a Unionist party, in the sense of wanting to maintain the integrity of Britain. However, the coming of the National Assembly presented Welsh Conservatives with an urgent challenge to find ways of making their Unionism compatible with a Welsh rather than English identity. Could they in fact become Welsh Conservatives and tap into what is undoubtedly a significant proportion of the Welsh electorate aligned towards the centre-right of the political spectrum? The evidence from the first term suggests that this should not be an impossible task.

There are clear signs that intellectual figures within the party and much of the leadership have not only embraced the changes but see virtue in aligning their party with a further advance for devolution. An outstanding example is Lord Griffiths of Fforestfach who headed Margaret Thatcher's Policy Unit in Whitehall between 1985 and 1990. In his lecture to the Institute of Welsh Politics quoted earlier he described why he had changed his mind on devolution. He said he had opposed the Assembly because he regarded it as an extra tier of government that would result in more bureaucracy, because it would be dominated by Old Labour, and because it could possibly lead to the break up of the United Kingdom. However, he had changed his mind for a number of reasons:

> "It became clear that a Welsh Assembly would provide a more informed debate on Welsh issues because it would draw on a greater number of people with first hand knowledge on the subject matter. It would also allow much greater time for matters such as education, health, agriculture and the language to be debated at a deeper level than was

---

[19] David Melding, op.cit.

possible at Westminster. It would encourage politicians in Wales to listen, at greater length and with greater care to the concerns of the electorate than had hitherto been the case. It would mean that un-elected bodies would be more transparent and accountable because of their new status. Finally, I believe that the very existence of an Assembly at the heart of Welsh political life must strengthen the identity of Wales and its language, which in my judgement are important, if not critical, for the preservation of Welsh culture."[20]

The South Wales Central AM, David Melding, also has a clear vision of the direction the party should be taking. Reflecting on the 2001 general election in Wales, he observed:

"It struck me when campaigning that what the people of Wales want is a light blue and genuinely Welsh Conservative Party. The spirit of one nation conservatism has attracted strong support in Wales in the past and could do so again. Given that there are now three left-of-centre parties in Wales, there is plenty of room for a moderate centre right party ... Perhaps our task is similar to that of the Anglican Church in 1920. Seen by many as a church for English brewers and landowners, Anglicans were somehow not authentically Welsh. However, after the shock of disestablishment, the Church in Wales became a successful Welsh institution. While holding true to its Anglican identity and remaining in full communion with the Church of England, it managed its own affairs and prospered. The Welsh Conservative Party must undergo is own disestablishment so that it can rebut all accusations of being an 'English' party."[21]

The party's future electoral objectives are clear enough. The regional vote of Conservative supporters in strong Labour areas must be more effectively tapped. Conservative abstainers must be motivated to vote on the basis that devolution is no longer a threat but a means of preserving the United Kingdom. Meanwhile, Plaid Cymru, largely disregarded in the first Assembly elections, will have to be confronted. In this context the Conservatives face a dilemma. Confronting Plaid obliges the Conservatives to adopt a stronger set of specific Welsh policies, which as we have seen a growing number of Conservative leaders and intellectuals wish to see developed in any event. Yet this could frustrate the party's attempts to motivate traditional supporters, who abstained in the first elections partly because of their weak sense of identity with Wales. Motivating its traditional supporters with policies they might not find congenial and simultaneously emphasising a stronger Welsh identity remains a challenge for the Welsh Conservative Party.

---

[20] Lord Griffiths *op.cit.*

[21] David Melding *op.cit.*

CHAPTER 14

PLAID CYMRU

Laura McAllister

The celebrations were bound to result in a hangover. In the first elections to the National Assembly in 1999, Plaid Cymru performed beyond even its own most optimistic expectations. It gained nearly 30 per cent of the total vote, winning 17 seats and becoming the largest opposition group in Cardiff Bay. And there was more. In the local elections held on the same day, Plaid took control of three of Wales's 22 local councils, including two in the south Wales valleys. A month later, it saw its first two MEPs elected to the European Parliament. For the first time in its history, Plaid Cymru had elected representatives at every level.

This unprecedented success created a novel environment and a rather different role for Plaid Cymru. It had grown accustomed to the pluses and minuses of being the perennial 'minority party'. Now it was central to the working of a new multi-level political settlement ,with its 17 AMs occupying a pivotal position in the Assembly.

Another factor informed its new role. Plaid was closely associated with devolution and the National Assembly, even more than devolution's official creators, New Labour. There was an irony to this since the new institution's flawed constitutional arrangements were very much the product of an internal Labour Party compromise. Publicly, however, the Assembly was seen as Plaid's 'baby'. This meant public judgements on the success or otherwise of the new body were intrinsically linked with a verdict on Plaid Cymru itself.

CHALLENGE OF OPPOSITION

These factors posed a few headaches for a party better accustomed to a back-seat role. One of the first, and most significant, decisions that faced the Plaid group was about the role it should play in the new Assembly. Was its priority to make the thing work or, conversely, to test the devolution settlement by creating difficulties for the minority Labour administration? Was it possible to conduct these two roles simultaneously? This debate within Plaid was also informed by an awareness of its role in a common drive to boost the public's fragile confidence in devolution, indicated by the wafer-thin referendum vote and a turnout of just 46 per cent in the first elections.

In some ways, Plaid had no choice. This was Wales's first democratically elected institution and, for all its limitations, the project was intrinsically linked with Plaid's longer-term goal of full national status within the European Union. Quite simply, Plaid could not afford for it to be labelled a failure. It had to work with the Labour administration, whilst simultaneously pressing the case for a more muscular Assembly to deliver the distinctive public policies it claimed Wales needed. This meant it had to perform as an effective opposition to Labour in Cardiff Bay, whilst studiously avoiding undermining the concept and legitimacy of the Assembly.

Many Plaid AMs found the task of constructive opposition essentially problematic. One described it as an "invidious position to be in", particularly when compared to the easier challenges facing the other two opposition parties. As well as eschewing destructive tendencies, Plaid had to make the case for additional powers beyond the limited ones afforded to the Assembly by the 1998 Government of Wales Act. The party was not helped by a perplexing array of 'clarifying' statements meant to explain the party's constitutional position. This had begun in the election campaign with Dafydd Wigley's clumsy denial of the status of "independence" in the party's aims.[1] It meant uncertainty reigned, inside and outside the party, as to what Plaid actually wanted on the constitutional front. All of this made for an uneasy compromise and is the critical backdrop for this account of Plaid Cymru's performance in the first term of the National Assembly.

Despite the challenges, Plaid hit the ground running, buoyed by its new status as the second largest party and having won from Labour talismanic seats like Rhondda, Islwyn and Llanelli. Pollsters suggest voters increasingly identify with parties through their leaders. Plaid's president, the experienced, popular and respected MP, and then AM, for Caernarfon, Dafydd Wigley had thoroughly enjoyed his campaign head-to-head with the beleaguered Labour leader, Alun Michael. Plaid had also successfully re-branded itself as 'The Party of Wales' which, with Michael in charge, allowed it to present Labour as 'The Party of London'. During the election, this had also helped Plaid Cymru loosen its traditional association with Welsh-speakers. The party had been the major beneficiary of Labour's self-imposed leadership problems. Wigley polled consistently higher than Michael in the popularity rankings for First Secretary. The elections confirmed Plaid had begun to establish itself as the party that many Welsh voters most closely associated with Wales and its best interests, giving credence to a phenomenon associated with 'second order' elections elsewhere.

[1] For further information, see McAllister, L., (2001), 'The National Assembly Elections: Plaid Cymru's Coming of Age', *Contemporary Wales*, Vol 14, pp.109-114; and McAllister, L., (2000), 'Changing the Landscape: The Wider Political Lessons from the Elections in Wales', *The Political Quarterly*, vol. 71, no. 2, pp. 211-222.

In many respects, Michael's decision to form a minority Labour government rather than seek a coalition agreement with the Liberal Democrats (as had Donald Dewar, his counterpart in Scotland) assisted Plaid. It immediately applauded the decision as one that recognised a "move to consensual politics" and confirmed it would not oppose Michael's nomination as First Secretary. Why? Plaid spied an opportunity, first to access and influence devolved policy-making; and, second, to transform itself into an alternative party of government in Cardiff. To what extent was it able to fulfil this role?

THE LEADERSHIP

Albeit in very different circumstances, each of the four political parties experienced its own leadership upheaval during the Assembly's first term. In May 2000, Plaid's 57-year-old president, Dafydd Wigley, who had held the post since 1991, stood down on medical advice, having been diagnosed with heart problems. He had been out of action since before Christmas leaving the party in the hands of its former manager in the Assembly, Ynys Môn MP and AM, Ieuan Wyn Jones, and not least through the critical weeks of Alun Michael's resignation during February. Ill-health was certainly a major factor in Wigley's decision to resign, but there had been murmurings of discontent at Wigley's leadership amongst the Plaid group. Some openly admitted that the experienced Westminster politician had found it difficult to adjust to the less formal and more consensual atmosphere in Cardiff Bay. There were suggestions that his leadership was less than strategic and, at times, divisive. There was also residual discomfort at Wigley's campaign outburst on Plaid's commitment to independence. However, most criticism centred on his management of the Plaid group. One AM described as "essentially problematic" Wigley's decision to appoint half of the group as Shadow Cabinet members, leaving the remainder with no official role. The result was that the leader communicated almost exclusively with his Shadow team, leaving the remainder of the group in the dark about tactics until the last minute. Communication problems of this kind caused the group some real problems.

Wigley's decision to step down as president spurred an election that was the first involving the party's whole membership. Every member had a vote to cast for one of three candidates: Ieuan Wyn Jones; Helen Mary Jones, AM for Llanelli and the party's spokesperson on equal opportunities; and Jill Evans, elected to the European Parliament as one of Wales's five MEPs in June 1999.

None of the three candidates were particularly well-known outside of the party. Of the three, Ieuan Wyn Jones had a head-start, having been an MP since 1987. Despite being the clear favourite, there was some doubt as to Jones's capacity to unite and develop the party at a crucial juncture in its history. There was concern that now Plaid had made its long-awaited breakthrough in the southern valleys, its priority had to be to sustain and advance this. Some feared that Jones would come across in public as signalling a return to the party's northern roots. He did not possess Wigley's broad appeal to different constituencies and sectors of Plaid's membership, or to the public at large. Crucially, however, he did have valuable parliamentary experience and plenty of popular support amongst Plaid's membership. He also possessed a sound managerial pedigree and had led the party relatively effectively during Wigley's enforced absence. His background and power base also worked to his advantage in garnering support from the most concentrated locus of Plaid's membership in north west and south west Wales in particular.

Helen Mary Jones was one of Plaid's early successes in the Assembly. A former Deputy Director of the Equal Opportunities Commission, she had taken to the new political arena with ease and quickly established herself as one of Plaid's most accomplished media performers. She was also popular with people outside the party. However, some within Plaid regarded her as too inexperienced, and some argued, erratic, to take over the leadership at this point. Still, Jones's performance before and during the leadership campaign showed that she had a broad level of support that many saw as an indication that she might become the party's first woman president in the future.

Jill Evans, meanwhile, was considerably disadvantaged by her position outside the Assembly. As a Brussels-based MEP, Evans was removed from the main focus of Plaid's attention. There was an understandable consensus that the new President had to come from within the Assembly group, since that was where the media, public and membership's attention now lay. In any case, the members knew less about Evans than they did about the other two candidates.

Both Evans and Helen Mary Jones lacked the influential backers Ieuan Wyn Jones enjoyed. He benefited from prestigious support from the Presiding Officer, Lord Dafydd Elis-Thomas, and AMs, Cynog Dafis, Elin Jones, Rhodri Glyn Thomas, Janet Ryder and Jocelyn Davies. This was a useful coalition representing most of Plaid's various geographical and political constituencies. On the other hand Helen Mary Jones was the choice of those inside and outside the party, including Phil Williams AM, who were aggrieved at Wigley's treatment and suspected a plot to oust him as president. This carried the legacy of internal rows in the early 1990s over the treatment of staff during a proposed party restructuring. Jill Evans's support came mainly from lower-profile members outside the Assembly group, although she did get the backing of Adam Price, candidate for Carmarthen East and Dinefwr, which

Plaid was targeting for its next Westminster breakthrough. Jill Evans presented herself as the left's candidate and was supported by many of the party's younger, southern-based members.

There was little of substance to distinguish the three candidates' personal manifestos. Each agreed that the party had to consolidate its position across Wales following the successes in the 1999 elections and continue its assault on Labour's heartlands, although, with their backgrounds, Helen Mary Jones and Jill Evans were better placed to convince on that. Each pledged to continue the modernisation of the party which had begun in earnest in the lead-up to 1999 and had helped deliver success. Each argued for a strong Plaid voice at every elected level with the objective of winning power in Cardiff in 2003.

The results of the presidential contest were announced in August 2000. Ieuan Wyn Jones won an overwhelming victory with 77 per cent of the vote. Jones gained 4,834 of the 6,273 votes cast (on a 60 per cent turn-out). Helen Mary Jones was a distant second, with 798 votes (13 per of the votes cast) and Jill Evans third with 598 votes (10 per cent).

Facing an unexpected presidential election forced the party to revisit wider questions about its leadership structure. It was clear that the leader needed to come from within the Assembly where public and media attention, not to say Plaid's own, was overwhelmingly trained. A row ensued within Plaid's *Pwyllgor Gwaith* (National Executive Committee) which rumbled on for over a year as to whether the President needed to be an AM. This was understandable given the composition of Plaid's Executive which had many members from outside the Assembly. It also underlined some of the early jostling and manoeuvring in the party post-devolution. Plaid's performance in 1999 brought with it higher expectations and greater career aspirations on the part of its activists, in short the price of success. The leadership debate, alongside various other constitutional and disciplinary questions, led to an internal Constitutional Conference in November 2001. This updated the party's constitution, dealing with issues such as candidate selection and disciplinary and appeal procedures. It also re-established the post of party vice-president in an attempt to bridge the gap between the party outside the Assembly and that within. The vice-president's role was to act as the leader outside Cardiff Bay, developing strategies for political campaigns, as well as overseeing the party's internal management and administration. The veteran activist and Gwynedd councillor, Dafydd Iwan, was elected unopposed to the post in April 2002.

Ieuan Wyn Jones's induction to the party leadership was not helped by the intervention of some Plaid members who sought a far stronger stance on the issue of in-migration to predominantly Welsh-speaking parts of Wales and its impact on housing, employment and the very survival of the language. Led by Gwynedd councillor, Seimon Glyn, there were calls for Plaid to adopt a far stronger stance on this issue. The pressure group, *Cymuned*, formed in 2000, argued for more public policy and legislative intervention in this area. As has been the case throughout its history on this issue, Plaid found itself between a rock and a hard place. Despite its aspirations to be 'the party of Wales', it had historically benefited from its association with those areas with a high concentration of Welsh speakers. Yet, its priority was to continue to broaden its appeal to the majority English speakers.

This is by no means an insurmountable problem, for the questions of secure jobs and good public services apply as much in Bridgend as Bala. However, this was also Jones's first real challenge and it happened to be one of the biggest he was likely to face. He was initially reluctant to discipline Glyn and others, like Ceredigion vice-president and Executive member, Gwilym ap Ioan who spoke against party policy. Not surprisingly, Labour seized the opportunity to make its main political opponent squirm and Jones's media limitations were horribly exposed on the BBC's Question Time programme in February 2001, with lasting discomfort within the party at his handling of this issue.[2]

The next real test for Jones was the General Election of June 2001. Despite increasing its share of the Welsh vote by 4.4 per cent and winning Carmarthen East and Dinefwr from Labour, Jones was horrified to see Plaid lose to Labour the Ynys Môn seat he had held since 1987. The symbolism was enormous. His critics argued that if the president could not safeguard his own seat, then how could he deliver advances for the party across Wales in the future? Plaid's two remaining 'dual-mandate' AMs, Dafydd Wigley and Ieuan Wyn Jones, who had simultaneously held Westminster seats for the first two years of the Assembly, stood down from the House of Commons.[3] In theory, this was designed to free up more time. However, in less than a year, Wigley and Cynog Dafis, plus the veteran, Phil Williams, announced that they would not seek re-

---

[2] During the programme on 15 February, Plaid Cymru leader Ieuan Wyn Jones came under intense pressure from Glenys Kinnock, a Labour MEP. He denied that Seimon Glyn had said some of the comments attributed to him, blaming 'Labour spin'. This backfired when David Dimbleby, Question Time's presenter, held up a BBC transcript of Seimon Glyn's comments for him to read.

[3] The MP for Ceredigion and Mid and West list AM, Cynog Dafis had resigned his Westminster seat at the end of 1999, precipitating a by-election in February 2000 that Plaid candidate Simon Thomas won, pushing Labour into a humiliating fourth place.

election in the 2003 Assembly elections. Whilst, as elder statespeople, their loss was bound to be felt, one senses that the Plaid group now has better experience, ability and breadth to cope with such a loss.

Jones's media performances remained the cause of some concern. Chief executive, Karl Davies admitted that Jones needed some media training to become a better television performer. Jones resisted the invitation, and many would now agree that he has improved his presentational credibility, certainly within the Assembly, and compares favourably with the other party leaders in this respect.

Plaid played a central and critical role in the no confidence vote on First Secretary, Alun Michael in February 2000. The background to this is rehearsed elsewhere,[4] but it did raise two significant issues for Plaid. In this first instance, Presiding Officer, and Plaid AM for Meirionnydd Nant Conwy, Lord Elis-Thomas played a decisive role, declaring it to be "the first day of devolution". Despite the impartiality of his post, this was seen to reflect a new political role for the Presiding Office and was subject to some sustained and vicious criticism from Labour in Wales. Secondly, it was the first time Plaid really flexed its muscles as an opposition party. It could scarcely have chosen a more potent time or an issue with such far-reaching implications.

PLAID CYMRU'S INTERNAL ORGANISATION

Like all the party groups in Cardiff Bay, Plaid's had strong and weaker members. Ieuan Wyn Jones's first task was to make the best of the human resources he had available. He immediately re-shuffled the group, a necessity given his own election to the leadership and Dafydd Wigley's retirement to the backbenches. He decided early on that the Plaid group should have relevant policy briefs that paralleled the policy structure of the Subject Committees and the Cabinet itself. This would enable the party to prepare itself for a future governing role. Thus his first reshuffle took into account some of the anticipated changes from First Minister, Rhodri Morgan, such as the merging of the two education briefs. Jones duly reorganised the Plaid group on this basis with two of his closest allies, Jocelyn Davies, AM for South East Wales, promoted to the important internal position of Business Manager; and Elin Jones, AM for Ceredigion, becoming Chief Whip and Shadow Minister for Rural Development.

Jones held another reshuffle in March 2002. This was to enable the party to

---

[4] See Chapter 10 in this volume, and the quarterly IWA report, *Devolution Re-launched: Monitoring the National Assembly December 1999 to March 2000.*, IWA, 2000.

take account of shifts in the portfolios of the Labour-Liberal Democrat coalition government set up through the Partnership Agreement of October 2000. It is fair to say that Jones is seen as having been more successful with his internal managerial reforms of the party than he has at raising the party's external profile. Jones is essentially a managerial politician, adept at organisational matters and with a clear focus on tactics, less so on visionary strategies. He proved better than Wigley at finding roles for all of his group, as well as improved communication systems overall. There are clear advantages to this. Several AMs commented that this led to a more stabilised group and more reliable communication networks. Jones also established new positions, such as three spokespersons for small business, sport and the Welsh language, and the Valleys, in an attempt to incorporate and placate those AMs not given shadow cabinet roles.

The Party's long-serving Chief Executive, Karl Davies left in May 2002 to take up a post with the National Association of Head Teachers. He was replaced in September by the Aberystwyth-based academic, Dr. Dafydd Trystan who, despite being a long-standing member of Plaid Cymru, had in his previous guise issued some rather critical judgements on Ieuan Wyn Jones's ability to lead the party effectively. This hardly made for a cosy start to the relationship between chief executive and president, although Jones was instrumental in Trystan's appointment and was known to favour him over the other main candidate, acting Chief Executive, Anna Brychan.

In reality, the advent of devolution meant little real organisational reorientation for Plaid. Unlike the other three parties, it was uniquely based entirely within Wales, save for support staff for its elected representatives in Westminster and Brussels, and a few branches of the party outside Wales. There were some changes, however. Formal arrangements already existed for liaison between the party's HQ in Cardiff and Westminster. Devolution required these to be formalised and extended, since policy issues often impacted on more than one level of government. A quasi-formal Liaison Committee was set up to ensure proper links between the Plaid Cymru representatives at Assembly, Westminster, Europe and local government levels. Although this has only met on an ad-hoc basis, it has helped set in place better systems of co-ordination and communication.

In addition, and perhaps more helpful, was a system of telephone conferencing that took place weekly between representatives from the party groups at every level. Interestingly, the driver for this came from councillors in Plaid-controlled local authorities. There was also bilateral liaisons. One AM described regular contact with the MPs and MEPs on her specific policy portfolio in the Assembly. This was multi-level governance in action, and having representatives at every level for the first time was the spur for Plaid's attempt to improve its internal liaison mechanisms.

Devolution also saw its overall staff complement associated with the party multiply considerably. New research and support staff based at the Assembly and in Europe, serving the party's AMs and MEPs, enabled an enhanced policy development capacity. With the additional funds the party received to boost its 1999 election campaign, it had recruited extra temporary staff for its Cardiff headquarters. Only some of these remained in post after the election, so Plaid continued to operate with a skeleton office staff of six. This clearly posed some problems since Karl Davies described the post devolution workload as "increasing significantly day by day". The successes of 1999 also raised expectations of what the party's headquarters could actually provide for its membership. Some difficulties were experienced in terms of the demarcation of roles between staff at each level while the Assembly staff were prevented from operating in a party political capacity. Overall, however, Plaid found itself far better served in a research, administrative and policy development sense after devolution.

THE NEW POLICY ENVIRONMENT

At one obvious level, Plaid was the party best geared-up to offer a platform of policies designed specifically for the Welsh context. That is the advantage all nationalist and regional-focused parties have in elections to that tier of government.[5] However, the new mantle of official opposition also meant Plaid Cymru faced different challenges in the policy arena. Previously, it had only experienced a governing role or official opposition to Labour within a few local councils. Now it had to develop its profile as a potential party of government. It could no longer act as a purely aspirational force.

The signs were good. Plaid's Assembly election manifesto was its most substantial ever and was certainly more weighty - in content and substance - than those of its rivals. It was helped by a long-standing Welsh policy focus and a widespread association in the public eye with the Welsh dimension. The manifesto looked beyond the scope of the Assembly and hinted at policies which, under the current devolution settlement, a government there would be unable to deliver. This underlines the party's essential dilemma: how to be Janus-faced in terms of operating within the existing capacity of devolution, whilst also looking to the future with its greater potential for distinctive policy-making.

The party benefited from a breadth and depth of policy experience, not only from its former MPs, but also within the Assembly group from the likes of

---

[5] See McAllister, L., (2000), op. cit. and Marsh, M., 'Testing the Second-Order Election Model after Four European Elections', *British Journal of Political Science*, 1998, pages 591-607.

Janet Davies and Pauline Jarman who had experience of leading local councils, Phil Williams on economic policy and European structural funds, Cynog Dafis on education, and Dr Dai Lloyd, a GP, on health. Others, such as Helen Mary Jones, Elin Jones and Janet Ryder, had worked in the public and voluntary sectors. Yet there remains a critical difference between design and delivery of policies. Plaid had little real experience of the latter. This meant it needed to recast many of its existing polices within a new, more pragmatic context.

The Assembly was naturally the main focus for such policy deliberation, although there was the new interface with the MPs, MEPs and local councillors to consider as well. Despite the *Cyngor Cenedlaethol* (National Council) retaining its role as the supreme decision-making body, there was a danger that the party's membership might feel alienated by the new focus in Cardiff Bay. With that in mind, Policy Consultation Forums were established which gave ordinary party members the opportunity to contribute to the policy-making process. The party was also helped by the establishment of a internal Policy Unit in 2002, funded by a Policy Development Grant from the Electoral Commission. The Unit conducted and commissioned research, focusing on education, public services, health, social services and the labour market as priorities. This has already made an important contribution to the party's research, enhancing the detail and depth of new policies.

In terms of influencing policy development under specific Ministerial and Subject Committee portfolios, Plaid's end of term report might read 'fairly effective'. Despite claims that the Subject Committees operate in a consensual and inclusive way, much is dependent on the Minister, the Chair and the wider composition of the committee in terms of broader input from across the party divides. One AM described many amendments made at Subject Committee level as failing simply because "they were Plaid-proposed", despite acknowledged Labour support for the principles involved.

It is fair to say, too, that the party has had little impact in plenary sessions. This is not surprising. As the Assembly has shifted away from its corporate roots, Plaid has begun to re-invent itself as the official opposition and has behaved accordingly. Its minority position has meant that it can have only a marginal role in influencing decisions taken at plenary. Inevitably, these project the coalition government's policies.

Plaid may well try to claim some of the credit for Rhodri Morgan's espousal of a distinctive, 'Welsh-way' of policy-making.[6] His claim that Wales eschewed the Treasury-driven public finance initiative, league tables and student tuition fees, preferring instead, comprehensive schools and health sector

---

[6] His 'Clear Red Water' speech at the National Centre for Public Policy, University of Wales Swansea, 11 December 2002.

reorganisation, certainly owed something to Plaid's promotion of a distinctive Welsh policy agenda. That is not to say that Welsh Labour's agenda was wholly reactive. Nevertheless, it had already learnt, to its cost, the lessons of London interference. Since Plaid was its principal rival, it was an important priority to compete on the new devolved terrain by distinguishing Welsh Labour more clearly from its London counterpart.

A MATURING PARTY

Overall, the first term of the National Assembly both precipitated and underlined an important stage in Plaid Cymru's maturing. This was a major and enforced growth spurt, for which the party had long yearned. Arguments over its proper role in Welsh politics, as either pressure group or political party, now seemed strangely anachronistic. It has almost completely transformed itself into a fully-fledged political party, despite showing occasional signs of its old weaknesses.

At the outset of the new era of Assembly politics, Plaid's priorities were clear, if problematic to achieve. It had to solidify and protect the considerable electoral mandate it achieved in 1999. It had to prove this was no fluke, that it was not just a protest vote, based on discomfort at Labour's leadership and candidate selection shenanigans.

The key tension for Plaid centred on whether to work within the framework of Ron Davies' devolution settlement or push for additional powers to transform the Assembly into a Parliament. It decided early on that it had to carry out the two roles. It was certainly helped by the *de facto*, if not *de jure*, move away from the Assembly as a corporate body and the creation in 2002 of the Welsh Assembly Government. It is fair to say that it was only in the latter part of the Assembly's first term that Plaid was able to consolidate a position as the official opposition.

Early on, the party certainly missed opportunities for bringing the ruling administration to account. It had been hamstrung by an almost unofficial coalition with the minority Labour administration at the start. During the early months, Labour was forced to consult with Plaid on an almost weekly basis to ensure its decisions could be agreed in plenary. However, the move away from corporate status allowed Plaid to consolidate a clearer oppositional role. It also helped shift the relationship between Plaid and Labour in a way that suited both parties. Their historic tension and distrust were always there. There is little doubt that the majority of AMs in both parties were happier to revert to their traditional adversarial roles. Incidentally, it may well be that this new context would have better suited Dafydd Wigley than Ieuan Wyn Jones.

Devolution meant Plaid was now operating under the glare of media and public publicity. The Assembly's first term shifted the party's policy focus away from the historically predominant constitutional question. This brought about some inevitable tensions, most notably over language and in-migration. In its preparations for the 2003 poll, Plaid determinedly set a public services agenda for itself. It did, however, return to the constitution in January 2003, pledging to establish under a Plaid Cymru-led government, a Constitutional Convention on the future powers of the Assembly. This was despite the ongoing deliberations of the Richard Commission on the Assembly's powers, set up in July 2002 and due to report by the end of 2003.

Critically, Plaid Cymru has had to acclimatise to coalition politics, surely a permanent phenomenon under the existing electoral system. This posed some initial problems as the party had planned to set out its stall as an alternative government for Wales. In reality, a single party forming a majority government is increasingly unlikely. Adjusting to coalition politics proved as much a culture-shock for Plaid as it was for Labour. It was further tested by having to transform itself into an effective opposition, scrutinising and challenging the government whilst not simultaneously undermining the fragile devolution project. It may be that the party needs to better divide these roles in future. Somehow it needs to better distinguish its role as the official opposition within the Assembly chamber during plenary sessions, while at the same time engaging in constructive policy debate within the Subject Committees.

In terms of personnel, some strong new politicians have emerged within the Plaid group, many of them women. This is an important development given the significant, but largely hidden, role women have always played in the party.[7]

As for the party leadership, Ieuan Wyn Jones's managerial skills may well be just what the party needs at this point in its history. His goal-orientated approach might better suit the moment. He is widely judged to have better awareness of short and medium term strategies than the more visionary Wigley. He is also deemed a more reliable and consistent leader than Wigley. Some of his AMs describe him as a greater risk taker than his predecessor. That is, he is willing to stake out new ground in relation to the party's tactics and strategies, and to measure the cost and benefit of pursuing each.

If we are to judge Plaid against the twin objectives outlined at the start, the verdict must be partial success. Yet, there is something inevitable about this judgement. Even without the upheavals of a leadership change and significant shifts within the Assembly's operation, the first term of the Assembly was

---

[7] See the chapter 'A Woman's Perspective: From the Outside Looking In' in McAllister L., *Plaid Cymru: The Emergence of a Political Party*, Seren, 2001.

always going to be the time when Plaid adjusted to a radically different environment and a changed role for itself. Its real task, which it is fair to say it accomplished in the Assembly's first four year term, was to lay the foundations for the future pursuit of power in Cardiff Bay.

PART 4

A CHANGING POLITICAL CULTURE

CHAPTER 15

A NEW POLITICS

Nia Richardson

When Ron Davies invited the then leaders of other pro-devolution parties to join him on stage at the Welsh College of Music and Drama to celebrate the Yes result in the September 1997 referendum, it was not just to thank them for their support. It was also to demonstrate the Secretary of State's intention that Wales should have a new 'inclusive politics'. A few months later, when presenting the Government of Wales Act to Parliament, he declared the Assembly would be:

> *"A new institution that will both herald a new style of more inclusive politics that better fits the needs and character of Wales and open to public scrutiny and accountability the machinery of government in Wales."*[1]

This chapter explores how far these hopes of creating a new political culture in Wales were realised in the first term. First it describes the new framework for Welsh politics that was put in place by the Assembly. It then examines the compromises that were required for devolution to be agreed by the Welsh Labour Party and argues that these led directly to the rhetoric of inclusion designed to engage Plaid Cymru and the Liberal Democrats in the project.

In practice, the fragility of the new politics was soon exposed by the Assembly's methods of operation. The new institution reverted to type and developed a parliamentary style. This was most clearly seen in the rapid emergence of a government and opposition. Paradoxically, the creation of the coalition in October 2000 re-inforced this more confrontational style. At the same time, however, there were real achievements in achieving a more consensual approach. There was a determination to bring a greater openness to government, procedures were established to involve outside interests, equal opportunities were given a high priority, and despite some disputes the Welsh language advanced its position.

To a large extent the advance of women in the Assembly produced this progress. As a result of new selection procedures in Labour and Plaid Cymru women achieved a critical mass of numbers in the new institution that, following the coalition, produced a female majority in Rhodri Morgan's Cabinet.

---

[1] Quoted in Dafydd Wigley, *Maen i'r Wal*, 2001, Gwasg Gwynedd.

A NEW FRAMEWORK FOR WELSH POLITICS

The idea that something new could be established in Wales that was innovative, imaginative and different in style to the more confrontational arrangements at Westminster became a shared aspiration of a loose coalition of interests in Wales. During the second reading of the Government of Wales Act in Parliament, the then leader of Plaid Cymru, Dafydd Wigley commented:

> *"At the very least, our own national Assembly will articulate the values that we hold as a people. It will be a bulwark against imposed dogma of the Thatcherite kind. When I say 'as a people' I mean all the people who live in Wales as citizens of Wales, and all are equal irrespective of race, creed, colour or language."*[2]

Ron Davies' vision for the new institution was one of:

> *"… power sharing, powerful committees, partnerships, proportionality, regional concerns, and a corporate body breeding consensus."*[3]

This new 'inclusiveness' also demanded an element of proportional representation in the Assembly elections. This was necessary not only to persuade Plaid Cymru and the Liberal Democrats to participate in what was essentially a Labour project, but also to buttress the legitimacy of the new institution. As Ron Davies told the 1997 Welsh Labour Conference that finally endorsed PR, it would reinforce the party's:

> *"… commitment to a new, more open style of politics that will ensure that the Assembly enjoys the confidence of all the people it serves."*[4]

Following the 1997 Referendum, Ron Davies set up the National Assembly Advisory Group which brought together 14 people from all walks of life with the remit to draw up recommendations on the working procedures of the Assembly. Their own composition reflected the aspiration for a more inclusive Welsh politics. Of the 14 members, six were women and eight were men, three were from north Wales and five from west Wales, with the remainder from industrial south Wales. All four main parties were represented together with the trade unions, business, local authority associations and voluntary bodies. The vice-chair of the "Yes' campaign, Mari James, was balanced by the chair of the Just Say No campaign, Nick Bourne,

---

[2] Hansard, 8 December 1997,Vol. 705-6. Quoted in John Osmond, *New Politics in Wales*, Charter 88 Reinventing Democracy Paper No.5, 1998.

[3] Ron Davies, evidence to the Richard Commission, 26 September 2002.

[4] Quoted in Kevin Morgan and Geoff Mungham, 'Unfinished Business: Labour's Devolution Policy' in J. Barry Jones and Denis Balsom (Eds.), *The Road to the National Assembly for Wales*, University of Wales Press, 2000, page 42.

while five members, including the chairman, John Elfed Jones, were also Welsh-speakers.

The way the Group went about its work reflected a belief that a new style of politics could be introduced in Wales. They consulted widely with more than 200 organisations and more than 100 individuals. Their 77 recommendations included the creation of a completely bilingual institution, family friendly hours for the members, and a public information office. The Assembly would not only be an inclusive corporate body, elected by proportional representation, but would also embrace bilingualism and equal opportunities, it would reach out to the regions, and in general be more open and transparent to the public. The emphasis on inclusiveness was as much a product of necessity as of aspiration. It was a tool used successfully by Ron Davies in order to build support for devolution.

INCLUSIVITY AND THE DEVOLUTION COMPROMISE

Much of Labour controlled local government was sceptical about a National Assembly. There was a belief that it would inevitably encroach upon local government territory. Other concerns that stretched back to debates in the 1970s also remained widespread within Welsh Labour's ranks, not least the idea that devolution was a concession to Plaid Cymru. What can now be described as 'Old Labour' believed that devolution did not rest easily with the belief that socialist change towards more equality in society required maintenance of a centralised British state. Others were lukewarm because they feared it would divert attention from the main task of winning the 1997 general election.

To appease sceptics within his own party, Ron Davies had to abandon any aspiration of achieving a Welsh Parliament with primary legislative powers. What emerged was an executive Assembly, closely related to the 1979 proposal based on a corporate local government model in which governmental functions would be vested collectively in the Assembly members as a whole. As Ron Davies himself commented later:

> *"During the period between 1995-97 within the Labour Party a 'legal corporate body' was more reassuring to people than a 'Parliament.'"*[5]

Ron Davies also used the concept of a corporate model to persuade other political parties in Wales to support the devolution proposals. Labour's lukewarm attitude meant the engagement of other parties was crucial to

---

[5] Ron Davies, evidence to the Richard Commission, 26 September 2002.

deliver a yes vote in the referendum. Plaid Cymru, which was nervous about a repeat of the 1979 debacle, and also the Liberal Democrats, needed to be persuaded that they would have an important part to play in the 'new politics' of Wales. A litmus test was the introduction of proportional representation. This was essential to convince the other pro-devolution parties that the Labour Party was committed to 'inclusive politics'. Davies also needed to win over the support of a public which had become increasingly averse to Labour local government and were concerned that the Assembly would suffer from similar problems. As Morgan and Mungham put it:

> *"There was also another problem, namely the poor reputation of Labour local authorities in several parts of Wales, linked to notions of 'cronyism', 'inefficiency', and being resistant to new ideas."[6]*

Davies needed to assure the public that the Assembly would not replicate the worst practices of certain Labour dominated local councils. Instead, the new body would be open, transparent, and accountable to the Welsh public. Proportional representation reinforced the argument. As Kevin Morgan, Chair of the Yes Campaign in the referendum, recalled:

> *"The Additional Member System gave us an argument against the No campaign's argument that the Assembly would be 'jobs for Labour boys'. The system made the Assembly a more inclusive body. That is the real value of PR."[7]*

CONFRONTATION REASSERTS ITSELF

Although the aspirations behind the principle of inclusiveness were genuine enough, it emerged as a fragile compromise within the Labour Party and between the Labour Party and other pro-devolution parties in Wales. Asked by the Richard Commission in September 2002 whether devolution had worked out the way he thought it would, Ron Davies replied:

> *"No, the vision was one of inclusivity, power-sharing, powerful committees, partnerships, proportionality, regional concerns and a corporate body breeding consensus. But since the coalition we have been seeing an increasingly parliamentary style and a de facto separation of powers. We have not just drifted from the corporate body, we have departed from it."[8]*

---

[6] Morgan and Mungham, *op.cit.*, page 47.

[7] Kevin Morgan, evidence to the Richard Commission, 26 September 2002.

[8] Ron Davies, evidence to the Richard Commission, 26 September, 2002.

The 'departure' had begun much earlier than the arrival of the coalition. In fact, its demise can be traced to the passage of the Government of Wales Act when a Cabinet system was grafted on to the corporate body. The road to consensus was also severely disrupted by Labour's failure to win a majority in the Assembly's first election. The party's plans for Welsh devolution had been predicated on the premise that it would have a majority and would be able to facilitate the new form of politics envisaged. After brief negotiations with the Liberal Democrats the Welsh Labour Leader, Alun Michael decided to lead a single party minority government. This resulted in several problems. In the first instance, the opposition parties discovered their ability to defeat the Labour administration with their early vote of no confidence in Agriculture Minister Christine Gwyther. In response Alun Michael accused the opposition parties of putting short-term political advantage ahead of consensus-building.[9]

The inclusive, corporate model was further weakened by the leadership style of the First Secretary himself. Coming from a Westminster background[10] he sought to control policy development, impeding the role of the Subject Committees by regulating the papers that officials prepared for the committees in order to ensure that they reflected the executive's preferred positions. As Ron Davies commented in a lecture in January 2000:

"There is a clear and growing perception that power is concentrated in fewer and fewer hands and that the Executive desires to downplay the role of Subject Committees both in effective scrutiny of its actions and in discharging their policy making role ... The National Assembly was not designed as a committee or cabinet model. It was designed as a hybrid – a cabinet and committee model ... "[11]

Disaffection with Alun Michael's rule came to a head in the no-confidence motion in the First Secretary in February 2000 over his inability to guarantee additional funding for the European Structural Fund Objective One programme. To a large extent, however, this issue merely presented an opportunity. Michael's Administration had failed to engage in the inclusive, consensual politics that had been anticipated. As Balsom and Jones conclude:

"The issue was not, in the end, one of Treasury money for Objective One, but one of leadership style. The Michael regime was perceived as

[9] Alun Michael, 'Dynamic Devolution in Wales', speech given to the Institute of Welsh Politics, University of Wales, Aberystwyth, 18 November 1999.

[10] He remained MP for Cardiff South and Penarth during his short-lived sojourn in the National Assembly and had previously served as Minister of State in the Home Office and Secretary of State for Wales 1998-99.

[11] Ron Davies, 'We Need a Coalition of Ideas', *Agenda*, IWA, Winter 2000. The article was based on an address given to the Welsh Governance Centre at Cardiff University on 17 January 2000, a matter of weeks before the no confidence vote in Alun Michael.

overbearing, dominant and incompatible with the minority status of the Labour Party in the Assembly."[12]

COALITION POLITICS

Rhodri Morgan was elected as the Assembly's new First Secretary in February 2000 and immediately went into coalition negotiations with the Liberal Democrats. A partnership agreement was finally agreed in the Autumn and provided a majority government with a detailed programme of action. At the same time the First Secretary was re-styled as First Minister. This was a far cry from the committee-led policy-making process originally envisaged in the Government of Wales Act.

The way the Agreement was ratified presented a further immediate contrast between the Liberal Democrats and Labour. While the Liberal Democrats debated the deal across the party in Wales and convened a special conference to ratify it, Labour kept it tightly under wraps. As Kevin Morgan reflected:

> *"The first time that most Labour AMs heard about the coalition deal was in a Group meeting at 9.30 am on Thursday 5 October when Rhodri Morgan summarily announced that he had struck a deal with the Lib-Dems. The process which spawned the deal – a process which had excluded all but the most trusted insiders on both sides – is without doubt the least acceptable part of Lib-Labism in Wales, at least from a Labour Party standpoint ... Sources close to the First Minister claim that had he offered a vote, the deal would have been dead, hence the secrecy."[13]*

In the event the deal transformed the old structures that had been built up to support the inclusive model. It ensured the independence of the Office of the Presiding Officer, sharpening the separation between the Assembly and the Administration. A House Committee was subsequently created to advise the Presiding Officer and to determine a separate budget for his office. The new First Minister was also anxious that the Administration's decisions and actions were being interpreted by the media and the public as coming from the Assembly as a whole. Consequently, he sought an acceptable form of words to denote the administrative or executive side of the Assembly - Welsh Assembly Government - and adopted a distinctive logo that was displayed on the Government's publications. The Assembly was moving towards a strong

---

[12] J. Barry Jones and Denis Balsom, 'Aftershock', in *The Road to the National Assembly for Wales*, University of Wales Press, 2000, page 273.

[13] Kevin Morgan, 'By Their Deeds Shall They Be Known', *Agenda*, IWA, Winter 2000/01.

executive government within a *de facto* parliamentary system.[14] It was accompanied by a more adversarial style of politics which was quickly reflected in the work of the Business Committee:

> *"All parties agreed that the Business Committee had initially been a genuine site for inclusive politics. However, with the formation of the Labour-Liberal Democrat Coalition in October 2000 party politics gained the upper hand. One party business manager complained that everything was now 'stitched up' by the Business Manager Andrew Davies, who was sure to get a majority."*[15]

However, consensus working has resumed on certain occasions. Debates in the Assembly often have a consensual tone. And occasionally unanimous votes have even occurred. For example, a motion to challenge Whitehall on funding the resources for free personal care for the elderly out of general taxation was passed unanimously in plenary in May 2002. There has also been a measure of consensus-working in the Committees. Most notable was the unanimous report on the Welsh language, one of the most controversial and divisive issues in Wales, produced by the Culture Committee in the summer of 2002.

It can be argued that the emergence of coalition politics demonstrated a new level of political maturity within the political parties in Wales. With little past experience of partnership working, and in the absence of a Constitutional Convention such as had done much of the spadework in Scotland, the coalition represented a new politics of co-operation between two parties in Wales. They managed to agree on a 25-page list of policy measures and shared Cabinet portfolios according to the relative size of the parties: seven for Labour and two for the Liberal Democrats. Certainly, Rhodri Morgan believed the coalition was indicative of a new politics:

> *"In moving our democracy forward we need a pluralistic view in which no party or groups of parties on the governmental side have any kind of monopoly on wisdom at all. The structure of the Assembly is very much orientated towards trying to develop a communal 'small nation psychology' way of working. In pushing the devolution process forward we don't necessarily want to keep the Westminster style for Wales."*[16]

Nevertheless, the coalition proved to be a shock to Wales' mainstream political culture, in particular grass-root Labour party members who

---

[14] John Osmond, 'In Search of Stability: Coalition Politics in the Second Year of the National Assembly for Wales', in Alan Trench (Ed.) *The State of the Nations 2001*, Imprint Academic, 2001

[15] Alistair Cole and Alan Storer, 'Political Dynamics in the Assembly' in John Osmond and J. Barry Jones (Eds.) *Building a Civic Culture*, IWA, 2002, page 252.

[16] Rhodri Morgan, 'Check against Delivery', address to the Institute of Welsh Politics, Aberystwyth 13 November 2000.

remained determinedly un-reconciled. They were not consulted during the negotiations and were especially angry at the agreement to consider proportional representation for local government elections.

Antagonism over the coalition soon made itself felt. Tom Middlehurst, Labour AM for Alyn and Deeside resigned from the Cabinet as Secretary for post-16 education. Mike German, the Liberal Democrat leader elevated to Deputy First Minister following the partnership agreement, claimed that accusations against him surrounding his previous position as Head of the European Unit at the Welsh Joint Education Committee were motivated by a wish on the part of some local government leaders to de-stabilise the coalition. He was forced to stand aside for a year whilst allegations that he had made improper claims for expenses were investigated by the police. Opposition to the coalition was also at the root of a threat by Blaenau Gwent AM Peter Law, a Minister in Alun Michael's Cabinet, to challenge Rhodri Morgan's leadership. As he put it:

> "Many sections of the Labour Party are very concerned about the way we're going now. We're going wider and wider away from the core membership, with the leadership taking us down the road that nobody voted for in the Labour Party – to be with the Liberal Democrats. You see the comfort zone is what Rhodri Morgan wanted by bringing in the Liberal Democrats – no Labour Party member was consulted on it. The Labour Party has voted against PR in local government but this leadership keeps on going its own way and forgetting about Labour."[17]

There is no doubt, however, that the introduction of PR resulted in a more accurate party balance in the Assembly. In particular, it brought the Conservative Party back into Welsh politics at a national level after its failure to gain a single Welsh seat in the 1997 Westminster election. All but one of the party's eight seats were gained through the regional lists.

INVOLVING OUTSIDE INTERESTS

The new politics have also taken the form of attempts to involve outside stakeholders directly in the work of the Assembly. The Government of Wales Act provided for statutory partnerships with local government and the voluntary sector. These have been supplemented by links with the Wales Social Partners Unit, which gives business and trade unions dedicated resources to help them work with the Assembly on policy development, and with other groups, such as the Gay, Lesbian and Bisexual Forum. A team from

---

[17] Interviewed on the BBC Wales *Dragon's Eye* political programme, 18 July 2002.

the University of Glamorgan which assessed the impact of the Assembly on local government in Wales concluded that those involved in the Local Government Partnership:

> "... felt it did provide a useful forum for trying to align the broad policy agendas for future intentions of the Assembly and local government."[18]

Organised interests with substantive resources behind them have been able to engage quite actively with the Assembly on policy-making. They have responded to an abundance of consultation documents and questionnaires circulated by the Assembly as part of its 'open government' policy and have often been successful in negotiating with the Government. For example, organisations representing the interests of the elderly persuaded the Assembly Government to create a sub-cabinet committee for the elderly in the autumn of 2002.

On the other hand, interest groups, organisations and individuals without the resources to dedicate the time and energy necessary to building a relationship with the Assembly Government have complained of consultation saturation and found it difficult to engage with what they would regard as 'inclusive' politics.

The Government of Wales Act provided for four regional committees to ensure that the Assembly would reach out beyond Cardiff. However, most Committees have suffered from low levels of attendance by AMs.[19] Equally, their their lack of power has hindered their contribution to the policy process:

> "The advisory nature of the Committees, the lack of formal mechanisms to feed into the wider work of the Assembly, and the range of topics covered, make it difficult to map the extent to which they have contributed to wider Assembly decision making. A major problem the Regional Committees have is lack of a clear purpose and how to feed their work into the main decision making process of the Assembly."[20]

The Assembly and its Regional Committees have not been able to overcome a deep feeling that exists in the regions, and especially in north Wales, that the Assembly is biased in favour of Cardiff and the south east. This perception was only reinforced by the Cardiff-centric character of Rhodri Morgan's Cabinet with five of its nine members representing constituencies either in, or close to, the capital.[21]

---

[18] Martin Laffin, Gerald Taylor and Alys Thomas, *A New Partnership? The National Assembly for Wales and Local government*, Joseph Rowntree Foundation, May 2002.

[19] For example in 2001 the South East Committee had an attendance rate of 69 per cent and the Mid and West Wales committee of 74 per cent. See Kathryn Hollingsworth, 'Connecting with the Wider Wales' in John Osmond and J. Barry Jones (Eds.) *Building a Civic Culture*, IWA 2002.

[20] Kathryn Hollingsworth, 'Connecting with the Wider Wales' *Ibid.*, page 218.

[21] Rhodri Morgan, First Minister (Cardiff West); Jenny Randerson, Minister for Culture (Cardiff Central); Sue Essex, Minister for the Environment (Cardiff North); Jane Hutt, Mninister for Health (Vale of Glamorgan); Jane Davidson, Minister for Education (Pontypridd).

OPEN GOVERNMENT

Open Government has been an important ambition of Rhodri Morgan's government, manifested by the presence of a Minister for Open Government, currently Carwyn Jones who combines the portfolio with responsibility for Assembly Business. It was noteworthy, too, that one of the first changes the First Minister made after entering office was to publish the minutes and the papers of Cabinet meetings. However they are only available after a time-lapse of six weeks, and are short and lacking in detail. Nevertheless, combined with background briefings that are published alongside they can provide a useful brief of what is currently on the government's agenda. The agendas, minutes and papers of the monthly management meetings of the Assembly Executive Board have also been published on the web since November 2002 as a result of the Assembly's new Publication Scheme.

In addition the e-mail addresses of all Assembly Members, including Ministers and the senior civil servants are also available on the Assembly's website. The Assembly as a whole has embraced 'e-government' rather successfully. In his evidence to the Richard Commission, the Presiding Officer Lord Elis-Thomas claimed that the Assembly's use of information and communications technology provided an 'exemplar' for other democratic bodies:

> "Our use of ICT has been an unalloyed success. We are able to do our business electronically in the Chamber, in our committee work and in our internal and external dealings – including our dealings with our constituents. We want to see this digital democracy develop further, and we are determined that the National Assembly should remain a world-leader. Democratic bodies must use the medium of the moment if they are to survive, let alone thrive."[22]

The Presiding Officer also praised the Assembly's education and public information service. The interface between the Assembly and its public was a preoccupation of the National Assembly Advisory Group. They were anxious that the Welsh public should feel welcome at the Assembly. They recommended the creation of a dedicated public information, research and education service within the Assembly. Between April 2001 and March 2002, over 4,500 members of the public visited the National Assembly building in Cardiff Bay. They included 2,695 visitors attending Plenary sessions in the Assembly Chamber and 1,854 people attending Committee meetings.[23] The Assembly has also developed an educational visiting programme which offers

---

[22] Lord Dafydd Elis-Thomas AM, Presiding Officer, evidence to the Richard Commission, December 2002

[23] Presiding Officer Annual Report 2001-2002, Assembly website www.wales.gov.uk

education groups the opportunity to visit the Assembly building. A designated education centre opened in May 2001 and bilingual education packs have been published. Lord Elis-Thomas emphasised the importance of these initiatives directed at a population which had only voted for the new institution by a margin of 0.5 per cent in 1997:

> "We have an excellent public information and education service in the Assembly in which we have invested considerable resources. Their effort is devoted to countering the corrosive and all too prevalent view that the National Assembly and our work as elected politicians within it do not matter."[24]

REPRESENTATION OF WOMEN

One of the most significant and visible changes to the political culture of Wales has been the better representation of women. The Assembly has the second highest proportion (46 per cent) of women elected to a national body in Europe. Not only that, but the Cabinet has a female majority, with five out of the nine Ministers.

There is no doubt that the critical mass of women in the Assembly brought a different tone to its proceedings than otherwise would have been the case. Debates have been less adversarial than in Westminster and topics such as family welfare, the rights and wrongs of smacking children and equal opportunities have been given a higher priority. The women members also added more weight behind the implementation of family friendly working hours.

This transformation of the Welsh political scene, which was previously dominated by men at every level, was the result of two initiatives: the introduction of proportional representation, and the use of 'twinning' by the Labour party. Proportional representation allowed the parties to manipulate their regional lists to allow women candidates to be placed at the top. Plaid Cymru, for instance, placed women alternately on their regional lists of candidates. The Liberal Democrats shied away from adopting a formal method of promoting women candidates arguing that it went against their 'liberal' values. However, they offered training days for women only and emphasised an informal route in order to encourage female applications.[25]

As part of the UK New Labour modernising programme, the Welsh Labour

---

[24] Lord Dafydd Elis-Thomas AM, Presiding Officer, evidence to the Richard Commission December 2002

[25] See Paul Chaney, 'An Absolute Duty' in John Osmond and J. Barry Jones (Eds.) *Building a Civic Culture*, IWA, 2002.

Party chose to use the twinning mechanism to achieve a gender balance amongst its candidates. This mechanism involved twinning constituencies which then established a joint selection conference to select a female candidate for one constituency and a male candidate for another. Twinning produced a total of 16 female out of a total of 28 Labour AMs. It should be noted that this was not achieved without causing a great deal of bitterness and anger amongst some rank and file Labour Party members who failed to obtain a candidacy. Many well known, established male Labour activists were, in effect, prevented from becoming a member of the Assembly. Nonetheless, the end result transformed what had often been perceived as a Labour-male dominated political culture in Wales.

EQUAL OPPORTUNITIES

Equality and equal opportunities were important elements of the 'inclusiveness' advocated during the referendum campaign. During the preparation of the devolution legislation, Ron Davies invited key figures from the Equal Opportunities Commission in Wales to draft an equality of opportunity clause. Endorsed by the National Assembly Advisory Group it was included in the Government of Wales Act 1998 and stated:

> "The Assembly shall make appropriate arrangements with a view to securing that its functions are exercised with due regard to the principle that there should be equality of opportunity for all people."[26]

The Assembly could thus be subject to a judicial review if it failed to comply with this equality duty. It has also enabled the Equal Opportunities Committee to push through radical changes to ensure that the Assembly sets an example of best practice in the way it embeds equality of opportunity in the conduct of its business and procedures.

The Committee oversaw the Assembly's equal pay audits which led to a three-year pay deal for civil servants, negotiated to promote equality and which had the effect of adding a further 22.3 per cent to the Assembly's pay bill.

The Assembly has also actively implemented some of the recommendations of the Roger McKenzie report *Lifting Every Voice: A Report and Action Plan to address Institutional Racism at the National Assembly for Wales*. Mandatory equality awareness training was introduced for all civil servants and the appointment process was opened up in an effort to attract candidates from a wider range of backgrounds. By January 2002, 97 new Assembly staff had been recruited through a new open external process. Of these appointments

---

[26] Section 120 of the Government of Wales Act.

50 were to positions at senior management level or within the top four civil service staff grades D to G.[27]

The Assembly has also taken this agenda beyond its own internal conduct and encouraged private companies to embrace equal opportunities by using 'contract compliance' with respect to outsourcing. Under these new arrangements, the Assembly Government has launched a voluntary code of equality practice. Companies and suppliers who sign up to the code receive constructive feedback if their tenders are unsuccessful, enabling them to be better placed to win contracts with the Assembly in the future. The Assembly's equality duty has also had an effect on local government, as one manager explained:

> "From local government's point of view the force of statute is very important. Sometimes it's a driver of reform. It does shake inertia where it occurs … we've only taken that view within the last 18 months and we've been pushed in that direction by the Assembly. What we've tried to do is to use the relevant pieces of legislation as the driver to say, 'wake-up local authorities, there are statutes out there and you are going to be in trouble if you don't comply with them'."[28]

In short, the Assembly Government's statutory equality duty has meant that equality of opportunity is beginning to be addressed in a systematic way at an all-Wales level of government for the first time. Whilst the statutory duty has been an important tool, a high level of political will and the consensus on the issue of equal opportunities within the Assembly, have also been essential in pushing the equal opportunities agenda forward. Carwyn Jones, chair of the Equal Opportunities Committee between June and December 2002, reflected:

> "It is easy, in many ways, to chair the Committee on Equality of Opportunity as we are all committed to the goal of fostering good equal opportunity policies. It is nice to be able to put party differences to one side and get on with the agenda."[29]

THE WELSH LANGUAGE

In the campaign running up to the referendum and during the Assembly's first year there was an impression that the Welsh language had been de-

---

[27] Paul Chaney and Ralph Fevre, *An Absolute Duty – Equal Opportunities and the National Assembly for Wales*, IWA, June 2002.

[28] *Ibid.*

[29] Paul Chaney 'An Absolute Duty' in John Osmond and J. Barry Jones (Eds.) *Building a Civic Culture*, IWA, 2002, page 229.

politicised. In part this was a result of the passing of a number of measures such as the Welsh Language Act in 1993 and the establishment of the statutory Welsh Language Board. In 1998 a member of the Board, Colin Williams, research Professor in Socio-Linguistics at Cardiff University, described one optimistic view of the place of the language in the new Assembly. This, he said, argued that:

> *"The Welsh language has been normalised and serves mainly as a medium of communication rather than as a symbol of a minority culture. It will have an important role within the Assembly as a functional means of expression, and consequently the old politics of confrontation will give way to a more accommodating approach to language choice. The previously fragmented nature of Welsh public life, divided by region, geography, history, and above all, language, may now be ameliorated by the establishment of a truly representative bilingual National Assembly.* "[30]

This impression was sustained during the early part of the first term. The Assembly operated bilingually from the offset, with simultaneous translation facilities in both plenary and committee meetings. All of the documents emanating from the Assembly or the Administration were translated. During 2001-02 more than eight million words were translated by the Assembly's translation service.

However, during the first half of 2001 the consensus that had been built around the language during the referendum campaign began to fall apart. In January the question of English immigration into rural Welsh-speaking Wales was articulated by a little-known Plaid Cymru councillor, Seimon Glyn, chairman of Gwynedd County Council's housing committee. This led to a furious row between Plaid Cymru and the Labour Party with accusations of 'racism' flying about in the run-up to the June General Election. During May and June a heated debate within the Education Committee over proposals for a Welsh–medium college within the University of Wales exposed a sharp gulf between Labour and Plaid Cymru. And in August the language issue was re-ignited once more when a substantial figure in Welsh political and economic life, John Elfed Jones, likened the impact of in-migration into rural Wales to the effects of foot-and-mouth disease.[31]

These were ill tempered disputes. Undoubtedly they registered deeply with AMs inside the Assembly. Undoubtedly, too, they were fuelled by party

---

[30] Colin Williams, 'Operating Through Two Languages', in John Osmond (Ed.) *The National Assembly Agenda*, edited by, IWA, 1998, page 102.

[31] For a full discussion of these issues see John Osmond, 'In Search of Stability: Coalition Politics in the Second Year of the National Assembly for Wales' in Alan Trench (Ed.) *The State of the Nations 2001*, Imprint Academic, 2001, pages 31-36.

rivalries at a time when a British general election was under way. Together they projected the Welsh language into the Assembly as a subject of political argument, making it more difficult to achieve a consensus. Certainly, one result was an interruption to what some had seen as growing agreement between Plaid Cymru and Labour on a range of policy questions, and not least on the future of the Assembly itself.

However, a certain degree of consensus returned to the Assembly in the Autumn of 2002 when the Coalition Government published its Action Plan on the language. This sought to 'create a truly bilingual Wales' and increase the number of Welsh speakers by 5 per cent by 2011 – from around 20 per cent to 25 per cent.[32] The publication of the plan, *Iaith Pawb* ('Everybody's Language'), supported by £27 million extra funding, was welcomed by all the political parties in the Assembly. The consensus was undoubtedly facilitated by the Culture Committee's review of the language which worked hard on drawing up a set of recommendations which were acceptable to all the parties.[33]

CONCLUSION

In many respects the aspirations for a new 'inclusive' politics in Wales, articulated by Ron Davies during the passage of the Government of Wales Act, were not realised during the Assembly's first term. A consensual style of politics based around a Corporate Model did not materialise. Instead the Assembly reverted to the UK Parliamentary model of a separate government and legislature.

Even so, the tone of proceedings has been different and less adversarial than in Westminster, due in no small part to the influence of a high representation of women in the Assembly. The Assembly Government also worked hard to achieve greater openness and transparency, and to include as many sections of society as possible in its policy development. Interests and organisations which previously had little access to the decision-making processes of the Welsh Office were now regularly consulted.

A new political class is developing in Wales. It is focused on the 60 Assembly Members and their researchers, secretaries, and press officers. The attention of the media, voluntary bodies, local government and businesses has moved

---

[32] These percentages were estimates, pending publication of the 2001 census in the early part of 2003. Published in February the census recorded a rise of two percentage points in those saying they could speak Welsh, from 18.5 per cent in 1991 to 20.5 per cent in 2001.

[33] See John Osmond (Ed.) *Dragon Takes a Different Route: Monitoring the National Assembly September to December 2002*, IWA.

from Westminster to Cardiff Bay. The BBC has a dedicated team working on regular broadcasts from the Assembly available on the web and S4C 2. The *Daily Mirror* changed the name of its Welsh edition to the *Welsh Mirror*. Many voluntary bodies, employers' associations, trade unions and other organisations now employ Assembly liaison officers. Five public relations companies lobby the Assembly Government and Assembly members on behalf of clients.

Yet whilst a distinctive political class is emerging, it will remain a small, and rather distant élite as long as the wider Welsh public feel that they are not part of the new political process. Although the Assembly has tried hard to create an open and inclusive political culture in Wales, only 34 per cent of Welsh people believe that the Assembly has given them more say on the way Wales is being governed.[34] The challenge for the Assembly's second term is to persuade the people of Wales that it is worth their engaging with the new political culture that is undoubtedly growing.

---

[34] Richard Wyn Jones and Roger Scully, *Engagement and Voting in Wales*, Institute of Welsh Politics, January 2003, a study prepared for the Electoral Commission.

CHAPTER 16

CULTURE AND IDENTITY

Geraint Talfan Davies and John Osmond

The devolution project, if such it is, has always been a fusion of functional and cultural strands. As Lord Crowther, the first chairman of the Royal Commission on the Constitution remarked after taking evidence in Wales and Scotland in 1970, "The difference I see is that the Scots want to do things, the Welsh want to be." Whether or not this was how the broader population of either country saw things at the time, there is little doubt that the last thirty years have seen significant changes in the texture of the civic culture of Wales. The world-wide paradox of the simultaneous homogenising impact of consumerism and the fissiparous search for distinct identity has been played out against the backdrop of globalisation in Wales as elsewhere. On the one hand, we have seen cataclysmic industrial change, a widespread sense of community as well as individual redundancy, rapid technological development and a new insecurity even among the prosperous. On the other hand, we see the undermining of the monolithic whether in party politics, religion or public organisation, the Welsh language fight back, the development of Welsh broadcasting, and a new exhibitionist sentimentalism - whether in the novel profusion of Welsh flag waving, Welsh number plates, the capturing of celebrities for Wales, affected outrage at Census organisers and media curmudgeons, or the mourning of a princess.

These economic, social and cultural narratives have coincided with three political phases: first, the experience of the 1980s with its serious disengagement between an undeveloped indigenous civic culture and the government of the day; second, in the 1990s, the generation of new expectations for change as the Major Government disintegrated; and third, the emergence of an additional potential for change following on the 1999 referendum and the creation of the National Assembly. The Assembly has been a means both to focus these changes and to accelerate them.

EMPOWERMENT

The decisive impact of the National Assembly on the development of civic culture has been the widespread acceptance (as Denis Balsom argues in the final chapter of this book) that there is "no going back." It can be argued that the 1997 referendum was not a choice between a constitutional innovation and the status quo, but a choice between that innovation and the status quo *minus*, since a 'No' vote would have settled nothing. The alternative scenario would have seen Wales trapped into further decades of the sullen, sterile recriminations of the powerless, the Welsh poker hand revealed as a miserable pair of twos. Whatever defects people choose to see in the current unsettled settlement, it has be judged against that alternative as well as against other criteria.

In this sense the creation of the Assembly has been an empowering and enabling force, almost regardless of the track record of government. Wales may be a long way from solving its deep-seated problems – as are most countries of the world - but within the Assembly, and outside it in the wider civil society, there are indications of an increased ownership of problems, an increased sense of responsibility for finding answers. Wales is not yet materially richer – the Welsh economy may not yet have bottomed out - but a case can be made that civil society in Wales is maturing under the pressure of that responsibility and the challenge of its objective circumstances.

The passion for 'partnership' – necessary in a small country where financial and human resources are in short supply – may, in the main, have affected only the political class, but it has had a wider impact: a routine and widespread engagement with a political process, a broadening of the critical constituency, and that ownership of problems referred to earlier. The number of organisations that now employ professional 'liaison officers' or lobbyists in Cardiff Bay has mushroomed, but more importantly, they are there because they have more to say. Their organisations have had to beef up their own policy development activity – whether they be the CBI, the IOD, The Federation of Small Businesses, farmers, environmentalists, architects, universities. It is now not only a question of persuading ministers but of ensuring that policies, strategies and plans hold water with 60 elected members.

The field of culture, more narrowly defined, demonstrates this qualitative change. For example, the decision by a lone Secretary of State for Wales in the 1980s to build new galleries for the National Museum in Cardiff, should be compared with the current consultation on the building of a new gallery for Welsh art. The shape of the issue this time round has been the result of an extended debate, feeding off the indefatigable work of the artist Peter Lord, who has attempted to document a 'tradition' of Welsh art. The word tradition is apostrophised not to disparage his work but to indicate that his views have been contested. That contesting has been an indicator of our wider cultural situation. It almost does not matter if he is right. A tradition has been invented and inserted into the consciousness of the cultural community. As a result the issue now has not just been about the availability of money for a building, but, significantly, about the whole idea of Welsh art, how it should be displayed, and where in Wales provision should be located. Similarly, under the previous arrangements the settling of budgets for a National Museum or, say, the Arts Council of Wales would have been a closed affair. There would also have been relatively little debate or scrutiny of the expenditure of that money. The National Assembly, on the other hand, has had to debate the definition of culture: its component parts, such as the arts, the language, sport, broadcasting, buildings, architectural standards, or the subsidising of publishing. It has also had to assess their importance relative to other pressing concerns.

CIVIL SOCIETIES AND THE LANGUAGE

Saunders Lewis famously predicted that unless the Welsh language was saved first, self-government might be fatal to it. Has the first term of the Assembly shown this to be far too pessimistic, providing testimony to the changes in attitude to the language over the intervening decades? It could be argued that before the Assembly, and despite the existence of the Welsh Office for more than 30 years, separate English and Welsh language civil societies existed in Wales. The English language cultural milieu had as much if not more in common with an 'England and Wales' context as with Wales itself. The Welsh language civil society was necessarily more enclosed. Though the two civil societies operated in parallel, they were, of course, divided linguistically, with the result that each had strikingly different territorial heartlands, at least in the imagination.

In this era the Welsh language civil society could negotiate deals at long range with London government whose main interest was avoidance of trouble, even at the expense of occasionally delving deep into its pocket. Arguably the creation of S4C in 1982 was a classic case. Had an Assembly been achieved as a result of the 1979 referendum it is hard to imagine that it would have countenanced the expenditure that S4C required. However, for Westminster £50 million-plus per year was a small price to pay for tranquillity in Wales. It was, in the words of the then Home Secretary, William Whitelaw, "an investment in social harmony."

However, the coming of the National Assembly put an end to such negotiations and accommodations. It was no longer possible to have two discrete civil societies living alongside each other but occupying different spaces. The question that was then posed was what would be the nature of the alternative? One commentator, Simon Brooks, Editor of the current affairs magazine *Barn* and a spokesman for the Cymuned language movement, was pessimistic:

> "The establishment of the Assembly, and the political project of creating a Welsh State, require these two civil societies to be merged and become one. It is hardly surprising that the minority civil society, the one that leads its life largely through Welsh, should lose out in the merger."[1]

Does this have to be the case? Is it inevitable that English-speaking Wales will simply absorb, and in the process extinguish, Welsh-speaking Wales? Simon Brooks' pessimistic view was inevitably conditioned by his absorption with the condition of what hitherto, has been known as Welsh-speaking Wales, the heartlands of rural Wales. The reality that we all now have to face, whether English or Welsh-speaking, is that this notion of a 'Welsh-speaking Wales', in the sense of geographical domain where Welsh is the dominant mode of discourse for a large majority of the population, no longer exists. Instead, we have a pattern of diverse bilingual societies within what used to be known as the Welsh-speaking heartlands. At the same time, southern and eastern Wales can no longer simply be described as 'anglicised' but are also becoming bilingual, though again according to widely varying patterns. It must be remembered that the one in five of the population recorded as Welsh speaking by the Census, are spread across a much higher proportion of households. The fact that a majority of Welsh speakers are in a minority in their own homes may, overall, be a source of weakness for the language. Yet it does mean that a very large percentage of the population are in a daily relationship with the language, even if they do not speak it. Moreover, the 2001 census recorded a small growth in the overall numbers speaking Welsh, from 18.5 per cent in 1991 to 20.5 per cent. That increase was undoubtedly due to the impact of Welsh medium schools in south eastern Wales, with the language continuing its decline, if partially arrested, in the rural west and north west.

The fundamental issue of the future of the Welsh language within the new milieu of bilingualism was addressed by the National Assembly's Culture and Education Committees in their policy review of the Welsh language, published in July 2002.[2] Within a few weeks of its publication the Assembly Government responded with a policy statement *Bilingual Future* that was immediately labelled a landmark document. In it First Minister Rhodri Morgan and Culture Minister Jenny Randerson pledged that:

> "The Welsh Assembly Government is wholly committed to revitalising the Welsh language and creating a bilingual Wales."[3]

---

[1] Simon Brooks, 'The Living Dead', *Agenda*, IWA, Spring 2002.

[2] *Our Language: Its Future*, July 2002

[3] *Bilingual Future: A Policy Statement by the Welsh Assembly Government*, July 2002.

This was highly significant since for the first time in the history of the Welsh language, a government was taking full responsibility for its future. And, as discussed in the previous chapter, the commitment also came in the wake of an 18-month period in the life of the Assembly when, contrary to expressed hopes at the outset, the language had become a matter of contentious dispute between the parties, especially Labour and Plaid Cymru. *Bilingual Future* agrees with the definition of what would constitute a 'bilingual Wales' as set out at the head of the joint report of the Culture and Education Committees' policy review *Our Language: Its Future*, published a month earlier:

> *"In a truly bilingual Wales both Welsh and English will flourish and will be treated as equal. A bilingual Wales means a country where people can choose to live their lives through the medium of either or both languages; a country where the presence of two national languages and cultures is a source of pride and strength to us all."*[4]

Three months later the Assembly Government published the Action Plan it promised in its immediate response to the Committee's report. '*Iaith Pawb* ('Everybody's language') sets out how this aspiration to make progress towards a bilingual Wales is to be achieved. It is based around three main strands: the national level, the community and the individual, and perhaps most significantly is supported by an extra £26.8 million funding. At the national level the Welsh language will be 'mainstreamed' through all policy sectors within the Assembly Government. A new unit will be established to be responsible for implementing the plan.

The Welsh Language Board is to be responsible for implementing the community dimension of the Action Pan. It is the main recipient of the additional funding, receiving an extra £16 million over three years which represents a 75 per cent increase in its budget. It will use the money to develop more *Mentrau Iaith* (community based language initiatives) and to set up nine new local language action plans. The Board will also be responsible for encouraging greater use of the language in the private sector and amongst young people in Wales. It will be setting up new regional offices in north and south west Wales to equip itself for these new challenges.

The third strand, empowering individuals to speak Welsh, is supported by £9.5 million funding. The greater part of it will go towards increasing the availability of early years provision through the medium of Welsh and increasing the number of staff available to teach in Welsh.

The Assembly Government's determination to create a bilingual Wales cannot be doubted. What remains in question is whether, in these circumstances, the Welsh language will flourish. To what extent will Welsh

---

[4] *Our Language: Its Future*, joint report of the Culture and Education Committees, June 2002.

continue to be a living language across Wales, rather than one that has a token and mainly symbolic role? The answer to this question must lie with Welsh people themselves and their wish or determination to use the language. Underlying this will be the extent to which their sense of identity rests on their attachment to the language.

Here the coming of the Assembly may make a difference. Devolution is part of a process that is changing Welsh society, both its Welsh and English language components, so that it feels and expresses itself in a more distinctive and autonomous way. In turn, a distinctive, and most importantly, autonomous, Welsh civil society, may be more open to the opportunities and advantages of bilingualism. This has demonstrably been the case so far as Welsh-medium education is concerned. Here we have numerous examples across southern Wales in particular, from Abergavenny, Caerphilly, Cardiff and the Vale, to Bridgend, the Rhondda, Port Talbot and Swansea, of English-speaking Welsh parents sending their children to Welsh-medium schools. Why do they make the choice? In some cases undoubtedly the motivation is a belief that the schools are simply better. But given the potential disadvantages and problems for monolingual parents – worries about being cut off from the educational experience of their children and being unable to help with their homework is one example – the decision surely reflects a deeply felt underlying impulse. At the very least in part parents make the choice because they want their children to have the opportunity of participating in a more rounded experience of being Welsh. Certainly, it offers a prospect that the emerging Welsh civil society will not simply be a mirror image of civil society in England.

A growing confidence of the Welsh in their identity over the past few decades has found its clearest expression in cultural forms where the Welsh language has been increasingly present, if only at times in emblematic form. We have seen this most clearly in broadcasting, but also in the increasing use of simultaneous translation for conferences, and the spread of bilingual signs into the private sector beyond what is legally required for the public sector by the Welsh Language Act. Certainly, when compared with the 1970s there is today a positive rather than negative attitude among English speakers towards the language. This was among the most important elements that explained why the four-to-one No vote in the 1979 referendum was turned into the slim majority we saw in 1997. And the National Assembly is now providing a fillip for the language, in its own usage as well as setting an agenda for a bilingual Wales.

A CULTURE IN COMMON

In the normal course of political debate in the UK limited financial resources tend to push debate and action on the cultural front to the sidelines. The reverse has been the case in Wales since the establishment of the National Assembly, and it is not difficult to see why. One of the Assembly's key imperatives in its first term was to demonstrate that it could make a difference to outcomes. This was demonstrably difficult in relation to the economy and health and, to a lesser extent in education. In the cultural field, however, there was a potential to transform the existing situation for sums of money that seemed tiny in relation to the total Assembly Government budget. Moreover, expenditures and policies in this field could underpin any burgeoning sense of Welsh identity and, therefore, be a unifying factor. It was no accident that the title of the cultural policy review by the Post-16 Education Committee, under the Chairmanship of Cynog Dafis, was *A Culture in Common* - taking up a phrase from a submission to the review by an historian of the left, Dai Smith. In this sense the report sought both to bridge the language divide and to extend the definition of culture beyond the arts. In the words of the report:

> *"... the Committee wanted to send out a clear signal that the arts and culture in Wales are of great significance and importance to 'Project Wales' and that an in-depth consideration was overdue."*[5]

It emphasised the need for a holistic definition of culture:

> *"... culture consists of all distinctive spiritual and material, intellectual and emotional features which characterise a society or group.......A definition of culture as synonymous with the arts is inadequate and can lead to an exclusive interpretation of culture and create barriers in achieving a creative society for the many as opposed to the few."*[6]

It emphasised the need for grass roots activity and community involvement, for spreading investment across Wales, for integrating cultural development with social exclusion, learning, economic and community regeneration and for the need to make bilingualism a living reality. It also put great store by the promotional value of culture:

> *"Wales' self-image, and its image on the international stage are of vital importance to the health and vitality of the nation as a whole."*[7]

In the narrower field of the arts the scope for significant and swift improvement was huge, and accidents of timing and circumstance were

---

[5] Post-16 Education Committee Report, A Culture In Common, November 2000, para. 1.9.

[6] *Ibid.*, paras. 2.1 and 2.2.

[7] *Ibid.*, para. 3.47.

much in the Assembly's favour. First, arts budgets had been under severe stress for more than a decade. Arts organisations lived at the brink of insolvency, and individual artists saw scant little patronage and scope for development. Second, Gordon Brown's 'prudent' stance in the first two years of the new administration at Westminster had only sharpened the frustrations of the arts community, as it had in many other public spheres. The loosening of the reins on public expenditure coincided with the first year of the Assembly's existence. Third, the Arts Council of Wales had been trapped by the earlier climate of public expenditure cuts into assured unpopularity amongst its own constituency. It was even denied sufficient funds to undertake root and branch reform of its own workings. It ended in a succession of crises that led to the departure of one Chief Executive only a short period after her appointment. As an organisation it had come perilously close to meltdown and had been subjected to a forensic and critical management review. New Assembly Ministers were reluctant to entrust it with more money. Referring to the evidence presented by arts organisations, *A Culture in Common* said of it:

> "*Very many felt that the Council was in need of overhaul particularly as regards: a perceived lack of openness with which it has operated - especially over the conduct of consultation and in providing feedback over grant decisions; its apparently bureaucratic, unresponsive, and managerially complex structure; its loss of direction over gaining and sustaining the confidence of the communities with which it should work in partnership; its centralised approach, which potentially detaches it from practitioners and audiences; its level of investment in high profile companies.*"[8]

With many pressing for the creation of a Minister for Culture there was even talk of abolishing the Arts Council, abandoning the arm's length principle and opting for a French style Ministry. All in all, the only way was up.

The final stroke of good fortune was that the completion of the cultural policy review, with its call for the establishment of a cultural ministry, coincided with the creation of the Labour-LibDem coalition administration, during which process Rhodri Morgan telescoped the Pre-16 and Post-16 Education Committees into one, creating room for a new culture portfolio. The new Cabinet brief, embracing culture, sport and the Welsh language, was given to one of the two Liberal ministers, Jenny Randerson, in October 2000.

In common with the cultural debate in the rest of the UK, *A Culture in Common* had laid great stress on the potential social and economic benefits of cultural investment – the arts as social service or economic regenerator. Any reservations in the artistic community about over-emphasis of these aspects

---

[8] *Ibid.*, para. 4.20.

were cast aside in the face of a planned 35% increase in budget of the Arts Council of Wales for the period 2000/01 to 2003/04. The introduction of free entry to the National Museums and Galleries of Wales from April 2001 was an added bonus. These developments went hand in hand with a restructuring of the Arts Council itself, on the basis of proposals made by a consultant, Anthony Everitt, a former Secretary General of the Arts Council of Great Britain. Responding to growing concerns about the concentration of government services in the capital city, the new structure involved considerable decentralisation, based around a three region structure – north Wales, mid and west Wales and south east Wales. Responsibility for drama and theatre came to rest in the North Wales Office, and the visual arts in Carmarthen in West Wales.

The last new piece in the institutional jigsaw was a Cultural Forum, *Cymru'n Creu (Creative Wales)* that, from February 2001, brought together on a quarterly basis a wide range of organisations in the field. These included the Arts Council, the WDA, the Wales Tourist Board, the National Museum, the National Library, the Welsh Local Government Association, the British Council, the Council of Museums, the broadcasters and Welsh National Opera. The Committee had proposed such a forum as a way of ensuring that:

> *"... the whole approach to arts and culture [is] broadened so that the Arts Council is not itself regarded as being solely responsible for the health of our artistic and cultural life..." [and] "... as a genuinely useful instrument for avoiding the pitfalls of centralisation, and as a way of keeping our sponsored bodies focused and working together."*[9]

A CULTURAL STRATEGY

The one missing element was a more operational cultural strategy, built on the philosophical basis of *A Culture in Common*. This gap was plugged in January 2002 with the publication of *Creative Future – A cultural strategy for Wales*. In broad terms this made a five-fold commitment to

1. making cultural development a cross-cutting theme for the Welsh Assembly Government

2. establishing cultural development as a primary task for local government

3. ensuring a strong, well-funded and efficient Arts Council of Wales

4. the effective coordination of planning and activity across all cultural bodies and

---

[9] *Ibid.*, paras. 4.8 and 4.15.

5. extracting cultural value from a wide range of public expenditure.

This was underpinned by no less than eight action plans that attempted to deal with gaps in the evidence base, investment in the young, stabilising and developing the professional arts, culture and communities, the Welsh language and cultural diversity, sport and recreation, the creative industries, and the development of an international dimension. Progress on these action plans is now subject to quarterly monitoring through the cultural forum, *Cymru'n Creu*.

This last action plan – the international dimension - underlined the Assembly Government's awareness of the potential of sport and the arts in raising Wales's profile abroad. The First Minister had already established a Cabinet sub-committee, under his own chairmanship, specifically "to raise the international profile and influence of Wales and establish it as a first class place to live, study, visit, and do business". Increased funding for Welsh Arts International, backing for Cardiff's bid for Capital of Culture status in 2008 and a first Welsh presence at the Venice Biennale were signs of the new approach. In sport the new Millennium Stadium in Cardiff was already proving a huge international marketing asset. The stadium had opened in 1999 just in time to host the Rugby World Cup, but the audience for that event was dwarfed by those for successive FA Cup Finals that came to Cardiff following the closure of Wembley Stadium. It was the spur to a concerted and ultimately successful attempt to attract golf's Ryder Cup to Wales for 2010. This has by now been broadened into an 'events strategy' that seeks to identify a hierarchy of international events, both sporting and cultural, to be attracted to Wales. The tourist potential of the big sporting occasions was clear but it has taken longer to develop a cultural tourism strategy, though one was expected from the Wales Tourist Board early in 2003. At the same time the Welsh Assembly Government was planning to appoint international "envoys" while the WDA commissioned the IWA to produce a "global Wales database" as a means of mobilising a rather hard to find Welsh diaspora of expertise and influence.

CREATING A CAPITAL

Creating an international dimension proved rather less controversial than the politics of geography at home. Much has been written about the "three-Wales model" developed by Denis Balsom – a split between y Fro Gymraeg (the Welsh heartland) British Wales and Welsh Wales.[10] Although this model was

---

[10] See, for example, John Osmond, *Divided We Fall: The Politics of Geography in Wales*, IWA, January 2003.

based largely on language and strength of Welsh identification, there is another cultural divide that does not coincide with the Balsom map: the split between i) rural Wales, ii) the industrial valleys of the south and iii) the coastal strip of the south east. Much has been written in recent years about the failure of urban Britain to understand the problems and plight of the countryside. That lack of understanding may not be as evident in Wales, because so many urban dwellers in Wales are a few generations closer to the land than many in the metropolises of England. In Wales the more dominant misunderstanding may be a failure to understand urban development, and the nature and role of cities in particular. That is not surprising given the absence of any history of large-scale urban development in Wales before the industrial revolution, the fact that the Welsh language and culture has been essentially rural, and that even the industrial valleys, topographically separated, can be characterised as big villages rather than cities. The discourse on urban development and city function has largely passed us by.[11]

This has impacted on a number of debates that involve the capital city. Ron Davies set the cat among the pigeons before the Assembly even opened its doors by encouraging a competition to house the new institution, appearing to suggest that its location in the capital was not a foregone conclusion. Whether or not this was merely a tactical game to strengthen his hand in negotiation with Cardiff's city fathers, the competition was joined in earnest, particularly by Swansea. When Cardiff was eventually chosen, disappointment elsewhere was sharpened by a feeling amongst the losers that they had been conned. In retrospect the debate does seem unreal and there appears to be a wholesale acceptance of Cardiff's capital status. However, there has been less agreement about what should flow from that status. The recognition in the EU Objective 1 boundaries of the essentially east-west split of Wales, has produced other echoes. There has been a commitment to disperse some government offices to the rest of Wales, as with the Arts Council, and bodies such as the WDA have shifted the geographical emphasis of their spending. The Assembly Government, in its allocations to local authorities has directed spending away from richer areas, including the capital.

For its part, Cardiff has been quick to emphasise an alternative case. It argues that despite recent growth it is still not a large city - it is about the size of Nottingham - and that it has its own very large areas of extreme deprivation. It has the largest influx of daily work commuters from outside its boundaries of any urban centre in Wales – 37,000 people a day, equivalent to 11.5 per cent of the city's population. In terms of the uniform business rate it is a net contributor, like most cities. Cardiff Council claims the city generates £110 million in non-domestic rates that go straight to the National Assembly. The

---

[11] See GeraintTalfan Davies, *The Capital Culture and the Nation,* National Eisteddfod Lecture. IWA 2002

city then receives back £64 million, with £46 million raised in Cardiff distributed to the rest of Wales. In this way Cardiff retains 58 per cent of its non-domestic rates, which compares with the 67 per cent retained by a much richer Edinburgh.

Whereas the suspicion of Cardiff in north Wales is based primarily on distance, in the upper Valleys it has focused around resentment at the scale of investment in Cardiff Bay. Both added fuel to the debate on a plan to build an arts counterpart to the Millennium Stadium in the bay area – the Wales Millennium Centre. The concept began life as the Cardiff Bay Opera House, the Zaha Hadid design that won Cardiff a degree of notoriety when the Millennium Commission turned it down. By the time the Assembly came into existence in 1999, an embryonic successor scheme had been on the stocks for three years. The planned building had metamorphosed into a multi-purpose arts centre, to house not only Welsh National Opera but also seven other resident companies, including a 130-bed residential centre for the Urdd, the Welsh youth movement. The fear of cost over-runs meant that the scheme was not popular with Assembly officials, while some Assembly members from beyond the southern coastal strip bridled at the prospect of further substantial investment in the capital city. However, in the end the scheme won overwhelming, though not unanimous support from across the political spectrum, the Liberal Democrats supporting their own Culture Minister, Plaid Cymru instinctively supporting a potential new cultural icon, and both Labour and Conservatives - following the sacking of Richard Rogers from the Assembly's own project for a new debating chamber - realising that yet another architectural debacle would be one too many. The commitment of capital and revenue funding to the project was carefully balanced with an additional £2m a year of revenue funding for arts projects elsewhere in Wales. Construction began in February 2002.

Referring to the legitimate concerns of elected representatives to defend the most disadvantaged communities, Patrick Hannan concludes in his diary of 2001:

> "The problem arises when the same people are engaged in the process of building, even inventing a place called Wales. They have to decide how they can sustain organisations that express a national existence, something that goes far beyond the mere occupation of a particular geographical territory. Common institutions are among the things that advertise what kind of people we are."[12]

The debate over the Wales Millennium Centre, in which both the Liberal Culture Minister and the Labour Finance Minister were steadfastly in favour

---

[12] Patrick Hannan, *2001:A Year in Wales*, Seren, 2001, page 17.

of the project, was also seen as a litmus test of Wales' ability to engage with architecture, the mother of the arts. Unlike Scotland, where an architectural policy was put in place by the Scottish Executive very early in its life, there was a great lacuna in public policy in Wales in this field. An IWA report, *Designing Success* - prompted by the WMC's architect, Jonathan Adams – criticised architectural standards severely and proposed a Design Commission for Wales to match England's Commission for Architecture and the Built Environment (CABE). The proposal was taken up swiftly by the Environment Minister, Sue Essex, herself a former lecturer in town planning. The new Commission was constituted by mid 2002, if with a limited budget.

By 2003, one could at least discern the possibility of a transformation: the Commission in place, the WMC under construction, Richard Rogers back on the case of the National Assembly's own building, Wilkinson Eyre - designers of Gateshead's award winning new bridge over the Tyne - designing the new industrial and maritime museum for Swansea, Richard Murphy designing an arts centre for Caernarfon, and the architects Austin Smith: Lord about to complete a new theatre for Newport.

COMMUNICATIONS

One area in which the Culture Minister's writ does not run is the field of broadcasting and communications. Broadcasting is not a devolved function and yet the advent of the Assembly has produced both long and short-term effects. In the short term it has provided a prime example of devolution pulling in additional money to Wales, with all the jobs that that entailed. Immediately after the referendum in 1997 BBC Wales was given a 10 per cent increase in its local programme budget - an additional £6 million - built into its baseline thereafter, to undertake the necessary journalistic task of covering the new National Assembly across radio and television in both languages, as well as launching new online services. The owners of HTV, then United News and Media, were given a new deal on their annual licence payments to the Treasury, which allowed them to put another £3million into their own programmes for Wales. That went into news, current affairs and drama. In 2000 the new regime at the BBC under Greg Dyke, allocated a further £11 million to Wales to develop local programming. At the same time there has been an added emphasis on increasing the supply of network programmes from Wales. Much of the new money is going into arts, music and drama. One can safely assume that the 'Yes' Vote in the referendum brought a devolution dividend of not less than £20 million to the broadcasting industry alone. This was not a one-off, but an additional, continuing, annual investment greater than the then published cost of establishing the National Assembly itself.

In newspapers some had hoped that an expanding policy community might have enlarged the commercial freedom of manoeuvre of newspaper owners by increasing demand. Immediately after the first Assembly elections the *Daily Mirror* assembled a small team of journalists in Cardiff, re-christened the paper *The Welsh Mirror*, marketed itself heavily on television, dropped its price and claimed to have increased its circulation in Wales by more than 10 per cent. This was undoubtedly a landmark development for the printed press in Wales, but less important in terms of raising the flow of quality information and debate than in the equally important task of reminding readers dependent on tabloid newspapers that Wales exists. Perhaps significantly, the *Daily Mirror* had been a key target for those managing the Yes for Wales campaign and had supported the campaign with high profile endorsements from Ryan Giggs though, tellingly in terms of the media issue, these appeared only in the papers supplied to South Wales. *The Welsh Mirror* is supplied to north and south. No sooner was it launched than Trinity - the owners of the *Western Mail* and the *Daily Post* - acquired the Mirror group, reinforcing its existing monopoly of indigenously produced morning and Sunday newspapers. From its 1960s sales heyday of more than 100,000 copies a day, the *Western Mail's* weekday circulation has fallen below 50,000, and yet has become more profitable on the back of greatly increased public sector job advertising. Despite this, in 2003 it is planning to repackage its historical editorial schizophrenia yet again in an attempt to reverse the trend. The new editor's task, in the words of media academic Kevin Williams,

> "... is to combine popular entertainment with intelligent and committed commentary and writing – not an easy objective in the UK newspaper market which has traditionally drawn a clear distinction between popular and broadsheet reporting."[13]

Coverage of the Assembly has quickly woven the new institution into the mainstream journalistic narrative in Welsh media, if not yet in London newspapers, to the extent that Welsh MPs at Westminster have complained that Wales' continuing home of primary legislation is being ignored. The Assembly has responded to the generous attention it has been given by paying a surprising degree of attention to communications issues – some would argue rather more attention than that given by the Scottish Executive or the Scottish Parliament. This was for both economic and cultural reasons.

On a conservative estimate broadcasting is already worth at least £400 million per annum to the Welsh economy. In terms of economic development the Assembly wants to ensure that Wales is not in any way disadvantaged in terms of communications infrastructure or technological take-up. It also takes an interest because of broadcasting's cultural impact, both generally – in

---

[13] Kevin Williams, 'What's Happening at the Western Mail?', *Planet* 157, February/March 2003.

disseminating information, debate and opinion – and specifically, in contributing to the arts and the Welsh language, both devolved responsibilities. In the Welsh speaking community there is a very substantial emotional investment in the Welsh language broadcaster S4C. And lastly, Assembly members are interested because, like it or not, broadcasting affects them directly. They use it.

As a result, despite its formal lack of powers in the field the Assembly debated the Communications White Paper that was published in December 2000. Reflecting the twin authorship of the paper by the Department of Culture, Media and Sport and the Department for Trade and Industry, responsibility for the Welsh Assembly Government response was shared between the Culture Minister and the Minister then in charge of e-commerce, Andrew Davies. It expressed concerns about the possibility that Wales would be disadvantaged in the roll-out of the new digital technologies, and the continuing porosity of eastern Wales to television and radio broadcasting from England. This last factor effectively allows many people to watch and listen to services devoid of any news of Welsh life and institutions. The Assembly Government has also pressed, though unsuccessfully, for Welsh representation on the main Board of the new communications regulator, Ofcom.

LOOKING AHEAD

It is too early to say whether all this ambitious cultural planning will pay off by producing a spectacular renaissance in Welsh cultural activity or by creating a sustainable bilingualism in Wales. One can argue that in its first term the Assembly has laid some very solid foundations for cultural policy. The task of the next term will be to maintain the momentum against a number of obstacles. The increase in the number of Welsh speakers recorded in the 2001 Census is the first increase recorded for more than a century. It may mark an historic change. It may prevent commentators talking about "inexorable decline". However, we have yet to see whether its potentially beneficial psychological effect will be greater than the depressing effect of the decline of the Welsh speaking 'heartland' communities.

In broadcasting the Assembly will need to be vigilant against the erosion of output for and from Wales, resulting from consolidation of ownership and other economic pressures. In the arts ambition is high and morale in the arts community is rising. Yet the new funding, large and significant though it is, in large part simply makes up for the atrophying of arts budgets over two decades. At the same time future lottery funds – which make up about half of the Arts Council's disbursements – look vulnerable to the weariness of the buying public and the machinations of the UK Treasury. The aspiration to establish cultural development as a primary task for local government is well-aimed, but will not be easily fulfilled, given the discretionary nature of cultural expenditure by local authorities, problems of definition and the absence of a standard reporting format that would allow robust benchmarking to take place. The one thing that cannot be guaranteed is the emergence of world beating talents, unless one believes that the talent quotients in all societies remain the same, and that it is only the level of opportunity that varies. If that is right, the odds look good.

CHAPTER 17

PUBLIC ENGAGEMENT

Richard Wyn Jones and Roger Scully

In terms of public acceptance the National Assembly passed the first hurdle in its first term. No major party now advocates its abolition. Even the Conservatives have reconciled themselves to "making devolution work". And in early 2003 the Wales CBI found that 41 per cent of its members support the current settlement, while 27 per cent wished to advance to a Parliament on Scottish lines with legislative powers.[1] The Wales CBI, of course, is an organisation that historically had been hostile to devolution, though in the 1997 referendum it adopted a neutral stance.

Yet, in the longer-term, if the broader aspirations of many for devolution are to be fulfilled, the National Assembly must do more than merely exist. It needs to be seen as generating a renewed sense of involvement and engagement in the political process. However, the ability of devolution in Wales to achieve this remains questionable. Unlike in Scotland, there was no clear 'settled will' that endorsed the establishment of the National Assembly. Instead, the institution emerged in an atmosphere combining disagreement with apathy in roughly equal proportions. The Assembly was supported by barely half of those voting in a low turnout referendum. When the time came to elect the chamber itself, in May 1999, turnout, at 45.9 per cent, was even lower than in the referendum.

Such low levels of participation were particularly striking given both that Wales has traditionally experienced higher turnouts than the UK average.[2] Not only that, the Assembly poll was conducted using a proportional voting system (additional-member) that is usually associated with higher electoral participation.[3] As one set of commentators observed:

> "The fact that Welsh turnout in the elections was lower than turnout in the previous round of local elections ... was certainly an inauspicious start for the Assembly."[4]

---

[1] *Western Mail*, 28 January 2003.

[2] Between 1945 and 1997 turnout in Wales was, on average, 2.8 percentage points higher than turnout across the United Kingdom.

[3] Farrell, D., *Electoral Systems: A Comparative Introduction*, Palgrave Press, 2001.

[4] Bradbury J., Denver D., and McAllister L., 'The State of Two Nations: An Analysis of Voting in the Scottish Parliament and Welsh Assembly Elections 1999', *Representation*, 37, 2000:page 9.

LEGITIMACY

However, before moving to a more detailed discussion of the evidence concerning turnout in Wales, it is worthwhile briefly reviewing the literature on electoral participation. The first point to note is that turnout is not a self-evidently important marker of the legitimacy of political institutions. There are political systems where low turnouts persist without the legitimacy of core institutions or the system as a whole being fundamentally challenged. Some critics cast aspersions on the United States's political system because of persistently low election turnouts, but few seriously doubt that the system enjoys widespread domestic legitimacy. In the UK, local government has survived many years of low turnouts in local council elections without the basic legitimacy of local government itself being questioned. In practice, therefore, there is no simple correspondence between turnout and legitimacy. Nor, it should be further recognised, is there agreement about the relationship between them at the level of theory. Rather, there are fundamental differences between theorists about the relative importance and desirability of the various possible forms of political participation in a democratic system, including voting. This in turn reflects different attitudes to the relationship between participation and legitimacy.

In her now classic study, *Participation and Democratic Theory*, Carole Pateman identified two broad attitudes towards participation in contemporary democratic theory.[5] She differentiated between the proponents of *representative government* on the one hand, and the champions of *participatory democracy* on the other. The former advocate a rather limited notion of popular participation. This position is upheld by a diverse range of thinkers motivated by very different concerns. These range from fear of the expropriation of property, to first hand experience of the power of fascist demagoguery. It also embraces classical liberal theorists, such as Jeremy Bentham and James Mill, post-war political scientists like Joseph Schumpeter and Robert Dahl, and left-leaning critical theorists such as Otto Kirchheimer and Franz Neumann. Whatever their other differences, all view participation in relatively narrow, instrumentalist terms, and argue that while some participation is vital, its role and scope must be strictly limited.

From this perspective, the function of public participation in the political system is a negative one. The ballot box and the resulting sanction of the possible loss of office, serve as the ultimate guarantor of public interests against any infringement by the arbitrary decisions of elected leaders. As such, theorists of representative government see no particular intrinsic merit in securing high turnouts at elections. All that is necessary is for turnout to reach

---

[5] Pateman C, *Participation and Democratic Theory*, Cambridge University Press, 1970.

"the minimum necessary to keep the democratic method (electoral machinery) working".[6] The success or otherwise of the system itself is judged on policy outputs rather than popular inputs via participation. Legitimacy is similarly closely linked with the stability and efficacy of the system.

In stark contrast, advocates of participatory democracy view ensuring the widest possible participation as an end in itself. They regard a system in which participation is limited to voting every few years as a rather hollow version of democracy. J.S. Mill, for example, was keen to underline what he regarded as the deep limitations of the model of participation characteristic of modern liberal democracies:

> "A political act, to be done only once in a few years, and for which nothing in the daily habits of the citizen has prepared him, leaves his intellect and his moral dispositions very much as it found him."[7]

This comment serves to underline a key aspect of the participatory democracy credo. For its advocates, a system based on broad democratic participation is not simply the most effective way of producing good government, although this is certainly claimed as one of its benefits. Rather, it is the means by which human capacities – our 'intellect' and 'moral dispositions' – can be developed. Participation plays a pedagogic role above and beyond any benefits accruing from efficacious decision-making.

But if this much is common ground among proponents of more participative models of democracy, there are also significant differences among them. Some of these differences are concerned with the extent of participation. Until recently most advocates of participative democracy, from Rousseau through Mill, to syndicalism and guild socialism, have advocated the extension of participation into the economic realm. But more recently, many advocates of enhanced participation have scaled back their vision of what degree of participation is either feasible or desirable.[8] For these thinkers, associated with so-called 'deliberative democracy', the focus is on delimiting more clearly the social realm from that of the economic. This is to ensure that the market mechanisms that regulate the latter do not encroach on the former, a realm that is properly open to greater participation.

Another key point of contention is the type of elections found in contemporary liberal democracies. In the past, many of the more radical advocates of participatory democracy have tended to be hostile towards 'bourgeois democracy'. At best, their attitude has been one of indifference.

---

[6] *Ibid*: page 14.

[7] Cited by Pateman, page 30.

[8] For example, Baynes, K., 'Deliberative Politics, the Public Sphere and Global Democracy', in Wyn Jones R., (Ed.) *Critical Theory and World Politics*, Boulder, CO.: Lynne Rienner Publishers, 2000, pages 161-70.

However, other advocates of participatory democracy, especially contemporary theorists, have adopted a very different view. For them, the election of members to some form of parliament or constituent assembly is viewed as a necessary – although not sufficient – condition for a properly democratic society. While in their view there is more to democracy than simply elections, and more to participation than voting, these are the cornerstones of democratic society. So while democratic participation may well need to be deepened, it is also important that it should be as wide as possible. In this view, therefore, ensuring high election turnout is crucial. High turnout is associated with a healthy political system, a system that is not only an effective deliverer for the public good, but also enjoys a high degree of public legitimacy.

The participatory view was, of course, at the heart of the case for the establishment of a democratically elected National Assembly for Wales.[9] As such, the relatively low turnouts witnessed in the 1997 referendum and the 1999 election inevitably raise questions of legitimacy. At the same time it should be noted that the equation of high turnout with public legitimacy is supported by a broad consensus of political opinion across the UK as a whole. This has certainly been the tenor of the wide-ranging expressions of concern that have followed the dramatic fall in turnout at the 2001 UK general election. And certainly, the studies undertaken of that election have painted a depressing picture for those interested in engaging the electorate with the political process.

THREE EXPLANATIONS FOR LOW TURN-OUT

It would appear that devolution had failed to engage the interest and support of a large section of the Welsh people. Yet while low turnout can hardly be seen as a good thing (except, perhaps, to die-hard opponents of devolution), the broader consequences depend heavily on the question why there were such high levels of non-participation. This is more complex than it may initially appear. In the specific context of Wales in 1999, there are at least three plausible explanations for the low turn-out. Each carry quite different implications for our understanding of what this says about the Assembly:

1. One view is that the low participation rate reflected, at least in part, a wider sense of apathy towards the political process. Participation rates in other elections in recent years have been poor, and some have

---

[9] See, for example, Davies, R, *Devolution: A process Not an Event*, IWA 1999, and Hain, P., *A Welsh Third Way?*, Tribune Publications, 1999.

diagnosed a "turnout time-bomb"[10] – one that appeared to detonate on 7 June 2001, for example, with the historically low participation rate in the UK general election. On this interpretation, the Assembly election was simply the victim of a much wider public alienation from the political process.

2. A second hypothesis locates the explanation for low turnout more specifically in the constitutional arrangements in the Government of Wales Act 1998: specifically the limited powers that the Assembly was granted compared to the Scottish Parliament. This is a classic 'second-order' explanation: in accordance with theories of second-order elections, where less is at stake fewer people bother to vote.[11] If confirmed, this hypothesis would suggest that only if the Assembly receives greater powers, or otherwise demonstrates its importance, would more people become engaged with it.

3. A third view, however, and potentially the most serious for the future of devolution in Wales, is that non-participation reflected a fundamental hostility to devolution on the part of many of the electorate.[12] Large numbers of people in Wales never wanted the Assembly, and abstention might therefore be seen as a conscious expression of alienation from, and hostility towards, an unwanted institution. This would suggest that among much of the population, the very existence of the Assembly was still essentially contested, rather than merely essentially ignored.

It is clear that how we interpret the causes of low turnout in Wales in 1999 influences our interpretation of its meaning for devolution in Wales. And our own research, investigating the reasons why so many people abstained in May 1999, suggests that while there is much support for both of the first two explanations raised above (apathy about both politics in general and the Assembly in particular), little support could be adduced for the third explanation (antipathy to the devolved body).[13] While this is not exactly good news for supporters of devolution, it is, perhaps, not particularly bad news: those who voted 'no' in the 1997 referendum and remain opposed to the

---

[10] Dunleavy P., Evidence to the House of Commons Select Committee on Public Administration, 15 March 2000.

[11] Reif K., and Schmitt H., 'Nine second order elections: a conceptual framework for the analysis of European election results', *European Journal of Political Research*, Vol. 8, 1980, pages 3-44.

[12] The then Conservative leader in Wales, Rod Richards, in the aftermath of the 1999 election ascribed the low turnout (particularly amongst Conservative supporters) to hostility towards devolution: "A lot of Conservative voters who didn't want devolution in the first place made the positive decision not to vote. This was their second opportunity to demonstrate their dissatisfaction with the Assembly." *Western Mail*, 8 May 1999.

[13] Richard Wyn Jones, Dafydd Trystan and Roger Scully, 'Turnout and Legitimacy in Post-Devolution Wales', Unpublished Paper (Aberystwyth, 2003).

principle of devolution are, nonetheless, participating in Assembly elections as much as those more favourable to devolution. Large-scale voter abstention thus indicates considerable apathy, but it is emphatically not evidence of a new division in Welsh politics, with opponents of devolution so alienated that they refuse even to take part in elections to the chamber.

THE 2001 GENERAL ELECTION

What about turnout in 2001, when voter participation fell drastically in Wales and the rest of Britain, when compared to previous Westminster polls? Clarke et al argue that the main factors that led to a low turnout in 2001 were policy dissatisfaction, lack of interest in the campaign and a decline in partisanship.[14] It is worthwhile reviewing their findings. One hypothesis might be the existence of dissatisfaction with the Labour party among that party's own supporters - in particular, 'Old Labour' socialists who were not supportive of Blair's 'New Labour' project for failing to 'deliver the goods' by improving public services. And indeed there did appear to be quite a lot of policy discontent with the government on issues of health, crime, taxation and education.[15] Furthermore, constituency-level returns show that the decline in turnout was somewhat larger in Labour-held constituencies, 13 per cent, than in those held by the Liberal Democrats or Conservatives, 11per cent.[16]

Another factor is the individual's level of interest in the campaign or in politics in general. Only 27 per cent of electors were 'very interested' in the campaign in 2001, compared to 76 per cent in the 1997 post-election survey. Respondents to the latter survey said they "cared a great deal which party won."[17] One of the reasons could be that the campaign was unusually long, as the expected May election date was postponed until June. Also, Labour were made the overwhelming favourites by media pundits and bookmakers alike long before the 2001 election was called. In turn this stigmatised the election as a boring 'non-contest', unlikely to capture public attention or energise partisan sentiments. Comparing data from the 1997 and 2001 British Election Study post-election surveys shows that the percentage of voters paying a 'great deal' or 'quite a lot' of attention to politics fell from 32 to 29 per cent. Meanwhile, the percentage of 'very strong' party identification fell from 16 to

---

[14] Clarke, H.D., Sanders, D., Stewart, M.C. and Whiteley, P.F., 'Turnout' in Norris, P. (Ed.) *Britain Votes 2001*, Oxford University Press, 2001, pages 211-224

[15] *Ibid.*, page 219.

[16] *Ibid.*, page 6.

[17] *Ibid.*, page 222.

12 per cent.[18]

In the context of devolution, however, the most important thing to note is that nothing about the fall in turnout was specific to Wales. Voter participation fell in 2001 by almost exactly the same proportion compared to 1997 in Wales as elsewhere in the UK. Thus general election turnout was still – at 61.6% - a bit higher in Wales than the UK average (59.4%) as it has generally been for many years. Devolution hasn't improved things in this regard, but nor has it made them worse.

PREFERRED CONSTITUTIONAL FUTURES

In this section we consider the development of public attitudes towards devolution and the National Assembly, drawing on several detailed surveys of the Welsh Electorate conducted in recent years. We begin by considering respondents' views on their preferred constitutional arrangements for Wales, indicated in Table 1. A number of salient points emerge. The first is that an executive Assembly without primary legislative power, of the sort established in 1999, has never been the favoured constitutional position of a majority of the electorate. While it was the most popular constitutional position in the immediate aftermath of the first elections to the body, even at this most auspicious juncture barely a third of the electorate thought an executive Assembly was the best way to govern Wales. Across the three years studied, support for the Assembly does not show a significant change.

TABLE 1: CONSTITUTIONAL PREFERENCES IN WALES (%S)			
	1997	**1999**	**2001**
Independence*	13	10	12
Parliament	19	29	39
Assembly	28	34	26
No elected body (i.e. pre-devolution position)	40	26	23
Base	637	1,192	1,039

* Respondents were offered the option of supporting Independence within the European Union or outside the European Union. The 'Independence' category includes both responses.

Sources: 1997 Welsh Referendum Survey (WRS);
1999 Welsh Assembly Election Survey (WAES); 2001 Wales Life and Times Survey (WELT).

[18] *Ibid.*, page 8.

However, while the notion of an Assembly fails to win new converts, support for a Welsh parliament increases significantly. In 1997, fewer than one in five of the electorate supported the establishment of a Welsh parliament. By 2001, support for this option had more than doubled, making it by a considerable distance the favoured constitutional position of the Welsh electorate. Alongside the growth in support for a parliament, the percentage of respondents wishing to see a return to the pre-devolutionary status quo has dwindled substantially.

What do these data tell us about the impact of the Assembly? The data could be interpreted in two rather contrasting ways. On one hand, if one accepts the evolutionary logic of Ron Davies' oft-quoted 'Devolution is a process and not an event',[19] one might suggest that the Assembly has been a success. It has used the powers within its grasp well and this has given the electorate confidence to support the transfer of further significant powers from Westminster to Cardiff Bay. In short, the Assembly has 'earned its stripes'. An alternative interpretation suggests that the Assembly has made little difference, and that a significant proportion of the electorate believes that devolution will only work if the devolved body is accorded greater powers.

On this second view, support for a parliament may be viewed as an indictment of the record of the Assembly, rather than a vindication. Of course, a third explanation might seek to combine elements of both of these previous explanations. The roof did not fall in with devolution. Indeed, the electorate seem to have become accustomed to it all remarkably quickly compared with, for example, the many years it took for the German and Italian regional tiers to establish themselves in public affections. In Wales, some seem to have developed a taste for devolution. Others may simply have decided that if we are going to have it, we might as well do it properly and have 'proper' powers. Either way, the data seem to suggest a pretty significant shift in favour of a parliament.

It is difficult to ascertain the causal processes that have led electors to shift their views in this way. However, a range of questions utilised in surveys carried out in 1999 and 2001 provide an opportunity to probe the competing explanations of the Assembly's performance. In 2001 respondents were asked whether they thought the establishment of the National Assembly for Wales had improved the way Britain is governed. This question provided an opportunity to probe more general views on the Assembly rather than in relation to particular policy areas.

---

[19] Davies, *op.cit.*

TABLE 2 : IMPACT OF THE ASSEMBLY ON HOW BRITAIN IS GOVERNED (2001)

	%
Improved it a lot	2
Improved it a little	18
Made no difference	59
Made it a little worse	7
Made it a lot worse	3
(It is too early to tell)	4
Don't know	6
Base	1,085

Source: WELT

The striking message here is that almost 60 per cent of respondents felt that the Assembly has made no difference to the way that Britain is governed. In comparison, only one in five respondents thought that the Assembly had improved the way Britain is governed. Given the Yes campaign at the referendum's focus on improving governance and addressing the democratic deficit, these figures will undoubtedly be a disappointment. They should surely not seek to draw much comfort from the fact that only one in ten believe that the Assembly has made things worse. Rather, the evidence suggests that, in general terms, a majority of the electorate perceive the Assembly as having little impact.

This finding receives further support when we examine responses to a series of other questions that explored respondents' expectations of devolution and their perceptions of the Assembly's achievements. The data relate to the voice that the Assembly would give/is giving Wales within the UK, and whether the Assembly would give/is giving ordinary people more say in government. A central plank of the pro-devolution argument was that ordinary people would be given a greater say in how Wales is governed, and that Wales would be given a greater voice in the UK. Recall that the 1997 White Paper was entitled *A Voice for Wales*. The data show that these expectations have so far been disappointed.

TABLE 3A : THE ASSEMBLY WILL GIVE/HAS GIVEN WALES A
STRONGER VOICE IN THE UK

	1997	1999	2001
Stronger	50	62	49
No difference	33	32	46
Weaker	12	5	3

TABLE 3B: THE ASSEMBLY WILL GIVE/HAS GIVEN ORDINARY
PEOPLE MORE SAY IN GOVERNMENT

	1997	1999	2001
More	54	55	34
No difference	36	39	60
Less	4	3	4

Sources: WRS, WAES & WELT. All figures are percentages.

In broad terms, Table 3a shows that by 2001 electors were equally split
between those who thought the Assembly had given Wales a stronger voice in
the United Kingdom and those who thought that it had made no difference.
The proportion thinking the Assembly had made no difference increased
from a third in 1997/1999, to nearly half by 2001. For those who advocated
that the Assembly would be an exercise in renewing Welsh democracy, the
findings of table 3b are even more discouraging. While a clear majority of
respondents thought that the Assembly would give ordinary people more say
in government in 1997, by 2001 the pattern had reversed. Now 60 per cent
responded that the Assembly had failed to make any difference to the say of
ordinary people in government.

TABLE 4A: IMPACT OF THE ASSEMBLY ON THE STANDARD OF
LIVING

	1997	1999	2001
Improve	29	29	33
No difference	51	61	54
Reduce	12	6	8

Sources: WRS, WAES & WELT. All figures are percentages.

TABLE 4B: IMPACT OF THE ASSEMBLY ON EDUCATION

	1997	1999	2001
Improve	50	41	22
No difference	37	48	62
Reduce	5	3	4

TABLE 4C: IMPACT OF THE ASSEMBLY ON HEALTH

All figures are %s	2001
Improve	29
No difference	61
Reduce	6

Sources: WRS, WAES & WELT. All figures are percentages.

When one considers the expectations of the Assembly in relation to specific policy areas one finds a broadly similar pattern. In terms of the impact of the Assembly on the standard of living, there has, in fact, been little change. While in 1997 29 per cent of the electorate thought that it would make a positive difference to the standard of living of people in Wales, the proportion in 2001 was broadly similar.

With education however, the picture is again one of disappointed expectations. In 1997, fully one half of respondents thought the advent of the Assembly would bring improvement in the standard of education. However, by 2001 almost two-thirds of electors thought the Assembly had made no difference, while fewer than a quarter thought it had made a positive difference. A similar question was asked about the health service in 2001, again eliciting a broadly similar pattern of responses. In this case, 61 per cent thought the Assembly had made no difference.

These findings are further reinforced by a series of questions in the 2001 survey designed to draw out opinions on how the NHS, the economy and education have fared since 1997, and, crucially, perceptions as to which level of government is responsible for any improvements. So, for example, respondents were asked whether the standard of the NHS had improved since 1997. They were subsequently probed further to ascertain whether they believed this was a result of the policies of the UK government or of the administration of the National Assembly. Given that the Assembly had only been in existence for two years, and also the well-advertised problems in the

Assembly's early months culminating in the political coup that deposed First Secretary Alun Michael, we might legitimately expect more respondents to ascribe primacy to the UK government. Even so the scale of the advantage (even on issues such as health where a great deal of responsibility has been devolved) is very considerable.

TABLE 5:CHANGES ARE THE RESULT OF UK GOVERNMENT OR WELSH ASSEMBLY ADMINISTRATION (2001)

	NHS	Education	Standard of living
Westminster	60	63	61
National Assembly	10	10	9
Other	16	14	17
Both	7	6	7
Don't know	7	6	6
Base	1,027	854	1,000

Source: WELT. All figures are percentages.

These data serve to demonstrate clearly that the majority of respondents do not believe that the Assembly has had a beneficial impact on key current policy areas. Respondents to the 2001 survey were also asked whether the result of Assembly elections and UK general elections would make a difference. This is important in the context of turnout, as the relevant evidence from elsewhere suggests that voters are less likely to vote where they perceive little is at stake in a given election.

TABLE 6: DIFFERENCE MADE BY GENERAL ELECTION AND ASSEMBLY ELECTIONS (2001)

	General election	Assembly election
A great deal	20	14
Quite a lot	28	23
Some	8	20
Not very much	26	31
None at all	8	12
Base	1,057	1,041

Source: WELT. All figures are percentages.

These data provide yet further confirmation of a widely held perception that the Assembly has little significant impact. It might of course be argued that these findings suggest that the electorate have a pretty realistic understanding of the limited power enjoyed by the Assembly. Indeed, the findings on growing support for a parliament for Wales, reported above, may serve to support such an interpretation. However, such a view is likely to prove cold comfort for Assembly Members of all parties seeking some kind of public recognition of their (considerable) efforts. They will perhaps be cheered by the fact that a somewhat less negative picture emerges when we compare public perceptions of Assembly Members to those of Members of Parliament.

TABLE 7: MPs/AMs LOSE TOUCH WITH THEIR ELECTORS (2001)		
	MPs	Assembly Members
Agree strongly	25	17
Agree	52	44
Neither agree nor disagree	13	25
Disagree	10	14
Disagree strongly	1	1
Net agree ±	+66	+47
Base	1,076	1,035

Source: WELT. All figures are percentages.

The striking feature of this table is, of course, that very considerable proportions of the electorate agree with the statement that MPs (and to a lesser extent) Assembly Members lose touch with the electors once elected. Fully 77 per cent of respondents agreed with the proposition in relation to MPs. Assembly Members fare somewhat better (at 'only' 61 per cent), though it is perhaps difficult to imagine how any group of individuals could fare much worse than MPs in the current climate.

GUARDIAN OF WELSH INTERESTS

Unequivocally good news for the Assembly emerges from questions seeking to probe respondents about which level of government they trust to champion the interests of Wales. When respondents were asked (Table 8) how far they trusted the UK Government or the National Assembly to act in Wales' best interests, almost 60 per cent said the Assembly acted in Wales' best interests at least most of the time. This was well over double the score achieved by the UK Government.

TABLE 8: TRUST UK GOVERNMENT AND NATIONAL ASSEMBLY TO ACT IN WALES' BEST INTERESTS (2001)

	UK Government	National Assembly
Just about always	2	12
Most of the time	22	48
Trust at least most of the time	24	59
Only some of the time	57	31
Almost never	16	6
(Don't Know)	3	4
Base	1,085	1,085

Source: WELT. All figures are percentages.

The National Assembly is regarded as the guardian of Wales' best interests by a clear majority of respondents. These findings are further underscored by data relating to respondents views on the potential future influence of the Assembly when compared with other levels of governance. Table 9 is based on a bank of questions that asked respondents to identify which bodies had the most influence on the way things were run in Wales, and which bodies *ought* to have the most influence on particular issues in Wales.

TABLE 9: LEVELS OF GOVERNMENT AND THEIR INFLUENCE (2001)

Base: 1,085	Does influence	Ought to influence	Will influence in 10 yrs	Food safety	Business start up grants	Welfare benefits
National Assembly	17	54	39	42	57	41
UK Government	61	26	38	31	14	40
Local Councils	14	16	4	20	24	16
European Union	3	1	10	5	1	1
Don't know	5	4	9	2	4	3

Source: WELT. All figures are percentages.

These are fascinating findings. While respondents are clear that the Assembly lacks influence and power, they believe that it should have such influence and expect it to gain influence over the next ten years. The responses on particular policy issues are also very revealing. In terms of food safety standards, while the largest proportion of respondents think that this should be an Assembly responsibility, a significant minority think that local councils should take the principal decisions. In terms of start up grants for business, respondents clearly identify the Assembly as the appropriate location for such powers. Particularly surprising in this regard is the fact that respondents are evenly split between the Assembly and Westminster in terms of who should be responsible for the level of welfare benefits. This is a power not even enjoyed by the Scottish Parliament. The data here suggest that respondents favour regionalisation and localisation. The challenge for the 2003 election will be to persuade electors that even without these powers, they should still vote.

CHAPTER 18

EUROPE[1]

Andrew Scott

The European Union continues to loom large in the on-going debate about constitutional reform in the UK. As the House of Lords Committee on the Constitution reported in January 2003:

> *"Many of the functions devolved in Scotland, Wales or Northern Ireland are heavily affected by the European Union - notably agriculture and fisheries ... the environment, economic development ... and, for Scotland, justice and home affairs. As well as the direct effect on devolved functions and policy, the European Union is important as a broader arena in which the devolved administrations may wish to act."[2]*

In Wales, of course, the EU dimension to public policy increased significantly with the designation of West Wales and the Valleys as eligible for up to £1.2bn from the Objective 1 programme over the period 2000-2006. However, as the House of Lords also noted, the European dimension in the devolved administrations extends considerably beyond the local administration of EU policy. This includes the implementation of EU legislation by the National Assembly. In short, the European dimension of policy is now so great that very few devolved policies are not affected by EU legislative or policy considerations.

It is vital therefore that the devolved administrations continue to play a central role in shaping UK Government policy towards EU legislative proposals and policy initiatives. The formal arrangements for this are set out in the relevant concordats, including the role of the Joint Ministerial Committee (Europe). In practice, however, much of the day-to-day policy process takes place via informal networks of officials from UK Government

---

[1] A draft of this chapter was presented in Aberystwyth (October, 2002) as evidence to the Richard Commission which is examining the Powers and Electoral Arrangements of the National Assembly for Wales. It draws on research being undertaken under the ESRC Devolution and Constitutional Change programme. The research project is entitled 'Asymmetric Devolution and European Policy in the UK' (Award L219 25 2003), and is jointly undertaken with Caitriona Carter (University of Edinburgh) Martin Burch, Simon Bulmer and Ricardo Gomez (University of Manchester); and Patricia Hogwood (University of Glasgow).

[2] House of Lords Select Committee on the Constitution, Devolution: *Inter-Institutional Relations in the United Kingdom*, HL Paper 28, para. 170

and the devolved administrations.[3] In the admittedly limited empirical work that has been published regarding the adequacy of the prevailing arrangements, two general conclusions have emerged:

- The first, and this is confirmed in the House of Lords report, is that the current arrangements are working reasonably well. The devolved administrations are 'in the loop' in matters of EU policy, and where tensions over policy have arisen they have tended to be results of administrative oversight rather than any conscious attempt at political gerrymandering.

- The second is that the inter-administration arrangements prescribed in the concordats, and the adjacent 'informal' arrangements, have not yet been fully tested. In particular, devolution has taken place in a benign political environment. The Labour Party is the principal political force in Westminster, Cardiff and Edinburgh. Consequently, we would not expect significant policy conflicts to arise between the administrations, and undoubtedly this has assisted the various inter-administration co-ordination and co-operation procedures to settle down.

In assessing the EU dimension to devolution at the moment therefore, the results are considered adequate by the principals involved, albeit they could always be improved upon. However, the EU is not a static governance structure. The devolved administrations' impact on EU policies depends on two related processes:

- Reform of UK constitutional arrangements, and the structure of inter-administration relations.

- Opportunities that arise for further engagement in the EU policy process directly as a result of changes to the *EU's* governance arrangements.

In this chapter Welsh involvement in EU policy will be approached from the internal (UK) perspective and the external (EU) perspective. What are the implications for Wales of debates about EU governance and the role of devolved administrations? Is this EU-level debate increasingly going to ascribe a greater role in collective governance for so-called 'constitutional' regions, or the wider grouping labelled the 'regions with legislative powers'? If so, what are the direct and indirect consequences of this for the UK's devolved administrations? These are important questions since they extend the focus of

---

[3] See House of Lords Report, op.cit. paras. 16-49. For a comprehensive review of UK arrangements for EU policy-making after devolution see Bulmer, S. *et al* (2002) *British Devolution and European Policy-Making* (Palgrave Macmillan, Basingstoke). For an analysis of the UK concordats, see Scott, A. (2001) 'The Role of Concordats in the New Governance of Britain: Taking Subsidiarity Seriously', *Edinburgh Law Review* Vol.5 Issue 1.

attention beyond the UK to include what might be described as the extra-territorial dimension of UK devolution. This is a dimension which is often ignored but which has considerable relevance for the future prospects of Wales, Scotland and Northern Ireland in an enlarged and reformed EU.

CONSTITUTIONAL REGIONS AND THE EU

The emergence of 'constitutional regions' is an important development in the current debate about the future governance arrangements for the EU. The debate is taking place within the framework of the European Convention established by the Laeken European Council in December, 2001. That convention met throughout the following year, and in December 2002 produced a series of preliminary conclusions from its eleven Working Groups.

The notion of a 'constitutional region' first appeared in the literature towards the end of the 1990s. It emerged from the various 'regionalist' debates of the preceding decade, debates that were animated by the Maastricht Treaty on European Union obligations to involve to a greater extent the regions of the EU in its governance architecture. Specifically, the Treaty provided for representatives from sub-state governments (sometimes called 'third level' government) to sit in the Council of Ministers and speak on behalf of national ministers (Article 203, *ex 146*), and the decision to create a Committee of the Regions (Article 263, *ex 198a*). Both decisions reflected and projected the debate about greater involvement by regions within the EU governance arrangement, a debate that originated in Germany, driven initially by the Lander Governments. The emergent language was one which saw the EU as an evolving system of 'multi-level governance' in which regions as well as nation states had a role to play.[4]

The debate about the role of regions in EU governance was underpinned almost from the outset by a parallel discussion concerning the principle of subsidiarity. That too found expression in the Maastricht Treaty (Article 5, *ex 3b*). Initially there was some dispute on exactly what scope subsidiarity was to have. Was it only about the EU member-state division of competences (as nation-state governments insisted), or was it also intended to inform the debate about assignment of policy competences within member states? This latter interpretation was consistent with the preamble to the Treaty (Article 1,

---

[4] In the EU policy process, it is important to distinguish between the policy formulation phase and the policy implementation phase. While the regions can and do play a direct part in the implementation phase (for example, via the structural funds, environmental policy, and fisheries policy), they do not formally input to the more important policy formulation phase. In discussion about multi-level governance, it is in the policy formulation phase that the relevant governance players are represented.

ex Article A) which elaborated the idea that decisions should be taken "... as closely as possible to the citizen." In the event, this interpretation found no political or legal expression within the Treaty or beyond, with the result that the subsidiarity question solely revolved around the division of competencies between EU and member state levels.[5]

However, as became apparent almost immediately, a central problem with 'multi-level governance' as a practical system within the EU was the wide disparities that existed between its various regions. These disparities were multi-faceted but were concentrated in two broad areas:

- Economic and population size, ranging from the populous and economically powerful German Lander to extremely small and relatively weak regions in, say, Greece and Portugal.

- Divergences in regions' constitutional authority, policy competence, and political mobilisation.

Indeed, in some member states the very conceptualisation of a region as a sub-national *government* was simply misplaced. A better characterisation in these instances would be administrative offices largely dependent on decisions made by central government. In short, therefore, 'multi-level governance' as an effective political argument suffered because 'regionalism' was not a uniform phenomenon across EU member states. As a result the issues of autonomy and policy authority of regions in relation to enhanced competences at the EU level has met with divergent responses across the Union. In some member states regions, and their central governments, reacted vociferously to the erosion of their constitutionally embedded policy autonomy. On the other hand, in others the trend went more or less unnoticed at the regional level.

Against this background of an EU of widely different regional types, attempts were made by some regional authorities to form themselves into regional groupings on the basis of specific criteria. These included economic status, geographic location, legislative authority, and constitutional autonomy. The purpose of establishing distinctive regional interest groups across the EU was to make an input, via lobbying, to the EU decision-making process on a matter of particular relevance to that regional grouping.

Such regional representation to the EU could take one, or both, of two routes: either directly at the level of the EU institutions, or indirectly through sympathetic member state governments. The latter would be most effective where the group included regions from federated member states in which

---

[5] The general principle is that the EU should act only insofar as member states acting independently through the enactment of domestic legislation are unable to achieve the aims of the common EU policy.

regions enjoyed (sometimes considerable) constitutional authority, as in the case of Germany. But beyond these informal (though nonetheless sometimes effective) arrangements, and notwithstanding the work of the Committee of the Regions, regions have thus far failed to gain an effective legislative foothold within the EU governance machinery.[6] Moreover, neither do the EU regions have any legal standing in matters appertaining to the often vexed question of subsidiarity which does expressly raise considerations of competence at the sub-national loci of policy-making.

Thus far, therefore, the debate about multi-level governance and the role of the EU regions remains unresolved, although discussions continue. Significantly, however, the role of the regions is not explicitly being addressed within the European Convention. As noted, the Convention was convened to review the EU decisional architecture (ahead of enlargement), and to seek arrangements whereby EU governance can be brought closer to the citizen, and thus command greater legitimacy. The Convention's conclusions will be discussed by a specially convened inter-governmental conference in 2004.

Set against these aspirations, it is surprising that there is no *explicit* recognition of the regional dimension to EU activities within the Convention's framework. This is despite a number of calls to establish a regional forum for this, for instance by establishing a Convention Working Group on regions in EU governance. But this is not to say that the Convention is entirely blind to the issues affecting the role of regions in EU governance. In particular, regional concerns are being touched upon in the Working Group examining subsidiarity and, although only indirectly, the Group examining the role of national parliaments. Both issues will be discussed later in this chapter.

CLAIMS OF THE CONSTITUTIONAL REGIONS

Within the various regional groupings currently active within the EU are the so-called 'constitutional regions' which have seven members.[7] In a recent report to the Flemish authorities, Boucke and Vos defined 'constitutional regions' in the following terms:

"... regions that possess a solid institutional basis (their own legislative

---

[6] Just as the extra-institutional political mobilisation of EU regions was frustrated as a result of wide divergences in competences and authority at the regional level, so the political 'voice' of the Committee of the Regions arguably has been compromised for similar reasons.

[7] It is worth stressing that constitutional regions are not recognised in any formal way either by EU member states or by the EU itself. The genesis and composition of the group is basically self-declaratory.

*assembly, more than purely administrative powers, a certain degree of
financial autonomy, etc.) and whose authority to set standards can only
be challenged by legal means: that is to say the German and Austrian
Lander, the Belgian Communities and Regions, the Spanish autonomous
Communities, Scotland, Wales.* [8]

It is arguable that Wales does not meet a *strict* interpretation of this definition,
because the National Assembly lacks primary legislative powers. Nonetheless
this definition does provide a useful starting place for a discussion of
constitutional regions. The underlying idea is that these are regions which
command considerable legislative authority and, as such, stand to lose most
as legislative authority gravitates upwards towards 'Brussels'. The concept of
the constitutional region was given political expression on 28 May 2001 when
the regions of Bavaria, Catalunya, North Rhine-Westphalia, Salzburg,
Scotland, Wallonia and Flanders signed a *Political Declaration by the
Constitutional Regions* which was aimed at influencing the Future of Europe
debate. The document puts forward a number of demands, including:

- Their direct participation in the preparatory work for the 2004 Inter-
  Governmental Conference.

- A general clarification and formalisation (to recognise and entrench
  the position of regions) of the principle of subsidiarity to facilitate a
  distinction between the competences of the EU on the one hand and
  the member states and the regions on the other.

- A review of the political responsibilities of the EU on the one hand
  and the member states and regions on the other, especially with
  respect to the approximation of laws that impinge on regional
  competencies other than with respect to the establishment and
  functioning of the internal market.

- Strengthening the role of the Committee of the Regions to give it the
  status of a fully-fledged EU institution, including the right to institute
  proceedings in the European Court of Justice.

In addition to this declaration, on 15 November 2001 some 51 EU regions
published a resolution whose contents mirrored in large measure the
declaration made by the seven constitutional regions. That regional grouping
defines itself not as constitutional regions, but as 'regions with legislative
power', and its membership extends well beyond the confines of the
constitutional regions grouping.[9] This group includes Scotland and Wales,

---

[8] Boucke, T. and Vos, H. (2001) *Constitutional Regions in the European Union: an examination of their
added value, of critical success factors, and political consequences* Final Report to the Flemish Authorities
(University of Ghent, mimeo).

[9] The regions with legislative power emerged in 1999 as a result of debates within the Council of
Europe's Congress of Local and Regional Authorities of Europe. Again, this group is self-constituted
and has no legal constitutional standing.

though not Northern Ireland. It is clear, therefore, that the regional question is a live topic within the broad debate over the future of Europe. Moreover, it is also clear that this debate is being led by those regions that command legislative competence. In turn this raises the question of how those regions will find a political expression to their demands. The following section considers this from the UK perspective.

INFLUENCING EUROPEAN UNION POLICY MAKING

In the main the *principal* source of influence of regions in the EU policy process is through (domestic) engagement with their national government.[10] Consequently, if that influence is to have an impact at the EU level, much will depend on the relationship between the administrations of the region and its member state. In this context four considerations impact on the devolved administrations' potential for influence:

1. Post-devolution arrangements for the devolved administrations to engage with UK European policy.

2. Ability of the Scottish Executive and Welsh Assembly Government to influence the UK Government.

3. Scope for the Scottish Parliament's Legislative Capacity to exert influence on UK European policy.

4. Role of the Brussels-based offices of the UK's devolved administrations.

1. ENGAGING WITH UK EUROPEAN POLICY

Under the 1999 devolution settlement, European Union policy is a reserved matter. However, it was understood from the outset that, because of the overlap between the devolved powers and EU legislative competence, the devolved administrations had a legitimate interest in UK EU policy. In both Scotland and Wales the interest went further as both the Scottish Parliament and the National Assembly would normally expect to implement EU obligations on devolved policies through their own (secondary) legislation, rather than through Westminster legislation. The upshot was the Concordat on Co-ordination of EU Policy Issues, signed between UK Government and the three devolved administrations. Although not legally binding, and devoid of formal constitutional standing,[11] the concordat was presented as a guide to

---

[10] This is notwithstanding regional lobbying powers and/or the policy 'window' presented to regions either through their duties as implementation agents of the EU or via the Opinions issued by the Committee of the Regions on EU legislative proposals.

[11] In the sense that nothing in the concordats affected in any way the devolution settlement as set out in the respective Parliamentary Acts.

sensible policy co-operation and co-ordination between the devolved administrations and the UK Government with a view to achieving 'joined-up' government, including an inter-administration 'no surprises' agreement. In the event of a disagreement between the UK government and a devolved administration which could not be resolved by officials, a Joint Ministerial Committee on Europe will be convened involving the relevant Ministers from UK government and the devolved administrations involved.[12]

In addition to concordats, a number of informal or *ad hoc* arrangements have evolved between individual Whitehall departments and the devolved administrations to ensure they are kept fully 'in-the-loop' with regard to pertinent UK government discussions on EU policy. These arrangements have arisen where the provisions of the concordats are insufficient to achieve the overriding aims of joined-up government. This is especially the case when sensitive issues are involved and where otherwise relevant information may not reach the devolved administrations, such as deliberations of Cabinet Committees. Beyond that, a Ministerial Group for European Co-ordination (MINECOR) has been established to bring together the UK Europe Minister with ministerial counterparts from the devolved administrations. Again, none of the deliberations from this group are binding, but it provides a forum for discussion of the strategic orientation of European policy. By general agreement these post-devolution arrangements are working reasonably efficiently. Certainly the *ad hoc* arrangements, in particular, have been welcomed.

2. INFLUENCING THE UK GOVERNMENT

The reserved status of EU policy implies that the UK government will consult equally with all the devolved administrations. However, Scotland has always tended to have a greater engagement in UK EU policy than has either Wales or Northern Ireland. This reflects a number of distinctive Scottish features including:

- Size and economic diversity
- A separate legal and educational system
- The significance of fishing and farming,
- Incidence of declining industries
- The scale of underdeveloped rural area

Scotland's capacity to engage in EU business was also buttressed informally after devolution because of the frequency and scope of previous inter-departmental discussion between Scottish Office and Whitehall officials. A

---

[12] Thus far no dispute-resolving meeting of the JCM(E) had proven necessary. At the same time the JMC(E) has convened regularly, typically immediately prior to a gathering of the Heads of Government and State (the European Council).

reservoir of mutual trust was inherited which eased the transition to devolution by minimising Whitehall reluctance to keep the Scottish Executive informed on European matters. In short, a cadre of officials in the Scottish Office had established deep-seated expertise in EU affairs over many years prior to devolution in 1999. This meant the Scottish Executive was well-placed to represent its EU policy interests both in Whitehall and, where appropriate, Brussels. In comparison, for instance, there was no Cardiff-based agricultural policy capacity until 1977. Prior to this there had simply been a Whitehall Ministry of Agriculture, Fisheries and Food office in Aberystwyth. This background bears on the different aspirations and capacity for agricultural policy-making in Wales as compared to Scotland.

Since 1992 Scotland Europa has developed considerable expertise and contacts within the Brussels policy community. This has the advantage of ensuring that relevant EU initiatives are spotted quickly, enabling lobbying pressures to be targeted. In contrast, Wales' representation has faced disruption since devolution because of major changes made to the Wales European Centre in Brussels. In April 2002 the Assembly Government resolved to pull out of involvement with the Centre, and instead to expand its direct representation in the European capital. The objective, to establish a stronger presence for the Assembly Government, may well be achieved in the longer run. However, the short term effect was certainly disruptive.[13]

An undoubted additional factor in the relative influence of Wales and Scotland in European affairs is the fact that the Scottish Parliament has primary legislative powers. Arguably this places the Scottish Executive in a more powerful position than the Assembly Government with regard to the UK European policy process. For instance, if the EU is considering legislating in a matter over which primary legislative competence is devolved to the Scottish Parliament, the UK government may feel duty bound to consider Scotland's views of the prospective legislation rather than risk being seen to undermine the concept of devolution. Moreover, if the EU legislative proposal conflicts with, or constrains, Scotland's actual or putative legislative competence, the UK government may feel under a greater pressure to respond to Scottish concerns than if an objection had come from the National Assembly. In the latter instance, Assembly concerns might be compensated in another area of UK primary legislation. That is to say, a policy 'deal' could be struck with the Assembly that could not be extended to Scotland because of devolution. It is worth noting that the Scottish Parliament does have sight of information from the Council of Ministers which plays a crucial role in the EU pre-legislative phase.[14] I will return to this issue in the next section.

---

[13] See the quarterly report, *Engaging with Europe: Monitoring the National Assembly March to June 2002*, IWA (www.iwa.org.uk), for an account.

[14] A current interest is whether regions with primary legislative competence should be involved in EU policy discussions which propose to utilise the so-called open method of co-ordination. See Carter, C. (2002) 'Institutionalist Dynamics: Policy Ideas, Institutional Change and Political Discourse', paper presented to European Consortium for Political Research conference, Bordeaux, September 2002.

The points made here suggest there are both historical and contemporary reasons why, in the aftermath of devolution, Scotland *might* be expected to have relatively more influence than Wales over UK European policy. Of course, there are counter arguments, the most persuasive of which is the respective political weights of the territorial Secretaries of State. While the offices of both the Scottish and Welsh Secretaries of State were retained at Cabinet level, the potency of the Scottish Secretary may be diminished simply because the devolution of legislative competence to Scotland has weakened the office within UK Government. This clearly is not the case with respect to the Welsh Secretary who has the task of presenting the interests of the National Assembly in discussions over primary legislation.[15] Ironically asymmetric devolution may have changed the balance of influence somewhat between these two offices inside the Cabinet.

On a more practical level, the scope for the relevant officials from the devolved administrations to attend Whitehall meetings may determine in part their ability to influence UK government European policy. While there may be no obstacle for them attending meetings of UK government officials, practical problems may militate against their regular attendance. Are there sufficient staff in the Welsh, Scottish or Northern Ireland departments to warrant attendance at every relevant Whitehall meeting? Is the subject under debate sufficiently central to their core functions? Does non-attendance contribute to a Whitehall culture that the devolved administrations aren't interested and therefore there is no need to keep them fully involved? Are there differences between Whitehall departments in their openness to, and communication with, the devolved administrations? In the political sphere, are there political reasons that will encourage UK government to be more or less open with any particular administration?

In general the Scottish Executive has (sometimes considerably) more resources with which to represent Scottish EU interests to UK government. However, this may be closely related to the next theme - the relationship between the Scottish Parliament and the Scottish Executive. The main problems may not stem from differential Scottish and Welsh influence in Whitehall, but rather a combination of the following two factors

- Both Scotland and Wales being kept out of sensitive Whitehall deliberations.

- The inability of either Scotland or Wales to change UK policy where their distinctive interests conflict with UK government's preferred approach (implicitly an approach that must benefit England).[16]

---

[15] In evidence to the House Of Lords Constitution Committee, Paul Murphy stressed that his role was to present to UK Government the views of the Assembly and of Wales, but not to *represent* the views of the Assembly - this being the role of the Assembly Government. See House of Lords Select Committee report, *op..cit.* para. 58

[16] Both issues are reported in Chapter 5 of Bulmer, *et al, op.cit.*.

3. Legislative Leverage in the European Policy Process

As a legislature, an essential role of the Scottish Parliament is to hold the Scottish Executive to account for the implementation of primary and secondary legislation, including that arising from UK membership of the EU. This raises the whole question of Parliamentary scrutiny of legislative proposals, and the extent to which the Scottish Parliament may seek to impose its position on the Scottish Executive.[17] It is well beyond the scope of this paper to go into a discussion of the procedures of the Westminster Parliament's European Scrutiny Committee. However, the legislative model of Scotland's devolution settlement, in particular the separation of executive from legislature, does carry with it important implications for legislative process in which scrutiny and accountability are key features. Of course, in Wales the executive role of government has been partially devolved while the primary legislative role remains with Westminster.

The role of scrutiny within a sub-national parliament opens a considerable range of possibilities for influencing outcomes, even where outcomes ultimately are determined at the UK level. Two paths are potentially open to the legislature. The first is to engage in scrutiny on the basis of policy interests distinctive to the devolved polity. In practice this might involve the executive making available to the legislature, in good time, all pertinent information as to the advantages and disadvantages of all EU legislative proposals likely to impact on devolved competencies or on the polity itself to facilitate parliamentary debate.[18] The results of this scrutiny are then communicated to the executive. At that stage, the legislature may leave matters alone, or it might require the executive subsequently to make representations to the UK government on the position agreed upon by the legislature. Of course, the executive can carry no responsibility if that position ultimately is overruled, but it does carry with it the possibility for potentially damaging backlash against UK government in the devolved polity should this transpire.[19] A second option for the legislature is to co-ordinate its scrutiny with the scrutiny activities of UK Parliament such that its opinions regarding an EU legislative proposal may be known to the UK Parliament as it undertakes its own deliberations. The UK Parliament, of course, does have a scrutiny reserve. In any event, the Scottish Parliament retains the right to call the executive to account with regard to the implementation of all legislation, including that giving effect to European law and this gives it some degree of leverage in the UK policy process.[20]

---

[17] This section draws extensively on Carter, C (2000) 'Democratic Governance beyond the Nation State: Third Level Assemblies and the Scrutiny of European Legislation', *European Public Law*, Volume 6, Issue 3.

[18] An example would be by having a 'local' regulatory impact assessment.

[19] In the Scottish realpolitik any repeated tendency for UK government to reject the Scottish Executive arguments would be bound to play into the hands of the SNP.

[20] The recent dispute between the Scottish Parliament and Executive with respect to tie-up versus decommissioning of fishing boats is an example of an EU-related matter where UK policy ran against the preferred Scottish policy option.

The question one might ask on the basis of this discussion is whether or not the political sensitivities attached to the preferences of a sub-national legislature carry greater weight than those attaching to the policy preferences of a sub-national executive. There are very good reasons for believing this indeed to be the case. For instance, the existence of a sub-national legislature encourages lobby groups within the devolved polity to engage with that legislature, and this is bound to increase the number of 'local' stakeholders than otherwise might be expected. Moreover, the existence of a devolved legislature is likely to 'crowd-in' a greater part of civil society to the political process than also otherwise might be expected. If this is the case, legislative devolution may well give greater implied powers to that polity than it does to a polity where only executive powers are devolved.

4. INFLUENCE OF BRUSSELS REPRESENTATION

A 'cardinal rule' in terms of member state EU policy negotiations is that all constituent parts of the member state adhere to a single negotiating line. The line is agreed upon in the national capital and thereafter represented in Brussels. Any tendency for the representation of a devolved administration to depart from the UK common negotiating brief almost certainly would be exploited by another member state and thereby weaken its influence within the EU. Accordingly, the formal position is that all UK devolved administration offices in Brussels are in fact parts of a single UKRep 'family' and each is singing out of the same songbook.[21]

The more important matter, however, is the extent to which the activities of the Brussels-based offices of sub-state governments informally influence policy outcomes. Two features are important here. The first is that an office will provide important information on EU legislative, and as important, pre-legislative, activity to the devolved administration. This will then be used by officials and Ministers in their discussions with the Whitehall lead department. It is common ground that by the time the Commission actually issues a legislative proposal there has already been extensive consultation with interested parties, and that it is by then too late to shape the content of those proposals. The presence of an office of the devolved administration has an important role to play in that regard. Second, the Brussels office may be delegated (or requested) to attend particular working groups in the Council or Commission where the issue to hand is of importance at home. Once again, this enables the office to make a contribution to the overall EU policy process.[22]

[21] See House of Lords Select Committee on the Constitution Report, *op..cit..* para. 174.

[22] I am ignoring here the impact that a Minister from the devolved administration might have should s/he be invited to represent UK Government within the EU Council of Ministers. This is because at that time the Minister is bound to represent the already agreed single negotiating brief of the UK Government. This is not, therefore, an opportunity of representing the views of the devolved administration, unless of course this has already been adopted as the common UK line.

Finally, there may well be an indirect influence if a Brussels office is part of an exclusive network which collectively can exert pressure on key players within the EU policy process. For instance, as a member of the group of self-declared Constitutional Regions, Scotland is taking its place alongside regions which command considerable political authority and influence in their own member state, in this case Belgium, Spain, and Germany. This raises the possibility that the network may shape the national policy position adopted by a member state, a position that - depending on the legislative procedure involved - could be decisive in determining the outcome.

FUTURE OF EUROPE

In this final section I want to draw together a number of strands involving the UK devolution process and the European Convention. There are, in my view, important points of overlap. It is likely that the European Convention will come forward with meaningful proposals on specific issues that impact upon the sub-state question in all member states, including the UK. Equally, it is likely that these conclusions will influence the proposals that come forward from the Richard Commission for reform of the National Assembly such as, for instance, the granting of primary legislative powers. The main point of overlap between the debate on the Assembly's powers and the discussions taking place within the European Convention revolve around the issue of subsidiarity. As we have seen this has been interpreted as the regulation of the division of competences between the European Union and the member states. It broadly states that the EU should act by common legislation only where the aims of the policy cannot be achieved by member states legislating themselves through national parliaments

During its initial phase the Convention established a Working Group on Subsidiarity and a Working Group on the Role of National Parliaments, both of which reported in September, 2002. The reports propose the following procedures should be introduced whereby a member state might appeal against an EU legislative proposal on the grounds that it violates the principle of subsidiarity:

- An obligation for the Commission to attach a subsidiarity sheet to legislative proposals after consulting all relevant players affected by the proposal – including local and regional authorities.

- Establishing an early warning system whereby national parliaments are able to give their opinions about the subsidiarity question before legislation is enacted.

- Giving national parliaments which activated this early warning system a right to appeal to the European Court of Justice following the adoption of a legislative act which it considers violates subsidiarity.

- Giving a right of appeal to the European Court of Justice to the Committee of the Regions in the case of legislative texts that fall within its remit.

Should these provisions be implemented within a revised Treaty following the 2004 Inter-Governmental Conference, it is likely that the legislative rights of sub-state administrations, as well as member states, will be better protected than currently is the case. It is a feature of EU governance that the gradual acquisition of competences at the EU level has occurred at the expense of the legislative authority of sub-state administrations (in federated countries) as well as at the expense of national governments. If implemented, the recommendations of the Convention will accord greater protection - *at least in the pre-legislative phase of the EU legislative process* - to sub-state administrations than before. At the same time these administrations will need to rely on domestic procedures and internal political discourse to ensure that their interests are both represented to, and taken account of by, their member state. Certainly the right of appeal to the European Court of Justice by member states will persuade the Commission to make sure that prospective legislation has gained wide consensus before being tabled. A similar outcome may flow from the right of the Committee of Regions separately to appeal to the Court on grounds of violations to subsidiarity. How might we assess these proposals in the context of UK devolution? Two main issues need to be addressed:

- First, to what degree will the UK Parliament feel it necessary to involve the devolved administrations in pre-legislative discussion on subsidiarity?[23] Arguably the UK Parliament will be bound to involve any sub-national parliament in this discussion to the extent that their legislative competences are being affected by prospective EU legislation. In the UK, this points to the involvement of the Scottish Parliament and the Northern Ireland Assembly, though not necessarily of the National Assembly of Wales because of its lack of primary legislative authority.

- Second, to what extent will the Committee of Regions be an effective mouthpiece for their membership in the EU subsidiarity discourse? The sheer diversity of regional 'types' in that Committee does not bode well for its active engagement. In the first instance many of the

---

[23] It is important to note that the subsidiarity discussion is to be with national parliaments and not national governments. In this context we are no longer primarily concerned with inter-administration correspondence and outcomes, but with inter-parliamentary outcomes - a fundamentally different proposition.

regions represented by the Committee have no primary legislative powers and therefore no recourse to the European Court of Justice, under the Working Group's proposals. Equally, the seven 'constitutional regions' or the 51 regions with legislative power might insist that a sub-group of the Committee of Regions be established to represent them in making referrals to the European Court of Justice. Almost certainly this will invite debate about which regions should be admitted to what would, by definition, become a very powerful and legislatively influential grouping within the Committee of Regions. A rather high eligibility test for membership of this sub-grouping of the Committee might therefore be applied. In these circumstances the question of Wales' admission to the group would be a moot point under the prevailing constitutional arrangements within the UK.

CONCLUSION

In many respects the idea of a 'Europe of the Regions' has failed to live up to the expectations of the early protagonists. The vision whereby the EU-level and the regional-level of governance would be enhanced at the expense of a weakened national-state level has not been realised. The EU remains a union of 'national states', albeit one characterised by powerful supranational institutions that enjoy considerable policy authority and autonomy.

To the extent that regions have a voice within the EU process per se, this remains essentially advisory, although it is the case that regions constitute a powerful interest group with the capacity to influence the EU policy process 'from the outside'. However, the real power of the regions to influence EU policy continues to reside within the domestic polities of the individual member states. Member states with strong regions will have to take greater note of their concerns than will member states with weaker regions. Consequently, the role of individual regions in EU policy depends primarily on the domestic relationship between region and nation-state government. Additional factors are, of course, the influence of that member state within the overall EU decision-making process and the relevant EU decisional procedures for whatever legislative proposal is under consideration.

The question about the powers of the National Assembly should, in my view, be debated within the context of both domestic UK constitutional considerations and the evolving debate regarding EU governance. Much attention has been given to the former; inadequate attention to the latter. If the Assembly is to maximise the welfare of the citizens of Wales, then it must enjoy a position within the EU debate at least as powerful - and certainly no weaker – as the other devolved administrations within the UK. Key European Union questions are looming which will impact as much upon Wales as Scotland and Northern Ireland, including the future of the structural funds, agricultural policy reforms, and state aid to industry. All of the UK devolved administrations should be equally placed to steer UK Government and Parliament's European Union policy both internally and, crucially, within the changing framework of EU governance.

CHAPTER 19

LEGAL WALES

Jane Williams

The expression 'Legal Wales' was coined early in the history of Welsh devolution, two legal establishment figures were largely responsible: Winston Roddick Q.C., Counsel General to the National Assembly, and Sir John Thomas, then senior presiding judge of the Wales and Chester Circuit. Sir John took it as his theme for the Lord Morris of Borth-Y-Gest lecture for the University of Wales in October 2000: *Legal Wales: Its Modern Origins and its Role after Devolution: National Identity, the Welsh Language and Parochialism.*[1] The proposition is that the development of law and legal institutions in Wales is an essential part of a trajectory towards nationhood, in which the 1998 settlement constituted the most significant step in centuries and provided a particular opportunity for the legal profession both to contribute to and benefit from that process.

'Legal Wales' encapsulates the repatriation of aspects of the administration of justice in Wales, notwithstanding that the administration of justice is not a field in which functions have been devolved under the Government of Wales Act. Sir John's 2000 lecture focused mainly on administration of justice issues such as the organisation of the courts and judiciary in Wales and the use of the Welsh language in legal proceedings. But other aspects, touched upon in the judge's analysis, are equally important. Sir Roderick Evans,[2] delivering the 2002 Lord Morris lecture,[3] identified the essential ingredients of 'Legal Wales' thus:

(a) The repatriation to Wales of law making functions.

(b) The development in Wales of a system for the administration of justice in all its forms which is tailored to the social and economic needs of Wales.

(c) The development of institutions and professional bodies which will provide a proper career structure in Wales for those who want to follow a career in those fields.

---

[1] Lord Moris of Borth-Y-Gest annual lecture, 2000, University of Wales, Swansea.

[2] Formerly a Presiding Judge of the Wales and Chester Circuit and now the only fully bilingual High court judge, of which more *infra*.

[3] University of Wales, Aberystwyth, 2002.

(d) Making the law accessible to, and readily understood, by the people of Wales

(e) The development of a system which can accommodate the use of either the English or Welsh languages with equal ease so that in the administration of justice within Wales, the English and Welsh languages really are treated on the basis of equality.

This chapter describes the changes and attempts to assess their impact. It will be argued that Legal Wales is both a significant consequence of devolution and essentially supportive of its further development. More than that, it is a necessary component in the social and economic development of Wales and a litmus test for the maturity of Welsh national government and administration.

MAKING WELSH LAW

Separate law and administration did not begin in 1998. There were both substantive and procedural differences between the law and legal system in England and in Wales in the years before devolution. From the last quarter of the 19th century there was gradual progress towards a distinct Welsh approach in a range of policy areas – from Sunday closing to the use and promotion of the Welsh language, education, culture and the Church. The establishment of the University of Wales, the disestablishment of the Church in Wales, the institutions of the National Library and the National Museum, and later the Welsh Development Agency, are all the result of Westminster legislation making separate provision for Wales. The creation of the Welsh Office in 1964 helped to establish Welsh administration of regulation in these fields and to provide a conduit for a Welsh voice in the development of Whitehall policy. The end product however remained precisely that – Whitehall policy - given effect, where changes in the law were required, by Westminster legislation. The sea change represented by the Government of Wales Act was that there was now both the opportunity and a political commitment to develop policy independently of Whitehall and to give effect to it, to the extent permitted under the Act, by legislation passed by the Assembly itself.

The particular structure provided in the Government of Wales Act for the devolution of law making powers relating to Wales is not the subject of this chapter and there is now a considerable and on the whole critical literature on it. There are few who would argue that the design is optimal in terms of producing accessible and coherent regulation in the fields in which it was intended that the new government of Wales should function.[4] The problems commonly identified include:

- The piecemeal nature of the original transfer of functions, based on the collection of functions previously carried out by the Secretary of State.

- The piecemeal and sometimes inconsistent method by which further functions have been conferred on the Assembly in subsequent Acts of the Westminster Parliament.

- The difficulties faced by the Assembly when seeking to secure policy aims through Westminster primary legislation.

- The horizontal division of powers which limits the Assembly's formal law making role to subordinate legislation.

- The complexity of the Assembly's own subordinate legislative procedures.

In the short time since the Assembly came into existence there has been a remarkable amount of review and reappraisal of the law making process for Wales. These include the Assembly's internal Review of Procedure conducted in 2001, an examination of the procedures for primary legislation for Wales by the House of Commons Select Committee on Welsh Affairs during 2002-03, consideration of the role of Parliaments and Assemblies as part of the remit of the House of Lords Select Committee on the Constitution during 2002-03, and of course the Richard Commission on the powers and electoral arrangements of the National Assembly which is due to report by the end of 2003.

However, the pertinent point in terms of Legal Wales is not that the current settlement produces difficulties in law making. It is that, imperfect as the structures may be, Assembly policies *have* been given effect using the vehicles of both primary and subordinate legislation. Furthermore, this process has generated a new creativity, with Assembly lawyers and other officials operating innovatively and independently of their Whitehall counterparts and engaging with them as equals.

A good example is provided by the Assembly Government's health policy.[5] The NHS (Wales) Plan set out policy objectives for the reform of health service structures in Wales. There were five key elements:

1. The abolition of the five Health Authorities and the establishment of 22 Local Health Boards.

2. A duty on Local Health Boards and local authorities to prepare a joint health and well being strategy,

---

[4] That is, those set out as the initial fields in Schedule 2 to the Government of Wales Act

[5] A detailed account of the legislative process of the Welsh health reforms is contained in a forthcoming article by Simon McCann for the Wales Law Journal – *Permissive Powers are Good for the Health Service*. The summary of that process in this chapter is much indebted to this text.

3. Reform of the Community Health Councils,

4. A new body to accredit training of nurses, midwives and other health-related professions.

5. A Wales Centre for Health to bring together expertise in public health and provide a focus for health research and public information.

The Assembly Cabinet set a deadline for implementation of 31 March 2003. It was originally hoped that a Welsh Health Bill would be introduced in the Westminster parliamentary session 2001–02, and that that Bill would contain all the necessary primary legislative provision. Such a Bill was heralded in the Queen's Speech on 26 June 2001. In the debate in the Assembly on the Queen's Speech, Secretary of State for Wales Paul Murphy made it clear that it was intended that the Assembly be given broad permissive powers to implement its policies through secondary legislation.[6] In other words this was to be the type of Bill that recognised: (i) the Assembly's capacity for law making through secondary legislation; (ii) the democratic legitimacy of that product; and (iii) the Assembly itself as a legislature.

In the event the aspiration for a Wales-only Bill dealing with all the necessary primary legislative provisions was frustrated. UK Cabinet drafting clearance was only given in the 2001–02 session for the publication of an all Wales *draft* Bill. The implication was that a Bill would then be introduced to Parliament in the 2002–03 session, which would be too late for the Assembly's implementation deadline. For that reason the key primary provisions that would enable the structural reforms to take place within the Assembly's timescale were included in the UK Government's NHS Reform and Health Care Professions Bill introduced to the Westminster parliament in November 2001. This meant there was a shorter than planned consultation. The rest of the primary provision was put into a draft Bill, published in summer 2002, for introduction in November 2002.

This unintended split in the primary legislative provisions meant that Assembly lawyers working with their colleagues in policy divisions had both the challenge and the opportunity of producing primary legislation for Wales through the traditional Bill process and through the novel procedure of a complete Assembly sponsored Bill. The outcome may be inconvenient in terms of accessibility of the eventual legislative product[7] but has undoubtedly been a learning experience of value to those now charged with review and reappraisal not only of legislative processes for Wales but for the UK

---

[6] *Assembly Record* 26 June 2001.

[7] See Baroness Finlay of Llandaff's eloquent plea, in the debate on second reading of the NHS and Health Care Professions Bill, for a consolidation for England and for Wales respectively, so that "someone simple like me could pick up the document and read it in its entirety instead of trying to rummage through what must be a lawyer's tea party but what, for a clinician, I am afraid, is a nightmare" – Official Record House of Lords 31 January 2002.

generally.[8]

In the case of each Bill, handling arrangements had to take into account the fact that the Assembly has no power to introduce or directly sponsor primary legislation. Neither do its officials have the right to instruct the Whitehall-based Parliamentary Counsel who would draft the relevant clauses. In each case the solution was found in section 41 of the Government of Wales Act.[9] For the NHS Reform and Health Care Professions Bill the Assembly lawyers and other officials acted as agents of the UK Government Department in carrying out the functions of advising Ministers, preparing drafting instructions and supporting debates in the parliamentary stages, working through the intermediary of the Wales Office. For the NHS (Wales) Bill the arrangements went a step further and provided for Assembly officials to exercise the functions of the Wales Office itself. The result of the experience was described by Simon McCann, leader of the Assembly team of lawyers with responsibility for the Bills, as follows:

> "In effect, the Assembly has been entrusted with the powers which it lacked, to exercise them on a quasi-agency basis on behalf of the Wales Office, whilst benefiting hugely from the very considerable political experience and influence which the Wales Office can provide. This is not only an excellent example of devolved and central government working together to achieve a shared goal, but also powerful evidence that the Assembly is coming of age and is ready, willing and able to exercise primary legislative powers of its own."[10]

It can be seen from this example that since 1998 Assembly lawyers and policy officials have had to develop significant new skills and to acquire expertise in 'doing legislation'. These simply did not exist previously in anything like the measure that would be required to exercise full legislative competence, but they have grown quickly. In the debate about whether primary legislative powers should be conferred on the Assembly, this very practical fact is often overlooked. The acquisition of the relevant skills by Assembly lawyers in particular is essential if that aspiration is to be given practical effect. The role of Assembly lawyers and other officials in relation to the health Bills was essentially that of a departmental Bill team in a Whitehall government department.

---

[8] The procedure for the NHS (Wales) Bill may be taken as a template for the kind of draft Bill procedure that the UK Government has recently committed itself to – see Modernisation Committee Report www.publications.parliament.uk/pa/cm/cmmodern.htm

[9] Section 41 provides that arrangements can be made between the Assembly and any other relevant authority for the carrying out of functions of one by the other, or the provision of administrative, professional or technical services by one for the other.

[10] Simon McCann, *op. cit.*

WELSH DRAFTING FOR WELSH BILLS

The other part of the equation in producing primary legislation is the actual drafting, and in this, the Assembly's first term has also seen a leap in the stock of skills and experience at the Assembly's disposal. Here too, only a certain amount could be learned from Whitehall. The novelties in the Welsh settlement include not only different subordinate legislative processes but also the requirement to draft bilingually. Nothing in the Whitehall experience could assist much in that regard. Instead, the Office of the Counsel General in the National Assembly has looked to the experience of bilingual legislatures abroad, forming in particular links with government draftspersons and the judiciary in New Brunswick where over 30 years a fully bilingual legal system has been established.[11] The Office has recruited bilingual lawyers and begun to work towards a system of co-drafting whereby English and Welsh drafters work together with policy officials from the earliest stage in the process of policy development.

The contrast with the position before the 1998 Act is stark. On the whole in those days, subordinate legislation made by the Secretary of State for Wales followed England. The work of the Welsh Office Legal Branch was essentially to process Welsh versions, sometimes including Welsh language versions, sometimes including agreed policy variations, but not to be heavily involved in the original policy process or to produce original drafts. The drafting style of the relevant Whitehall department, informed by standards policed by the relevant Westminster committees, would be followed.

By contrast drafting original legislation bilingually – for equal legal effect in both languages[12] - implies a whole industry of activity. Assembly lawyers are now much more likely to be centrally involved with colleagues in administrative divisions in the formulation of the policy. Scrutiny of legislative style as well as policy substance is carried out exclusively by the Assembly's own committees.[13] There is also an obvious need to achieve consistency in the use of legal terminology in both languages. In this the bilingual drafters and the advisers to the Assembly's Legislation Committee have acquired a particular expertise, but it is recognised that external assistance is also needed.

In other parts of the world where bilingual legislation has been introduced –

---

[11] See Paul J.M.Godin, *"The New Brunswick Experience: the Practice of the English Common Law in the French Language"* (2001) 1 Wales Law Journal 40, based on a paper given at the first of the Lord Morris seminar series following Sir JohnThomas's lecture.

[12] See section 122(1) of the Government of Wales Act – the English and Welsh texts of any Assembly subordinate legislation is of equal legal standing.

[13] By virtue of section 44 of the Government of Wales Act which disapplies, in relation to Assembly subordinate legislation, the established Westminster procedures.

New Brunswick being but one example – university law and languages departments have been enlisted to work in partnership with government agencies to provide language training for lawyers and official translation services. The role of the law departments of the University of Wales in this respect has yet to unfold, but the potential for partnership has been recognised.[14] In 2002 the Assembly invited tenders for a standardisation project for Welsh legal terminology. At the time of writing no contract had emerged, apparently due to the cost of providing a service which combines the requisite legal and linguistic expertise, rather than any lack of such expertise or willingness to engage on the part of the academic departments in Wales. Provision of bilingual legal education is also under active consideration by the University law departments, and it is recognised that collaboration will be necessary to produce the "critical mass" required.[15]

ADMINISTRATION OF JUSTICE IN WALES

The legal system of Wales remains absorbed within a system for England and Wales for which constitutional responsibility and administrative arrangements reside with the Lord Chancellor. There is a gathering debate as to how long that position can be sustained in the light of developments under the current settlement, and whether it would be tenable at all if primary legislative powers were conferred on the National Assembly.

Since devolution there have been changes in the arrangements for court sittings and for the issue of some types of legal process but without altering the Lord Chancellor's dominion. The changes that have occurred since 1998 have had the effect of bringing the physical processes of the higher courts into Wales. They include the establishment of a mercantile court in Cardiff, regular sittings in Wales of both civil and criminal divisions of the Court of Appeal and of the Employment Appeal Tribunal, and the establishment of an Administrative Court and a Chancery Court in Wales. A Practice Direction was issued in 1999 enabling and encouraging the issue and hearing of Administrative Court proceedings in Wales.[16]

There are two main drivers for greater separation and for a degree of formal

---

[14] For example, Iwan Davies *"The Challenge of Legal Wales"* – annual lecture for the Law Society, National Eisteddfod, 2001. For a consideration of how the University law departments could play a crucial role in the development of bilingualism within the legal community in Wales, see R. Gwynedd Parry *Hyrwyddo'r Gymraeg Ym Myd Y Gyfraith: Beth Yw Cyfraniad Adrannau Cyfraith Y Brifysgol?* (2001) 1 Wales Law Journal 388.

[15] See, for example, Sir Roderick Evans' 2002 Lord Morris lecture.

[16] Practice Direction 1 July 1999 and Note for Guidance issued by the Administrative Court July 2001.

devolution of functions in the field of administration of justice. The first is the emergence of distinct Welsh substantive law, and the second is the Welsh language.

As to the first, there is a steadily increasing output of separate, bilingually drafted legal regulation across a range of fields, all of which are capable of generating issues requiring legal advice and representation in the courts. The argument runs that at the very least this means that Welsh law will become more and more of a specialism. Not only practitioners but also judges hearing cases at first instance in Wales will develop a familiarity with those Welsh laws and the Welsh government policy environment in which they are made and administered. Elsewhere in the United Kingdom, as well as abroad, a separate body of substantive law is generally associated with a separate body of procedural law and a separate court system – as the position in Scotland and Northern Ireland reflects. The present limitation of the Assembly's law making powers to subordinate legislation may well be successfully argued, at least at a political level, to provide a sufficient difference to justify this particular manifestation of the asymmetry of devolution in the United Kingdom. In practice, even without primary legislative powers, there will increasingly be sufficiently different legal regimes in place to produce anomalies in the conduct of 'Welsh' cases within a unified system.

As to the second, it is official policy of the UK as well as the Welsh Assembly Government to promote the use of the Welsh language in law and administration, although it can be assumed that the policy is never likely to enjoy as high a priority in Whitehall as in Wales. The 'problem' of the Welsh language in court proceedings in Wales had rumbled in various reports, inquiries and legislative proposals for more than a century before the first limited concession to the use of Welsh oaths and the provision of state funded interpretation.[17] The position after the Welsh Language Acts of 1967 and 1993 is that the English and Welsh languages should be treated on the basis of equality[18] and that in any legal proceedings in Wales, the Welsh language may be spoken "by any party, witness or other person who desires to use it".[19]

There has been a striking change of judicial attitude to the use of the Welsh language over the last thirty years. The point can be neatly demonstrated by reference to two extracts from judgments, one at the beginning and one at the end of that period. In an appeal from the Merthyr Tydfil Justices in 1967, Mr Justice Widgery stated that:

> "... the language difficulties which arise in Wales can be dealt with in

---

[17] The Welsh Courts Act 1942. See Sir John Thomas's 2000 lecture for a detailed account of the debate over the use of the Welsh language in court proceedings in Wales in the course of the 20th century.

[18] Preamble to the 1993 Act.

[19] Section 22(1) of the 1993 Act

exactly the same way as language difficulties at the Central Criminal Court where the accused is a Pole".[20]

By contrast in a case reported in 2000 Mr Justice Judge, commenting on the lack of provision for the use of Welsh in proceedings on appeal from a Welsh employment tribunal, said:

"This prolonged suppression [of the Welsh language] presumably contributed to the continuing inability of many Welsh men and women to converse fluently in the Welsh language ... The infamous Act of 1535 is indeed being rolled back, perhaps it may be said, not yet far enough, but at an ever increasing pace ... Welsh people ... take a loyal pride in their language, both for itself and for what it means to them and their nation."[21]

The approach of senior judges is now one of positive encouragement, which the Welsh Assembly Government's commitment to a fully bilingual Wales[22] can only strengthen. The problems are now of a practical and technical nature. There is at least some doubt as to whether they can be adequately addressed while policy and administrative responsibility remains outside Wales. For example, there is an issue about Welsh speaking juries. The argument is that it ought to be possible to select a jury comprising Welsh speakers of sufficient fluency to hear and evaluate evidence given in Welsh. One counter argument is that this would offend against the principle of random selection of juries. The arguments have been conducted at very senior levels amongst the judiciary in England and Wales and were summarised by Sir Robin Auld in his Review of the Criminal Courts.[23] His conclusion might be cited in support of the development of Welsh governmental competence in the field of the administration of justice, recognising as it does that the answers to the problems should be found from within Wales:

---

[20] Widgery J in *R v Merthyr Tydfil Justices ex p Jenkins (1967) 1 All ER 636.*

[21] Judge Igor in *Williams v Cowell* (2000) 1 W.L.R. 187. The case concerned an appeal from an employment tribunal in which the appellant was denied what he asserted to be his right to use the Welsh language because the Employment Appeal Tribunal did not sit in Wales. Although the case was a 'Welsh' case, originating in Wales, the geographical limitation of section 22 of the 1993 Act meant that the Welsh language could not be used in the appeal which, under the administrative arrangements then in place, would only be heard in England. Since the appeal was heard arrangements have been put in place for the Employment Appeal Tribunal to sit in Wales, and it has done so regularly. For a further discussion of the case, see R Gwynedd Parry, *Yr Iaith Gymraeg a'r Tribiwnlys Apel Cyflogaeth – Ystyried Y Penderfyniad* (2001) 1 Wales Law Journal 178.

[22] *Our Language; Its Future: Policy Review of the Welsh Language,* the Assembly's Culture Committee and Education and Lifelong Learning Committee, 2002; and the Welsh Assembly Government Policy Statement *Bilingual Future,* 2002.

[23] www.criminal-courts-review.org.uk paras 63 – 72. For a further discussion see R. Gwynedd Parry *"Random Selection, Linguistic Rights and the Jury Trial in Wales",* [2002]Crim LR 805.

"As a non Welshman, I approach this debate with timidity. My view, for what it is worth, is that the proposal of a power to order bilingual juries in particular cases is worthy of further consideration - but not by me. It should be developed and examined, with appropriate consultation, in Wales."[24]

The use of Welsh in court proceedings is an issue which like all others exists not in a vacuum but in a context. Promotion of the use of Welsh in court proceedings is linked to issues of Welsh education. and especially Welsh higher education, and to the development of specific projects such as the standardisation of legal terminology referred to above. These are fields in which the Assembly currently has functions. Other key elements are judicial appointments and the administrative arrangements made to support access to justice. In these fields the Assembly has no powers. The question, which will certainly be exposed to the Richard Commission in the course of its consultation in Wales, is whether this position is tenable.

Furthermore, as the case of *Williams v Cowell*[25] demonstrated, the geographical limitation of the right to use the Welsh language will undermine the exercise of that right in practice unless the necessary institutions and administrative arrangements are in place for the hearing of cases in Wales – in particular this means that it must be made possible for cases to be heard both at first instance and on appeal within Wales. The changes in arrangements for court hearings, and the official encouragement for Welsh cases to be dealt with in Wales, referred to in this section, are therefore crucial. However, it seems increasingly inappropriate for the decisions and directions to come solely from Whitehall.[26]

The pressure for change should not be exaggerated. Presently there is no more than an active debate amongst senior judiciary and other members of the legal establishment, feeding into the various reviews that are under way, in particular the Richard Commission. Concluding his 2002 Lord Morris lecture Sir Roderick Evans expressed confidence that there was room for further development with or without a unified system:

---

[24] Para 72 of the Report.

[25] See footnote 21.

[26] Whitehall itself, or at least the Lord Chancellor's Department, is not lacking in appreciation of the issues – see the extract from Sir Roderick Evans' lecture at the end of this section. A further example can be found in the White Paper, *The House of Lords, Completing the Reform*, issued in December 2001 by the Lord Chancellor's Department: para 43 *et seq* deal with the representation of the regions in a reformed second chamber and it is there postulated that in future there may be a need for inclusion amongst the Appellate Committee of the House of Lords (if that Committee is to be retained as a part of the second chamber) law lords having particular expertise in Welsh law. The Paper was debated in the National Assembly in plenary on 7 March 2002. If it is recognised that Wales specific legal expertise is required at the highest level of judicial decision making in the UK, it must surely follow that there is a similar need at the intermediate levels – that is, the High Court and Court of Appeal. Those who argue for a separate division of the High Court for Wales may draw some comfort here.

"At present the development of Legal Wales can proceed within a unified English and Welsh system. The senior judiciary are supportive of the development of indigenous institutions in Wales. The Lord Chancellor has played a major role in the formation and implementation of the Government's policy on devolution and none of the developments which have so far taken place could have occurred without his support and that of his Department."

Further evolution rather than radical change should be expected. Yet, the momentum, sedate as it may be, is towards at least partial separation of the system especially if significant further law making powers are conferred on the Assembly.

THE PRACTISING PROFESSION

Devolution ought to have provided a stimulus for the legal profession in Wales, and there is some evidence that it has. One example is the establishment of new professional associations: the Wales Public Law and Human Rights Association, the Welsh Personal Injury Lawyers Association, the Wales Commercial Lawyers Association. All were established in 1999 or 2000. The Wales Law Journal, established in 2001, has as part of its mission the dissemination of information and comment of particular relevance to legal practitioners in Wales. The Centre for Welsh Legal Affairs[27] in Aberystwyth and the Welsh Legal History Society[28] are further devolution-linked developments in legal academia.

Senior members of the legal profession have been active in seeking to promote the contribution that law and legal services can make to the economic and social development of Wales.[29] Projects such as IP Wales[30] and BRASS[31] are examples of inter-disciplinary partnerships where law and lawyers play a key part in supporting and promoting economic activity in

---

[27] Department of Law, University of Wales, Aberystwyth.

[28] Based at Cardiff Law School.

[29] See for example the addresses given to the IWA in 2002 by Sir John Thomas and by Carolyn Kirby, then President Elect of the Law Society of England and Wales – published in *Agenda*, IWA, Summer 2002 and in (2002) 2 Wales Law Journal respectively.

[30] See Marc Clements, Iwan Davies and Andrew Beale, *Intellectual Property Activity in Wales: A Report on the Support for Innovative SMEs Project* and Andrew Beale and Alison George, *IP Wales Report: A Web Based Project*, (2001) 1 Wales Law Journal, pp256 and 423.

[31] The Centre for Business Relationships, Accountability, Sustainability and Society - a multi-disciplinary project involving the business, law and planning schools at Cardiff University, funded by the ESRC. See Robert Lee, *Brass Trumpets New Approach*, Agenda, IWA Summer 2002, and Ken Peattie, *The BRASS Centre at Cardiff University: A Multidisciplinary Approach to Business Sustainability* (2001) Wales Law Journal 264.

Wales, aspiring also to export best practice. The promotion of Welsh legal services themselves, representing as they do almost one per cent of GDP, can also contribute to economic growth.[32]

The most obvious growth opportunities are in the field of public and administrative law, including planning, local government, health and education. Here it must be said that there has not been much change in the volume of litigation – which is the most obvious, but not the only, measure of activity. The number of public law challenges to administrative decisions in Wales remains "surprisingly low".[33] Writing in early 2001 Tessa Shellens, a solicitor with Morgan Cole in Cardiff, said:

> "… the under-usage of the administrative courts facilities in Wales remains a cause for concern. Part of the problem lies in the fact that there is not a tradition in Wales of administrative law challenge. Specialist practitioners are thin on the ground and, even two years post devolution, understanding of the significant changes to the constitutional position in Wales and the extent of the Assembly's powers is limited."[34]

She postulated further that where, as in Wales, the potential for challenge exists largely in relation to decisions made by the Assembly affecting other publicly funded bodies, those bodies may be inhibited by the fact that the Assembly is an elected body representing the people of Wales and that the use of public resources to challenge Assembly decisions may lead to criticism. On the first of these points, the existence of the new associations and the encouragement of senior judiciary may help. The second is more difficult, and, as Tessa Shellens goes on to state, more worrying:

> "In the absence of legal challenges coming before the courts, the Assembly will not have the benefit of scrutiny and input from the judiciary in developing its approach to the exercise of its powers. The Assembly itself may be at a disadvantage if its processes are not from time to time subject to the checks and balances of litigious challenge."[35]

The message is that a more litigious population, advised and represented by a creative and vigilant legal profession, is good for the constitutional health of the nation.

The National Assembly has taken some steps which ought to encourage

---

[32] Figure produced in 1999 for the Welsh Development Agency by Cardiff University.

[33] Report of the third Lord Morris seminar, 2001, *The Courts, the Legal Profession and the Economy, the Challenge of Legal Wales* (2001) 1 Wales Law Journal 240.

[34] Tessa Shellens, *The Importance of Public Law Challenges in Wales* (2001) 1 Wales Law Journal 64.

[35] *Ibid.* Not everyone would agree with the assertion that there is a deficit in skills: Nicholas Cooke Q.C. *"From the Courts in Wales"* (2001) 1 Wales Law Journal pp 66 and 402 proselytyses the capacity of the profession in Wales, when given the opportunity, to meet the challenges.

conduct of Welsh public law cases in Wales and by Welsh practitioners, adopting a general policy of having all litigation to which it is a party conducted in Wales and appointing a panel of Assembly Counsel mirroring the existence in England of the Attorney General's Panel of Counsel. Beyond that there is little that the government of Wales could do even if it wished to address the issues to which Tessa Shellens referred, given its lack of formal functions in the field of the administration of justice.

Pressure for support for changes which would help create the desired dynamic may then need to find different, informal channels. In this regard the establishment in 2002 of the Standing Committee for Legal Wales is interesting. Chaired by the Counsel General this informal association of practitioners, judiciary, academics and professional bodies has as its aim

> "...to provide a forum for the discussion of views and proposals for action on issues affecting the administration of justice, the teaching of law and the provision of legal services as they affect Wales and, in particular to co-ordinate responses to consultations on such matters by the National Assembly for Wales or the United Kingdom Government; and where the Committee think it appropriate to make representations on such matters to the National Assembly for Wales, the United Kingdom Government or any other relevant body."[36]

Already the Committee has made representations on subjects such as the Joint Home Office/Cabinet Office Review of the Police and Criminal Evidence Act 1984. It argued for official recognition of the Welsh language version of the PACE codes[37] and support for standardisation of the Welsh language terms used in charging and cautioning suspects. A further opportunity for the Committee to establish itself as a conduit for the collective voice of the 'Welsh legal community' will be found in responding to the current Richard Commission consultation. The Committee's position can be expected to give support for proposals that will further the causes identified as 'Legal Wales' – that is to say, the development of Welsh law and legal institutions, and the promotion of the Welsh language in the administration of justice. The Committee may prove to be a driving force for change in these matters.

---

[36] Draft constitution of the Standing Committee for Legal Wales, October 2002.

[37] Issued under the Police and Criminal Evidence Act 1984, prescribing rules for investigation, arrest and questioning of suspects.

IMPACT ON THE DEVELOPMENT OF WELSH DEMOCRACY

A modern democratic state contains three core elements – legislature, executive and judiciary. The extent to which these are supplied within Wales for Wales is an important feature in any progress towards greater national governance, towards a new Welsh constitution within a reconfigured constitutional arrangement for the UK. Law and legal services form an integral part of the development of each of these core elements. In the development of the Assembly as a legislature, they are represented by legal advisers to the Welsh Assembly Government, by practitioners and by judges who supply the legal checks and balances that guard against misuse of executive power. It is therefore reasonable to assert that the range and volume of Welsh law and the strength of Welsh legal institutions and legal practice are indicators of the development of Wales a nation.

When Lord Bingham, as Lord Chief Justice of England *and Wales* (adopting the full title which had been dropped in practice by many of his predecessors), celebrated the opening of the mercantile court in Cardiff in 1999 he saw it as part of a

> "... *long overdue recognition of the need for the Principality of Wales to have its own indigenous institutions operating locally and meeting the needs of its citizens here ... another step towards recognising Wales as a proud, distinctive and successful nation".*[38]

The same could be said for all the aspects of Legal Wales identified at the beginning of this chapter. To that extent Legal Wales is a symptom of devolution. It is, however, also supportive of further change because it has stimulated the development of technical skills and knowledge and of an active, cross disciplinary engagement in the process of policy development, thereby removing some of the earlier objections to conferring greater powers on the National Assembly. Legal Wales is therefore an integral part of the unfolding story of Welsh devolution, of a growing sense of nationhood and an essential nutrient for the healthy development, both *ante* and *post* natal, of Welsh democracy.

---

[38] Quoted in Winston Roddick QC, *Creating Legal Wales*, Agenda, IWA, Spring 2002.

CHAPTER 20

NO GOING BACK

Denis Balsom

The outcome of the first elections to the National Assembly for Wales has been characterised as 'A Quiet Earthquake'. The seismic metaphor is pertinent for, not only did the result hugely disrupt past patterns, it was also unexpected. Like any major earth movement however, the impact has been absorbed and the resultant political landscape now constitutes a new status quo. The establishment of the National Assembly and this new pattern of party politics have transformed the political topography of modern Wales. As with any such seismic upheaval, there can be no reversal. These new circumstances now define our political system. Whatever follows must start from here. The term 'devolution' in Wales has always been articulated to rhyme with evolution; in contrast to Scotland where they tended to favour a pronunciation closer to revolution. Even if the achievements to date of our new political institutions may have disappointed enthusiasts, devolution and political change is a process in train and there can be no going back.

A TIMELESS OBJECTIVE

When the Queen formally opened the National Assembly in May 1999 Wales had finally secured a democratically elected, representative institution. A body had been created through which a degree of self-government over a range of domestic and economic issues could be exercised. It was in truth the birth of the political nation.

Since the dawn of representative politics in the mid 19th Century, and in every decade during the 20th Century, Welsh political leaders have sought recognition of the country's of difference and individuality through the establishment of a national representative institution. In the late 19th Century these included Tom Ellis, David Lloyd George, Keir Hardie and others who supported a Welsh Parliament. In the 1930s Welsh MPs, including the Liberal leader at the time Clement Davies, pressed the case for a Secretary of State for Wales. In the 1950s many endorsed the mass petition of the Parliament for Wales campaign, including Labour MPs S.O. Davies, Lady Megan Lloyd George, Goronwy Roberts, and Plaid Cymru's leader Gwynfor Evans. The incoming Labour Government in 1964 saw the creation of the Welsh Office with James Griffiths as the Charter Secretary of State for Wales. In 1967 his successor Cledwyn Hughes and others attempted to engineer local government reform to accommodate an all-Wales Council or Assembly. The 1970s saw the publication of the report of the Commission on the Constitution advocating an elected Assembly, culminating in the ill-fated referendum in 1979.

But for all the longevity of these aspirations, the establishment of a National Assembly has never been the driving issue of the Welsh political agenda. Throughout this period there would appear to have been a fatal contradiction at the heart of Welsh political ambition. The demand for greater recognition for Wales seemed in perpetual conflict with an ideological and political desire to participate in the governance of Britain. In particular, the ambition of Welsh Labour leaders such as Aneurin Bevan and Neil Kinnock, to lead the British working class combined with their pragmatic acceptance of the social realities of the fragility of the Welsh economy. Furthermore, many Labour leaders from Wales were, *de facto*, major British politicians with aspirations to Cabinet and Government rank. Ramsay McDonald sat for a Welsh constituency, Jame Griffiths was Deputy Leader, Nye Bevan was an icon for a generation, whilst the Cardiff MP James Callaghan became Prime Minister having already held the posts of Home Secretary, Foreign Secretary and Chancellor of the Exchequer. Three successive Leaders of the Labour Party – Callaghan, Michael Foot and Kinnock – all sat for Welsh seats. When seeking to govern Britain, aspirations for a more autonomous Wales seemed, at best, a distraction.

When the devolution question finally came to be put, initially in the referendum on the Wales Act 1978, the proposition of an elected Assembly for Wales was overwhelmingly defeated by a margin of 4 to 1. That defeat contributed directly to the collapse of James Callaghan's Government and the election of Margaret Thatcher. Thereafter, the Conservatives were in power for eighteen years, during which time Wales was transformed both economically and socially. The previously ambivalent Labour Party re-adopted devolution in Opposition and the election of Tony Blair's Government in May 1997 saw simultaneous moves to fundamentally change the government of Wales and Scotland. A subsequent pre-legislative referendum in September 1997, on whether the principle of devolution to Wales should be accepted succeeded by only the narrowest of margins. The majority voting 'Yes' exceeded those voting 'No' by less than one percent, in a poll where barely half of the electorate had bothered to vote. The creation of a Scottish Parliament was widely welcomed for a once historic nation and captured the popular imagination in a way not found in Wales's lukewarm endorsement of the proposition. While the United Kingdom is formally a union of Great Britain and Northern Ireland, the place of Wales within that union is perhaps, the least recognised or understood.

CREATING THE WELSH IDENTITY

A now infamous entry in an early *Encyclopaedia Britannica*, once advised readers 'For Wales – see England', an epithet that embodies both the reality and the paranoia of much of the history of Wales. Unlike its fellow partners in the United Kingdom, Scotland and Ireland, Wales was never an historic nation with a developed Court, distinct legal system or institutions of state. Wales was primarily a feudal society, the aristocracy of which, following the Union, were largely integrated into the English nobility. Against the longevity of the legal entity 'England and Wales' and the weakness of its own internal structures, it is remarkable that the individual character of Wales remained intact and distinct within the modern United Kingdom. Pivotal to this persistence has been the survival of the Welsh language.

In 1536 very few people in Wales spoke English. The Act of Union forbade holders of any office from speaking Welsh, but did not ban the language. Thus while acculturation into a wider British society absorbed the gentry of Wales, it was the persistence of the Welsh language amongst the common people that sustained a distinct society and identity. Later reinforced by the translation of the Bible into Welsh, the predominance of non-conformist religion kept the majority of the people of Wales in the security of their farms and chapels and detached from pressure towards Anglicisation. Economic development brought with it internal migration from within Wales as well as immigration from England and Ireland. Such population shifts diluted the proportion of Welsh speakers, but at the turn of the twentieth century in 1901, half of those resident in Wales still spoke Welsh.

The Industrial Revolution created powerful forces of modernisation and homogeneity. At the same time, the rapid economic development of Wales also helped define a particular and unique Welsh identity. Within a few decades Wales was transformed from a predominately rural society into one of the most advanced industrial regions in the world. The discovery and exploitation of coal and iron resources gave rise to a heavy industrial economy, but it was for the international export of coal that Wales became renowned. Much of the nature and character of Wales today still derives from the impact of the Industrial Revolution and its coal and steel communities.

The switch from coal to oil as a primary fuel source, which occurred between the First and Second World Wars, bore within it the demise of the traditional Welsh economy. The decline of the coal industry took until the 1980s. Steel-making, on a much-reduced basis, continues to the present day, but from a greatly reduced number of plants and with a fraction of the previous labour force. The steel industry also migrated from the coalfield to the coast, where imported ore and, eventually, coal were easily available and replaced the indigenous resources. Indeed, the run-down of coal mining in the mid twentieth century facilitated a second, manufacturing, industrial revolution in Wales. However, the key changes that occurred were to the wider sociology of Welsh society, particular the impact of the decline of trade unionism and the increased employment of women

Following Britain's accession to the European Common Market in 1973 and further development of the European Union, the economic regeneration of Wales continued and, in total, almost constitutes a third Industrial Revolution. Heavy manufacturing has largely been replaced by light engineering and assembly work. New technology has fostered development in the electronics industry and further growth in the cities has supported a burgeoning services sector. Even in rural Wales, European initiatives and changes in consumer demand have affected traditional produce, whilst the disastrous outbreaks of BSE and foot and mouth disease in the late 1990s and early part of the new century further undermined traditional farming. The rural economy is now highly dependent upon tourism and farm diversification. Endeavours are being made to focus agricultural output into niche markets, such as organic and specialist food production as well as green energy, concepts and products that draw explicitly upon the continued existence of a sense of Welsh identity.

Wales has a population of slightly less than 3 million, of whom about 500,000 speak Welsh. The language is taught in all schools, as part of the national curriculum, but the dilemma at the heart of the contemporary language debate is the nurturing of bilingualism. Though such a goal has yet to be fully realised, the formal recognition of the place and role of the language in contemporary Wales has been one of the major achievements of the last twenty-five years. The creation of *Sianel Pedwar Cymru* (S4C) in 1982 and the enactment of *The Welsh Language Act* 1993, which legally requires public bodies to operate a bilingual policy, represent landmarks in the continued development of a modern Welsh identity.

EMERGENCE OF A TRULY WELSH POLITICS

It is against this background of economic and social change that the first elections to the National Assembly were held. The result produced a minority Labour Party administration. More significantly in electoral terms, Plaid

Cymru recorded its highest ever vote. Hitherto, Plaid Cymru had been regarded as an extremist party in a constitutional sense, advocating the case for Welsh autonomy that has been variously described as independence, self government, freedom or separation, depending on the outlook of the commentator. Officially the party campaigns for 'full national status within the European Union', seeking an equivalent status for Wales to that given to Denmark or Ireland.

On the other hand, to a greater or lesser extent the other political parties in Wales have been branches of their London parent bodies. The Assembly is changing these relationships, however. The Liberal Party, followed by today's Liberal Democrats have always operated on federal lines and have adjusted most easily. Meanwhile, the steps currently being taken by Welsh Labour and the Welsh Conservative party to develop greater autonomy from their London head offices is one of the most visible demonstrations of the impact of the new Welsh politics.

The contrast in results between the Assembly and UK elections in 1999 and 2001 shows that the Welsh electorate views the different levels of government from markedly different perspectives. In the British context, Wales remains staunchly Labour and returned 34 MPs to Parliament out of a total of 40 in 2001. In the Assembly however, Labour secured only 28 seats out of 60, whilst Plaid Cymru won 17 seats and became the official Opposition. Welsh people, and Welsh politics, have developed a bifocal perspective through which to view the new politics. The local, almost parochial, remains important, more so perhaps than in many other parts of Britain. Yet Wales also remains part of, and engaged in the wider British and European economic and political system.

After four years of living with a National Assembly, Wales has changed. No single decision or policy initiative can be identified as having decisively swung public support, but opinions have changed and the Assembly is now widely accepted as an integral part of Wales. No serious political group is campaigning to have the Assembly dissolved and Wales return to the *status quo ante*.[1] Indeed, the consensus would appear to be that it should assume greater powers, in order to operate more effectively.

In May 2003 the second Welsh general election will be led by a Welsh political élite. It will be based upon manifestos for Wales, setting out what each party would wish the National Assembly to achieve in the following four years and will be a largely internal political contest conducted separately from the influence of London. As in any democratic election, the incumbent regime will be defending its record against the opposition parties who would seek to replace it in office.

---

[1] It should be noted that the UK Independence Party will be fighting the May 2003 election on a platform of abolishing the Assembly.

These points are so straightforward that they barely need making. The fact that they do is because of one qualification. This is the difficulty that all the parties will have in getting their message across in the absence of a comprehensive national press or media. Most of the newspapers read in Wales emanate from London, and apart from the Welsh edition of the Daily Mirror, give scant attention to Wales. The Western Mail purports to be the country's 'national' newspaper, yet it only circulates in the southern half of the country and then has a circulation of less than 50,000. Television and radio have a greater reach, but some 40 per cent of the population in the eastern half of the country live in what is termed an 'overlap zone'. That is to say, they can choose to have their aerials tuned into Welsh or English transmitters, and many choose the latter. The take up of digital satellite television in Wales is also higher than the UK average. Consequently, a significant proportion of the electorate do not participate in Assembly election campaigns because they do not hear or read about the debates. The issue of turn-out in the election should be considered against that context.

Wales has long felt itself to be a nation subsumed within another state. Its unique character however, derived from its history and particular linguistic and cultural heritage, has resisted submersion within an homogeneous British identity. Yet a sense of being part of Britain remains an important ingredient of the identity of modern Wales. The country is highly integrated into Britain and lacks the self-sufficiency, and perhaps self-confidence, of Scotland. As has been stated, it has a weak indigenous daily press and, although well served by broadcast media, lacks a forum for internal, intellectual, critical debate. Few professions, be they in law, business or technology, can wholly be pursued within Wales alone. It remains the case that professional career development will, inevitably, take the most talented and aspiring to London and beyond. Traditionally teachers, preachers and poets have been projected as a particular Welsh stereotype and, sadly, this often remains true today.

In politics, however, the infrastructure of Wales has been totally transformed. The National Assembly has provided a democratic focus and its further evolution as an institution will inevitably create a more distinctive history and collective memory. Irrespective of the future development of the Welsh economy or society, Wales now has a political identity that will define the country and project it to the wider world. Compared with the political reality of its existence, constitutional questions concerning its powers and functions are relatively unimportant. It is no longer possible to say 'For Wales, see England'. The 2001 census saw a stabilisation of the number Welsh speakers, with a small percentage increase compared with 1991, up two percentage points to 20.5 per cent. But even if the Welsh language were to further decline or perish, Wales and Welshness within the United Kingdom is now secure. In all likelihood, the distinctiveness of Wales, especially in the cultural field, will become more pronounced as more support and endorsement is secured from the National Assembly. Businesses and other organisations will also learn to accommodate the local institutions of Wales, as they would if they were to operate, in a similar context, in Texas or Bavaria.

AN EVOLVING POLITICAL CULTURE

The British political tradition is a fluid concept as befits a state with no written constitution. While political and constitutional practice has evolved, almost by stealth over many decades, the day to day reality of political discourse has been one of confrontation. The British parliamentary model is characterised by a highly adversarial style of engagement between Government and Opposition. At the same time it has also been defined as an 'elective dictatorship'. This Westminster model is also reinforced by the first past the post electoral system which is more likely than any other to produce a majority Government and inflate the number of seats the winning party secures, relative to its share of the vote.

What at first appears an indefensible constitutional structure has been tolerated for many reasons. There has been an explicit assumption that power will alternate between the major parties. If it operates, this 'swing of the pendulum' implicitly introduces a balance and a fairness to the system and may inhibit parties from pursuing too radical an agenda. However, such constitutional optimism did not prevent there being long periods of Conservative Government in the 1950s and throughout the 1980s into the 1990s. In essence, a largely two party system has accepted this system because of the power it gave parties when in Government. Even when defeated, they still retained the expectation of a return to Government in due course.

While this sense of long run equilibrium has persisted in Westminster, in Wales no such internal balancing mechanism applied. Since the coming of popular democracy and mass suffrage, Wales has been characterised by one party politics. The Liberal dominance of Welsh parliamentary representation in the nineteenth century, gave way to the hegemony of the Labour Party for most of the past eighty years. There were only occasional intimations of a wider, multi-party politics following the limited successes of Plaid Cymru. This inherent partisan imbalance, for example, inhibited the debate over devolution in Wales for fear that any new elected body would be dominated by the Labour Party. Such concerns certainly played a large part in the massive referendum defeat in 1979 and in the less than wholehearted endorsement of devolution in 1997. Indeed, Ron Davies, and the drafters of the proposals that went on to form the basis of the 1998 Government of Wales Act, consciously set out to create an institution that did not engender an automatic presumption of Labour dominance. In particular, the adoption of partial proportional representation for the National Assembly held out an olive branch offering greater integration and inclusivity. The Labour Party never really believed it would not win a majority in any Assembly election, but the adoption of partial PR diminished the fear of one-party dominance. Quite genuinely there was an intention to ensure the engagement of the other parties in the Assembly's affairs.

UNCHARTED TERRITORY

The outcome of the 1999 election took Welsh politics and to some extent, the British political tradition, into uncharted territory. The advent of the first Labour minority administration, and the eventual recourse to coalition, forced a shift in the style and character of Welsh politics. What was uncertain was whether the 1999 result was a fluke or a statement of a new reality. Rhodri Morgan has claimed that, under the new election system, he would expect Labour to win outright in three out of four elections. The coming election in 2003 will be the great test of this belief. Given the experience of the first four years, it is doubtful whether the electorate will wish to return to single party dominance, nor that the electoral system will facilitate it.

The adjustments that each party has had to make to accommodate the new parameters of Welsh politics have been detailed in earlier chapters in Part 3. Although the Assembly set out to be an inclusive, corporate body it was, perhaps, no surprise that the fundamental separation and divisions of the British Parliamentary model asserted themselves. Three of the four parties in the Assembly were led by MPs of long standing, some of whom had ministerial experience. Inevitably, therefore, some of the familiar patterns of Westminster procedure were bound to emerge. Though not compatible with minority government, they were perfectly workable with a majority, coalition, government. Yet, while the business procedures of the Assembly have fallen into line with more general British practice, it remains arguable that the parties and the wider political culture have not.

The political parties approach the 2003 election with each maintaining the fiction that they are campaigning to form a single party, majority Welsh Assembly Government.[2] Such claims on behalf of the Conservatives and the Liberal Democrats are clearly preposterous. They are barely credible for Plaid Cymru, while even the Labour Party remains pessimistic of a successful,

---

[2] Or, in the case of Plaid Cymru, the 'Government of Wales': nomenclatures have a high salience in Assembly politics.

majority, outcome. Successive research has shown that the 1999 shift in public opinion and party preference was not a fluke, but a rational response to the reality of Welsh politics. Mathematically, it is doubtful that the Assembly election system will ever produce a substantial majority for any one party. Politically, the First Minister has recognised this fact and has stated that there might be merit in forming a coalition, even if Labour secured a bare majority. As the public becomes more familiar with the opportunities offered by the electoral system, so their responses will become more sophisticated. Parties, likewise, will have to come to terms with a system that will reward collaboration, while penalising excessive, narrow, partisan self-interest.

In these respects, the politics of Wales are becoming more European in character and less the creature of the traditional British political culture. In time, there is every probability that similar trends will feed back into Westminster politics as, for example, the emergence of a much stronger third party and pressure for an elected second chamber have shown. As ever, however, such change will be slow and incremental.

The British political system is changing, but the essential evolutionary character of the process persists. For once, Wales is in the vanguard. As their manifestos for the 2003 election demonstrated, all the parties have accepted that the National Assembly will continue to pursue its own agenda, not quite in step with London. Significant pressure points remain and important fault lines have still to be crossed. For the devolution process itself the central issue is when and how the Assembly will acquire the essential legislative powers to turn itself into a proper parliament. There is a clear majority across the parties in the Assembly for this to happen. For the time being the responsibility for charting a course has been handed to Lord Richard and his Commission. In turn, he will be keeping a weather eye on the outcome of the May election. Politics is not a logical business, but in a democracy it has a way of responding to the force of argument. And on this question the arguments all point in the direction of the Assembly acquiring greater powers. What is unknown is the timing. It is inescapable, however, that the Westminster Parliament will have to agree, and legislate to replace or amend the 1998 Government of Wales Act. To do this one of the British parties, most likely the Labour Party, will have to place a commitment in a Westminster general election manifesto. The earliest this could happen would be ahead of the next election in 2005 or 2006, with legislation going through in the following parliamentary term. The next Assembly election is then in 2007, which seems the earliest point that a legislative National Assembly or Welsh Parliament could come into being.

It remains to be seen, too, how a Welsh Assembly Government of a markedly different political hue from that prevailing in London would fare. Again, this may well have to wait until beyond 2007, although in politics it is always 'events' that upset the most informed predictions. What is not in doubt is that the new Welsh political nation, born in 1999, has taken its first tentative steps and has begun to grow. In the coming years it will cross many bridges. There can be no going back.

PUBLICATIONS

AGENDA

The Institute's regular journal appears three times a year – March, July and November. Contains more than 25 articles covering the themes: Economic Development; Politics and Policy; Environment; Social Policy – health and education; and Culture and Communications. £5 for a single issue, £15 yearly subscription. IWA Members (subscription £30 per year) receive *AGENDA* as part of their membership package.

CURRENT RESEARCH REPORTS

The Future Development of Air Transport in the United Kingdom: A Response by The Institute of Welsh Affairs, January 2003, £10

The Welsh Potential for Renewable Energy Edited by Eilidh Johnston, Dec 2002, £30

Competing with the World: Final Report, July 2002, £10

Equal Opportunities and the National Assembly for Wales by Paul Chaney and Ralph Fevre, June 2002, £10

A Guide to EU Funding in Wales 2000 - 2006 New Edition by Nia Richardson, May 2002, £10

The Third Mission: Creating a Business Culture for Higher Education in Wales by Dr Gareth Jones , April 2002, £10

Tools for the Learning Country, IWA/Basic Skills Agency, December 2001, £5

The Search for Balance: Taxing and Spending across the United Kingdom by Ross Mackay, June 2001, £10

Knowledge and the Welsh Economy by Professor Sir Adrian Webb (Jun 01) £10

A Guide to European Funding in Wales 2000 – 2006 by Dr Gareth Jones, May 2001 £10

An Icon for Modern Wales: Realising the Benefits of the National Botanic Garden by Neil Caldwell and John Stoner (Feb 2001) Summary Report £10 Main Report £20

Craft As Art: Projecting the Makers of Wales Within the Global Economy by John Osmond (February 2001 £10

Small Loans for Small Businesses: Developing Micro-Credit in Wales by Dr Nigel Blewitt, July 2000, £10

Designing Success: the Case for a Welsh Commission for Architecture and Design, IWA Report, June 2000, £10

The Irish Experience of Objective One by John Osmond, June 2000, £10

Waste in Wales – A National Resource, ECOTEC consultancy, February 2000, Summary report £10, Main Report £30

Innovating to Succeed: Creating Competitive Advantage in the Welsh Economy, by Nigel Blewitt, December 1999, £10

Building a Knowledge-Driven Welsh Economy by Gareth Jones and John Osmond, November 1999, £10

Unravelling the Knot: The Interaction of UK Treasury and EU Funding for Wales by Dr Gillian Bristow and Dr Nigel Blewitt, November 1999, £10

Uniting the Nation: Improving the Cambrian Way North-South Links in Wales WS Atkins, May 1999, Full Report £40, Summary Report £10

Quality of Service, Bilingualism and the Public Utility Services in Wales IWA/Welsh Consumer Council, September 1998, Bilingual, £10

The Other Wales: the Case for Objective One Funding Post 1999 by Adam Price and Professor Kevin Morgan, July 1998, £10

A Competitive Edge: Why Welsh Medium Schools Perform Better bilingual, June 1998, £10

BSE: The Welsh Dimension, edited by Gillian Bristow published with the Institute of Rural Studies, University of Wales, Aberystwyth, October 1997, £10

Bridging the Technology Skills Gap: Changing the Perceptions of Young People to Modern Manufacturing Industry, September 1997, Bilingual, £10

Making the CAP Fit: An Integrated Development Strategy for Rural Wales, by Dr Gillian Bristow, July 1997, £10

Wales Information Society, by John Osmond, June 1997, £10

Building Our Future: The Housing Challenge for Wales by Malcolm Fisk and Dale Hall, February 1997, £10

Wales 2010: Three Years On, Dr Gareth Jones, December 1996, £%

Bread and Roses: Making the Case for a Millennium Centre for the Arts in the Welsh Capital, May 1996, £5

THE GREGYNOG PAPERS

Wales: One Nation by Professor Phil Williams AM, March 2003, £7.99

The Future of Welsh Conservatism by Jonathan Evans MEP, April 2002, £7 99

Creating an Entrepreneurial Wales by Professor Dylan Jones-Evans (September 2001) £7.99

Our Welsh Heritage by Richard Keen (Feb 00) £7.50

Devolution: A Process Not an Event by Ron Davies MP (Feb 99) £7.50

State of the Arts by David Clarke, October 1998, £7.50

The Welsh Image by John Smith MP, June 1998. £7 50

Lessons from the Sea Empress by Neil Caldwell and Clive Morgan, March 1997, £7 50

NHS Wales: Business or Public Service? By Professor David Cohen, February 1997, £5

The Place of North Wales by Huw Vaughan Thomas, July 1996, £5

IWA DISCUSSION PAPERS

Divided we Fall: The Politics of Geography in Wales by John Osmond, December 2002, £10

Developing a Partnership Approach to Primary Legislation between Westminster and the National Assembly by Keith Patchett, Oct ober 2002, £5

The Future of Welsh Devolution by John Osmond, June 2002, £5

A Reorganisation Too Far: IWA Response to the National Assembly consultation document Structural Change in the NHS in Wales by Gareth Jones, October 2001 £5

Variable Geometry UK, by Rhodri Morgan AM, March 2000, £5

Funding, Fairness, Farming and the Future by Professor Gareth Wyn Jones, December 1999, £5

Welsh Politics in the New Millennium, by John Osmond, August 1999, £5

Swansea Bay in the 21st Century, March 1999, £5

The Hole at the Centre: IWA Response to the Welsh Office Enterprise and Training Action Group's Plan for Wales, February 1999, £5

Broadcasting in Wales and the National Assembly: IWA Evidence to the House of Commons Welsh Affairs Select Committee, Discussion Paper No 4, October 1998

Rural Wales and the Agricultural Crisis, January 1998, £5

Why Snowdonia and North Wales Need a New Tourism Strategy by John Osmond, Gareth Wyn Jones and David Williams, October 1997, £5

NATIONAL EISTEDDFOD LECTURES

The Capital, Culture and the Nation by Geraint Talfan Davies (delivered at St David's, 2002), £7.50

The Role of Universities in the Modern Economy by Professor Deian Hopkin (delivered at Denbigh, 2001), £7.99

WELSHBAC PUBLICATIONS

Beyond the Border: The Acceptability of the WelshBac to Higher Education Institutions outside Wales (bilingual) by Cerian Black and John David, September 2000, £10

The WelshBac: From Wales to the World, August 1999 £5

The Hole at the Centre: IWA Response to the Welsh Office Education and Training Action Plan for Wales Consultation, Discussion Paper No 9, January 1999, £5

The WelshBac: Educating Wales in the Next Century by Colin Jenkins, John David, John Osmond and Juliet Pierce, June 1998, £7.50

The Welsh Baccalaureate: Matching International Standards by John David and Colin Jenkins, October 1997 £5

MONITORING THE NATIONAL ASSEMBLY

Building a Civic Culture: Institutional Change, Policy Development and Political Dynamics in the National Assembly for Wales edited by J Barry Jones and John Osmond, March 2002, £15.00

Inclusive Government and Party Management: the National Assembly for Wales and the Work of its Committees edited by J Barry Jones and John Osmond, March 2001 £15

Adrift But Afloat: The Civil Service and the National Assembly, John Osmond, May 1999, £10

The National Assembly Agenda : A Handbook for the First Four Years, November 1998, edited by John Osmond. £10

The Operation of the National Assembly: Reponse of the IWA's Constitution Working Group to the National Assembly Advisory Group's Consultation Paper, Discussion Paper No 6, May 1998, £5

Enhancing Welsh Input into Westminster Legislation by Professor Keith Patchett and John Osmond, March 2001, £5

The Bonding of Wales: Housing the Assembly, Discussion Paper No 5, January 1998, £5

Making the Assembly Work, IWA Constitution Working Party, November 1997, £10

An Effective National Assembly: Key Amendments to the Government of Wales Bill, Discussion Paper No 3, IWA Constitution Working Party, October 1997, £5

Wales in Europe: The Opportunity Presented by a Welsh Assembly by Sir John Grey and John Osmond, June 1997, £10

The Economic Impact of a Welsh Assembly by Professor R. Ross Mackay, May 1997, £10

The Road to the Referendum: Requirements for an Informed and Fair debate, October 1996

Quarterly Reports:

Dragon Takes a Different Route: Monitoring the National Assembly, December 2002, £10

A Bilingual Wales: Monitoring the National Assembly, August 2002, £10

Engaging with Europe: Monitoring the National Assembly, June 2002, £10

Education Policy Breaks Loose: Monitoring the National Assembly, March 2002, £10

Coalition Creaks over Health: Monitoring the National Assembly, December 2001 £10

A Period of Destabilisation: Monitoring the National Assembly, August 2001 £10

Farming Crisis Consolidates Assembly's Role: Monitoring the National Assembly, May 2001, £10

The Economy Takes Centre Stage: Monitoring the National Assembly, March 2001 £10

Coalition Politics Come to Wales: Monitoring the National Assembly, December 2000) £10

Devolution Looks Ahead: Monitoring the National Assembly, September 2000 £10

Devolution in Transition: Monitoring the National Assembly, June 2000 £10

Devolution Relaunched: Monitoring the National Assembly, March 2000 £10

Devolution: A Dynamic, Settled Process? Monitoring the National Assembly, December 1999 £10

To order a report (there is a p&p charge of £1.50) contact:

IWA, Ty Oldfield, Llantrisant Road, Llandaff, Cardiff, CF5 2YQ

Tel 029 2057 5511 Fax 029 2057 5701

E-mailwales@iwa.org.uk

For up-to-date information on IWA publications contact our website: www.iwa.org.uk

PUBLICATIONS

WORKING PAPERS:

The Welsh Governance Centre disseminates information arising from its research activities through the WGC Working Papers. The research is undertaken by members of WGC, university associates, honorary research fellows as well as colleagues from university institutions in Wales. Research is funded by the Economic and Social Research Council and private consultancies.

I Devolution and Development: the Welsh Assembly & the Governance of Regional Economic Policy by Robert Huggins, Kevin Morgan & Gareth Rees (July 2000), £5

II A New Electoral Profile?: the Welsh voters at the polls, 1997-1999 by David Broughton (February 2001), £4

III Devolution and Health in Wales: the first year of the Health and Social Services Committee by Susan Burnett (February 2001), £4

IV Analysing the Welsh Identity by Carwyn Fowler (May 2001), £4

V Institutional Evolution: The Operation of the Welsh Executive by Alan Storer & Mark S. Lang (November 2001), £4

VI Wales and the European Union: Refining a Relationship by J Barry Jones (November 2002) £4

VII Constitutional Dilemmas: Decentralisation, Devolution and Federalism (November 2002) £5

VIII Welsh Devolution: Balancing Opportunities and Frustrations by J Barry Jones (November 2002) £4

ST DAVID'S DAY LECTURES:

The St David's Day Lecture is an annual event hosted by the Welsh Governance Centre. It was fitting that the Presiding Officer of the National Assembly for Wales, Lord Elis-Thomas, gave the inaugural St David's Day Lecture. To him fell the onerous responsibility of setting the political course for the future development of the National Assembly, and of balancing the needs for modernisation with the forces of tradition. Professor Robert Hazell of the Constitution Unit, University College London gave the second St David's Day Lecture at a time when the National Assembly had embarked on a review of its powers, specifically the efficacy of executive devolution and the extent to which the ability to draft primary legislation would enhance the aspiration of 'good governance' in Wales.

A New Constitution for Wales? by Lord Elis-Thomas (Bilingual Copy) (March 2000), £5

The Dilemmas of Devolution: Do the Welsh have an answer to the English Question? by Professor Robert Hazell (Bilingual Copy) (March 2001), £5

Devolution: The View from Whitehall and Torfaen by Paul Murphy, Secretary of State for Wales (March 2002)

JOINT PUBLICATIONS WITH IWA:

Inclusive Government and Party Management: The National Assembly for Wales and the Work of its Committees edited by J. Barry Jones & John Osmond (March 2001), £15

Building a Civic Culture: Institutional Change, Policy Development and Political Dynamics in the National Assembly for Wales edited by J Barry Jones and John Osmond (March 2002) £15.00